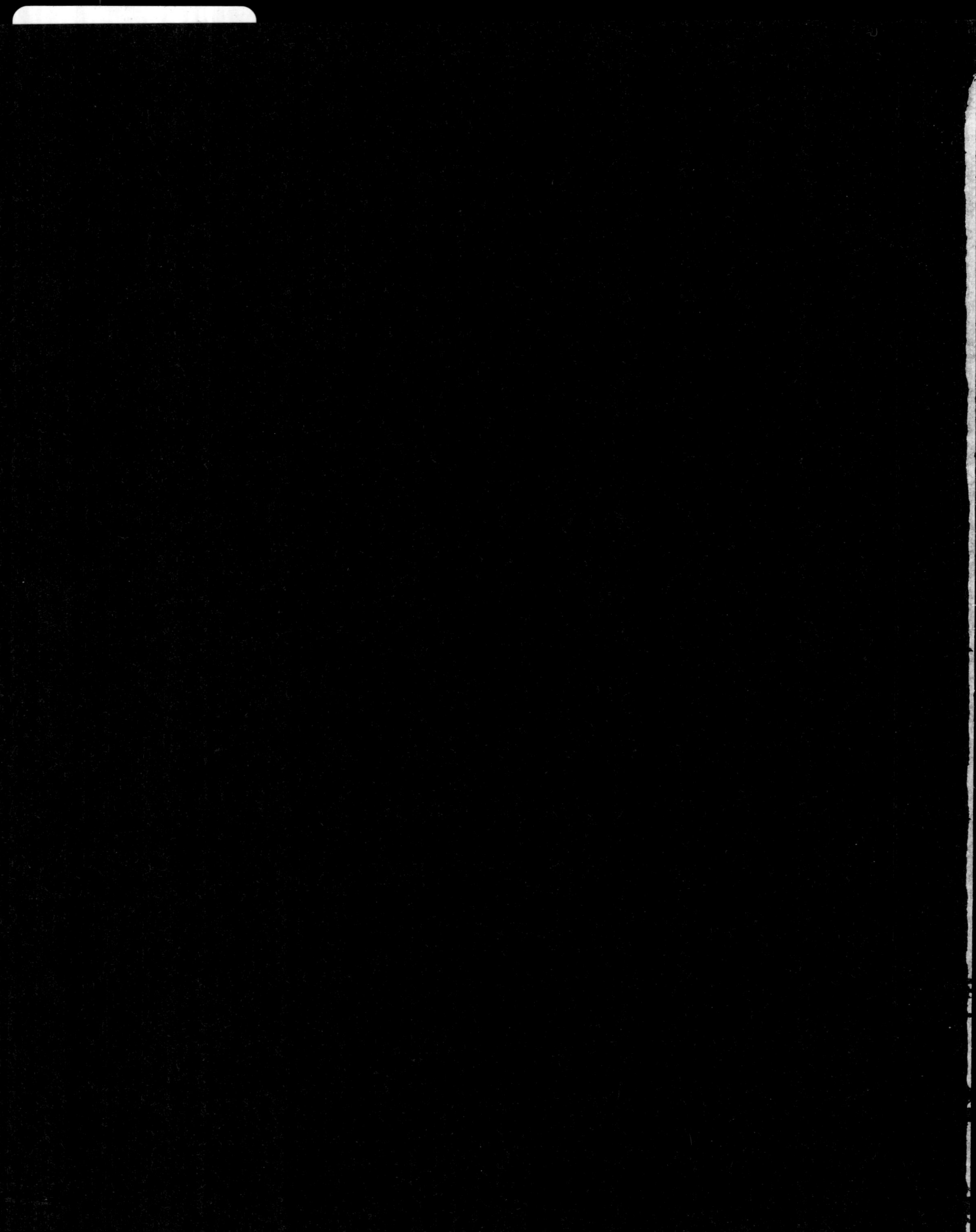

DESIGNING MOBILITIES

DESIGNING MOBILITIES

Ole B. Jensen

Art and Urbanism Series no 4

ISBN: 978-87-7112-098-1

ART AND URBANISM SERIES
ISSN: 1904-3732

LAYOUT
Jacob Bjerre Mikkelsen

COVER PHOTO
Jacob Bjerre Mikkelsen

PRINT
AKAPRINT a/s

FINANCIAL SUPPORT
Realdania
Department of Architecture, Design and
Media Technology, Aalborg University
GRUS fonden
Center for Strategisk Byforskning (CBS)

PUBLISHED BY
Aalborg University Press
Skjernvej 4A, 2nd floor
9220 Aalborg Ø
Tel: 99407140 / 99407141
aauf@forlag.aau.dk
www.forlag.aau.dk

ART AND URBANISM SERIES

Art and Urbanism is a multi-disciplinary series that focuses on urban living, art and architecture and their relation to cultural understanding and social behaviour. The content includes Urban Culture, City Life, Architecture, Urban Design, Media Art, Performance Art, Social Technologies and more. It highlights artistic practice and research on the various concepts, methods and theories on art, culture and urban design enhancing mutual experiences, learning and cultural exchange.

Gitte Marling, Hans Kiib and Ole B. Jensen, 2009, Experience City. DK, No. 1

Hans Kiib, 2010, Performative Urban Design, No. 2

Gitte Marling and Hans Kiib, 2011, Instant City@ Roskilde Festival, No. 3

Ole B. Jensen, 2014, Designing Mobilities, No. 4

DESIGNING MOBILITIES

Ole B. Jensen

TABLE OF CONTENTS

Preface & acknowledgements

This book is the outcome of several years of thinking about the relationship between the phenomenon of mobilities and what it means for social identities, social interaction, and embodied practice as well as how the phenomenon's spatial and material embedding seems to be under-researched (at least within a mobilities theory perspective). To put matters a bit crudely: there are many fine scholarly works theorizing mobilities within geography, sociology, and anthropology. There are also many fine books on architecture and urban design illustrating the creation and staging of practical mobilities. However, not much connection seems to have been made yet between the 'academic' and the 'design' world, as is it were. What I am thinking is that the theories and concepts from academic research might help enlighten designers and architects to get deeper into an understanding of their practice. But likewise the practices, designs, and buildings made by architects and urban designers may explain, illustrate, and elaborate upon the theories and concepts of mobilities scholars. Being a sociologist within an urban design environment working together with architects and engineers alike for the last decade, I have come to realize that someone needs to make this connection in order to lay bare the benefits for research in exploring design as well as for design in exploring research. The book presented here is step two in a process where, with the book *Staging Mobilities* (Jensen 2013a), I created a theoretical framework for understanding and analysing situational mobilities. I have titled this book *Designing Mobilities* since the focus here is to apply the theoretical framework to specific cases of mobilities design. Both volumes have been written as 'standalone' books. However, I do consider them integral to the work I have been doing for a little more than a decade, namely, to reach a deeper understanding of the phenomenon of contemporary mobilities. From these two books I have now embarked on a longer journey in order to articulate a new and emergent research field of 'mobilities design', where the aim will be to work more collaboratively, with outreach to the different professions and disciplines. Taken together, the two volumes *Staging Mobilities* and *Designing Mobilities* form the first step in articulating this relationship with the overarching aim of understanding the meaning of mobilities within its material contexts.

As always when one finalizes a book, the contributions made by other people and institutions become evident. Thus I must thank many people and organizations for supporting this piece of work. Firstly, I want to thank the Department of Architecture, Design and Media Technology (AD:MT) where I have been Professor of Urban Theory since 2004. AD:MT is truly an inspiring environment and there is so much potential for further cross-disciplinary research within the frames of this organization. Thanks to the former Head of Department, Michael Mullins, who supported the work in its early phases and never has said 'no' when more resources were needed. Also thanks to the present Head of Department Hans Jørgen Andersen for continuing this support, but equally for being a good colleague and for teaching me the value of true cross-disciplinary research. Thanks to the Urban Design Group/Section from which most of my 'design' knowledge derives. It is great to have such a creative group from which to learn and to which to present ideas. Also I want to thank the many students I have had the privilege supervising in the Urban Design master's program. Most of my ideas for the articulation of 'mobilities design' may be traced back to things I have learned from supervising urban design projects and studios. Thanks are due to the members of the Research Cluster for 'Mobility and Tracking Technology' (MoTT) for creating yet another cross-disciplinary platform on which I could explore my ideas. The Faculty of Engineering and Science at Aalborg University has been a perfect venue for exploring not just social theory, but equally importantly the technical and design-oriented dimensions to mobilities. The people in the 'Centre for Mobilities and Urban Studies' (C-MUS) have been very supportive and in particular I will mention Antje Gimmler, Henrik Harder, Lea Louise Holst Laursen, and Claus Lassen as well as the growing number of C-MUS Ph.D. students. Thanks for being such great colleagues.

Thanks to Centre CEO Mille Schou and Steen & Strøm Danmark A/S for granting access to do field studies in the Friis shopping centre and to Architect Søren Askehave for explaining shopping centre architecture and design. In relation to the case on bike systems design, I want to thank Victor Andrade, Henrik Harder, and Jens Christian Overgaard Madsen for fruitful collaboration in the 'Bikeability' project from which the empirical material originates. Publishing a book such as the one you are holding in your hands is not only hard work but also financially challenging. Therefore I wish to thank Realdania, GRUS Fonden, Centre for Strategisk Byforskning (CSB), and the Department of Architecture, Design and Media Technology for direct financial support for the printing of this fine book.

During my years as academic researcher I have supervised a number of Ph.D. students whose work also has had positive influence on this book. I want to thank Bo Stjerne Thomsen, Esben Skouboe Poulsen, Anne-Marie Sandvig Knudsen, Ditte Bendix Lanng, Simon Wind, Christian Fisker, Martin Trandberg Jensen, and Salmiah Hamid for inspirational collaboration. Also research assistants Simon Wind and Jacob Bjerre Mikkelsen did most valuable work on many of the empirical cases presented in this book. Jacob Bjerre Mikkelsen did not only create the layout of this book, but also produced empirical material for many of the cases and gave most useful feedback on the written texts. He truly has done a great job.

Ditte Bendix Lanng, whom I supervise on a Ph.D. project related to mobilities design, needs to be thanked in particular. Through our many discussions and joint work the emergence of the new research field 'mobilities design' is materialising and the articulation of my thoughts in relation thereto has been very dependent on our fruitful collaboration. Also Ditte has been helpful in setting up the institutional anchoring for the next phase of articulating a research strategy for mobilities design, namely the formation of the 'Mobilities Design Group' (MDG) under C-MUS.

Over the years strong links of international character have shaped the global context for this book. In the United Kingdom, the connections to Sheffield University have been valuable, and in particular the collaboration with Malcolm Tait. I must thank John Urry of Lancaster University for immense inspiration and encouragement; I hope to bring some small contribution to the field created by him. Also thanks for good company and collaboration to Mimi Sheller, Drexel University, Philadelphia. In terms of organizations and networks I thank the members of the 'Cosmobilites Network' as well as the growing number of members of the 'Pan-American Mobilities Network', and here I must mention Phillip Vannini, Christian Fisker, and Jim Conley in particular. It's a great comfort to know I can run into you guys almost anywhere on the planet and enjoy intelligent company.

Over the years a number of institutions have hosted me as a visiting scholar. Thanks to the 'mCentre' (Centre for Mobilities Research and Policy), Drexel University, Philadelphia; the Department of Sociology and Anthropology, Swarthmore College, Philadelphia; the Graduate Program in Urban and Regional Planning, Iowa University; the Department of Town and Regional Planning, University of Sheffield, United Kingdom; the Graduate School of Architecture, Planning and Preservation (GSAPP), Columbia University, New York; and the Faculty of Architecture, Chulalongkorn University, Bangkok.

At Aalborg University Press I want to thank Pernille Herold for great support and for believing in the project. I also want to extent gratitude to an anonymous reviewer whose critical comments on the manuscript surely have improved the end result. Thank you the editor of the Art & Urbanism book series at Aalborg University Press, Professor Hans Kiib, for encouraging me to publish in this book series.

As always the final word of gratitude goes to my family: Lone, Christine, and Julie. Whether we travel or are at home I never grow tired of your company, and I am much obliged that you have not grown tired of mine either!

Despite the fact that many where called upon no one else is to blame for shortcomings, errors, or omissions but yours truly.

Ole B. Jensen

Aalborg
December 2013

1 DESIGNING MOBILITIES: INTRODUCTION

Scientific thought in recent years has continuously led us further into the realization of the dominance of space and movement and to the notion that matter is really the product of movement in space.

Ed Bacon (1967) *Design of Cities,* p. 34

Access is the prerequisite to using any space. Without the ability to enter or to move within it, to receive and transmit information or goods, space is of no value, however vast or rich in resources. A city is a communication net, made of roads, paths, rails, pipes, and wires. The economic and cultural level of a city is in some proportion to the capacity of its circulation system.

Kevin Lynch & Gary Hack (1984) *Site Planning,* p. 193

A metro system is an excellent demonstration of how the built environment influences the quality of our lives. The building of tunnels of trains is usually seen in isolation from the provision of spaces for people – even though they are part of a continuous experience for the traveller, starting and ending at street level.

Norman Foster (2007) *Norman Foster Works 3,* p. 484

Introduction

Contemporary society is characterised by multiple and complex systems of mobility of goods, people, symbols, and messages. This is a dominant feature across urban societies as well, as it links (or decouples) local places to/from global networks. *Designing Mobilities* is a book that explores how places, sites, and systems 'hosting' these multiple and complex mobilities are designed and how they stage these in terms of their physical layout. By analysing specific cases of 'mobilities design' related to the four modes of moving -- *Walk, Bike, Train,* and *Car* -- the book uncovers important and heretofore neglected areas of social and cultural importance. The book is titled *Designing Mobilities* and is the empirical and case-based companion to the book *Staging Mobilities* (Jensen 2013a). The two books *Staging Mobilities* and *Designing Mobilities* are based on more than a decade of research within the fields of urban studies, mobilities research, and urban design. This first chapter briefly reviews the 'mobilities turn' and explores its relationship to theories and ideas about design. In particular the relation between urban design/architectural design and mobilities theory is presented. The chapter identifies the theoretical understanding and framing used in the rest of the book and links this to the approach of *Staging Mobilities* as the key analytical perspective for the book.

Background

The background to this area of research has matured during the last decade or so as a growing research interest has emerged within the so-called 'mobilities turn'. This is a cross-disciplinary field covering geography, sociology, anthropology, urban studies, urban design, architecture, and cultural studies to name but a few of its underpinning lines of thought. Put very simply, the main issue is that mobilities is much more than just movement from A to B. Moving from A to B (either as person, bit, good, object, or image) is essential. However, by focusing on the *'more than'*, the 'mobilities turn' has come to document and explore how intimately mobilities are linked to issues of identity, culture, and social norms as much as to the instrumental acts of organising flows of traffic, passengers, goods, information, or other types of mobilities. Within this realm of thinking I have worked for more than a decade much inspired (and have been personally encouraged) by one of the seminal thinkers and founders of this academic field, English Professor of Sociology John Urry. Since his ground- breaking book *Sociology beyond Societies* in 2000, Urry has been vocal in articulating this particular perspective on contemporary society (see Urry 2000, 2007, 2011, 2013). Also the works by Adey, Cresswell, Sheller, Vannini and others help to identify the 'mobilities turn' and its intellectual currency (e.g., Adey 2010; Cresswell 2006, 2010; Cwerner, Kesslering, and Urry 2009; Larsen, Urry, and Axhausen 2006; Sheller 2011; Sheller, and Urry 2006; Vannini 2010). My own contribution to the field has been widely published (e.g., Jensen 2006, 2007, 2009a, 2009b, 2010a, 2010b, 2011, 2012a, 2012b, 2013a; Jensen and Richardson 2004). In terms of the institutional embedding of my research in mobilities I have cofounded the Centre for Mobilities and Urban Studies (C-MUS) at Aalborg University in 2008, and a member of the international network 'Cosmobilities' and 'Pan-American Mobilities Network', embedding my research in international networks.

In my work I have come to test a number of the ideas underpinning this book, and in particular I have come to articulate a field of study and research that to my knowledge is nonexistent, namely what I term 'mobilities design'. In this book the aim is to explore and document the usefulness of applying my established theoretical framework of 'Staging Mobilities' (Jensen 2013a) to concrete cases of mobilities design. In the *Staging Mobilities* book the mobile situation is at the centre and the analysis is divided into three areas: material spaces, social interactions, and the human body. This corresponds to the claim that situational mobilities affect and are affected by questions of identity (Self), society (Others) and our relations to the environment (Material Space). The framework can be illustrated in the following model (fig. 1.1).

The model frames the basic assumptions about placing the actual and practical mobile situation at the centre of the analysis and deals with it in three analytically separated themes:

> Mobilities do not 'just happen' or simply 'take place'. According to the Staging Mobilities framework we should think of mobilities as carefully and meticulously designed and planned 'from above', as one might say. However, they are equally importantly acted out, performed, and lived 'from below'. Mobilities are staged and people performing mobilities are engaged in social interactions of staging mobilities. Staging mobilities is therefore a process of creating lived mobility practices and the material preconditions to these. In this research, contemporary urbanism is understood as highly influenced by the staged mobilities of planning, design, architecture, governance systems, and technological networks as well as by the social interactions, cultural meanings, and the production of social order. Staging mobilities is a socio-spatio-temporal process designing mobile lifescapes 'from above' and performed mobile engagements and interactions 'from below' (Jensen 2013a, 5).

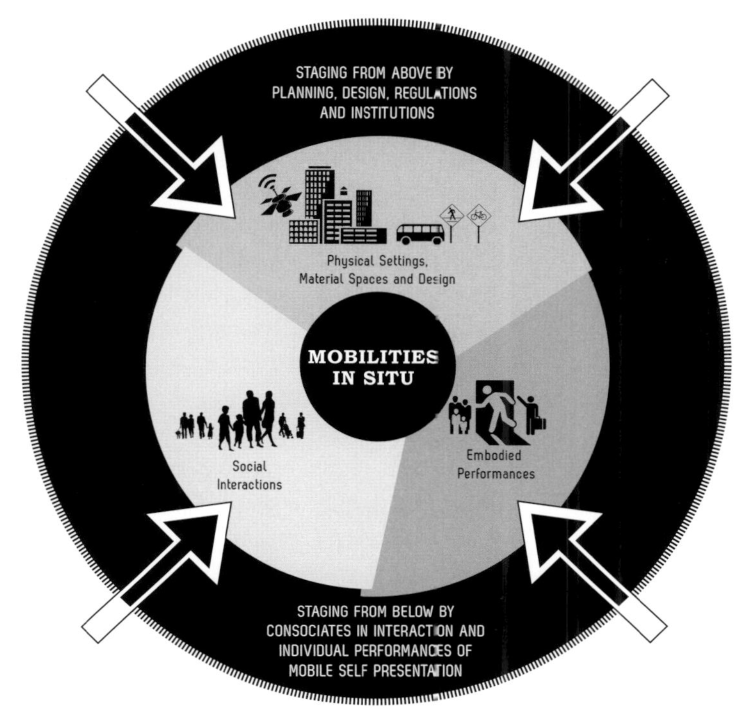

Fig. 1.1: The *Staging Mobilities* model (first published in Jensen 2013a)

In brief, I shall explain how this theoretical framing will be used in the book you are holding in your hands. The key point is to focus on the actual and situational mobilities. By looking at the mobile situation I unpack the underlying assumptions on the design side as well as exploring how social agents perform mobilities in specific situations. The model obviously is an abstraction since we may imagine many more analytical dimensions. Moreover, we might argue that the notion of staging from above and below is an artificial and simplistic dichotomy. However, the model is not to be understood as an ontological postulate but rather as a methodological devise and an analytical heuristic. If we, for example, think of a person riding a bike in the city this is the 'mobilities in situ' that has our attention. According to the model such a situational practice may be staged from above by means of the layout and design of the bike paths, the traffic light system, and the general rules for traffic. The subject biking through the city is moreover also engaged in a practice of staging as she or he 'performs' mobilities by means of the bike chosen, the style of driving, the attention (or inattention) to other fellow mobile subjects in the city. Only in analytical terms does it make sense to separate such staging from above and from below since the mobile experience is perceived in one whole stream of situations without any dissections of the situation into legal compartments, research discipline, or design doctrines. That is seen from the point of view of the mobile subject, which is what I put at the centre of this work. As Norman Foster pointed at in the introductory quote to this chapter, the designed environments facilitating everyday life mobilities are experienced by the 'user' as a holistic experience. If we zoom in on the underlying layers of the model, we see that the mobile situation may be explored with a focus on three particular fields, namely the physical settings, material spaces, and design; the social interactions; and the embodied performances. As before, separating a situation into such dimensions is an act of abstraction that we perform only when looking analytically at the object of research. In a research project on how and why people move in their everyday life, it seems justifiable to argue that the material and physical settings of such practices should be included. Moreover, as the research background for this work lies within situational sociology (much inspired by Erving Goffman; in particular, see Jensen 2010a, 2013a), the social interactions that take place as we are mobile must be addressed. However, it may seem unnecessary and trivial to point this out, but any social and material practice is an embodied performance. We perform mobilities with our bodies in time and space, and the way we position ourselves, sense the environment and other fellow mobile subjects, cannot be grasped without a firm understanding of the importance of the human body. As mentioned other dimensions may be imagined, but from the research interests of this work this is sufficient.

Also I feel an urge to remind the reader that 'the map is not the world'. In other words, we need analytical models and theoretical frameworks to reduce the complexity of the reality studied if we are to handle analysis of complex social practices at all. This is not an act of omission or bias. But what is an act of omission and bias is to pretend not to reduce and simplify. So coming back to the cycling example cited above, I shall pay attention to the fellow bike riders, the pedestrians, and car drivers in the environment as they communicate their 'mobile intentions' (or as they do not, which equally affects the mobile situation). Obviously this may be done in very reflective and overt ways such as giving signs, verbal exchanges, or direct physical engagement. But it may also be performed in much more subtle and implicit ways such as a quick gaze, fleeting eye contact, or a particular way of positioning the body. In other words, by looking at the person cycling we understand that certain things in the situation have been designed, planned, and 'put down' as conditions for the subject; similarly, certain elements of the situations are derived from the habits, norms, intentions, and cultures shaping any sort of social and human practice (including cycling). The body and the interactions with other bodies in the situation (either very directly face-to-face or mediated by technologies) are the touchstones for the *Staging Mobilities* framework that is the analytical background for this book's focus on the design of mobilities.

From these theoretical assumptions I propose in this book to explore concrete cases of mobilities design as well as to investigate more design-oriented dimensions of the research framing. Coming from a practical engagement with mobilities teaching both within 'analytical' disciplines (sociology, geography, and planning) and 'interventionist' disciplines (urban design and architecture) as well as many years of academic mobilities research, I have come to the conclusion that there is a need for a book illustrating and exploring how mobilities are being designed with a huge implication for human culture, identity, and social life. The book *Designing Mobilities* will investigate how the staging of mobilities by means of very specific design solutions and choices not only affects contemporary urban life, but actually shapes cultures and social interaction. Mobility is culture, and the design of the frame conditions for mobilities therefore becomes about much more than rational organisation of traffic flows. *Designing Mobilities* fills a gap in which much other research either is very theoretical or very design oriented, but where the connection between mobilities theory and design literally is non-existent. (Exceptions are Merriman's 2007 study of motorways and Adey's 2010 work in airports.) Due to the complexity of the matter as well as resource restriction, I have chosen to explore Danish cases only in the empirical section. However, I have compiled an appendix on global reference projects to put things into perspective by illustrating how the analytical model may be applied beyond Danish cases. Moreover, the analytical points and details found in the Danish cases are not valid only for or restricted to this study. Needless to say, the cases chosen have generic and global properties which afford inference of results from the Danish cases to other global examples of mobilities design. The visual illustrations in terms of images, photos, and diagrams are furthermore a distinctive feature partly to utilise such techniques for communicating the message of the book, partly to engage with a key design element: graphic representations and diagrams as a method of reflection and analysis.

Materialities of mobilities

In this section I address the relationship between mobilities and design in a broad sense. Speaking from the vantage point of urban design and urban theory, the sort of 'design' I have in mind is related predominantly to urban design, architecture, and urban planning (see Bacon 1967; Carmona et al. 2010; Cullen 1996; Gehl 2010; Halprin 1963; Krieger and Saunders 2009; Lang 2005; Lawson 2001; Lynch 1981; Madanipour 2003; Shane 2005, 2011; Whyte 1988). However, I believe we also should include wider arrays of professions and practices such as traffic engineering, urban logistics, and wayfinding systems designers. The key idea behind this book is partly to illustrate empirically how mobilities are being staged from above by planners, designers, and regulations as well as from below by humans in motion. But I also want to contribute to the emerging articulation of a more distinct research field that I want to call 'mobilities design' (for beginning discussions of this notion, see Jensen 2013a; Lanng, Jensen, and Harder 2012). This means exploring the very physical and tangible layouts and designs of, for example, transit spaces, bike systems, metro stations, and shopping centres. As delimitation to this book's approach to 'mobilities design', I would point to the many interesting accounts of the aesthetics, technologies, and interior designs of vehicles (e.g., Votolato 2007). I do find such perspectives interesting but tangential to this work with its focus on urban space and mobilities in the built environment. To the extent that the interior design of, for example, train compartments or cars, affects the mobile social interactions, this is relevant to the perspective on 'mobilities design'. The analytical angle chosen on mobilities design is the mobile situations as they are staged within a context of public spaces and urban meeting places in their broadest sense. I will go more deeply into the substantive matter of what 'design' might mean in chapters two and three, but for now the key issue is to clarify that the 'interventions' of design and the 'analysis' of mobilities theories might benefit from a mutual exchange of ideas. But let me start in an altogether different place with the reflection by British geographer Nigel Thrift on the lack of experiments and interventions in the social science curricula:

> Experiments have never been a big thing in the social sciences – with some exceptions. But they could be. And that could be very interesting ... I would love to see Master's courses which gave people the ability to do these kinds of things [experiments]. For example at the moment we do not often teach Master's students to construct things, to make things. We don't teach them to draw; we don't teach them to program; we don't teach them all sorts of things which might be interesting if you believe that what we need is an experimental social science (Nigel Thrift in Farias 2010a, 111-112).

As a matter of fact, programs in Urban Design do just these things: teach students to make things, to construct spaces and objects, to draw and make diagrams, to make interventions and installations in urban space to scale (1:1). Conversely, a strong pragmatist undercurrent shapes the understanding of real space, the meaning of design, and the complex relationships between infrastructural systems and lived experiences. So my argument is that, by engaging with the design practices and their interventionist and experimental approaches, mobilities theory arrives at a deeper understanding of the substance matter. But equally, designers may learn to operationalize and utilize concepts and theories in a much more informed design process. But the story does not stop here. I would argue that beyond the usefulness of increased mobilities/design interaction there is an ontologically deeper relation between these fields. Put differently, the mobilities practices in the contemporary city are created, enacted, and afforded (as well as they may be obstructed, prevented, and confined) by the very layout and design of sites, systems, and spaces. The notion of 'affordance' coined by Gibson has been shown to be of relevance to the understanding of mobilities elsewhere (Jensen 2013a), and here I shall refer to the Canadian cultural sociologist Rob Shields when he argues that:

> Affordances are the kind of interactions you can engage in conjunction with a given site or element. For pavement, you can walk on it; you can sit on it; you can drive on it ... And what de Certeau says about the material city is that you have to actualize it as this or that. What will it be? It is your choice at any given time. So, in the actualization of things, people may play essential roles. But one should not underestimate the materials: their hardness, their softness, their ability to maintain a shape. All this makes the material a player in a way that is significant, causative not causal (Rob Shields in Farias 2010b, 297).

The complex interrelatedness of 'things' and people, materialities, and socialities needs to be addressed, and increasingly this is being done from the vantage point of 'Actor Network Theory' (Latour 2005); Assemblage Theory (DeLanda 2006; Farias and Bender 2010); and types of mobilities research exploring these new assemblage/ANT perspectives (Vannini et al. 2012). Moreover, some design historians have now started to see things in line with the perspectives of ANT and Assemblage Theory (Fallan 2010). What emerges is an understanding of the importance of materialities, artefacts, objects, and ultimately the design of sites and places. Such an understanding has been voiced as a critique of the mainstream social science perspective where objects, artefacts, and even embodiment seem to fall beneath the radar. Or in the words of Bruno Latour:

> The social sciences have an amazingly narrow definition of what <u>is</u> in the world; there is a very small list of inhabitants. I mean for them there are no objects, no animals (or very little), so it's only humans. But they are naked humans, often even just heads, something with a body but not with clothes on or without internal organs (Latour in Halsall 2012, 965-6).

So I would argue that a research practice engaged with interventions, material design, and experiments holds the potential for reaching deeper into the meaning of mobilities and the socio-cultural significance thereof. Such potential may not be actualized unless scholars from within the mobilities field embrace and engage with the designers and interventionists since the theories and concepts may facilitate, guide, and stimulate the experimental design work. This is precisely where this book seeks to fill a gap and open a new frontier at one and the same time. The underutilized potential of linking design intervention with mobilities theory may be enacted in multiple ways (see Svenstrup et al. 2008; Poulsen et al. 2012a, 2012b; Jensen and Thomsen 2008). What is important is to move beyond the dichotomies of seeing the material and the social, the technical, and the human, as separate realms. Instead, they are explorations into how complex socio-technical systems and networks may establish new assemblages of humans, objects, spaces, and design. The ideas of the 'sentient city' (Shepard 2011), Code/Space (Kitchin and Didge 2011), and Performative Urban Space (Jensen and Thomsen 2008) illustrate new technologies, new types of urban experiments and interventions. As mentioned above I will engage with the notion of 'mobilities design' in a much deeper manner in the chapters to follow. For now I want to emphasize that there are practical as well as profound epistemological and ontological relationships between mobilities research and design that have only started to be explored.

Coming from the notion of *Staging Mobilities* as a sociological perspective and relating this to material mobilities design, I believe a set of interesting questions starts to emerge. In the next section I shall elaborate on the general research question and its subsets.

The research questions

The research question and the subquestions underpinning this book are the following. In general terms the book is concerned with the overall question;

> How is design affording and/or preventing particular mobile practices in everyday life?

As subthemes to this very general question I shall explore the following in greater detail:

> I. How is the design of various modes of mobilities and sites affecting the mobile situations of everyday life?
>
> *II. How are mobilities represented and 'captured' in analytical and methodological terms?*
>
> *III. How does the design of mobility modes and sites of mobilities influence the social and cultural interactions and exchanges of the contemporary city?*
>
> *IV. How does the design of mobility modes and sites of mobilities enact and engage with the human-embodied performances in the mobile situations of everyday life?*
>
> *V. How can we, on the basis of the investigations and explorations carried out in this book, start to articulate a field of 'mobilities design' and which theoretical, methodological, and disciplinary inputs may be needed?*

These subquestions are addressed across the empirical cases as underpinning and guiding issues. In the wake of the analysis, I hope to be able to provide sufficient answers to these questions and issues. However, the nature of 'critical mobilities research' (Jensen 2009a, 2013a) is partly to provide answers of a factual and practical nature, and partly to be creatively exploratory and seek the borders of new and unfamiliar territories.

The content and organization of the book

The book is organized into four parts and eight chapters. Part one contains the introduction and research questions and part two focuses on representing mobilities. Part three is the empirical analysis of cases and part four contains the conclusion and perspectives.

In part one I present the key issues and the theoretical framework for analysing these issues. The theoretical perspective on how to 'read' the cases is presented so that the reader will be familiar with this line of thinking from the outset. In the first chapter, the link between mobilities theory and design is presented as a key nexus of the book. The growing field of mobilities research is described briefly, and the key rationale behind the book is presented together with the key questions driving this research. The chapter focuses on the *Staging Mobilities* framework and how this can become operational in relation to analysing specific cases of mobilities design. The chapter goes through the three analytical areas of the model: material spaces and design; social interactions; and the embodied performances in order to present how these areas and themes may be explored in cases of mobilities design.

In part two, I look at how mobilities are being represented and 'captured'. Chapter two focuses on various mapping approaches, methods, and technologies in order to comprehend how mobilities design may be understood and represented in research and design efforts. The chapter gives a short overview of a wide array of mobility mapping approaches and methods, some of these being both qualitative and quantitative (e.g., GPS, Songlines, Mental Maps, Serial Vision, RFID, Bluetooth, Video Surveillance, heat sensitive video, computer vision, and Social Signal Processing). Secondly, the chapter's focus is on ideas of representing mobilities and flows in a visual and graphic format. From early visual representations of movement studies of humans and animals to the diagrammatic vocabulary of architects and urban designers, the chapter explores how motion is 'captured' in two-dimensional graphic representations. In the third chapter the notion of 'mobilities design' is presented as a particular emergent research field. On the basis of the analytical and theoretical *Staging Mobilities* framework (Jensen 2013a), this chapter works toward an operational discussion of key concepts and levels of the framework. My own mobilities diagrams are also presented in this chapter. The chapter connects key concepts from the *Staging Mobilities* framework to visual diagrams in order to facilitate the development of an operational framework that will be applied to the analysis of the cases in part three.

Part three of the book contains four detailed case studies all explored using the analytical framework. The case studies cover four modes of mobility: *Walk, Bike, Train,* and *Car.* Chapter four explores the notion of the 'Extra Large' building upholding urban characteristics and features due to its scale and mediating function as transit space in an urban context. The case is the urban shopping mall 'Friis' in the centre of Aalborg, Denmark. Friis is a node of horizontal and vertical mobility of goods and customers. The people frequenting Friis come mostly by private car or on foot. A key feature of Friis is its linking function between areas of the city, making it host both to people in transit as well as shoppers. The chapter mainly explores the pedestrian flows within and through the building complex. Chapter five explores how cycling as a mobility mode is being designed very differently in three Danish cities. The relationship between the moving body, the cycle as an artefact and material vehicle, and the wider system of cycle paths and traffic information systems make up complex socio-technical assemblages that are designed carefully and with the clear agenda of trying to shift car users to bikes in inner cities. The empirical data is from the 'Bikeability' research project on which I worked, and the material used in this chapter is some of the unused and less frequently published material from this project (Andrade et al. 2011, 2012a, 2012b). In chapter six, the busiest train and metro station in Copenhagen, Nørreport Station, is the case used to illustrate how 'metroscapes' are designing, hosting, and orchestrating mobilities. By exploring in detail how the Metro Company has approached the aim of almost 'pure circulation' with no public activities and programs, the case of Nørreport Station is used to show the staging and designing of mobilities within complex assemblages of socio-technical infrastructure systems creating habitats of mobilities in urban everyday life. In chapter seven the interurban freeway that shapes and affords a very large part of the contemporary urban development on a global scale is explored. The key themes are to understand the (interurban) motorway as a space on its own, governed by both formal regulations as well as 'cultures on the move' and the 'grammar of the motorway'. (I want to acknowledge the borrowing of this term from Urban Designer Peter Frost Møller.) The case explored is the motorway stretch from Vejle to Aarhus, Denmark, also dubbed 'the 100 km City'. Chapter seven investigates how material conditions of the motorway design, such as off-ramps, gas stations, and the built environment alongside its path, together with the complex interactions in and between the mobile subjects occupying the 'motorway assemblage', are illustrative of 'mobilities design'.

Part four of the book collects the elements presented in the book and draws conclusions based on these findings as well as pointing forward to perspectives for mobilities research and identifying a new research field of 'mobilities design'. The concluding chapter will draw upon the analysis made so far to engage in a discussion about the education and curricula of the many different disciplines engaged with mobilities design. In the chapter it is argued that many more professions may be considered 'mobility designers' than actually appreciate this. Moreover, the chapter illustrates the cross-disciplinary advantages and potentials that accompany such new insight. The chapter returns to the overall research questions and lays out further implications of mobilities research. In particular, the empirical findings will be linked to the theoretical perspective of *Staging Mobilities*, aiming at contributing to mobilities research by offering a new research perspective focusing on how spaces and sites of mobilities are laid out, designed, and materially constructed. The concluding chapter presents the double research strategy of *Staging Mobilities/ Designing Mobilities* as illustrative of 'critical mobilities thinking'. The final chapter also points to future challenges for theoretical as well as empirical research, arguing for the establishment of a new field of enquiry. The chapter ends by stipulating how such a research area of 'mobilities design' may contribute to both theory and conceptual innovations, as well as to practical and material investigations of how designs shape, afford, and hinder various forms of future mobilities.

From this introductory chapter I now move on to part one of the book where I start in chapter two by shedding light on how mobilities are represented and 'captured' by various analysts over time.

ARRÊT
ARRÊT
ARRÊT
ARRÊT
ARRÊT

2 'CAPTURING' MOBILITIES

MAPPING, NOTATIONS AND RE-PRESENTATIONS OF FLOWS

Ever in flux and process, reality cannot be approached directly. Reality is too vast, and direct means fail. Suitable tools are needed, as in the raising of an obelisk

Siegfried Giedion, Mechanization Takes Command, 1948, p. 14

There is no single best method – questionnaire, interview, simulation, or experiment – for studying people's adaptations to their environments. One chooses methods to suit the problem and the people and not vice versa. These methods are generally complementary rather than mutually exclusive

Robert Sommer, *Personal Space. The Behavioral Basis of Design,* 2007, p. 221

Even today architecture is still mediated above all via photographs in magazines, books or on slides. The space and sequences of movement that these generate are neglected, and so are the processes that an architecture stimulates or prevents

Christian Gänshirt, *Tools for Ideas. An introduction to Architectural Design,* 2007, p. 179

Introduction

This chapter examines various mapping approaches, methods, and technologies in order to comprehend how mobilities design may be understood and represented in research and design efforts. The chapter gives a short overview of a wide array of mobility mapping approaches and methods, some of which are qualitative and some quantitative. Secondly, the chapter focuses on ideas of representing mobilities and flows in a visual and graphic format. From early detailed visual representations of movement studies of humans and animals to the diagrammatic vocabulary of contemporary architects and urban designers, the chapter explores how motion is 'captured' in two-dimensional graphic representations (I want to acknowledge the terminology of 'capturing mobility' in Cresswell's (2006) work.). The short and illustrative examples run from Muybridge's nineteenth-century motion studies, through Halprin's choreographic notations systems, to abstract diagrams of urban flows. Dynamic visualisation tools such as 3D animation and moving images in general have not been included in this chapter. The omission is neither because they are not relevant tools, nor because they do not hold a prominent position within some areas of mobilities design and architecture. Dynamic visualisation tools are excluded solely due to the confinements of this book (and the medium of moving images should be a website, for example).

Mapping mobilities

In this section I present a short overview of a wide array of mobility mapping approaches and methods (e.g., GPS, Songlines, Mental Maps, Serial Vision, RFID, Bluetooth, Video Surveillance, heat sensitive video, computer vision, and Social Signal Processing). As a point of departure I will consult Büsher, Urry and Witchger (2011, 8-12) who mention a number of methods:

- Observing people's movements ('follow the people')
- Participating in patterns of movement (e.g., 'walking with', 'travelling with')
- Mobile Video Ethnography
- Time-space diaries
- Virtual Mobility through texting, web sites, blogging, e-mails, etc.
- Art and Design interventions and experiments
- Mobile Positioning methods (e.g., GPS)
- Capturing 'atmosphere'
- Researching mobile memories (e.g., souvenirs, postcards, letters, etc.)
- Mapping 'real' places
- Examining conversations of the mobile situation
- Researching slowing-down, redirecting, and refocusing places and routes

Obviously some of these methods relate to 'classic' notions of field studies and situated ethnographies, where the key instrument in describing the phenomena is the researcher's own presence as well as the researcher's own embodied sensing of what takes place. Parallel to these are approaches reliant on various levels of technologies as well as quantifiable data collection approaches. What I think should be noticed are not the relatively well-known approaches but rather those approaches where something significantly new is created. An example might be Phillip Vannini's eminent mobile ethnography of the British Columbia Ferries (Vannini 2012), in which he not only elegantly creates a narrative of theory and ethnographic findings, but also offers some sobering remarks on the difficult issues of methods and epistemology:

> Just like I believe that as cultural researchers we are first and foremost storytellers, I do not believe that as researchers we can separate ourselves from our research. Hence in this book I have chosen to engage in a reflexive, *public ethnography* … I take inspiration for my

> writing and organization from the tradition of impressionist and confessional ethnography ... I have opted for a situated, embodied, reflexive, dialogic, and performative strategy of representation ... Indeed, I am less interested in ethnographic *representation* than I am in ethnographic *creation* (Vannini 2012, 26-28, italics in original).

Another innovative contribution is from the urban designer and architect Gitte Marling (2003), who seeks inspiration in the notion of the 'songline' that Bruce Chatwin saw as the predominant way Australian aboriginals related to their environment. By 'singing' particular songs relating to particular sites, the songline created a complex and operational navigation tool creating collective narrative accounts for wayfinding and location. In Marling's interpretation, the songline becomes an 'urban songline' where interview subjects reflect upon the movement lines within the city and how they relate to particular sites, areas, or neighborhoods along the road (Marling 2003). My own studies of, for example, the everyday mobilities at a city square in central Aalborg (Jensen 2010b), the field studies conducted in the Metro of Copenhagen (Jensen 2012a), or the field work capturing how the Bangkok Sky Train establishes a segregated mobilities system (Jensen 2007c) are illustrations of other attempts to fuse ethnographic field work with mobilities theory. All of these approaches have in common the qualitative, embodied, and classic ethnographic mapping perspectives. The foreground issues are how people move, why they do so, how this may feel and affect their understandings of self and other.

In my research I have deliberately sought collaboration with researchers within fields as diverse as computer vision, robotics, and GPS to challenge my understanding of mobilities research and methods. In a project utilizing heat sensitive cameras, we set up a system detecting people's motions and movements across a public square logging and mapping the data as input for urban design parameters (Poulsen et al. 2012a, 2012b). I have also been supervising a geographer on a Ph.D. project applying GPS technologies to map movement patterns in a neighbourhood of Aalborg. A number of interesting maps have been created that illustrate the potential of location-aware technologies (Knudsen et al. 2011). In the project the GPS maps are partly expressions of real-time information on the whereabouts of the interviewees and partly evocative objects facilitating conversations about people's emotions and subjective perceptions of sites and routes. This is so because the respondents more often than not relate to the maps and projections of their own bodily movements in emotional and affective terms.

In this project, the respondent's occupancy of various sites has been registered using GPS and is illustrated here by the 'hot spots' of concentrated activity in the city centre and the suburban areas (fig. 2.1). The same research project also utilizes a website where respondents may upload their routes and trajectories

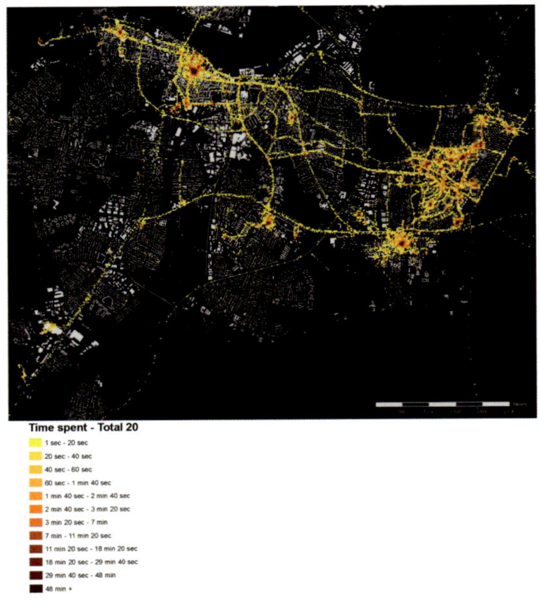

Fig. 2.1: GPS Measurement of staying time in the city (courtesy of Anne-Marie Sandvig Knudsen)

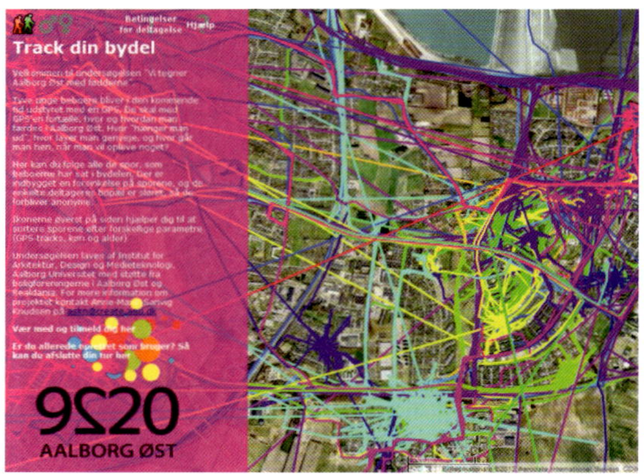

Fig. 2.2: Draw your neighbourhood with your feet (courtesy of Anne-Marie Sandvig Knudsen)

and thus 'draw their neighbourhood with their feet' as the slogan for the project tellingly presents it (fig. 2.2).

By logging routes with GPS and uploading these to a website, a mobile representation of the respondent's whereabouts was created. This representation then proved very interesting for post-registration reflections and interviews about how the respondents feel about particular places and sites in the neighborhood. Another project bridging field observations, interviews, and sophisticated technologies was the study of a mobile robot 'set loose' in a public transit space (Svenstrup et al. 2008). By studying people's interaction with a mobile robot dressed as Santa Claus (dubbed 'Santabot') we explored both the complexities of having a mobile robot in a nonlaboratory environment as well as how people interacted with the robot and how its presence challenged people's notions of what may take place in a regional bus terminal on a gray December day. Taking to GPS I engaged with an artist and architect, Christian Nold, who combined GPS technologies with the technology gained from the 'lie detector' (Nold, Jensen, and Harder 2008). By combining geolocational GPS data with registrations of pulse and body heat, Nold created 'emotional maps' showing how mobile subjects reacted physically and emotionally to various places. The visual maps of such emotional mappings were then used in community dialogues about how various parts of neighborhoods may be frightening, scary, or otherwise in need of redesign.

As mentioned in chapter one there is an experimental dimension to these research projects, where the analytical theorizing becomes inspired and challenged by the pragmatic and material hands-on experiments. Gänshirt argues in his insightful book *Tools for Ideas* (2007) that architecture and design should be thought of as much more integral to research and theorizing. He finds that the theory/practice distinction is rather unhelpful if it leads to unreflected and atheoretical design, as well as to unpractical and abstract theory. Gänshirt distinguishes between three types of design research (2007, 25). Firstly, there is design research based upon cases and examples (what designers and architects often refer to as 'references'), typologies, and individual designers. Secondly, there is design research based upon principles such as specific standards, certain approaches, methodologies, and 'ways of doing'. Thirdly, there is design research based upon theories where 'accountability' is the key word and the inspiration may vary from natural sciences through cultural and humanistic theories to social sciences. Each of these dimensions corresponds to three basic questions: what one can design? (example), how one can design? (methodology), and how design can be accounted for? (theory).

To the list of more explorative research utilizing new technologies must be added research applying Bluetooth technology in mobile phones to collect data, Radio Frequency Identification (RFID) technologies applied to monitor and track movement of people or objects (Suenson and Harder 2011), and the developments of software technologies that will be able to track, monitor, and recognize persons and particular patterns of behavior based only on automated, camera-based monitoring and tracking. One example of this would be the so-called 'Social Signal Processing' (SSP) field, in which work is being done on the development of software in order to recognize predefined types of body expressions, gestures, movements and even facial expressions (Moeslund et al. 2011). The research within this field is, however, still in its infancy and therefore not sufficiently developed (and thus the many Orwellian 'big brother' scenarios are in the distant future). In general the emergence of location-based and location-aware technologies as they are found on smart phones via Internet linking is another field of potential research tools and methods. (See Farman 2012 and Gordon and Silva 2011 for comprehensive accounts of location-based technologies and their social impact). The development and application of GPS and CCTV (closed-circuit television) for military operations and urban policing (e.g., crowd control) is well known and could equally be put to use as mobile methods. In his highly critical but also very timely book *Cities under Siege: The New Military Urbanism*, Steve Graham illustrates how many of these surveillance technologies are expressions of a Focaultdian 'boomerang' in the sense that they are being 'tested' in Iraq, Afghanistan, and the Gaza Strip before 'returning' to the Western urban agglomerations (Graham 2011). Technologies varying from CCTV, remote-controlled flying drones, biometric identification systems, etc., are in the 'toolbox' of the military and surveillance business. Needless to say, this raises huge ethical questions about their application, both in foreign warfare as well as in urban surveillance. But regardless of those questions, these technologies also offer new potential for increasing our understanding of contemporary mobilities and are therefore potentially methods of the future in mobilities studies. (Most people did not realize the potential for research in the GPS when it was launched as a 'military technology'.)

This is not the place to develop a full list of mobile methods. Rather, I would like to stress that there is something very fruitful and important in connecting the very sophisticated and technologically innovative tools to well-known qualitative methods such as observation and interviewing. So rather than turning our backs on the new technologies, I would (despite the fact that my personal preference is the classic in situ observation method) recommend as much experimentation and cross-fertilization between these different fields as possible. Hybrid mobile methods are needed to understand hybrid mobile practices. In much performance art, interaction design, and artistic practice these new technologies are often coupled with very longstanding issues of what is a city, what does it mean to be human, what is life? etc. On a more practical note, I have been instrumental in establishing a research cluster for 'Mobility and Tracking Technologies' (MoTT), where issues of the development and testing of software and hardware for tracking is set into a larger theoretical frame raising social and ethical questions. The point is, however, that in order to understand the potential for research as well as the societal implication of these new technologies, we need to engage in cross-disciplinary dialogue.

A full study could be made of the many methods existing for mobilities research. However, in this context I want to use this short outline of the methods as the stepping stone for a discussion about representation. The technologies and methods for 'capturing' mobilities are rather useless if the data and information acquired are not selected, packaged, and represented in ways that makes sense to an observer. Moreover, I would claim that representing mobilities is not just an issue of communicating results. It is a window into the underlying ontology at play. Put differently, the ways we capture and represent mobilities are reflections of how we comprehend and understand the phenomenon of mobility at a very profound level. However, the notion of 'representation' needs to be qualified here since I am interested in visual techniques for 'capturing' mobilities albeit not from the epistemological standpoint of naïve or 'accurate' representation. As I mention in chapter three, this work is partially inspired by the 'nonrepresentational' or 'more than representational' streams of thinking (Andersson and Harrison 2010; Thrift 2008). So aligned with the epistemological critique of 'mirror accurate representation' I must put emphasis on the fact that all the following ways of representing mobilities are related to technical limitations, subjective choices, and methodological blind spots that we need to remember in order not to become naively seduced into thinking that these ways of 'capturing' mobilities are objective and accurate.

Representing mobilities

In this section I will focus on ideas of representing mobilities and flows in a visual and graphic format. From early detailed and visual representations of movement studies of humans and animals to the diagrammatic vocabulary of architects and urban designers, this section explore how motion is 'captured' in two-dimensional graphic representations. The short and illustrative examples reach from Muybridge's nineteenth-century motion studies, through Halprin's choreographic notations systems, to Lynch's abstract diagrams of urban flows. I am primarily interested in the visual and graphic representations of movements, and thereby plead guilty to a visual bias for and a selective attention to methods of diagrammatic and visual representation (e.g., excluding audio-mappings and real-time living images). The justification is twofold. First, I need to delimit the discussion due to lack of space. And secondly, I chose to focus on the visual and diagrammatic since this is one of the key fields of representations with which mobilities designers engage. The notion of 'diagram' and its epistemological and methodological status is very complex (Garcia 2010) and will be touched upon both here and in chapter three. Often the visual diagrams printed on a two-dimensional surface are completely inadequate for capturing the dynamism of the mobile situation. However, diagrams are not only about representation. They are often active design tools and may be abstract and conceptual attempts to express mobile situations or envision future mobilities. We might think of diagrams in these two very different ways: to capture, represent, and report something held to be already in existence, and secondly as a performative intervention and contribution that moves beyond the representational and into the interventionist realm as is the case when an architect or designer uses a diagram to create form, or when a theoretical, conceptual, and reflective practice includes the diagram as a 'vehicle for thinking'. To put matters simply, the first notion of the diagram is my concern in this chapter and the second dimension will be at the centre of chapter three.

Tim Cresswell shows in his seminal work *On the Move* (2006) how mobilities have been attempted to be 'captured' by various devices and technologies. I return to these examples but first note that these attempts to 'capture' mobilities in representations were by no means the earliest accounts of such endeavours. Thus, according to Sigfried Giedion, we find the first graphical representations of movement in the works of Nicolas Oresme writing in the fourteenth century (Giedion 1948, 16). In particular the treatise *On Intensities* contains an interesting attempt via a graphical method to determine the 'changing qualities of a body'. Oresme studied change over time and, thus, ultimately speed and acceleration -- two key components of material mobilities.

The innovation of this system was that '*Oresme was the first to recognize that movement can be represented only by movement, the changing only by the changing*' (Giedion 1948, 16). This was achieved by representing the same subject repetitively over and over again. From the works of Renaissance painter, engineer, and philosopher Leonardo da Vinci, we also know of early motion studies and diagrams depicting mobilities. This is, for instance, the case when da Vinci studied the flight of birds to get input for his designs of various flying devices (Cianchi 1984, 58). Following Giedion's account of the history of mobilities diagrams, we move swiftly to the nineteenth century to learn that the material pulse of nature was then 'captured' in much more dynamic ways. In 1860, the French physiologist Étienne Jules Marey invented a device termed the 'Spygmograph', by which the heartbeat and pulse of a body (animal or human) could be represented on a smoke-blackened cylinder. He also made a version of the device that represented muscular movements.

Marey worked intensively on 'capturing' mobilities in all sorts of ways and included human and animal as well as nature's movements and flows (e.g., airstreams). According to Giedion, Marey reflected upon the Cartesian heritage but the novelty springing from his work was how he *'translated organic movement into graphic form'* (Giedion 1948, 19). This becomes particularly effective with the advent of the technology of photography to which Marey turned in the 1880s. There was a certain affinity to the work of Muybridge even though the former was more concerned with representing movement on a single plate/screen and the latter developed multiple-camera recordings that produced the now almost-iconic representations that have become the hallmark of Muybridge's motion studies. But there was a divergence of interests since Marey strived for a three- dimensional form of representation, leading him to complex experiments with camera settings. He also explored what he termed 'time photography' or 'chronophotographie' (Giedion 1948, 24). A major breakthrough was, however, dependent on two things: firstly, the moving image or what we today term film. Secondly, the strict, scientifically oriented interest of Marey and his colleagues was boosted significantly with the advent of the attempts within the industrial sphere to monitor and ultimately optimize the workflows of the modern production process. The American production engineer Frank B. Gilbreth started this work around 1912, and with the founding of 'Scientific Management' the detailed study and representation of motions and mobilities gained its most sophisticated expression. Many seem to connect the development of 'Scientific Management' with Frederick Taylor, but his efforts are to be understood in relation to the ground-breaking work done by Gilbreth. The 'time-space studies' of Scientific Management dispensed with stop watches and started exploring more 'objective' measuring devices such as the 'Cylograph', which in all its simplicity was recording a worker's motions with an attached light bulb, representing the absolute path of movement (initially only recorded by an ordinary camera (Giedion 1948, 103). For a more detailed account of the study of workplace motion, see Creswell 2006, chapter 4.

Giedion argues that Gilbreth was the first to provide deeper insights into the 'pure path' as well as the time element of a movement. In the words of Giedion:

> A line leads from the fourteenth century to the present: Oresme – Descartes – Marey – Gilbreth: The theologian-philosopher – the mathematician-philosopher – the physiologist – the production engineer. Three of these men arose in the country that is outstanding for visualization in all of its domains. The fourth, an American, appeared as soon as efficiency demanded knowledge of 'the best way to do work' (Giedion 1948, 24).

To Giedion this is a significant new realm that draws lines to the works of Marcel Duchamp and Wassily Kandinsky within art, or Henri Bergson and James Joyce in philosophy and literature, as well as to the Italian Futurists' obsession with speed and technology, but also the dynamic paintings of Joan Miro and Paul Klee (Giedion 1948, 25-29; 106-113).

The English photographer Eadweard Muybridge made some unusual and substantial contributions to this discussion. Cresswell delivers a very detailed analysis of the work of Muybridge in his book *On the Move* (2006), so here I mention him only in passing. Muybridge was a British-born, American working photographer who was a pioneer in the development of photographing humans and animals in motion. Actually, his choice of motifs was rather exotic, e.g., nudes carrying objects like buckets of water or a nude woman spanking a nude child (Adam 2010). The animal studies and very detailed exploration of the physiological and almost mechanical dimension to living mobilities that occupied Muybridge is perhaps his most well-known legacy. Muybridge studied humans, cows, horses, birds, kangaroos, deer, lions, elephants, giraffes, tigers, raccoons, and many more moving animals.

The grid and the framing of mobile bodies in time-space by Muybridge are, according to Cresswell, an expression of the 'epistemology of the grid' (Cresswell 2006, 62). This is in fact a very old technology and lends itself to the Cartesian division and rational organisation of elements within a greater whole. Having the grid as the background to the mobile bodies would 'make mobility legible'. As with the representational technique of 'perspective', the grid revolutionizes the way architects and designers may represent their inner ideas.

I want to move from the arts toward urban design and its concern for 'capturing' mobilities. Here the American urban designer and planner Lawrence Halprin and his interesting applications of insights drawn from his wife Anna Halprin and her practice as a dance choreographer are of particular interest. (See Merriman 2011 for an insightful story of the urban designer and his choreographer wife and their interchange). In particular Halprin is interesting in this context because he put the mobile body within the ordinary mobile situation at the focus of his analytical endeavour, thus aiming to understand 'Mobilities in Situ'. Halprin (1963, 1966) examined mobilities under the heading of 'choreography' and worked with both artful and expressive photographic attempts to capture flux and mobility intensities; he also worked with 'dance notations', capturing the movement patterns of bodies in time and space. (See also the standard-setting work on dance notation written by Ann Hutchinson Guest (2005) on the 1920s German dance notation developer Rudolf Laban and his 'Labanotation'.) The attempt to capture flux in photographic representation was inspired by the visual arts, and painting in particular. However, Halprin also developed an abstract system of representation and notation much closer to sheet music.

Also Halprin, like Lynch, saw infrastructure and transportation artefacts as having sculptural qualities (1966, 16). Halprin explained that *'in order to design for movement, a whole new system of conceptualizing must be undertaken'* (1963, 208). Halprin thus worked toward creating an abstract tool, putting movement before the environment, and he specified the challenge for urban designers and planners this way:

> We need a system to program movement carefully and analyze it, a system which will allow us to schedule it on a quantitative as well as qualitative basis. Since movement and the complex interrelations which it generates are an essential part of the life of a city, urban design should have a choice of starting from movement as the core - the essential element of the plan. Only after programming the movement and graphically expressing it, should the environment - an envelope within which movement takes place - be designed. The environment exists for the purpose of movement (Halprin 1963, 209).

The ambition of representing 'arrested motion', so to speak, by utilizing techniques similar to music is interesting. The American avant-garde musician and composer, John Cage, illustrated both the diversity of music notation as well as the different attempts to capture the very dynamic nature of music in his book *Notations* (Cage 1969). Clearly one should be careful about extending the analogy between musical notes and moving humans too far. But after all music is an issue of time-space organisation of notes in flow. So seen from the point of 'capturing as representation', it does makes sense. Needless to say the whole discussion about embodied and practiced mobilities, how they are sensed, and how mobilities are highly effectual leads to a different analytical trajectory. However, staying with the analogy of music, Lynch stated rather frankly that one, as an architect/urban designer, should organize infrastructures 'as a melody' (Lynch 1960, 99).

The urban designer and city planner Ed Bacon uses the terminology of 'movement systems' in his book *Design of Cities* (1967). The book is interesting due to its emphasis on mobilities for both architecture and urban design. In relation to the issue of representation and 'capturing' mobilities, Bacon draws heavily on the artwork of Paul Klee. The inspiration from art in recognizing its potential for 'capturing' motion is also seen in other works, such as the paintings of Kandinsky, which influenced both the Bauhaus School as well as the Situationist movement (Sadler 1998). Bacon quotes Klee in order to verbalise the importance of mobilities in this manner:

> A man of antiquity sailing on a boat, quite content and enjoying the ingenious comfort of the contrivance. The ancient represents the scene accordingly. And now: What a modern man experiences as he walks across the deck of a steamer: 1. His own movement, 2. The movement of the ship which may be in the opposite direction, 3. The direction and velocity of the current, 4. The rotation of the earth, 5. Its orbit, 6. The orbits of the moon and the planets around it. Result: an interplay of movements in the universe, at their centre, the 'I' on the ship (Paul Klee in Bacon 1967, 11).

Here Klee articulates with great sensibility the multiscalar and relational sense of embodied mobilities characteristic of contemporary infrastructural systems. In the seminal book *Site Planning* by Lynch and Hack (1984), they similarly discuss how to map mobile practices in the city. One of the recommendations is that the designer should make careful observations, traffic counts, and diagrammatic illustrations of people moving in and out of the space under observation. They compare the diagrammatic notation to that of 'dance notations' and are thereby close to articulating viewpoints similar to the ones found in Halprin's works. Lynch and Hack acknowledge that 'automatic cameras' may be used, but also that there is no real substitute for the 'sympathetic experience of real places in action', as it is said (Lynch and Hack 1984, 86). Other classic studies of urban life on smaller scales are, however, less afraid of embracing the technologies of the day as in the case of William Whyte's studies of a small urban space in Manhattan (Whyte 1988). Whyte used camera observation widely and was in many ways a forerunner to the work of architect and urbanist Jan Gehl, who also studies the way people appropriate urban spaces in general, and in particular how designs may encourage or discourage activities and movements (Gehl 2010). Lynch tried to capture the 'highway experience' in his study with Appleyard and Myer: *The View from the Road'* (Appleyard, Lynch, and Myer 1964) where the mobile perception of movement spaces such as the highway was at the forefront. The research project of Lynch and his colleagues is however not only about the isolated mobile individual but rather takes the analysis to a more general 'birds-eye' view of highway choreography (a perspective I will return to in chapter seven).

The *View from the Road* study has been very influential in shaping many later explorations of motorway and highway experiences (see Nielsen et al. 2005; Houben and Calabrese 2003) and is as such ground breaking in its efforts to 'capture mobilities'. Sommer describes the efforts made by Lynch and his colleagues this way:

> In their studies of highway experience, Appleyard and his associates believed that their first task was to develop techniques for recording, analysing, and communicating the visual and kinaesthetic sequences of highway travel. Without such techniques, it is difficult to express or refine design alternatives short of building full-scale roads. Sensing the inadequacies of photographic recording for detailed analysis of visual experience, they have developed an intriguing system analogous to the music

> notations used by composers in which the road becomes a spatial and kinaesthetic rhythmic experience – a symphony (Sommer 2007, 213).

It is interesting that Sommer in fact sees the representations of 'photographic recording' as inadequate when compared to the diagrams and notation techniques applied by designers. To Sommer, the 'realist' representations of photographs may fall short of facilitating the creative process of 'mobilities design'. The representation of flows in space and time share similarities with ideas as diverse as 'capturing music' and 'staging movies'. We might talk about a particular 'cinematic urbanism' representing the city and mobilities in accordance with basic principles of moviemaking and film editing. A number of architects and designers compare auto-mobilities to a cinematic experience (Appleyard et al. 1964; Halprin 1963; Ingersoll 2006; Lynch 1990; Schwarzer 2004; Venturi et al. 1972). Halprin writes of urban mobility as similar to frames in a motion picture (1963, 199) and Ingersoll (2006) uses the term 'jump-cut urbanism' to capture the cinematic 'staging' of auto-mobilities as well as the creative 'editing' that is the job of the architect, planner, traffic engineer, or urban designer. Ingersoll argues that:

> For a driver, buildings, signs, and background perspectives are arranged much like a sequence of shots assembled for a film, and when the driver uses the rear-view mirror, the extraordinary phenomena of seeing forward and backward simultaneously occurs just like the montage of a cinematic jump cut … With the advent of the automobile, the theatrical order of the urban street was converted into a cinematic one, composed of long shots, close-ups, pans, tracking shots, and above all, the accelerated montage of jump cuts (Ingersoll 2006, 75).

To Ingersoll the driver resembles the film director, assembling bits of disconnected shots (Ingersoll 2006, 80). With a reference to the Soviet cinema icon Dziga Vertov's notion of 'Kinopravda', Ingersoll points to the fact that montage and 'jump-cut urbanism' may be seen as a modern liberation from human immobility (Ingersoll 2006, 84). Seen from the perspective of Vertov, 'jump-cut urbanism' and the fragmentation by way of the montage is a new code of perception surpassing the norms of the perspectival code (Ingersoll 2006, 85). Christian Gänshirt explains that the Dutch architect Rem Koolhaas also describes his work as that of a film maker, thinking through his buildings as a sequence of scenes and 'cuts' that he arranges along an elaborate path (Gänshirt 2007, 179). The work of Gordon Cullen under the heading of 'serial vision' is precisely an attempt to capture the almost scenographic and cinematic visual experience of a person moving through a built environment and the vistas and sights (favouring the visual, for sure) that emerge as one, for example, turns a corner to find new sights and impressions (a method I shall apply both in chapter four and six).

In relation to the codification of design knowledge and representational diagrams, the internationally recognized 'manual' from Neufert and Neufert termed *Architect's Data* (Neufert and Neufert 2000) is a study worth considering on its own: it lays down very detailed and quantified design standards on everything from kitchen sinks and toilettes to airport terminals, but also utilizes the diagram of the human body much inspired by both Leonardo da Vinici's Vitruvian Man and Le Corbusier's much later diagrams of the human body as the yardstick for design (Neuftert & Neufert 2000, 15).

Diagrams and representations of mobilities may be abstract or concrete, and they may refer directly to human bodies in movement or objects and artefacts on the move. The architectural diagrams of Bernard Tschumi are of particular interest and relevance here. Cook sees an analogue to the 'choreographic diagrams' of ballet in Tschumi's work (Cook 2008, 25)

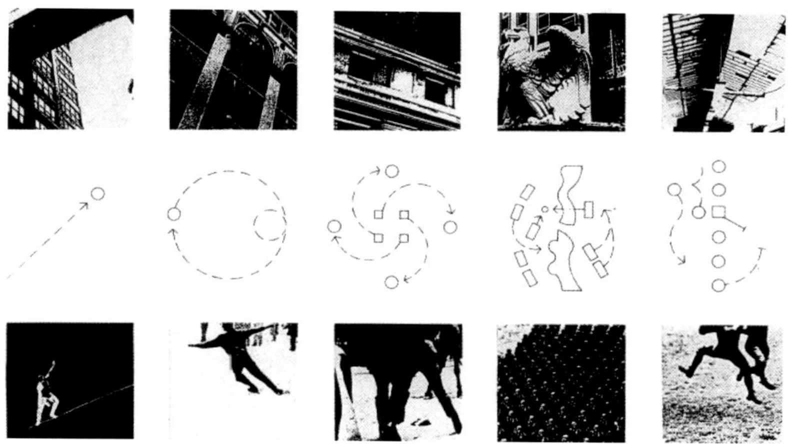

and highlights the so-called *Manhattan Transcripts* as iconic examples of an attempt to 'capture' mobilities (fig. 2.3).

In *The Manhattan Transcripts*, Tschumi (1994, XXI) articulates a view of architecture in which it is an '*organism passively engaged in constant intercourse with users, whose bodies rush against the carefully established rules of architectural thought*'. Centred on the human body and mobilities, Tschumi develops a complex movement notation (fig. 2.3). In this work he speaks of the accuracy of recording bodies' movements and their relationship to architecture and, like Halprin and others, Tschumi develops his vocabulary into one inspired by dance and choreography:

> Rather than merely indicating directional arrows on a neutral surface, the logic of movement notation ultimately suggests real corridors of space, as if the dancer has been 'carving out of a pliable substance'; or the reverse, shaping continuous volumes, as if a whole movement has been literally solidified, 'frozen' into a permanent and massive vector (Tschumi 1994, XXIII).

The *Manhattan Transcripts* by Tschumi are also inscribed into the previously mentioned cinematic perception of architecture and mobilities. In the complex diagrams of Tschumi, there is furthermore much sensitivity to the embodied performances of mobilities. In reflecting upon the relationship of mobility and the diagram, Tschumi argues that:

> Before time and narrative comes the body and the movement of that body in space. If I define architecture as space occupied by bodies and the motions of bodies in that space, then inevitably I need a vehicle, an instrument, a tool in order to describe the interaction between that space,

Fig. 2.3: The Manhattan Transcripts (Tschumi 1994:46)

> and the movement of the body. So immediately the necessity of introducing a mode of notation becomes apparent (Tschumi 2010, 198).

Tschumi thus developed a more intuitive notation technique, in which he substituted by the diagrams of superimposed 'layers' used in his most well-known project, Parc de la Villette. The diagrams of the UN Studio are a further development in the direction of embracing the mobile and fluid. Their diagrams of 'time-based architecture' are essentially maps of movements (van Berkel and Bos 2010, 227).

In the architecture and urban design of the 1990s, there is an increasing experimentation with visual diagrams as both creative tools and representations; experimentation is done often by superimposing large quantitative data sets and statistical information onto the diagram, creating a hybrid mix between descriptive 'data scapes' and creative twists on 'realism' such as MVDRV's notion of 'Metacity/Datatown' (MVRDV 2010, 246). The practices of Koolhaas (2004), OMA (Patteeuw 2004; Wouter and Garritzmann 2010), MVDRV (Maas 2003; MVDRV 2003), and other predominantly Dutch 'new pragmatists' are the examples here. I will not move deeply into that territory since it would require a very comprehensive exploration. The practice of the architectural company BIG that fuses cartoons and diagrams in an attempt to re-narrate their project for popular appeal would also fall into the category of visualisation and 'creative diagramming' (BIG 2009). Among these 'new pragmatist' experiments with the diagrams, there is one publication I find of special interest in this context: the book *Five Minute City* by Viny Maas and MVRDV (Maas 2003). The book contains the result of a workshop that focused on the relationship between mobilities and architecture from the vantage point of what would happen if everything in a city could be reached within five minutes.

The workshop on the '*Five Minute City*' is also interesting because it captures some of the creative and explorative approach that is much more developed among designers than it is within more analytical disciplines such as sociology and geography. I see this as a clear example of what I term 'mobilities potential thinking' (Jensen 2013a), referring to the open-minded exploration of mobilities. Having said this, however, *Five Minute* City -- even with all its interesting workshop entries -- stays on the 'conceptual' level, as the designers like to say. By this I mean that even though the proposals are bold as well as creative and playful, they are rather abstract and not very tangible in a physical and material sense. There is still one point from the workshop, though, that I like to emphasize. That is the question posed by workshop leader Winy Maas to a group of students: 'What is the design-speed of this proposal?' I find this specific question quite illustrative of the imminent relationship between design and mobilities. In this particular case the 'design-speed' is 120 km/h, meaning that we are dealing with a motorway space where the human capacity to filter and process information and data at such a speed requires large signage and redundancy in the wayfinding information system. The question of the 'design-speed' is a profound example of the key point being made in this book, namely, that designers work with mobilities in a very practical sense and that mobilities scholars from the 'analytical disciplines' may learn a lot from engaging with this way of thinking. Winy Maas has also engaged the relationship between architecture and mobilities in another interesting and thought-provoking project termed 'Skycar City'. In this project Maas and Grace La conducted a studio where the city was designed around an imaginary mobilities technology of the 'Skycar' (i.e., a flying personal vehicle). The studio provokes new ideas about the change from car city to skycar city and changes the perception of fixed armatures for mobility to fluid, layered, and visually intangible pathways of connection. With this studio the imaginary is almost stretched toward a science fiction scenario akin to Luc Besson's blockbuster movie, *The Fifth Element*.

Another architectural company working explicitly with flow and mobilities in relation to its projects is the Foreign Office Architects (FOA), with its globally recognized and prizewinning project for Yokohama International Ferry Terminal (Zera-Polo 2010). In this work FOA uses the diagrams to describe relationships and performances of space in order to anchor their practice in a new hybrid method. Consequently the ferry terminal with its mix of urban mobilities design and landscape architecture (see the appendix where this project is one of the global references) is a 'project developed diagrammatically' (Zera-Polo 2010, 240). The architecture and planning projects of Norman Foster need to be mentioned here as well since they partly are very often directly related to mobilities and infrastructures (Foster 2007), but also because the way this company works with mobilities is related to the linkage between mobilities theory and design practice that I aim to explore in this book. Moreover there seems to be a predominant understanding of infrastructure spaces as 'scenes' of the everyday life and of mobilities as being more than A to B, which fits the research agenda of *Staging Mobilities* and *Designing Mobilities* with much precision. The projects of Foster are often directly related to transit, transport, and mobilities with a large number of terminals and intersections in the portfolio (among which are Kansai International Airport, King's Cross Masterplan, Bilbao Metro, and Stansted Airport, to name but a few). Projects that often are equally related to mobilities but with a more explorative form of representation are the works of Zaha Hadid. In a particular way of creating 'parametric diagrams', the work of Hadid is often represented in diagrams of high sensitivity to flows and mobilities (Schumacher 2010).

Here I have to end this short expedition into the vast territory of mobilities 'capturing' by means of diagrams that would require book-length explorations to be fully realized. However, my intention for bringing in this select number of diagrams was not to tell the full story of architectural diagrams but rather to use the diagrams as illustrations of the ambition long present within architecture and design, namely to 'capture' mobilities.

Concluding remarks

As is now clear, the notion of 'capturing' mobilities is much more complex than what may be dealt with within one chapter. There are huge epistemological and methodological disputes about the status of acts of representation as well as what may be the adequate method for such 'capturing'. Given the complexity of the field as well as the multiple diagrammatic efforts made within architecture and design, I shall sum up only in brief.

The first thing I want to highlight is the multiplicity of methods that are available to scholars of contemporary mobilities. I am aware that it has been advocated by many other scholars, but I am a strong believer in the cross-fertilization of various methods. One important dividing line that needs erosion is the (simplified) notion of qualitative versus quantitative methods. From my own research experience it seems that we have moved beyond the point of no return; combining qualitative and quantitative methods is a must and should not need to be defended as either provocative or novel. Moreover, even though most of my own research is grounded in the ethnographic tradition, where the researcher's own embodied perceptions form a key path to 'data', I want to acknowledge the new and digital networked technologies. GPS and the many other types of 'tracking' that are predominantly related to quantitative data need to be explored and related to the more classic ethnographic perspectives. Some of the new and very technologically led methods for mapping and 'capturing' mobilities may fade away as the technologies on which they rely are outsmarted by new technologies. But this is no excuse for not exploring the potential of any given new technology presenting itself as a potential tool to mobilities scholars.

The second point I would like to direct attention to is the complexity of diagrams and their potential for mobilities thinking and design. In this chapter I have discussed a very rough and selective array of diagrams ranging from very early scientific ambitions to much more expressive design diagrams. Regardless of whether one is trying to introduce the very abstract understanding of flows into a diagrammatic vocabulary of a certain scientific level of ambition or exploring the underlying and abstract dimensions to flow of a more general nature, the framing means selections and emphasizing of certain elements. Additionally, the diagrams expressing the material relationship between mobile bodies and a sense of place could have been made in a different manner, expressing dimensions other than the complexity of mobilities. Diagrams also carry the potential for more expressive dimensions and they may be communication vehicles for complex design parameters. Across any selection of diagrams I believe we find illustrations of the complexity and the key features of any 'map': selection and choice (Jensen and Richardson 2003). Therefore, the more conceptual and theoretical concepts the diagrammatic attempts to capture and to present mobilities are not just neutrals nor are they simple acts of 'mirroring'.

My third and final point is that the diagrams and representations contain a lot of knowledge and underutilized potential for mobilities thinking. Beyond performing and playing an often very interventionist role, the diagrams also become 'vehicles for thinking'. This capacity (or at least potential) is what I address in the next chapter, where I explore the problem of trying to capture and represent mobilities in more depth, and where I also address the notion of 'nonrepresentational' diagrams and discuss how diagrams may facilitate thinking mobilities as well as mobilities designs.

ALLER HOTELGÄSTE SIND
100 % SPAREN IM SCHLAF.
DANK 30 % FIRMENRABATT.
HRS.de
Das Hotelportal
Berlin Hauptbahnhof

3 MATERIALITIES OF MOBILITIES

TOWARDS MOBILITIES DESIGN

The Design of Buildings, which must be stationary, should be based on the movements that will flow through them.

Steen Eiler Rasmussen (1959) *Experiencing Architecture*, p. 150

Movement is the law of our existence: nothing ever stands still, for if it does it begins to go backwards and is destroyed, and this is the very definition of life.

LeCorbusier (1929) *The City of To-Morrow and Its Planning*, p. 243-4

The road is the construction that is most involved in the architecture/mobility relationship. Many mobility problems often derive from the fact that the road is not considered architecture, or at least not an integral part of the overall architectural fabric.

Gino Finizio (2006) *Architecture & Mobility*, p.102

Introduction

In this chapter the notion of 'mobilities design' is presented as an emergent research field. On the basis of the analytical and theoretical *Staging Mobilities* framework (Jensen 2013a), this chapter works toward an operational discussion of key concepts of the framework. The chapter connects key concepts from that framework to visual diagrams in order to discuss an operational approach that will be applied to the analysis of the cases in part three. This chapter is divided into four sections. After the introduction the second section discusses the relationship between design and mobilities in order to point toward a notion of 'mobilities design'. In the third section of the chapter the notion of 'mobilities design' will be made operational by engaging the theoretical framework of *Staging Mobilities*. In this section the key concepts will be explained and visual diagrams presented. The chapter ends with a few concluding remarks pointing toward part three and the empirical case analysis.

What is mobilities design?

In coming to terms with the complex relationship between mobilities analysis and design, I draw from chapter nine of my book *Staging Mobilities* (Jensen 2013a) as well as earlier writings on design research (ed. Jensen 2010) but elaborate further on the key concepts and ideas behind the mobilities/design relationship. In this work I do not engage deeply with the difference between architecture and design. The reason I chose the 'design' label is, however, because I find this more general than the label 'architecture' (even though the definition of architecture is equally elusive). Since I consider highway engineers and traffic systems programmers as much 'mobilities designers' as more classic architects and urban designers, I think this justifies a broader category. Such broad categorisation may be provocative to some professions, but here the aim is to ask for a new perspective on the fields or professions that are either contributing directly to the design of mobilities technologies or infrastructures, or indirectly contributing to design decisions shaping the built environment of mobilities. In other words, I am not only interested in architecture and urban design. That said, I do refer to the literature within architecture and urban design. Gänshirt (2007, 10) points to the fact that there is an underutilized potential for research reflection within architecture but stresses that *'design is so centrally significant in today's society that research into it can no longer be neglected'* (2007, 11). The societal transformations during the last three to four decades make it inevitable that design and research activities are closely related, not least because the programs of design education often are university programs and thus intimately linked to research environments.

But what is 'mobilities design' in more precise terms? We may start by noting like Lawson that 'design' is both a noun and a verb, and refers to both processes and products (Lawson 2006, 3). What seems common to design activities is furthermore that they in one way or another aim at making an intervention, an act, or at least an imprint on the world. Design is an interventionist field at some point (or at least it may become so if the projects are being realized).

Obviously the definition of design and thus ultimately of design research will not be sufficiently dealt with, given the limits of this chapter. There are close to as many thoughts and viewpoints on this issue as there are institutions and environments hosting design research and educational programs (Lyon 2011). Moreover, the definitions vary within fields of, for example, architecture, industrial design, or urban design. There are generic definitions to be found and there is common ground among some of these fields of design. Here I only scratch the surface and invite a few definitions into the argument for the simple reason of fuelling a reflection upon the research related to these types of design. According to Webster's dictionary, 'design' reaches back to the Latin word '*designare*', which means to 'mark out or designate'. Likewise the Oxford English Dictionary points toward 'design' as a verb implying 'to set something apart for someone, to intend, to make an imaginary sketch . .' (Shane 2005, 104). As mentioned, this is not the place to enter upon a comprehensive design discussion. Instead, I shall present a few definitions as point of departure:

> Design: The deliberate shaping of the environment in ways that satisfy individual and societal needs (Norman 2007, 171).

> The conscious process to develop physical objects with functional, ergonomic, economic, and aesthetic concern (Rune Monö in Molotch 2005, 263, note 1).

> Designing means devising a form for an object without having that actual object in front of you (Gänshirt 2007, 57).

> Design is the playful creation and strict evaluation of the possible forms of something, including how it is to be made. That something need not be a physical object, nor is design expressed only in drawings. Although attempts have been made to reduce design to completely explicit systems of search and synthesis, it remains an art, a peculiar mix of rationality and irrationality. Design deals with qualities, with complex connections, and also with ambiguities (Lynch 1981, 290).

I want to focus on the design definitions coming out of urban design and such related disciplines as these do fit the general aim of identifying 'mobilities design'. Therefore I have found Lynch's definition most useful since it captures both the material and immaterial, as well as the play between the rational and irrational or should we say creative leaps in the design process. So from this it should be clear that I am subscribing to a very broad notion of design and that the objects and scales are not something that defines this in a positive sense. In the words of Lella and Vignelli:

> We believe that the designer should be able to design anything, "from spoon to the city" because the basic discipline of design is one, the only things that change are the specifics (Lella and Massimo Vignelli in Gibson 2009, 17).

Moreover, I take the interaction between the 'analytical' and 'interventionist' perspectives to be very promising but also that such simple nomenclature of course may cloud the fact that these may have more in common than what surfaces in this distinction. (See Caliskan 2012 for a reasonable critique of the upholding of the 'analytical/constructive' distinction). Elsewhere I have argued that:

> … there can be no such thing as 'pure practice'. Thus we neither chose to start with clean theory and pure abstraction, nor start with concept-less practical examples. We need to understand more about the complex nature of utterances and concepts in relation to practices and actions as for example Austin (1962/75) highlights. Likewise the later work of Wittgenstein demonstrates language use is a 'form of life' (1953) and hence separation between knowledge and action, of theory and practice, is impossible. As the observation of Kurt Lewin goes, 'there is nothing as practical as a good theory (Jensen 2004a, 255)!

So even though separating the analytical and the interventionist perspectives is an artificial distinction, I will keep it for the sake of the argument. This is in parallel with Eisenman, who sees a double dimension to the diagram: *'In architecture the diagram is historically understood in two ways: as an explanatory or analytical device and as a generative device'* (Eisenman 2010, 94). The definition of 'mobilities design' requires more work indeed, but for now the working definition applied here reaches back to the notion of situational mobilities and is basically concerned with answering the pragmatic question: *What design decisions and interventions afford, enable, or prevent concrete mobile situations?* In light of such a pragmatic and situational understanding, 'mobilities design' reaches across fields of practice and disciplines and may include architecture, urban design, and planning as well as traffic engineering, interaction design, software design, product/industrial design, and service system design. This is admittedly a broad notion but just as the disciplinary underpinning of the 'mobilities turn' is diverse, so are the design practices and professions of relevance to 'mobilities design'. Or put differently: the design decisions and interventions affecting and creating 'mobilities in situ' are the ones of interest and relevance to research into 'mobilities design'.

One of the ways to build a bridge from the predominantly analytical 'mobilities turn' toward the more interventionist design disciplines is to look into one of the very dominant and widespread methods of design: the diagram. Obviously we may find diagrams within the social sciences but rarely of the detail and level of entwinement with analytical reflection that we find within the design field. (Diagrams within social sciences are often descriptive as in organizational studies or highly abstract theoretical constructs.) Social sciences diagrams are most often rather abstract, conceptual, and distinctly not 'spatial'. So in order to comprehend the materialities of mobilities, I propose a link between design and mobilities theory via the notion of the 'diagram'.

Diagrams for a research agenda

In this section key concepts from the *Staging Mobilities* framework will be deepened with visual diagrams, etc. Accompanying the *Staging Mobilities* model presented earlier (fig. 1, chapter one), there are a number of theoretical concepts and ideas that form a new analytical vocabulary for mobilities analysis. Some of these are listed below and are connected to a diagram. This form of presentation is very much inspired by Kevin Lynch in his book *Good City Form* (1981). However, the diagrams are not meant to work as representations by means of iconic or realist similarity. There is no naïve goal of representation taking place with these diagrams, but rather an attempt to supplement the linguistic vocabulary with visuals that may work to inspire further reflection. Diagrams may obviously mean a lot of different things, but here I want to position myself within the field of diagrammatic thinking that considers them to be much more than representations (Garcia 2008; Lynch 1981; Rendgen 2012). As Shane argues, '*A diagram, like a telegram, compresses a lot of information about a proposition or argument into a small space*' (2010, 80). To put matters differently, the way I intend to engage with diagrams in this chapter differs fundamentally from the 'representative' discussion of chapter two. Thus I engage with the performative and 'more than representative' and interventionist potentials of diagrams. There is definitely a link between nonrepresentational perspectives, pragmatism, diagrams, and experiments (McCormack 2010) that needs to be explored through the new field of 'mobilities design'.

Notes on the status of the diagram

The issue of how diagrams enter design processes and communication interaction with users and the public is complex and cannot be adequately explored here. Several works discuss how diagrams may also enter directly as the catalyst of a creative process as well as a visual outcome. (See Ingold 2007 and Ingledew 2011.) Bernard Tschumi, whose diagrams for *The Manhattan Transcripts* we saw in chapter two, argues that: '*For me the diagram is a device, a tool that I am always using, that I am improving, this is an extension of my mind*' (2010, 202). In other words, they are both a practical tool and a powerful mental technique. I am leaning on the general interpretation of diagrams as something much more intrinsic to the design process than simple communication devices (and find support for this understanding in the works of, for example, Cook 2008; Garcia 2010; Gänshirt 2006;

Renden 2012). Shane captures neatly the potential as well as the ambivalences of diagrams (within urban design) this way:

> Diagrams of the city can be both magical or scientific, or a strange hybrid combination of these two, like urban design guidelines that manipulate the city image to create a desirable, marketable scenography. Diagrams can be of great use to urban designers in clarifying the structure of the city, its genetic code in small patches and its dynamics between patches. They can show individual paths, complex sections and collective shared maps. At the same time they have their limitations like any analytical device. Diagrams are inevitably reductive and simplistic. The life of the city and local conditions easily escape their net. Diagrams help us see the city, but at the same time can blind us to its real complexity and fluidity (Shane 2010, 87).

Here is a hint to the epistemology of diagrams as they in certain respects are active in creating knowledge and statements about the world; Shane also points to the reductive nature of diagrams (which applies to theories in general). Likewise, Bowring and Swaffield argue that the diagrams from Halprin, Lynch, and later writers neglect what they term the multisensate and emotive (phenomenological) dimensions (Bowring and Swaffield 2010, 142). This has its obvious limitations in the static nature of two-dimensional graphics and needs more technologically advanced components added. The literature on diagrams is rich and here I will only be able to touch upon a few (e.g., Amoroso 2010; Garcia 2008; Ingledew 2011). There is of course a tension between looking toward the diagram as 'representation' in rather simple terms of 'mirroring' reality, and then to understand the potential of the diagrams as 'vehicles for thinking'. The former function may be relevant and quite adequate for some purposes, but here I am more interested in the latter dimension of the diagram. Dean and Garritzman (2010) argue, with reference to Koolhaas and OMA, that the diagram in design is equivalent to the metaphor in language use. In this sense the diagram (like the metaphor) works as an organizing principle assembling the components of a particular project. Furthermore, I explore an idea that I have been developing for a while, namely, that there is an interesting affinity between the diagrams as 'vehicles for thinking' and the so-called 'nonrepresentational' strand of thinking that has emerged within social science in general, and human geography in particular (Berkel and Bos 2010, 224; Malnar and Vodvarka 2010, 112). Key thinker and 'nonrepresentational' exponent par excellence Nigel Thrift put it this way:

> ... nonrepresentational theory asks three main questions. First it questions the divide between theoretical and practical work ceding certain theoretical conundrums to practice. Second, by questioning what is in the world, it exposes a whole new frontier of human endeavour, what might be called the construction of new matterings, along with their typical attachments, their passions, strengths and weaknesses, their differences and indifferences. Third, by intensifying the intensity of being, it is able to question the load of precognitive conditionings that make up most of what it is to be human. In other words, or so I will argue, it is possible to boost the content of bare life, making it more responsive, more inventive and more open to ethical interventions (Thrift 2008, 22).

The point about including 'nonrepresentational' perspectives is thus that this strand of thinking shares the ambition to move beyond naïve representation as well as pointing toward a pragmatic understanding of concepts and theories. The influence on the field of study through the development of theories, concepts, and methods is in this sense both performative and pragmatic. These are two key terms I also find of relevance to understanding design. The relevance of 'nonrepresentational' thinking is also evident when it comes to the inclusion of notions of ambience, affect, emotions, and atmospheres. These are not alien to design fields, but they are only slowly beginning to become embraced by mobilities theories. Furthermore, Anderson and Harrison (2010, 5-13) argues that 'nonrepresentational' theories are antisubstantialist, non-subject based, give equal weight to humans and 'things', are experimental, and increasingly concerned with effect. I think we are starting to see the coming-together of rather interesting elements like mobilities analysis, design thinking, 'nonrepresentational' and performative aspects, awareness of effect, embodiment, and practices all within or affiliated with some sort of 'mobilities pragmatism'. Obviously such diverse thinkers and perspectives may not be lumped together under one epistemological heading. Nevertheless, I do find the pragmatic dimension quite commonplace and cross-cutting in relation to many of these thinkers (see also Caliskan 2012). For instance, the landscape designer James Corner argues that '*... the function of mapping is less to mirror reality than to engender the re-shaping of the worlds in which people live*' (Corner 1999, 213). So maps are performative as '*...mappings do not represent geographies or ideas; rather they affect their actualization*' (Corner 1999, 225). This is significant since a whole set of disciplines within architecture, landscape design, and urban design are utilizing the notion of 'mapping' and the diagram as key tools for making design proposals and to reflect upon the realities faced. I should be careful to mention that maps and diagrams are not necessarily the same thing, but they may be, as for example, when relatively 'realist' representations in maps are overlayered with icons, words, and graphics to add semantic layers to the map/diagram (such as the standard topographic atlas or 'Google Maps' with its layers of information and icons). In his book *Becoming Place*, Dovey argues for utilizing Deleuze and Guattari's notion of the diagram as an 'abstract machine' to disentangle elements of places as assemblages (Dovey 2010, 27). Quite a few people have noticed the powerful potential in thinking of diagrams like 'abstract machines' (Kwinter 2010, 124; Eisenman 2010, 97). This is indeed interesting in this context but what is more so is the fact that Dovey connects the diagram to the design practices in much the same manner I am doing here. Dovey sees the diagram as a 'design driver'. Actually Dovey treats the diagram and the map under the same heading and refers also to the work and thoughts of Corner, Deleuze, and Guattari. In line with this he discriminates between 'mapping' and 'tracing', the former being related much more to the creative and performative (and one might say 'nonrepresentational') whereas the latter refers to the 'mirroring' aspirations of various representations (Dovey 2010, 29). The notion of maps as acts of representation and power is very well described (Jensen and Richardson 2003). Maps might be acts of bureaucratic homogenization and thus governmentality or part of *Seeing Like a State*, to use the evocative title coined by James C. Scott (1998). Maps and mapping may also be understood as subjective engagements with the world as in the *derivé* of the Situationist movements (Sadler 1998). Much detailed discussion may unfold in relation to the differences and similarities between maps and diagrams. Here I want to move toward a more tangible agenda and explore the potential of diagrams in relation to the mobilities thinking already articulated elsewhere (Jensen 2013a). It should be noted that this is very much an experiment and there is no guarantee that these diagrams are of a quality and a nature that will work as communicative devices. Having said so, there is no doubt that they worked as facilitators for exploring how to connect the theoretical concepts with the empirical analysis.

From the work thus far, both here and in *Staging Mobilities*, I turn now to an attempt to expand the linguistic definitions and understandings of key terms within this theoretical perspective. The diagrams have worked for me in a pragmatic sense to facilitate and support the 'thinking work' of bringing my ideas together. Here I am inspired (albeit post facto) by the way Tim Ingold speaks about 'lines' and visual images:

> Drawing is fundamental to being human – as fundamental as are walking and talking. For whenever we talk we gesture with our bodies, and insofar as these gestures leave traces or trails, on the ground or some other surface, lines have been, or are being, drawn. Yet contemporary western society attaches little value to drawing, and those who have been educated into its values are happy to admit not only that they 'can't draw' (even though they can and do) but also that there is no particular reason why they should … Why draw, indeed? If your purpose is to describe and explain, you can do it better with words. If your purpose is to represent, illustrate, or display, you can do it more quickly and accurate by photographic means. Drawing, to the extent that it persists at all, looks like a survival, rendered more or less obsolete by the keyboard and the camera (Ingold 2011, 177).

Without comparing my skills to those of a trained designer and architect, I do find an element of resonance with the way Ingold describes the sketching of an architect and its complex relationship to reflection and thinking:

> Most contemporary architects love to draw but hate to write. They always carry pencils with them, and are constantly doodling and sketching … They draw as they think, and think as they draw, leaving a trace or trial both in memory and on paper (Ingold 2007, 162).

There is obviously an element of generalisation in the quote and I do not claim to have mastered the drawing skills of an architect, but the expression of 'drawing as thinking and thinking as drawing' is a rather accurate description of my work with diagrams.

I present a large number of diagrams knowing well that more could have been made, and that less might do, for setting up an analysis and making my point, which is ultimately that the diagrams are 'vehicles for thinking' as well as openings toward design analysis. As a means of introduction to this, I return to the point of diagrams as 'vehicles for thought'. Seen this way, the drafting and sketching of these diagrams have facilitated my articulation of the theoretical concepts and nomenclature for one thing, but they have also suggested themselves as useful tools for organizing empirical case studies (chapters four to seven). I think of these diagrams as 'more than representational' as they do not presume to resemble or 'mirror' the concept as a picture. There might be iconic similarities, such as when the human body is depicted, but yet still in a totally abstract manner. As will be seen later in the analysis of the four cases, I draw upon other diagrams created by various research assistants over the years (all with a background in urban design, though). In retrospect I probably have come to appreciate the usefulness of diagrams for both communicating findings and registrations from field studies. The discussion of diagrams and their revisions also proved to be an intellectual stimulus to the conceptual development of my theoretical work. The diagrams became both a medium for exchange and deliberation of concepts and ideas as well as becoming 'mediators' (Latour 2005; Tait and Jensen 2007). I lean on the notion articulated by Garcia when he writes that '*a diagram is the spatialisation of a selective abstraction and /or reduction of a concept or phenomenon. In other words, a diagram is the architecture of an idea*' (Garcia 2010, 18). This notion of 'the architecture of an idea' is not only intuitively appealing; it also links to my understanding of how diagrams may facilitate thinking. Coming back to the main diagram (fig. 1, chapter one), all of the theoretical concepts are subsumed under this key diagram and represent various dimensions and facets of the three analytical fields: material spaces and design, social interaction, and embodied performances. Moreover, they refer in different ways to the idea that situational mobilities are staged from above by planning, design, regulation, etc., and staged from below by mobile subjects and their multiple decisions and actions.

Critical mobilities thinking - Dark sides of mobilities/ mobilities potential thinking

This diagram is actually comprised of two dimensions since the hallmarks of 'critical mobilities thinking' are both to engage with the 'dark sides' of mobilities, such as social exclusion or failure and breakdown, and to explore mobilities potentials in seeing new opportunities for socially enriching designs and experiences previously overlooked. Simply put, 'critical mobilities thinking' works with both problems and potentials (fig. 3.1).

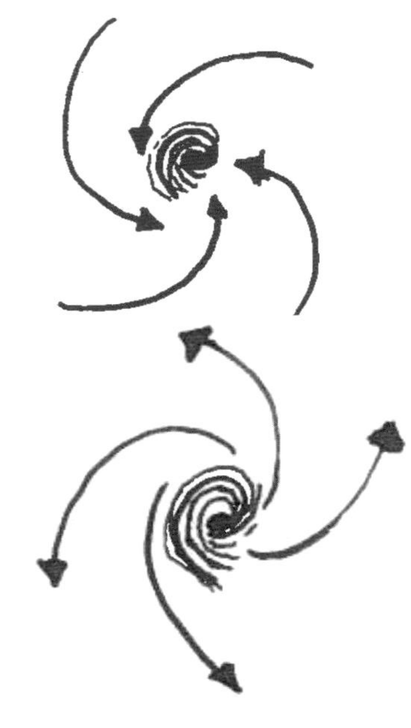

Mobile sociopetals and mobile sociofugals

The notion of mobile sociopetals refers to how some sites and settings function particularly well in getting people to go there and unfold their activities (fig. 3.2). In a metaphorical sense the sites are attracting and 'drawing in' people and things where they are the epicentre of a magnetic field of gravity or a whirlpool. As the opposite of the sociopetal notion, the mobile sociofugals tend to 'push' away people, goods, etc. or distribute them from their centre of gravity.

Mobile body semiotics

The concept 'mobile semiotics' concerns how signs (in their broadest possible sense) afford, process, and coordinate (or obstruct) the physical circulation and movement of people, vehicles, and goods in more or less codified systems of infrastructure. Related to the notion of 'mobile semiotics', I speak of 'mobile geo-semiotics' as a way to think about material locations (hence the 'geo') of signs as well as the fact that signs are interpreted in motion. Semiotic systems modify and interact with the human body and sensations as the subject moves and thus afford particular motions, directions, speeds, modes, and routes. This leads me to speak of an increasing number of semiotic techniques, designs, media, symbols, and signs coming together in an emerging 'mobile semiotic grammar'. This may be likened to a semiotic vocabulary of a more or less generic nature as, for example, the well-known international standards of airport signage and wayfinding or traffic signs. Reading these requires a certain level of skill in applying the mobile semiotic grammar. Across all cases of mobilities research, the moving and perceiving body is crucial. However, what becomes even more interesting about the notion of a 'mobile body semiotics' is that human bodies do not only move and sense the material and semiotic environment (fig. 3.3). The body on its own also becomes a 'sign vehicle', communicating intentions and norms. Therefore, the codified regulatory principles governing the gestures of the mobile bodies as they move in traffic become an interesting and illustrative case of a 'mobile body semiotics'.

Mobile assemblages

The term 'mobile assemblages' captures how systems and socio-technical networks that 'host' contemporary mobilities are complex and how large material environments where technologies, humans, software, codes, semiotic and communicative systems, objects, and artefacts are assembled in specific combinations that facilitate and afford certain mobile practices and restrict or prevent others (fig. 3.4). The key issue is how systems and networks assemble humans and non-humans in an attempt to 'stage' mobilities.

Mobile with

Our movement in the city is a dynamic and socially complex affair that has more repercussions than 'just being traffic'. Humans make sense of their environment as they move and this is important to the way we engage with our consociates whether or not we know certain things. To describe this, let me coin the phrase 'mobile with' for the particular interaction dynamics that are created when a 'party of more than one' is on the

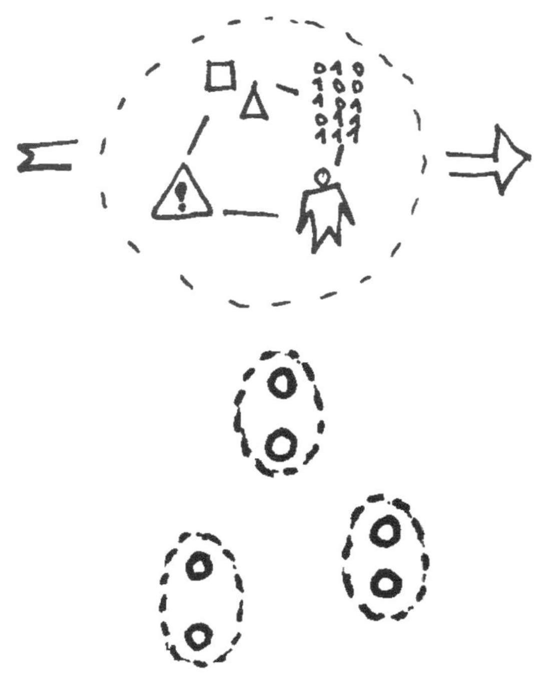

move (fig. 3.5). The fact that groups move together affords particular social dynamics that are captured by the notion of the 'mobile with'.

The networked self

Using the notion of the 'networked self' (fig. 3.6) I want to focus on how urban everyday life mobility is deeply embedded in all sorts of networks (from 'hard' infrastructure to 'soft' digital communication systems). Some of these are the 'channels in which we move', so to speak. Others are leisure-time communication and entertaining systems (e.g., commercials or digital gaming). The performative act of networking as we move, coupled with the effects of network connectivity on mobilities, are at the centre of this concept. As it seems that more and more of the networking in digital systems becomes mobile, the mobile subject to a large extent is becoming what he or she is while being on the move. We are 'linked-in-motion' and

Left page from top: Figs. 3.1, 3.2 and 3.3

Right page from top: Figs. 3.4 and 3.5

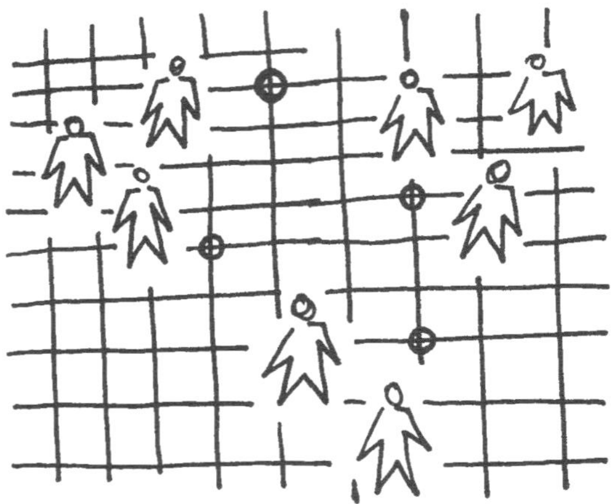

Fig. 3.6

carry networks in socio-technical systems, sorted by software leading to new interactive practices. The notion of being 'linked-in-motion' is thus the 'systemic' property and dimension related to the individual notion of the 'networked self' presented earlier. In the midst of the complexity of 'negotiation in motion', people tend to cluster and interact in very swift and volatile situations that nevertheless offer a minimum of stability and are recognized as situations on the go or what I term 'temporary congregations'. Such meetings are ephemeral and may be the shared waiting for a bus, the sharing of a train compartment, an elevator ride, or other types of loose and temporal situational mobility. Often the staging by design has prepared for specific modes of interaction in such temporary situations where mobile subjects are known to congregate. The working of such protocols is due to the stretching of technologies taking place across time and space, thereby facilitating a new dimension to the 'proximity-connectivity nexus'. By this is meant a new dynamic relationship between physical copresence and mediated connections across time and space and how those connections affect the mobile situations. Connections and distances have been influencing each other for long time, but now networked technologies create a new and dynamic interface and mediation, or what I term a 'nexus'. The distinction refers to the difference between topography (proximity) and topology (connectivity). As a result, adjacent to the logic of closeness and proximity lies a new potential in distanced connectivity mediated by networked technologies. This affords new ways of engaging, for example, the 'friction of distance' as connections and communications may occur across time and space.

Mobility cultures

Each of the specific mobilities modes involves a set of practices and normative regulating principles that one needs to master for practical reasons. So there are 'walking-codes', 'cycling-codes', etc. Clearly, these are ways of acting that we could see as more or less explicitly articulated cultures (fig. 3.7). Such 'mobility cultures' are linked to official and legal sanctions and mobility regulations, and are installed and inscribed into material environments from above. However, they are also embedded in the body as tacit mobility cultures, and thus individual acts of self-staging from below. Some are more globally generic mobility codes, while others are locally anchored and, as such, are expressions of local norms and customs. The key insight is therefore that mobilities are signifying and meaning-producing performances that create culture as much as they are instrumental acts of physical displacement.

Mobility aesthetics

The realm of aesthetics becomes highly relevant as we engage the wider production of subjectivity and the meaning of movement to perception. We are looking at 'life in motion' and the body plays a pivotal role in creating the situational touch points for the creation of cultures and practices related to mobilities. The mobile body produces and reproduces a 'mobile aesthetics' that creates new subjectivities and new ways of perceiving the world (fig. 3.8). Moreover, the mobile experiences lend themselves to new ways of thinking about infrastructure spaces and mobility technologies as having aesthetic properties. So rather than morally condemning these 'non-places', the mobile experiences afford new aesthetic experiences and ways of relating to self and other. Experience in motion has to do with the way that new mobile embodied perceptions are creating systems, patterns, and models of moving and being moved. That is to say, embodied mobilities afford particular normative and social interactions that aggregate into cultural patterns of 'mobilities meaning'. Such embodied and collective 'cultures of mobilities' are at one and the same time very different for particular modes of mobility (cars afford different experiences than walking shoes) and identical since we interact with systems, technologies, and artefacts that have the same 'body interface' regardless if we are driving, sailing, or flying).The individual mobile subject thus experiences the world (or significant parts hereof) in motion.

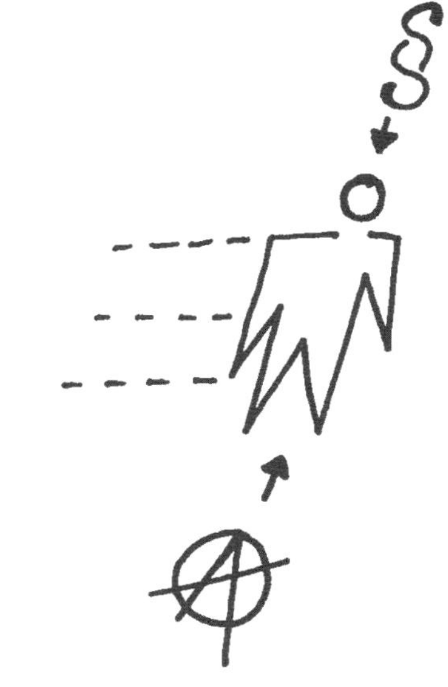

Mobility affordances

The material sites and the technologies that our bodies negotiate in mobile practices may then be thought of as 'mobility affordances' (fig. 3.9). By this is meant how the specific relation between the moving body and its material environment opens up to particular modes of mobility, different speeds, trajectories, temporalities, etc. 'Mobility affordances' illustrate the very specific and material dimensions to mobile situations.

Mobilities divides

The staged mobile situations of everyday life relate to networked technologies of different sorts. In relation to such technologies, issues of 'mobilities divides' (fig. 3.10) are socially stratifying practices that relate to mobility differentials that come about either as a function of economic resources, intellectual and knowledge capabilities, practical skills, geographical

Figs. 3.7, 3.8 and 3.9

location, or cultural frames all contributing to the fact that some people know how, can, and will be mobile while this is out of range for others (or even fully constrained, as with immobile subjects in jails or nursing homes). 'Segregated mobilities practices' are the mobility patterns segregated along the lines of income and social hierarchy often wedded in a complex way to the infrastructure systems of the city with respect to both 'switched off areas' as well as to the more general urban social strata. The notion points toward an understanding of the staging of mobilities as an expression of mobile power-geometries. Segregated mobilities practice may also come about as a function of mobilities skills reaching from cognitive operations to bodily capacities.

The river

Seen from a 'birds-eye' perspective, an infrastructural flow space with its actual layout of curbs and urban furniture might be likened to a 'riverbed', shaping the flows of people as water in a 'river' (fig. 3.11). The 'river' is coined as a metaphor for seeing mobilities from the vantage point of a 'bird's eye' and will therefore intentionally homogenize the elements of the stream. In other words, the analysis may benefit from the abstract, aggregated, and homogeneous understanding of a collective stream of bodies, bikes, cars, or the like. However, grasping the embodied experiences of mobilities requires a shift to the 'ballet' metaphor.

The ballet

At eye level with the mobile subjects, I coined the notion of the 'ballet' because I find the gestures, gazes, and embodied negotiations and micro-interactions that take place ever so swiftly (fig. 3.12). The 'ballet' metaphor places in the foreground the bodily interactions and situational dynamics of situational mobilities. It puts the embodied and lived perceptions and sensations of the individual mobile subject at its centre. The mobile and situational interactions that take place in everyday life often come into existence swiftly, but dissolve just as quickly, in the blink of an eye. However, as mobile subjects share the same spaces and pass each other in often confined space and with high-speed interactions, exchanges of reciprocity become essential for the mobile order of the everyday life. This is covered by the notion of 'negotiation in motion'. The swift and almost ephemeral social interactions are equivalent to negotiations-in-motion.

From this list of concepts and diagrams an analytical vocabulary emerges. This is a set of concepts and a 'language' that makes it possible to explore and engage with empirical cases of mobilities design in a richer way than what has been the case until now. Moreover, these concepts are operational and applicable to any analysis of 'mobilities in situ'. The test for this claim constitutes part three of the book, where I use these new terminologies in the analysis of empirical cases.

Concluding remarks

In this chapter I have engaged in a discussion where I admittedly at times have not felt that I am on my home turf. However, many years of working together with architects and designers have fuelled my appetite for exploring the diagrams and also for moving more deeply into the territory of design thinking.

Here I have attempted to connect the mobilities research agenda with the design field, utilizing the tool of the diagram. It goes without saying that I do not consider the diagrams just presented as 'designs'. Rather I have made a case for understanding spatial but also abstract images as 'vehicles for thoughts'. In no way can I substantiate that all mobilities researchers should engage with such an exercise of diagrammatic thinking. But I do find the diagrams a viable route to reconnecting what needs to be connected: the analytical and theoretical sensibilities of the 'mobilities turn' with the material, physical, and interventionist awareness of design and architecture. In more practical terms I have developed the concepts and diagrams in a process of mutual and circular interaction. I have, for example, used the diagrams in their various visual forms as a form of theoretical 'scribbling' when developing a new term and concept. Afterwards I have used the diagram to 'question' and challenge the concept. Admittedly this may seem like a rather introverted process and I cannot expect readers to 'see' the exact same thing in a diagram as I do. However, this is a beginning exploration of the potentials of 'diagrammatic thinking', leading to the articulation of 'mobilities design'.

Let me end this chapter by applying some of the concepts presented to a short pedagogical example. Imagine that you are driving a car into a city centre, looking for a parking space. Being in your car is an example of staged mobility as you are present in a material artefact (the car, possibly networked by GPS and perhaps with a link to an ITS system) and all the infrastructural systems supporting and sustaining automobility (e.g., roads, traffic lights, and parking spaces). You are also inhabiting the car with your body and the skills invested in this body-car nexus (and representing a particular way or style of performing mobilities dependent on personal traits, individual temper, and experiences). Rarely would you be looking for a parking space if you were solely on your own, so the social interaction perspective becomes a vivid and important part of this (from the lane crossing dramas on the way into town to the often quite power-laden chase for a free parking space). During this imaginary trip into town, you have performed mobilities and enacted situations of mobility within frames created by someone else (e.g., the road spaces and the traffic signals). This is what I term staging 'from above', and the defining point here is that your actions and performances are enacted and afforded (or the opposite) by systems, rules, and frameworks outside your control. But, for instance, giving way to a pedestrian or driving swiftly in front of someone else in line for a parking space are acts of the mobile subject with a relatively free will. (This assumption cannot be discussed at length here, as it is one of the major issues in the history of

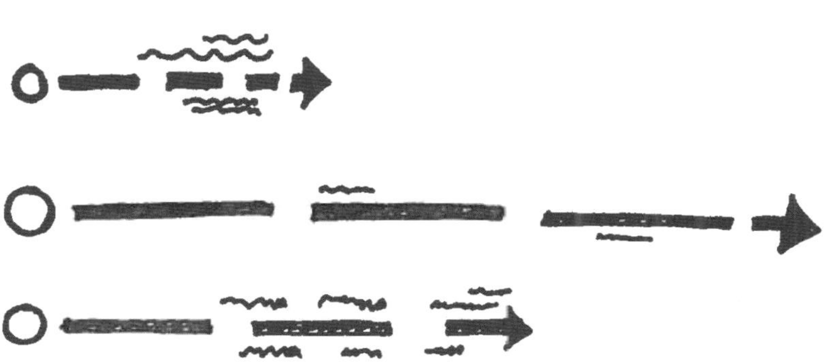

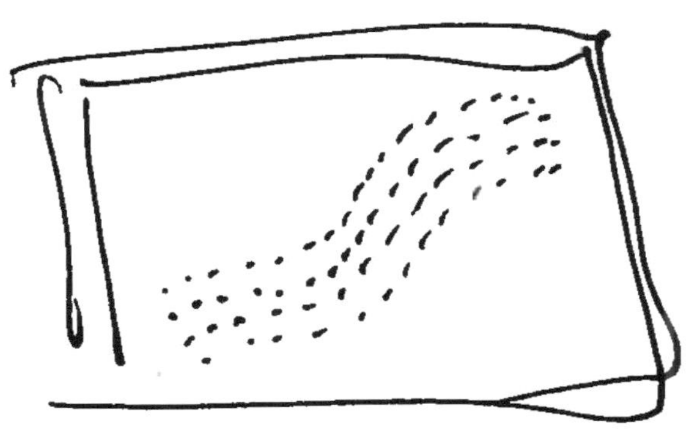

Figs. 3.10, 3.11 and 3.12

philosophy.) The point is that these autonomous and situational acts are staged 'from below' in the sense that they are expressions of the individual traits of the mobile subject. Thus far, the simple act of driving your car into town looking for a parking space contains a number of situational properties that we may describe using the staging mobilities framework and the three spheres of materiality, sociality, and embodiment. Moreover, these situations are always performed within a field of tension spanning the staging from above and below. This is what is captured in the notion of 'staging mobilities' and the accompanying diagram (fig. 1.1, chapter one).

Basically, I have 'walked around' the general diagram from chapter one in this example in order to argue for the three dimensions of material design, social interaction, and embodied performance, and with a view to the way that all situational mobilities play out in a field between staging from above and below. If we then zoomed in on, for example, the embodied handling of the car and the wider traffic system as, for example, the city's wayfinding and information signs system guiding you to a parking lot with vacant space, we may open up the analysis to include more detailed concepts. One might be the 'mobile sociopetals' as when multiple cars gravitate toward the parking spaces of the city. But we may also think about the 'mobility affordances' being created by the fact that you actually have a car and thus are able to perform particular forms of mobilities such as riding in a sheltered vehicle if it is raining or carrying large and heavy items, for example, compared to a bicyclist. So the concept of 'mobility affordance' becomes an example of how certain acts and practices of mobilities are being afforded and sustained by the materialities of mobilities design.

As this is only meant to be a short example I cannot include all diagrams and concepts (even though most of them might become operational in relation to a particular situation illustrating how this theoretical framework is quite complex and multidimensional). So I end the example here by including the notion of the 'networked self' (and under this notion also the idea of 'temporary congregations'). The 'networked self' may exist when you are queuing up with other fellow drivers on the access road awaiting the green light, or it may be when you step up in line to the ticket machine after having succeeded in finding a parking space on this short and imaginary car trip into town. As cities are complex socio-technical systems, the many mobile subjects inhabiting these are coming into more or less ephemeral situations of social interaction characterized by the 'networked self' and its engagement within 'temporary congregations'.

The diagrams and their accompanying concepts are only a selection of the concepts developed in the *Staging Mobilities* book. One could obviously develop diagrams to match all concepts, but the point of this exercise is to illustrate a particular way of thinking and reasoning. The general idea is to relate all the diagrams and concepts to the overall model of 'staging mobilities' as a theoretical and methodological tool for understanding and analysing 'mobilities design'. Therefore I have plotted the diagrams developed in this chapter onto the 'staging mobilities' model as a way of visualising how these concepts are parts of a wider theoretical and conceptual understanding that I term 'Staging Mobilities/Designing Mobilities' (fig. 3.13). To put matters simply, the 'staging mobilities' framework is the theoretical frame and the diagrams now 'added' or 'mapped onto the model' are the operational tools and concepts to open up the empirical case analysis which I understand to be the exploration of 'mobilities design'.

Coming out of a pragmatic and situation-oriented stream of thought, I shall use no more intellectual energy on setting up arguments, preparing agendas, and paving the way for a specific understanding. Rather I propose that we from here move into part three of the book and start applying the theories and concepts to empirical cases.

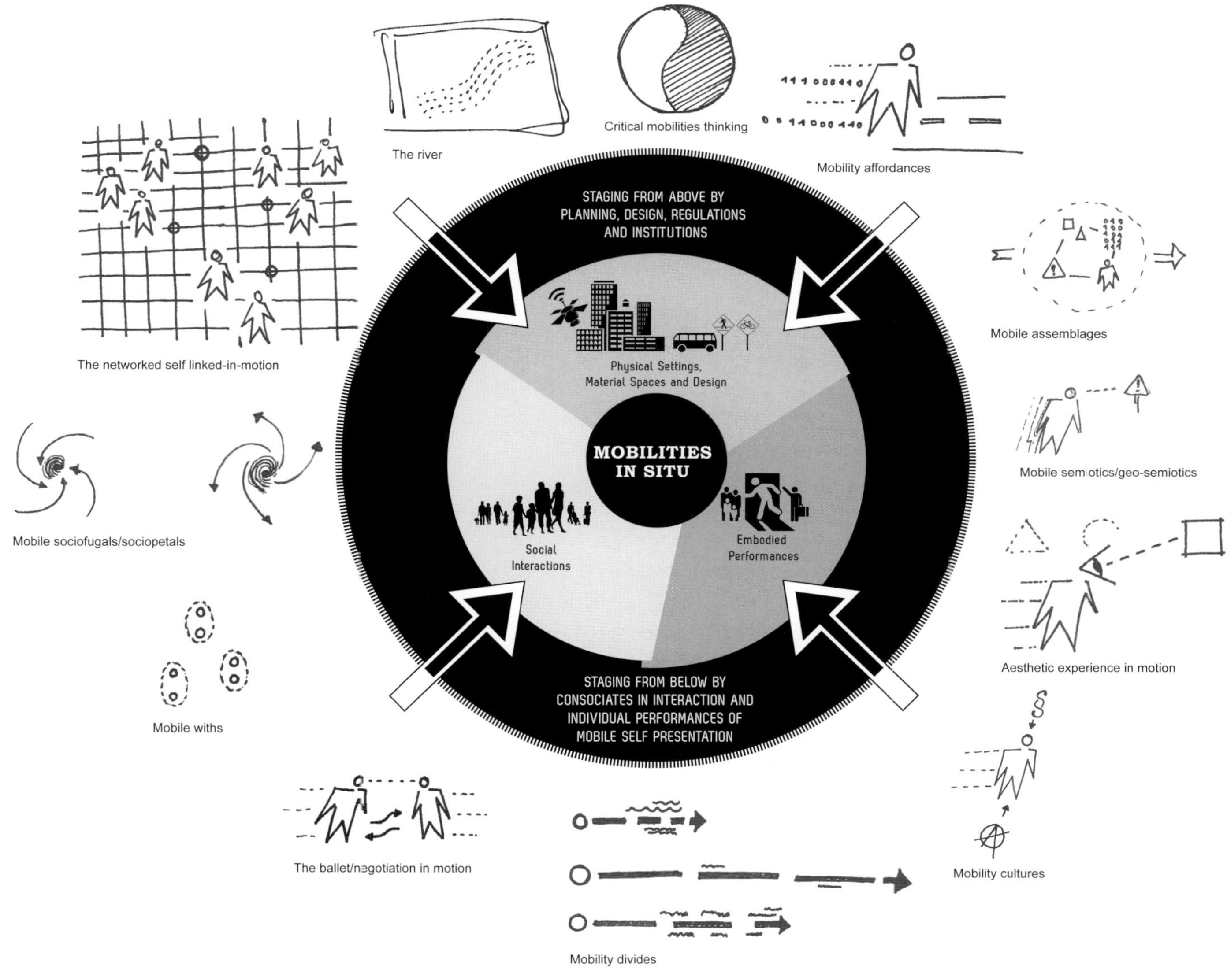

Fig. 3.13: Designing Mobilities diagrams mapped onto the Staging Mobilities model

Friis
Sony Center
FEMILET
SALE

4 WALK

COMMERCIAL FLOWS IN THE XL BUILDING

Nothing is more fundamental to the survival of shopping than a steady flow of customers and goods. The correlation between the amount of foot traffic and volume of sales has made the relationship between shopping and urbanism indistinguishable from the issues of mobility: how to move people about, whether by foot, moving sidewalk, underground, or car. Shopping's effectiveness in generating constant activity has made it an indispensable medium though which movement in the city is enacted.

Sze Tsung Leong (2001) *Mobility, in Project on the City 2. Harvard Design School Guide to Shopping*, p. 477

The problem with buildings is that they look desperately static. It seems almost impossible to grasp them as movement, as flight, as a series of transformations. Everybody knows - and especially architects, of course - that a building is not a static object, but a moving project.

Bruno Latour & Albena Yaneva (2008) *"Give me a gun and I will make all buildings move": An ANT's view of Architecture*, p. 80

Now we are left with a world without urbanism, only architecture, ever more architecture. The neatness of architecture is its seduction; it defines, excludes, limits separates from the "rest" – but it also consumes. It exploits and exhausts the potentials that are generated finally only by urbanism, and that only the specific imagination of urbanism can invent and renew.

Rem Koolhaas & Bruce Mau (1995) *Whatever Happened to Urbanism?*, p. 967

Introduction

Chapter four explores the notion of the 'Extra Large' building upholding urban characteristics and features by virtue of its scale and mediating function as a transit space in an urban context. This chapter explores mainly the pedestrian flows within and through a building complex. The case is the urban shopping mall 'Friis' in the centre of Aalborg, Denmark (fig. 4.1). Friis is a node of horizontal and vertical mobility of goods and customers. The people frequenting Friis come mostly by private car or on foot. A key feature of Friis is its linking function among areas of the city, making it host to both people in transit as well as shoppers. In other words, Friis serves as a 'hinge' between various urban areas, affording a certain amount of transit mobility (people simply walking through the centre on their way from A to B in the city). However, most people go there to buy goods and a fair amount of younger people go there as well to meet and mingle.

In terms of material design the mall is a multistorey and multilayered building complex with three stories of underground parking and two stories of shopping mall within two large building bodies connected horizontally by skywalks and bridges and vertically by escalators and lifts (see fig. 4.2). Within this rather complex setting, an interesting shopping scenography takes place as people meet and mingle, shop, and are in transit. We see the staging from above in form of wayfinding systems and hierarchies of movement paths, and we see people appropriating the spaces with their own logic and desires to interact as if this were any other urban space (i.e., staging from below). The social interactions and the embodied mobilities within the mall illustrate how the material design of an urban shopping mall affords certain mobile practices and discards others.

The chapter is structured in the following way. After the general introduction, I explain in some detail the

Fig. 4.1: Friis

field work and methodological approach followed. The empirical case analysis will follow in this structure: urban context - 'getting there' (serial visions) - the inside of the building - social interaction - mobile semiotics. The chapter ends with concluding remarks in which the case is related in more general terms to the overall analytical framework.

Conceptualising the commercial XL building

The case of the Friis shopping centre in the downtown area of Aalborg is in many ways related to a number of classic topics within urban planning and design other than mobilities. The Mall actualizes for example the question of public space and commercial exchange as a key urban feature; this discussion is as old as urban centres themselves (Kjærsdam 1995; Weber 1978). In the context of *Staging Mobilities* and *Designing Mobilities*, I will, however, forego mobilities and touch primarily upon other themes insofar as they are being motivated by the analysis of mobilities. This means that I only touch lightly upon the urban mall's deeper rationale. For explorations into the origin of the shopping mall and analysis of the functionality of these urban commercial sites, I recommend other sources (e.g., Chung et al. 2001; Wall 2005).

The postwar urban shopping mall

The postwar period in Europe and North America witnessed a dramatic transformation of consumption patterns. Many of these are related primarily to the spreading of the new and 'game changing' technology of mobilities -- the private car (Buchannan 1964; Urry 2000, 2007). The city as a trading node, commercial centre of commodity exchange and capital accumulation obviously was already a key feature of urbanism and urban agglomeration. It lies well beyond the confinement of this book to explain this development (see Clarke 2003; Harvey 1989; Kjærsdam 1995; Marx 1887/1972; Simmel 1903/50; Soja 2000; Weber 1978). However, with the advent

Fig. 4.2: Observation areas

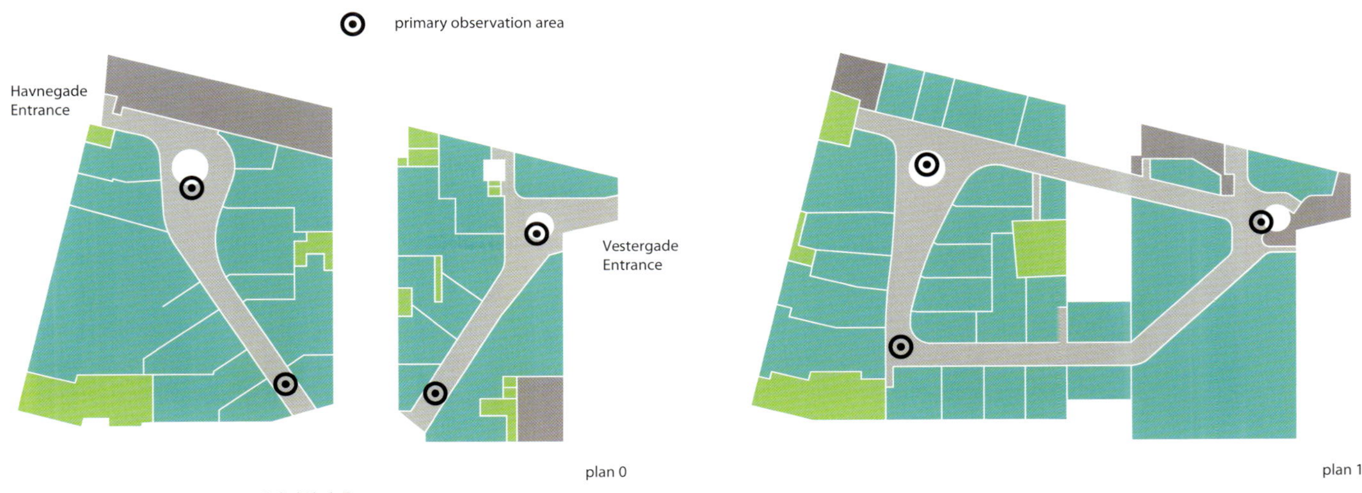

of the modern division of labour, the increased urban agglomeration, and the new modes of mobilities, the postwar economies of 'westernized' societies took on a particular trajectory, creating new ways of inhabiting cities as well as consuming the surplus from material production. Concentrations of goods and easy access created as a result the huge shopping areas and centres out of town known as 'malls' or shopping centres. Thus, from viewing the exchanges of goods and commodities as a primarily inner city phenomenon and often deeply intertwined with urban culture (see Benjamin 2002; Simmel 1903/50), the world witnessed a mushrooming of car-dependent megastructures and out-of-town shopping facilities and malls (Ben-Joseph 2012, 81; Olesen and Lassen 2012, 225; Whyte 1988, 206-8). Increasingly, urban shopping centres and malls are located near infrastructures and thus near traffic hubs (Allingham 2006). This is not, however, the case with Friis, and perhaps this might be stipulated to be one of the reasons why the centre has had some difficulty in attracting a significant number of customers. In fact a smaller urban mall (the Kennedy Arcade) was built adjacent to the rail station in Aalborg, but this never had an urban ambience and feel to it (which is the case with Friis).

Despite the serious economic problems with inner city economies in the 1970s and 1980s, city centres have for more than two decades experienced what might be termed the 'return of shopping'. Obviously it is not in the sense that the huge extra-urban shopping malls are history, but rather in the sense that many city centres are becoming 'mallified' (as critics would put it) or, put in more neutral terms, regaining commercial focus. Urban centres may either 'mallify' existing building areas by, for example, connecting areas with pedestrian zones, covered walkways, and roofs or by constructing large building complexes with big volumes -- what I term the 'XL Building' (see Koolhaas and Mau 1995 for a discussion of 'XL'). Friis is such an XL building (in fact it is two building volumes connected by skywalks) and an 'in-town' centre (Lynch and Hack 1984, 324). Koolhaas points to the 'bigness' of buildings and architecture in the postwar period as a force eroding the strict distinction between architecture and urbanism (Koolhaas and Mau 1995). In her study of airports as architecture 'beyond big', Smith (2003) finds that scale in itself is not an absolute phenomenon but a relative term that, together with the new large buildings and their multiple network connections, requires a new 'reading. Besides being a large and complex technical and architectural achievement, the contemporary urban XL building also becomes an interaction zone and a habitat for small-group ecologies, as has been the case for more traditional types of public urban spaces (Gehl 2010; Goffman 1963, 1972; Hall 1966; Lawson 2001; Sommer 2007).

Whether they are out of- or in-town, malls are now taking on a number of extra-commercial functions such as meeting spaces, public squares, experience and entertainment sites (Krange and Strandbu 1996; Lynch 1990; Marling et al. 2009; Shields 1991). Critics of this development point to the issue of privatization of space and risk of social exclusion as well as lack of 'true' public sites where the population may gather and speak in a participatory and democratic spirit. In light of such critiques, malls have been defined as 'non-places' (Augé 2005), 'cathedrals of consumption' (Ritzer 1999, 2001), a threat to the public sphere (Olesen and Lassen 2012; Sorkin 1992) and securitized spaces of surveillance and 'panopticon malls' (Davies 1992; Graham 2011). Others would argue that shopping is precisely a public activity:

> Shopping is arguably the last remaining form of public activity. Through a battery of increasingly predatory forms, shopping has infiltrated, colonized and even replaced, almost every aspect of urban life. Town centres, suburbs, streets and now airports, train stations, museums, hospitals, schools, the Internet, and the military are shaped by the mechanisms and spaces of shopping (Chung et al. 2001, 0).

As an antidote to the rather pessimistic interpretation of malls as non-places, privatized, and socially exclusionary sites, Hajer and Reijndorp (2001, 45) argue that it is debatable that justice is done to urban spaces deemed to be non-places and Kolb (2008) also voices a similar critique as do Degen et al., who point to the multimodal, performative, and practice-oriented experiences of thoroughly designed environments (Degen et al. 2008). This is not the place to engage in a complex debate over the future of public space; however, it should be mentioned that, as an increasing number of urban sites are becoming managed, designed, and under private ownership (as is the case with shopping malls), there are fewer sites of public engagement and voice. The big issue is whether cities are planning and designing for privatized spaces only, or if they keep insisting that the public realm, the city square, and the urban plaza are important urban typologies. There is thus a rather substantial academic critique of shopping malls being inauthentic as well an expression of place commodification (Crawford 1992; Sorkin 1992; Urry 1990). This debate is complex and I find the tendency to lump together critiques of aesthetics, authenticity, and instrumentalism to be rather problematic. However, counterarguments are found in particular in relation to the tendency of automatic criticism of anything commercial (see Kolb 2008 for a more open-minded view). Shopping centres truly are sites of commercial activity, but according to some analysts are also sites of community interaction and thus perform as social spaces (Lynch and Hack 1984, 323). Some may say this is a more American tradition; however, Benjamin (2002) also pointed to Parisian arcades as sites of more than instrumental acts of economic transactions. These were significant sites of urban culture and social interaction. Urban malls and arcades are eminent sites of the ostentatious display of what Veblen termed 'conspicuous consumption' (Veblen 1889/1994).

I think, however, we need to realize that there is more to these sites than simple commercialization. The identity of the contemporary urban dweller and the cultural codes of social interaction are being created in such public and semipublic spaces, like it or not. Moreover, it is rather naive to perceive of commercial activity as only acts of market interaction. Trade and commodity exchange, as well as the consumption and attachment to goods, are cultural features that reach very far back into human history. It seems like only recent commercial activities are falling prey to moralizing judgements, whereas ancient cultures' consumption practices are seen as 'authentic' and integrative to society. The space allocated here cannot justify a deeper engagement with this, but it is similar to the discussions with which I engage later in relation to 'transit spaces'. This is a tendency (in particular within 'critical' social science) to become moralizing rather than to try to understand how the urban and built environments as habitats of the contemporary human may often be much more sophisticated and complex than a simple deductive analysis of sites as alienating and inauthentic may suggest. Rather than knowing in advance who are the 'suppressed and alienated' and which sites are inauthentic, I would recommend a research strategy of 'critical mobilities thinking' with its focus on problems as well as potentials, and not least its pragmatic focus on the real-life situations (Jensen 2013a). So I will leave this discussion for now in order to return to issue of moving and navigating in the urban mall.

Wayfinding and mobile semiotics

XL buildings such as transit hubs and shopping malls obviously 'direct' people by their very physical layout: *'the combination of obstacles, open spaces, and bottlenecks organizes places in a way that steers people along paths, keeping them out of certain areas, moving them past shops and advertisements, and allowing them to stay for an extended period of time in certain places'* (Frers 2009, 7). Obviously I pay attention to these spatial qualities. However, since the moving human body takes in quite a lot of information through the visual register, we need also to focus on the semiotic dimensions and layout of the material environment. Needless to say, we may learn to 'read' objects and spaces on their own (as, for example, knowing how to 'read' a door as exit or entry point to a building. (See Venturi and Scott-Brown 2004 for a position in this debate). But in relation to mobilities and navigation within XL buildings, we need to pay attention to designed systems of signs -- or 'wayfinding' design as the terminology goes. In an urban mall such as Friis, the semiotic system is predominantly one of 'directional signs' staging and controlling the flow of visitors, customers, and goods deliveries (Gibson 2009, 50). Moreover, the whole commercial semiotic system of shop window advertisement, company logos and brands obviously are important in an urban shopping centre (Fuller and Harley 2004, 126; Lynch and Hack 1984, 187). Additionally, the need for identifying the shop or mall as a legible destination calls for identification signs. There is thus a need for semiotic systems and signs that are regulatory, directional, and commercial (Gibson 2009; Scollon and Scollon 2003). As explained in more detail elsewhere (Jensen 2013a, chapter 3) a semiotic system has what Fuller terms 'decision points' as the points where sign systems mediate physical routes demanding crucial decisions to be made (e.g., 'something to declare?' at Customs, or the off ramp on the freeway). At such points, finding one's way requires plotting predictable paths and 'decision' points within the signage systems (Fuller 2002, 235). To understand semiotic systems as collections of 'decision points' parallels the notion of 'Critical Point of Contact' or CPC (Jensen and Morelli 2011). In Friis there are a number of 'CPCs' such as the entry doors from the street, the car park ramp into the underground parking; however, 'inside' the building spaces in front of escalators and lifts are important CPCs as well as, of course, store fronts and their entry and exit points. Looking at the shopping centre and its circulation of goods and people from the point of view of the *Staging Mobilities* framework means to understand how material connections and openings/closings are mediated and nested within symbolic or communicative dimensions of the environment such as signage and wayfinding systems. In the case of Friis, the architecture of two main buildings, underground parking, multiple entrances and two parallel skywalks require a certain level of legibility and an operational wayfinding system. The latter has been a challenge since many users keep having difficulties in 'reading' the site and understanding precisely how to negotiate the space. Much more is said about the semiotic dimension to mobilities sites elsewhere (Jensen 2013a). Here I want to move closer to the empirical case. However before that, I need to explain the approach and method of collecting data.

Stepping into Friis - methodology and data collection

One of the key premises of empirical field work is gaining access to the field itself (Burgess 1991). So the approval from the owner of the centre (Steen & Strøm Denmark A/S) and in particular Centre manager Mille Schou has been crucial. The provision of background data as well as permission to conduct fieldwork has been essential to this case. As the aim of this case study is to explore Friis as a place where multiple networks and flows in the city meet and overlap and where capital is generated and people engage in city life, coming to terms with this way of seeing an urban shopping mall was the first step. After meetings and exchange of data and information, the actual fieldwork was conducted.

Practical setup

The main method applied is the ethnographic field study. Observation was carried out by a research assistant from February to May 2011 (the background of the research assistant is in urban design). During February and March, the surrounding areas of the Friis Shopping Centre were mapped mainly through photography but also observations of traffic flows (pedestrians, bikes, cars, and buses). From March to May a series of observation sessions were conducted inside the Friis Shopping Centre. One of the main aspects was to document the different flows of people passing through Friis. In order to gain a detailed understanding thereof, observations were conducted on three different days during the week and at different times:

Wednesday before noon (very light visitor load, 500-1,000 visitors/hour)

Thursday afternoon (medium visitor load, 1,200-1,500 visitors/hour)

Saturday at noon (heavy visitor load, 2,000-2,500 visitors/hour)

The main objectives of the observation sessions inside Friis were: to document and 'capture' the aesthetics and design of the spaces; to 'capture' interaction and movements between Friis and users; to 'capture' interaction between users of Friis; and finally to gain data for sorting visitors into general subcategories (types). Each session was between 2-4 hours depending on visitor load and consisted of photography and hand sketching (for quickly noting and 'capturing' encounters). Six areas in the shopping mall (fig. 4.2) were selected as critical nodes where the most flow, encounters, and interactions would occur. These areas were bases from which most of the photography and sketching were conducted. The areas with escalators and elevators connecting the two levels were selected as primary nodes because of the highest amount of traffic. To cover the most ground at each session rotations were used, staying only 10-15 minutes at designated locations before moving on to the next. The specific placement of the research assistant at the six areas was either chosen for the most expanded view or to be the least visible, depending on the situation.

Data collection

The data gathered for the case study of Friis was conducted from March to May 2011. The data was concurrently analysed and gathered for presentation in a fieldwork report. The case study consists of several types of data from various sources: Photos (Aalborg University), Observations (Aalborg University), Sketching (Aalborg University), Visitor Statistics (Friis Centre Management, data used from February 2011), Traffic Statistics (Aalborg Municipality, counted 2010), Technical Drawings (Friis Centre Management), Planning Documents (Aalborg Municipality), and Design Manuals (Friis Centre Management) The technical drawings, design manuals, and planning documents served as a background for understanding the physical building and its surroundings. Photos, sketching, observations, and statistics helped gain an understanding of the different flows, their volume and rhythm, and the interaction and encounters that occur in Friis. Most observations were done from a stationary point (the six areas mentioned above). Also obtaining knowledge of people's choice of routes through 'shadowing' (Jiron 2011) was utilized. The hand sketching was used to either remember or detail what happened in a situation already documented through several photos, or it could be used exclusively as a more covert way of 'capturing' a situation since it did not attract the same kind of attention as the camera.

Reflections on observer bias

When 'capturing' interaction and encounters between user-object (understood here as, for example, a visitor and the escalator) and user-user (e.g., two visitors), it seemed that there could be a great deal of interference from the research assistant affecting or simply dissolving the situation. While people did not directly confront the research assistant it seemed clear that they often felt watched due to the presence of a person with a camera. This was dealt with in two different setups: A) To be very visible (seeming official), mounting the camera on a tripod or B) to photograph quickly and with a hand-held camera, often without anyone noticing it. The A setup clearly did not register any special practice besides walking from A to B even though a few extraordinary situations could be 'captured', because the users did not notice the research assistant. The B setup could 'capture' the more rare use of space in Friis but often not directly because of distance and angle (as a reflection of the assistant's attempts to remain unnoticed). This effectively meant that the A setup was particularly good for mapping the design, space, and general flow within the building, while the B setup was better for 'capturing' extraordinary situations and practices. Alternative techniques that were not used were smaller compact cameras (with reduced picture quality because of the inability to use flash) and access to the Friis CCTV surveillance system. Almost every square metre of the shopping areas at the Friis Centre is fully monitored from several angles. While this might incite other ethical questions, it could give insight and 'capture' almost unbiased practices (since people are mainly not aware or simply forget they are being monitored in Friis). These sources of data would undoubtedly have enriched the empirical material for presenting the case. There are also heat sensitive cameras at all entrances measuring the peak of flows and the distribution of use among the entrances. Needless to say, access to this data could also have been explored. That I did not try to access such data was exclusively my decision in order to keep the empirical material at a level with which I could cope.

Reflections on seasonal changes

Due to the fact that the fieldwork was undertaken in a relatively cold season, the urban life observed surrounding Friis is of lower activity levels than would have been the case if the study had been conducted during summer. Little urban life occurred, especially at the plaza Gabels Torv in front of Friis but also at the Nørregade entrance. The few pedestrians who used the space did so in an instrumental manner only moving from A to B. Had the study been carried out in the summer, a higher frequency of pedestrian use and outdoor social activities would have been the case, offering a more nuanced understanding of Friis and its urban context. A more detailed analysis of flow and rhythm in Friis could be extracted from this.

Choice of methods

The methods employed for the field studies both outside and inside Friis were based primarily on observations and could therefore have been extended with a confrontational and direct method such as the interview. More detailed information of visitor´s practices and use of the Friis could have been gained via informal onsite interviews. Interviews could have been employed at different situations for different purposes. An organized semistructured interview could, for instance, have been applied to understand a visitor's activity, sense of wayfinding and direction, experience of Friis, choice of route, etc. Or the interview could be employed ad hoc, engaging with visitors in specific situations (meeting, playing, transgressive use, drifting, etc.), asking them what they are doing and why. However, the method applied in all the cases of this book is the field study observation technique where the key idea is to document how mobile subjects move in their urban contexts and well as how they interact in mobile situations rather than enquire into what they think about this and how they would verbalize it. I stay aligned with the basic theoretical and methodological approach presented in Jensen (2013a) as well as the seminal urban studies of Whyte, where he proclaimed that looking at people rather than asking them to reason and rationalize was, for him, the key to, for example, show that people most often stop to chat in the middle of crowded flows. Given the opportunity to reflect, many people would have said that they act differently (Whyte 1988, 10). So the naturalized and nonreflective practices of everyday mobilities may be studied better with the observation method rather than the interview approach.

A final note on the methods applied is that most of the registrations, photos, and mappings have been carried out by a research assistant with an academic background in urban design. In part, this ensures a higher quality of the registrations related to the build environment (i.e., hand sketching and general awareness to design impact on people's practices).

In part, this obviously means that I have had to rely on someone else's registrations. However, multiple discussions and deliberations between the research assistant and me have taken place; I also designed the observation instruction and discussed this thoroughly with the assistant. Needless to say, I have walked the routes for the 'serial visions' and the other types of registration in person to set up the data collection procedure. And, finally, even though the main registration has been carried out by an assistant, I am a regular visitor to Friis and I have been there very often to test out ideas and points for my interpretation of the registrations, as well as to confirm the stories from Friis that you are about to read.

Mobile Life in the Commercial XL Building - The case study

In the following I organize the case material into five themes. By way of introduction I look first at Friis in its urban context. Next I approach the building as the customer or visitor experiences it, utilizing 'serial vision' analysis. After this, the third theme focuses on the experience of the inside of the building, exploring the workings of the XL architecture and its flows. The fourth dimension concerns how visitors and customers move and interact within the building and here I explore the situational and interactional perspective from *Staging Mobilities* in some detail. The final theme concerns the semiotic and the systems of communication that enable the visitors to navigate and find their way within and through the building complex. All five dimensions will connect to the three analytical themes from *Staging Mobilities*: the physical settings, material spaces and design; the social interactions; and the embodied performances illustrating how situational mobilities in Friis is a matter of both staging from above as well as from below. It should be mentioned here as a delimitation that I will not go into the logistics of providing shops with goods and the disposal of their waste even though these are very important features and without these the mall would not function at all. However, the case has to be delimited and this is one of its boundaries.

The XL building in its urban context

Even though there are good reasons to be critical of a notion of 'context' that seems to suggest a fixed gaze and a static understanding of an object's 'nestedness' within a fixed structure, or as Koolhaas states, 'context stinks' (Koolhaas in Latour and Yaneva 2008), I think it does make sense to explore the way Friis is inserted into a wider urban ecology. Admittedly the problematic notion of context suggests that an 'object' and its environment are almost hermetically sealed off from one another. Latour has a point in stating that any project 'brings its own context' (Latour 1996, 133). This understanding goes hand-in-hand with the understanding of place as a relational and mobility-defined assemblage that I discussed elsewhere (Jensen 2012a, 2013a). The object (and in this case the urban XL building) brings with it a number of connections and a complex internal and external set of relationships. From electricity, water, and power to supplies of goods and customers, the urban XL building is networked and thus not neutral, to neither its imprint on its environment nor the environment's imprint on the XL building. Friis is thus a complex building operating through multiple 'critical points of contacts' (Jensen and Morelli 2011) as well as a complex set of 'service ecologies' (McCullough 2004). One of the first places to look to gain an understanding of the context for Friis is the official document issued by the Municipality termed the 'local plan'. In a highly regulated society such as Denmark, the most profound and legally binding level of planning and land use is to be found in the local plan. In 'Lokalplan 1-1-102' covering downtown Aalborg and with a particular focus on Friis, the urban context is meticulously described as an area within and next to large urban transformations (Aalborg Municipality 2008). I cannot go into detail here but a key feature of the urban transformation in Aalborg since the late 1980s is the closing down of

Fig. 4.3: Friis in its urban context

many industrial work places and production facilities on the one hand, and the building of cultural institutions, new office spaces, and housing units alongside the harbour front and reaching further out along the fjord (fig. 4.3). I have analysed the planning, power, and branding dimensions related to this very common path of postindustrial urban development elsewhere (Jensen 2007a). Friis is not located at the quayside, but is relatively close to both the very attractive harbour front and new cultural institutions such as the House of Music, the Utzon Centre (the last building made by the famous Danish architect), and the culture house Nordkraft. This is the area north of the site. To the west, Friis is linked to the pedestrianized shopping areas of midtown. Connections run through the site as both gangways and streets pass the building and connect it to the public library and the City Hall assembly to the east of the building.

The building itself is as mentioned put together of two larger building bodies each with their own particular characteristics. The northern building hosts both Friis shopping centre but also the low-priced chain hotel 'Cap Inn'. There are also a number of office spaces in the building which, at the time I wrote this book, were rented out to Aalborg University. The northern building contains a very large internal atrium located several floors up and disconnected from the Friis shopping centre (fig. 4.4). It creates a sealed-off yard with grass and benches that are completely detached from its urban context. The southern building also contains the Friis shopping centre as well as a fitness centre and the office of the architectural company C. F. Møller.

The construction of Friis was finalised in 2009. At this time the general economy was good and there was a lot of optimism in the retail sector. (The situation changed radically in 2013 when the Danish retail market struggled with empty spaces and a more

Fig. 4.4: Internal atrium and roof gardens

stressful financial situation.) The two building bodies have very different histories since the northern building was built from scratch at a site where, for almost 20 years, there had been a multistorey concrete parking garage for which it was hard to find any advocates for its aesthetics and contribution to the city's atmosphere (fig. 4.5). Thus the parking garage was completely demolished and four floors of underground parking were dug out before the erection of the northern building. The story of the southern building is different; basically, it is a renovation of an earlier store. 'Magasin' which runs high-end retail stores in Copenhagen and Aarhus, decided to withdraw from Aalborg; before 'Magasin' there was yet another local store named 'Anva' in the southern building.

Left behind from the old structures was a skywalk connecting the 'Metax' parking garage to the 'Magasin' store. Instead of keeping one path, the architects decided on two smaller skywalks contributing to the unique circulation system of the centre. The two skywalks pass over a street where most traffic is public busses, bikes, and cars going to nearby shopping centre parking at 'Salling' or 'Føtex'; due to the traffic abatement design of the underpass street, the number of private cars is limited. As the skywalks are equipped with large glass windows, people at street level can see shoppers dining and moving up in the mall, as well as people in the mall can see the traffic passing below. The two skywalks and the two large building envelopes create an almost void-like space in the middle used mainly for transit traffic and bike parking.

An architect from the architectural company C. F. Møller, who drew the house explains, that Friis is a very complex entity and there have been a number of difficult issues to deal with, from interests related to developers, the city, and the companies to legal, functional, and architectural challenges (research interview, March 12, 2012). From his explanation it becomes clear that the complexity of the building in technical as well as in planning terms was challenging, and so were the internal flow structures of the two houses. This goes in particular for the many levels of underground parking combined with two large buildings that are connected with two skywalks. According to the architect, this complexity has meant that some visitors have difficulty finding their way and navigating in the centre. From my own experiences as a regular visitor who both comes to shop but also uses the centre as transit space, I tend to agree. Friis is more difficult to find your way through due to its complexity and layers than due to its actual size. Much larger malls may be navigated much more easily. However, this is not necessarily a bad thing since this 'maze-like' property also gives the centre identity and character. In times of generic transit space and shopping design, a unique layout and a not-so easily overseen spatial organization might be what customers recognize as unique. As always things do have to be 'legible' within design, whether a building or an urban neighbourhood, balanced design is essential for the successful use of a place (Lynch 1960). The complexity of navigating Friis is obviously due to its physical layout but this again actually stems not only from the usual confinements and restrictions (e.g., money and space) but also from the conscious wish to design a building seeming larger and more complex than 'it actually is' (research interview, March 12, 2012). One of the keys to providing visitors with a sense of largeness and XL is to create slightly more complex circulatory systems and paths than one would do if the only aim were to move in the fastest possible manner between point A and B. So the mobilities design of Friis not only solves the necessary logistical tasks, it also provides customers and visitors with an experience of 'place'.

When building an urban shopping mall, one crucial issue obviously is parking. Looking at the local media one might get the impression that there are almost no more parking spaces left in the inner city of Aalborg. However, the municipality continuingly monitors the parking supply and demand, and with recent large scale projects the provision of parking in the shopping areas does seem adequate. However, access to parking with nearby proximity to the shops is only one dimension of the 'parking issue'. Cost is the other, and here Friis shares its fate with the rest of the downtown shops as they suffer stiff competition from the out-of-town mall and shopping facility 'City Syd' who boast that they have 4,500 free parking spaces. The regional retail magnet of 'City Syd' has expanded dramatically during the last decade and was with its creation in the 1970s defined as a 'secondary centre' to take off the pressure off the city itself. With access to the national motorway system and huge, classic big-box chain stores, 'City Syd' has proven to be a serious competitor that on a 'good day' matches the downtown shopping area in both number of customers and turnover. So when Friis was established, the 850 underground parking spaces immediately beneath its many shops was a compelling feature. In the very early days of the centre's existence parking was free precisely in order to compensate for the competitive pressure from 'City Syd'. This cannot be explored in great depth here, but obviously the ownership and control of the underground parking space need to be understood in relationship to the ownership and control of the shopping centre as well as to management operation and control.

Friis was officially opened on March 23, 2010 and was developed by A. Engaard & Braaten+ Pedersen. The architect is C. F. Møller and the engineering company COWI. The owner is Danica Pension Properties and daily operations are administered by the company Steen & Strøm. They ooperate and manage several malls and shopping centres internationally and are engaged in very meticulous performance monitoring of the centre. On regular intervals they perform measurements of customer flow and stop interviews and correlate this data with information about turnover in shops and the like. The result is a rather finely-grained monitoring device that helps the centre management find out anything from potential renegotiation of square metre rental prices, to the need for signage improvement or internal logistic

Figure 4.5: The 'Metax' parking garage before and after demolishing in 2008, author's photos

interventions. From one such 'tracking' report based on research done on two days in December 2010, it was concluded that customers were becoming increasingly aware of Friis and that they were reasonably distributed in terms of age groups; more than half of the customers are however below the age of 35. The largest competitors were other nearby shops ('Salling' in particular) but also the aforementioned 'City Syd'; the issue of parking, the central location, and the covered facility were the key reasons for customers to choose Friis (bearing in mind this was conducted in December) (Steen & Strøm 2010). As a separate issue of particular interest to this work was the mode of transport among the customers interviewed. Unsurprisingly, 56 percent of the interviewees came by car, 24 percent on foot, and only 15 percent by bus. This of course illustrates that the accessibility and car-oriented design of the centre are key to understanding its market performance (and a vital competitive parametre). This report was of course a snapshot of the 2010 Christmas retail situation, where more money was in circulation than today, as well as the fact that the centre was still working to position itself in the minds of the potential customers.

Today the picture might look very different, but that is not a central issue to this particular work. Steen & Strøm also conducts very detailed 'footfall' surveys of the daily numbers of customers, their preferred entrances and many other detailed levels of information. This is not unique to Friis but is rather a standard operating procedure within contemporary retail business as the optimization of everything from rent to shop logistics depends on accurate and detailed information. In this case I have chosen not to go more deeply into these materials as the key interest is the situational mobilities performed by the visitors and customers rather than aggregated statistics of more general nature. However, it speaks of course to the knowledge of how such shopping facilities are dependent on not only a steady flow of customers and goods meeting and marrying, but also of carefully configured protocols of data and information processing. The layer of the building that comes closer to 'software' or an 'operating manual' is not central to this case study, but should be understood as key to the notion of a building as a 'moving project' rather than a 'static object' (Latour and Yaneva 2008, 80).

Opposite: Fig. 4.6: Facades from Gabels plaza, Fjordgade and Nyhavnsgade

From this contextualisation of Friis I 'move in closer' and utilize the method termed 'serial vision', developed by architect Gordon Cullen.

'Getting there' - serial vision analysis

As explained elsewhere (Jensen 2013a) the method developed by Cullen termed 'serial vision' (Cullen 1996; Bosselmann 1998) may be utilized to illustrate how a mobile subject will experience the visual shifts of scenery as he or she moves through an environment. The method is obviously limited by its visual focus and its 'frame-by-frame' presentation as opposed to a moving picture (or a full-range sensorial experience that is the 'normal' way a mobile body perceives and registers the environment in motion). However, the method is very often used within architecture and urban design and works well as a way of presenting the site and in particular the 'getting there' issue. In a broader context (fig. 4.3), it is clear that even though many paths may lead to Friis there are a limited number of key access routes. These then again are different depending on mode of transport, as the pedestrians and bicyclists have more route choice options than, for example, cars.

The first 'serial vision' (SV) I explore is '*on foot to the Gabels Plaza entrance*' (fig. 4.7). In this serial vision I move from the west toward the east of Nytorv, passing the other large shopping centre 'Salling'. From this SV we see that Friis presents itself to the approaching pedestrian with a distinct architectural identity. The large scale and volume of the building are countered by the relative lightness of its design, utilizing the surface colour of white and transparent glass for the ground level façade and the skywalk.

THIELE
30
Zone

HOTEL CABINN
TAXI
Forbeholdt
politiet

Friis

The modernist form-language of Friis contradicts some its neighbouring buildings that date back more than 100 years. However, other adjacent buildings are much newer and thus contribute to the creation of a rather mixed architectonic expression within the whole area. Sightlines are clear and led by the 'beacon sign' of the red 'Friis' on the white background. There will be no doubt about how to get to the centre from this direction. The revolving glass doors are generic entry technologies that filter, sort, and control the accessibility to the centre with ordinary doors for wheelchair users and other disabled people adjacent). In contrast to the automatic doors operated by the photo sensors often seen at shop entrances, the revolving glass door stages a slightly complex choreography for the user body. Speed and number of people entering need to be calibrated carefully to the capacity and speed of the revolving door. Failure to comply with these underlying design assumptions will cause the door to halt, thus leaving people stranded on public display. Mostly the operation moves along smoothly but occasionally people get too close to the glass door triggering the sensor to stop – at times by accident, at times deliberately to play a trick on the other people forming the 'mobile with'. Thus the revolving door becomes a crucial design feature and a 'CPC' connecting and mediating the XL building's inside and outside as well as affording the creation of 'temporary congregations' quite similar in nature to the ones that occur at lifts inside the building (however, mediating vertical movements as opposed to the door that mediates horizontal ones). At this side toward the south and west, Friis has its most open and welcoming facade. When the skywalks and the two anchor buildings are seen in section as here from the west, they stand out as rather powerful and strong foreground images that most people will think of when speaking of Friis. This image (fig. 4.1) is the semiotic and iconic visual identity that creates an identity for the mall in the midst of the rest of the urban fabric. This has, however, suffered a severe blow with the closing down of the Sony Centre as they had huge LED screens in the skywalk and thus contributed to the ambience that splits urbanites into advocates of the high-tech metropolitan image versus the critique of 'visual pollution' and generic design.

The second SV is *'on foot to the Nyhavnsgade entrance'* (fig. 4.8). The urban fabric I pass through here is of an altogether different nature and much more car-oriented and includes more rear views of buildings that give a less appealing and pleasant impression. I move from the fjord going first in the direction north to south passing a hotel and then turn right, moving from east toward west alongside the major traffic artery Nyhavnsgade (which has been downgraded from a four-lane to a two-lane road as part of the whole transformation of the harbour front area). The entry at the Friis building toward the street is a traditional automatic door and the design around this entry breaks the façade which is all white, rather massive, and closed along the rest of the building body toward the west. However coming from the fjord, the passing of Nyhavnsgade (despite its downgrading) makes it necessary to negotiate a rather busy street full of cars and street lights that mediate the entry flow of pedestrians to the centre that is staged 'from above' as part of the wider traffic regulation system. As the street is a vital east-west traffic axis, the periods of green and red are not experienced as being in favour of pedestrians. You will have to stand waiting much longer and less comfortably as a pedestrian using this entrance when compared to using the Gabels plaza entrance. In fact there have been some issues in the public debate about the intervals of the traffic lights at the southeastern building corner toward the public library. In the early days of the centre's existence, many car drivers and cyclists coming from west toward the east, passing under the two skywalks, felt they were waiting in vain for long periods without any traffic to wait for. The centre management has been in a running dialogue with the municipal Traffic Department about the setting of these intervals so that the delivery of goods into the centre and the street traffic are in synchronicity. Likewise, the cars 'coming up' from

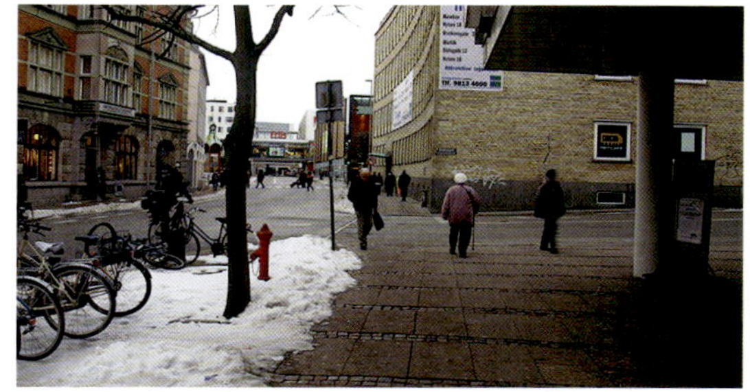

Fig. 4.7: Serial vision 'by foot to Gabels Flaza entrance'

Fig. 4.8: Serial vision 'by foot to the Nyhavnsgade entrance'

the underground parking spaces toward the north have been subject to changed traffic light intervals. This has been a particular challenge since these cars surface directly at the busier traffic junction between Rendsburggade and Nyhavnsgade. Much more could be said about these attempts to calibrate the external traffic flows, but here I have deliberately chosen the pedestrian as the mode of mobility to be studied. In chapter seven I shall explore the larger scales of car-based mobilities.

The facade facing toward Nyhavnsgade was a challenge for the architects and we can see from the serial visions that the interest in maximizing shelf and display space inside the shops has been prioritized over open facades connecting this part of the building to its immediate surroundings. Such transparency and openness may also not be as attractive because this adjacent road is a rather congested space. However, one might turn the argument around, stating that if the mall had opened up toward the north and the streetscape of Nyhavnsgade, new and interesting opportunities for engaging the city may had been inspired. It does seem as though the materialised design is at odds with the requirements laid down in the local plan section 6.2 with its explicit requirement of transparency and visual connection into the shops from the street so that passers-by may see an exhibit of goods at display (Aalborg Municipality 2008, 18). However, this is a reflection of the post-decision implementation negotiations to which such a large scale project is subject, as well as the fact that there might have been dispensation for this item (something I have not explored as it is outside the focus of this case analysis).

The third SV I present is the one made *'by bike to the Fitness World entrance'* (fig. 4.9). As mentioned, this is a well-travelled path to the building complex due to the fitness centre entrance. The SV illustrates the view of the building as one pass under the skywalks as well as it shows the 'bike parking void'. As the route is rather

Fig. 4.9: Serial vision 'by bike to the Fitness World entrance'

similar to the first SV where I followed the pedestrian path that runs parallel to the street route of this SV, the real difference is first noticed as I bike under the westernmost of the two skywalks and park the bike in the space between the two skywalks. The Fitness World entrance is a little unusual since it is a door to a lift placed directly at street level. This entrance often creates quite a few 'temporary congregations' as people queue up on the sidewalk in order to take the lift up to the fitness centre.

The fourth and final SV is *'on foot to the Nørregade entrance'* (fig. 4.10). This is very different from the other SV presented as this goes through the pedestrian areas at which the Friis centre is located, creating a 'hinge' as a transit link between north and south. I embark on the SV from the end of the pedestrian street and pass a number of smaller shops where quite a few of these have changed ownership and faced closings over the last years. The eastern end of Nørregade is on the edge of the shopping district and many of the shops here seem to struggle for survival. Without any research documentation for this claim, it does seem as if the increasing flows of pedestrians along the east-west axis due to the opening of the Nordkraft culture centre only a few hundred metres west of the street is changing all this. As I pass the series of smaller shops I come to the community centre that houses the main public library and the municipal assembly hall on my right. The building complex is close to being the same size as Friis but made from very different materials (predominantly red bricks and concrete pillars). Turning right after the community centre, I reach the Nørregade entrance of Friis where two things immediately spring to mind. First of all, one cannot help but notice the old half-timbered house on the left hand side of the small path leading to the entrance. The juxtaposition of the Friis centre and this old house is striking and is a reminder that this is the very heart of the historical centre of town. Next to this, the revolving door is the most dominant feature. The door uses the same technology as the one at the Gabels plaza

Fig. 4.10: Serial vision 'by foot to the Nørregade entrance'

entrance, filtering and sorting the flow of visitors and customers in a similar fashion. The building façade at this entrance of Friis is rather narrow and the big red logo on the white background is almost squeezed in between the old historic house to the west and the modernistic red brick and concrete building of the community centre to the east. The entrance is more hidden and inconspicuous than the one facing Gabels plaza; however, as one progress either east or west through Nørregade, the sight of the building and the glass façade are clearly communicating 'entrance' and not much signage is needed to make visitors and customers understand where to go.

Summing up these serial visions, I think it is safe to say that Friis is centrally located and mediates a number of different modes of mobility both as a destination and a 'hinge' facilitating transit in the city. Also the staging of these flows are carefully thought through in a choreography attempting to balance immanent interests that may be different for the different mobility modes (e.g., car drivers have wishes for accessibility different than those of pedestrians or cyclists). The key issue is the scale of the building. As an 'XL building' the centre orchestrates and stages a number of flows. These may include the delivery of goods and food supplies to customers and transit visitors. The access points and CPC facilitation vary in terms of ramps to the car park, revolving or automatic sliding doors. The design and architecture of this huge layered complex of flows have been made with a number of restrictions and choices to be balanced against each other since building a downtown urban shopping mall is quite different from constructing one on an open field out of town. The staging 'from above' must balance many interests, motives, and practicalities. However, at the end of the day the real interesting issue (at least in this research) is how people move and position themselves and thus how they appropriate the building. In accordance with the *Staging Mobilities* framework, I will therefore 'zoom in' on the mobile situations and the ways that customers and visitors in Friis actually act and interact. It is time to move inside.

Inside the building – the XL architecture and its flows

Friis has a rather complex geometry and spatial layout. The two main buildings and the underground parking form, with the double skywalk system, the backbone of a complex circulation system. In architecture and design a key distinction is between 'plan' and 'section'. Plan is the layout on a two-dimensional surface to which we may have become accustomed when reading maps on paper (a 'bird's-eye' perspective). The section is the imagined 'cut through' of what we may see in plan at a specific given line of intersection. One of the key points in designing and building spaces is that you need to think and work in three-dimensional space. Therefore, you need both plan and section in order to comprehend a site's spatial configuration. To show section drawings of Friis will, however, complicate matters a great deal, and I personally think that the story of how people inhabit Friis is much better told by relying on visual accounts in the form of photo registrations (regardless of the fact that photos obviously are not neutral and objective proofs; see Harper 2012). So understanding '*life within the walls of Friis'* may require that, along with the visuals of photos and textual accounts of observations, we engage with plans for the physical layout and structuring of the interior of the building in the 'programming' of this. The notion of 'programming' refers to the physical placement of activities and functions such as shops, amenities, infrastructure, technical facilities, etc. To build an overview of this complexity, the first thing to look at is the overview plan (fig. 4.11). From this we see that the main artery of the Friis building is the circular path system (marked in light grey). On the surface level ('plan 0') this is punctuated by the street crossing between the two building elements, whereas the path system is unbroken as we move toward the first floor ('plan 1'). In this plan drawing we find the location of important facilities such as toilets and lifts. I shall return

Fig. 4.11: Friis Overview Plan

in more detail to the wayfinding dimension at the end of this chapter. Also we need to notice that the actual names of the shops on the plan are a snapshot of the location and distribution in 2011. This has changed since due to shop relocation and some shops closing while new ones open. I will not list the shops that were there at the time the map was made, but rather point to one eye-catching feature: the composition of relatively many smaller shops and a few larger ones. This is in accordance with much mall design practice and theory since the placement and the size of shops are subject to complex design decisions. From established shopping research and mall design it is clearly documented that the precise location and relative positioning of certain shops compared to others are by no means trivial. Instead, they may be the key to the success of the mall (Chung et al. 2001; Wall 2005). Thus professional mall managers and designers talk about 'anchor stores' with very detailed monitoring of the location of stores and their internal flows of customers. In the literature, malls are typically divided into two types: the dumbbell and the cluster. The former separates building masses with circulation along linear pathways (or armatures in Shane's 2005 terminology). The latter type bundles building masses into groups with circulation in a network of intersections. These are abstract typologies, meaning that in empirical terms we most often see a conglomerate of these types (Herman 2001, 462). In the specific case of Friis we are looking at a predominantly 'cluster type' mall. However, as we zoom in, the circular and two-level path system may resemble the dumbbell structure. Furthermore, if the point was to assess Friis' performance as shopping centre, a plan like figure 4.11 would be useless since it is not updated. Anchor stores and the complex assemblage of smaller chain stores and independent shops need to be represented quite precisely to assess if the mall is performing in an optimal setting. However, here I am interested in the underlying mechanisms for mobilities design and how such principles materialize and become subject to complex social negotiation and appropriation. Therefore a plan with the principal layout of shops at any given time will suffice.

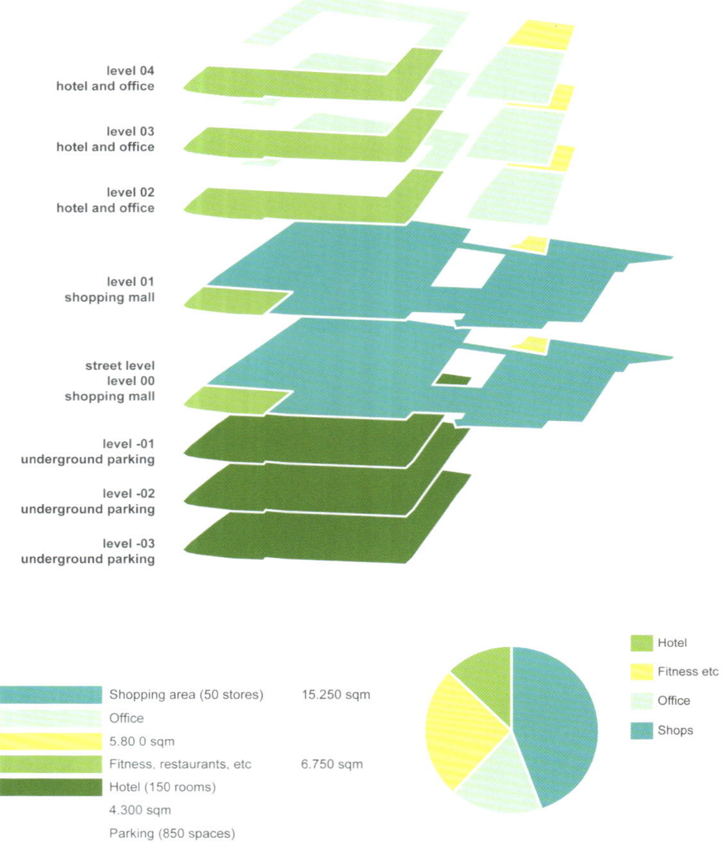

source: Steen & Strøm Danmark A/S

Next in importance to the plan is the so-called 'programming' of the site. Given the fact that changes have occurred, this map is not a precise representation of the actual situation in Friis (fig. 4.12). However, as in the case of the plan, I am looking for the underlying principles for staging mobilities rather than the actual performance of Friis. The layered 'stacks' of program illustrate that the mall actually takes up only two floors within the XL building but also that the mall is by far the largest program within the overall building envelope.

One of the first impressions a visitor gets as he/she moves inside the building are the large horizontal surfaces that make a strong statement due to a rather short distance between floor and ceiling. This is a feature accentuated by the choice of dark colours in most of the ceiling surfaces and a substantial part of the floor area. Furthermore, the shape of the horizontal surfaces strikes the first-time visitor as being different from the large and rectangular malls we may be familiar with particular in out-of-town malls. The interior spaces in Friis are curved and shaped in nonlinear ways that give the space a particular identity and ambience (fig. 4.13). These almost organic shapes are enforced by circular 'windows' perforating walls at seemingly random sites. The transparent shop facades are working to enhance visibility and light in the pedestrian

corridors at the same time that they fulfil their primary target: displaying goods and merchandize.

As one moves around in the centre, the relatively few key elements -- two main buildings, two floors of mall, two skywalks and the vertical operation of lifts and escalators -- create a rather complex space where the ability to navigate and recognise one's location can be a challenging task. Large windows supplying the corridors with daylight from above work to (partly) compensate for the lack of daylight that one experiences when moving in the deeper interiors of the buildings. The CPCs connecting the horizontal layers with vertical armatures for movement are important sites. Thus around and adjacent to the entry points of the escalators and lifts we find 'temporary congregations' as a function of people queuing up for moving to a different level of the building (fig. 4.14). As one rides the lift, the transparency of the glass walls makes legibility from the inside-out a key feature while other visitors in the centre may stop to gaze at the people being transported up and down in the lift. On the escalators people are 'on display' too, but in a less confined space and with a more open view to the surrounding space.

If we move even closer to the visitor's and customer's experience, we may see how people are exposed to each other's gazes and visual recognition when moving up on the one side and down on the other side of the escalators (fig. 4.15). Furthermore, the open escalators serve the purpose of giving visual orientation as one moves slowly and builds an overview from one level to the other.

While walking along the corridors and the paths in the centre, other visitors are obviously obstacles' to avoid colliding with. However, a number of supportive columns that are key structural features of the building as well as smaller pieces of urban furniture such as benches and flower pots all work to divide and separate the flows within the building. As a visitor, one embarks

Left page from top:

Fig. 4.12: The 'programming' of Friis

Fig. 4.13: Mall interior

Right page from top:

Fig. 4.14: Temporary congregations at the escalators

Fig. 4.15 The mutual 'up and down gaze' on the escalator

Fig. 4.16: Negotiating human and non-human objects

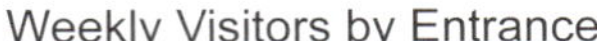

50.000

Weekly Visitors by Entrance

16,000
14,000
12,000
10,000
8,000
6,000
4,000
2,000
0
Nyhavnsgade
Parking elevator
Parking escalator
Gabels Plads
Fjordgade
Nørregade

Nyhavnsgade entrance
750 visitor/week
1.5%
Elevator entrance
3.500 visitor/week (7%)
Escalator entrance
12.500 visitor/week (25%)
Gabels plads entrance
15.000 visitor/week
30.5%

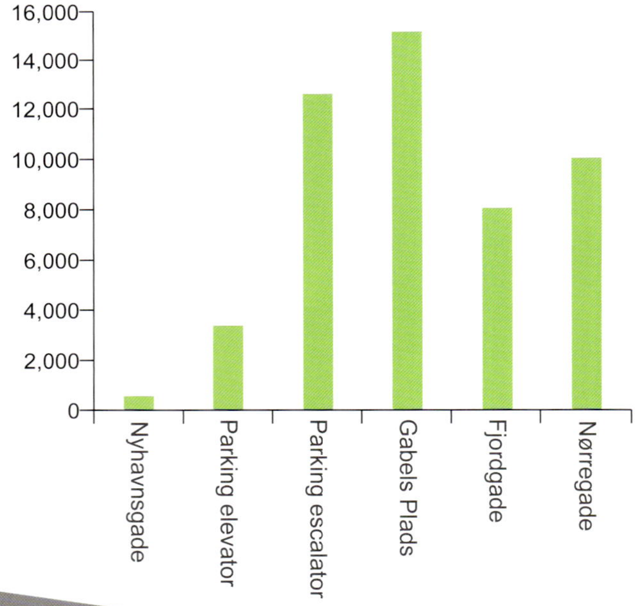

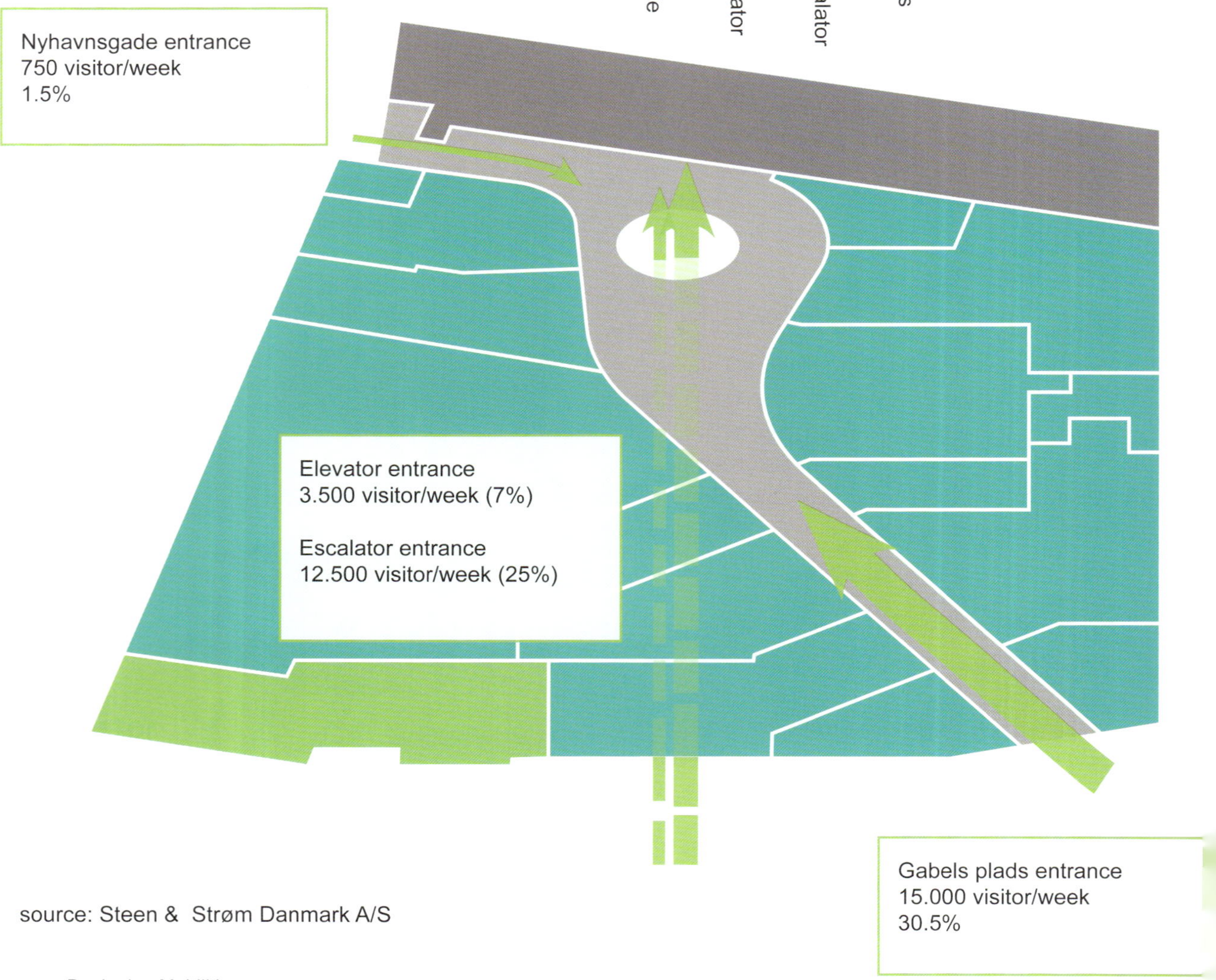

source: Steen & Strøm Danmark A/S

Daily Visitors

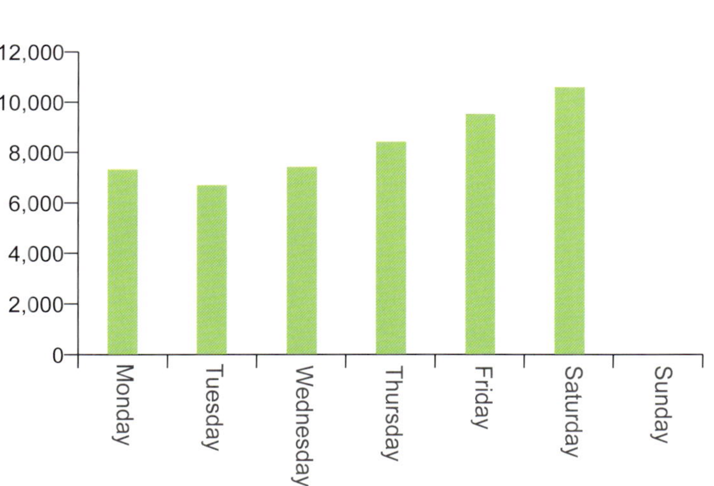

Hourly Visitors

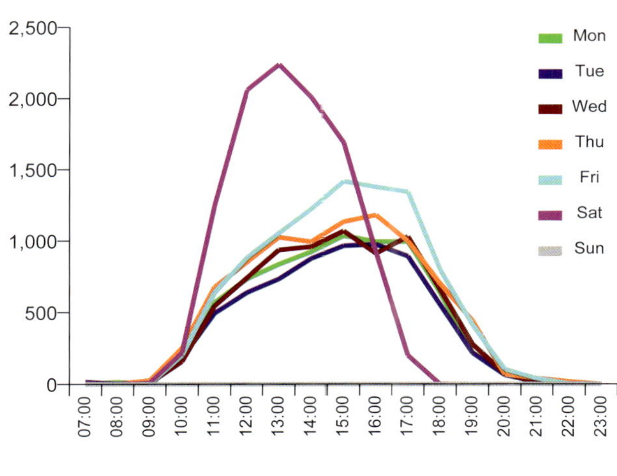

street level
level 00 -
shopping mall

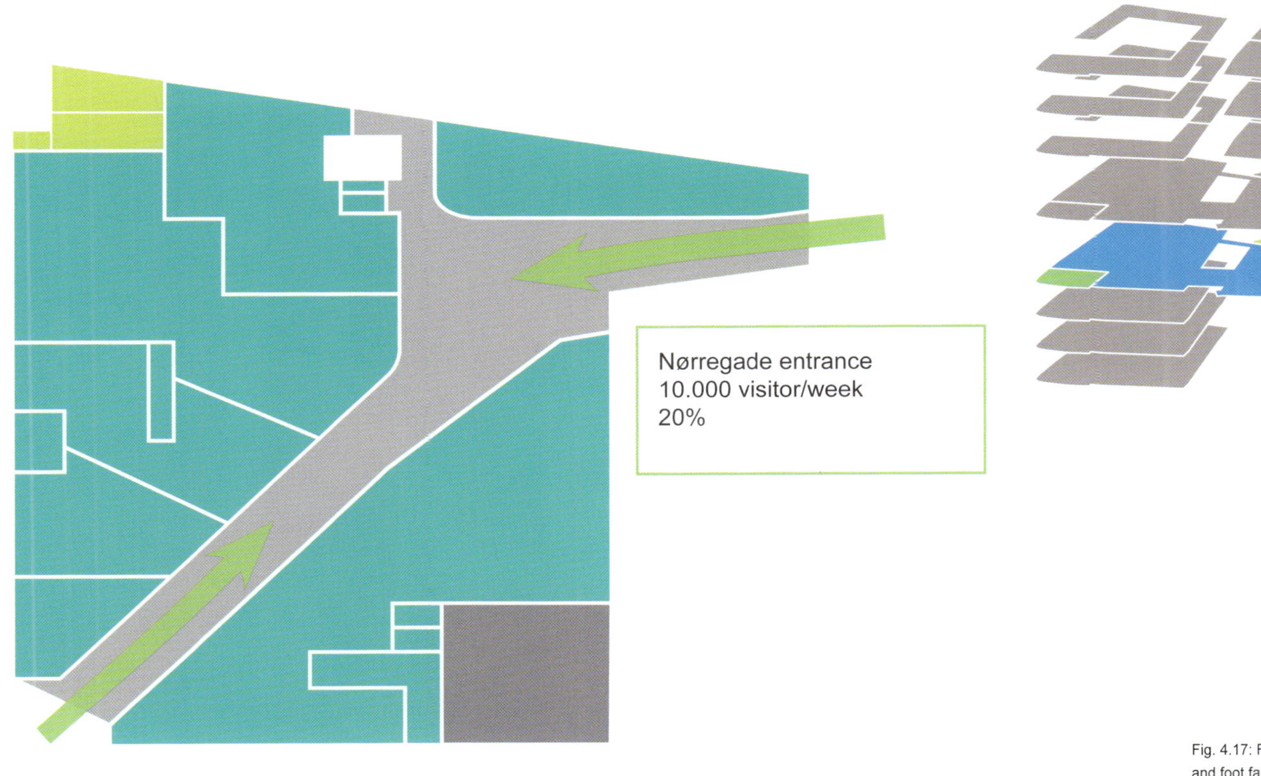

Fig. 4.17: Flow analysis and foot fall into Friis

on a number of microscopic interactions, twists of the body, speed and direction changes within this armature space in order to negotiate human and non-human 'objects', making one's way through the building (fig. 4.16).

The centre is, as mentioned, monitored rather closely and this also applies to the flows of visitors through the centre. In figure 4.17 we see weekly flow by entrances (Gabels plaza and parking being the main entrances), the peak weekdays (Friday and Saturday), and the peak hours in the so-called 'footfall' studies. Here I have chosen only to show data for level 00 since it is the principle of monitoring flows that I find interesting.

An even more interesting representation of the internal flows that also includes the complexity of horizontal and vertical mobilities is the illustration of both levels 00 and 01 (fig. 4.18). Here we see the functionality of the main artery and circulation armature that keeps the centre running. We learn also that the escalators in the north building and the south building are moving different volumes of visitors on a weekly basis (25,000 in the north versus 30,000 in the south building). The two elevators also differ in their carrying activity (2,000 in the north versus 2,500 in the south). The importance of the escalator cannot be overestimated in relation to shopping malls. In a chapter on the escalator's profound importance for shopping mall development Weiss and Leong quote the following from a 1940s promotion brochure made by the Otis escalator company:

> The elevator is ideal for the 'man [sic!] with a mission'. He knows what he wants. It's a specific floor; he goes to that floor, makes his purchase and leaves. If *he* wants to go upstairs because he has business there, then give him an elevator. But if *you* want him upstairs, then you must reach down and pick him up. The Escalator does this

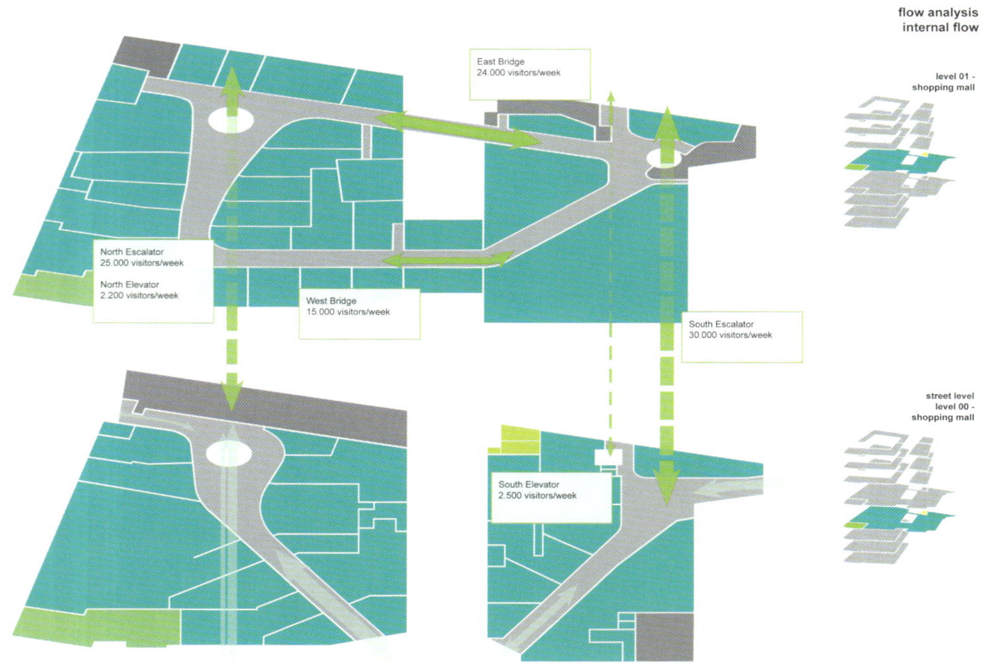

Fig. 4.18: Flow analysis – internal flow

job for you – and it does it better than any other vertical transportation equipment available today (Otis advertisement, quoted in Weiss and Leong 2001, 346, italics in original).

From the footfall studies we also saw that the escalator's carrying capacity is greater than the elevator. The elevator/lift is, however, needed to cater to less mobile people, disabled people, or people with prams. In Friis the design solution with transparent glass in the lifts that run in the centre of the building envelope compensates for the lack of visual orientation and helps to facilitate impulsive purchases; as you are slowly moved up or down you have ample time to gaze at goods and shop windows. Also an escalator within a shopping centre is an excellent device for displaying goods to potential customers in a clever way as goods are fixed and customers mobile! If we add to this the distinction between the eastern skywalk and the western skywalk, we get a fuller picture of the aggregated levels of weekly flows in the centre. Here the eastern skywalk facilitates the flow of 24,000 weekly visitors versus only 15,000 in the western skywalk. Needless to say, such information is vital for the centre management and for the price setting of the rent for the individual shops (assuming that most shops would want to be close to the main flows but also that the centre management would want to utilize anchor store effects of the key shops to 'draw in' visitors passing less popular shops).

A number of more detailed flow studies could be presented here at this level (for instance, flows within centre sections). However, I wish to move toward the social interactions and movements of visitors and customers at the more detailed level.

Mobile situations, user mindsets, and mobile practices
From the *Staging Mobilities* perspective upon which this work is based, there are two key principles of

Fig. 4.19 (left): The River

Fig. 4.20 (right): The Ballet

mobilities observation to be made. One I termed the 'river' and the other the 'ballet' (these were presented in chapter three). From the perspective of the 'river' (fig. 4.19), mobilities are seen from a 'bird's-eye' view and we noted the layout of the site with all its details; for example, columns, escalators, and benches may be likened to a 'riverbed' shaping the flows of people as does water in a 'stream'. I also noted that this metaphor deliberately homogenizes people within the situations as if they were all identical. The analysis of the 'river' gives us an abstract, aggregated, and homogeneous understanding of a collective stream of mobile bodies in the Friis centre.

From the perspective of the 'ballet', we move toward being at eye level with the mobile subjects (fig. 4.20). When looking at the mobile practices in Friis through the metaphor of the 'ballet', we start noticing the gestures, gazes, and embodied negotiations and interactions that take place ever so swiftly. What becomes the focal point then are the embodied and lived perceptions and sensations of the mobile subject.

Friis (as any other material arena of mobilities) may only be understood fully if we aim to couple the two perspectives of the 'river' and the 'ballet'. As architectural and spatial analysis need both plan and section, so do situational mobilities analysis need both the 'river' and the 'ballet' perspective. As one of the key ambitions of the 'mobilities turn' is to document that mobilities are much more than acts of physical displacement, the notion of the 'ballet' becomes particularly important. However, we fail to understand the structuring principles and the mobile affordances created by architecture and design if we don't take the bird's-eye view of the 'river' into account as well. In order to move in even more closely on the mobile subjects and the way they negotiate the place, I propose an even more micro-oriented level of analysis. This is the analysis of user types and detailed mobile practices. What follows here is an attempt to categorize the mobile subjects in Friis into three different user groups or typologies based exclusively on visual observation. From the mappings of situations I propose three types of mobile subjects: the drifter, the transiter, and the determined. The key has been the embodied mobilities, or in other words how people 'carry their bodies' as they move about. The work of Goffman is central to the theoretical underpinning of *Staging Mobilities*, and it is very much in his spirit that I make inferences on how people move, pause, break up, stand still, overtake, and interact with relation to the user typologies. I shall give more detailed examples in the analysis below. For now, key words describing the drifter are a relaxed body attitude, a somewhat unfocused gaze, and a slow pace of walking. In contrast I see the determined as being busy, focused in his or her gaze, and with a medium pace. Finally, I would argue for the transiter to be one that is busy, focused, and moving at a relatively high speed. According to these key features we may see specific mobile situations and acts such as 'hanging

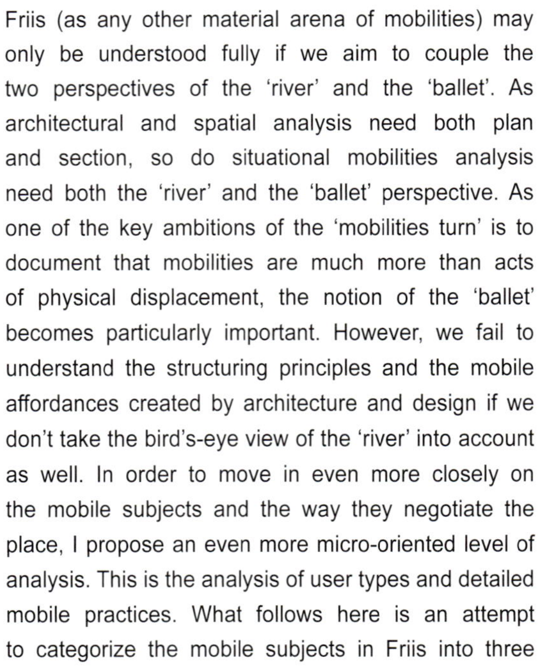

Fig. 4.21: User mind-sets and mobile practices

out', staying/resting, meeting, and playing for the drifter. We may see shopping, meeting, and wayfinding as key activities for the determined. And finally the transiter is, as the name suggests, in transit and thus mostly concerned with finding his or her way through the building. This simple structure of three types and their related key words supplies us with a vocabulary for analysis (fig. 4.21).

I realize this is a rather crude categorization and that more fine-grained ones could have been made. Having said so, they fulfil the pragmatic criteria of lending themselves to an understanding of the situational mobility of people in Friis at the time of observation. In the process of observing and registration in Friis, much more material has been produced than I can manage to present in this book. So I shall pick a few illustrative examples of how the nomenclature of user mind-sets and mobile practices can be coupled with the theoretical concepts from the *Staging Mobilities* framework in order to emphasize relatively detailed studies of mobile situations and the design/architecture affording these. Before focusing on social interaction I will present three examples of the user types: the drifter, the determined, and the transiter.

The drifter that was observed here (fig. 4.22) was observed for approximately 5 minutes at 16:30 in the afternoon on March 17, 2011 at level 0 close to the north escalator area. The person is slowly strolling along without any apparent direction, stops as the railing and watches other people. After a short pause the person starts moving again and walks toward a shop window that seems to have caught the person's attention rather coincidentally.

The determined that was observed here (fig. 4.23) was observed for only 20 seconds at level 0 close to the Gabels plaza entrance on March 17, 2011 at just after 16:30. What we observed here was a 'mobile with' where one person pushed another in a wheelchair. As is seen from the diagram, they passed another 'mobile

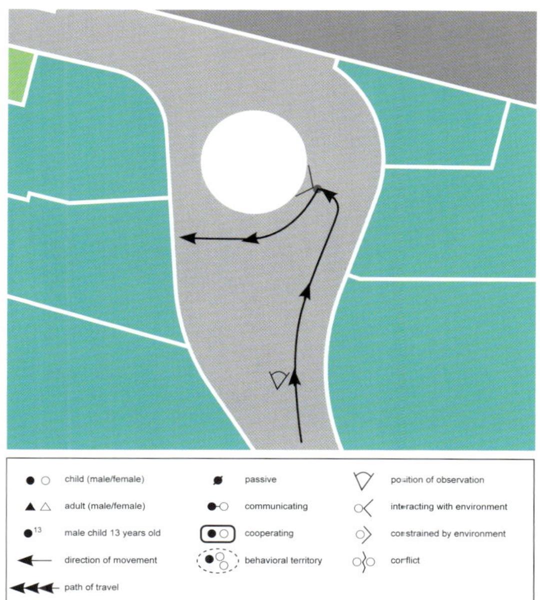

Figure 4.22: The Drifter

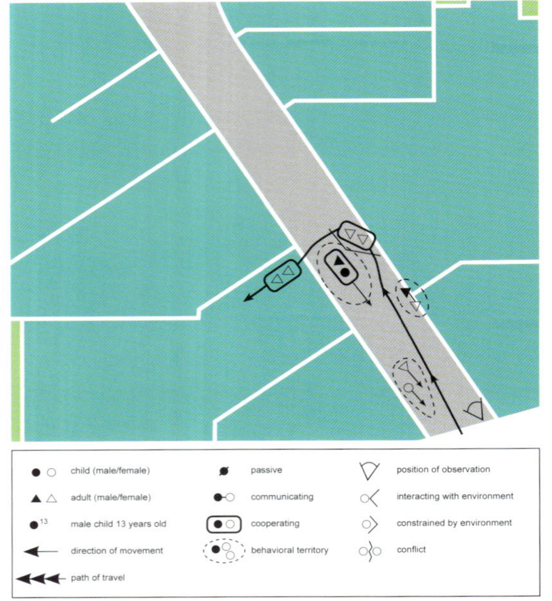

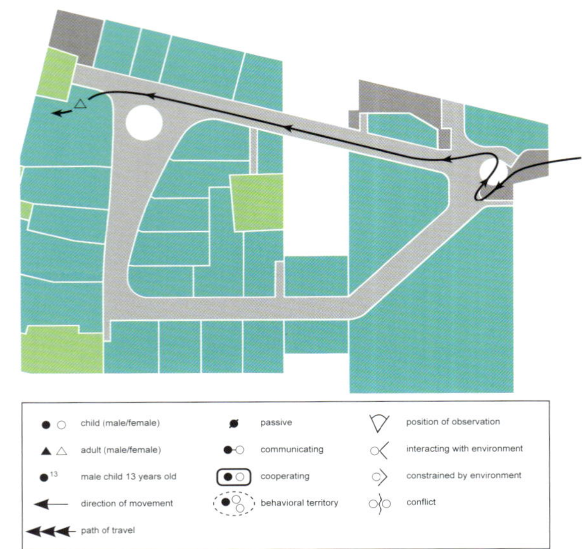

Figure 4.23 (left): The Determined

Fig. 4.24 (right): The Transitter

with' (an adult with a child) very closely and thereafter took a sharp left turn into a shop. Judging from their speed and the trajectory, these people were not window shopping but entering Friis specifically with a determined goal.

The transiter presented here (fig. 4.24) was observed on March 30 at 11:30 for approximately 2 minutes at level 1 by the Nørregade entrance. The person observed entered the building through the revolving doors at the Nørregade entrance, went to the first floor by escalator, walked down the eastern hallway where she stopped and waited for the elevator, and rode down to the underground parking.

From these three types we see how mobile subjects appropriate the space passing through the building with an eye to objects and space as well as to other mobile subjects. I will explore the mobile interactions occurring in this space very shortly but before coming to this, let me present illustrations of common mobile practices such as shopping, transit, stay/rest, wayfinding, meeting, play, and hangout (figs. 4.25 – 4.31).

As we find people using the mall, all these various mobile practices suggest that there is more to a mall than shopping. In line with the general understanding of transit spaces as sites of more than merely A to B movement, so are shopping malls urban habitats, where the movement and interaction of people is a part of contemporary culture and urbanism. Coming from this more general observation, I want to end this section with more detailed accounts of mobile social interaction between shop visitors and customers.

We have observed seven different situational interactions (collision, occupying space, queuing at escalator, meetings, privacy, cleaning up, and appropriation of space). Here I want to present three that are distinctly illustrative for the mobile situational interactions. The first one I term 'collision' (fig. 4.32). This observation lasted approximately 20 seconds and was conducted on March 30, 2011 at 12:23 at level 1 in the east hallway. What was observed was three elderly ladies standing and chatting in the middle of the hallway. As they start to move across the hallway, four younger children are moving in the opposite direction causing the two 'mobile withs' to meet in the middle of the hallway, leading to some confusion and disruption of their movements. In this particular situation the children avoided collision by utilizing the close proximity 'sliding off' body turn. The application of this rather well-known technique is performed in perfect synchronicity by the children as if this were a well-rehearsed mobile act almost on the level of a sports routine. From earlier observation studies in public spaces, this mobile performance by the 'mobile with' is by no means exotic (Jensen 2013a, 143). Instead, this seems to be a very ordinary example of 'negotiation in motion'.

Another standard theme in the study of urban spaces is the issue of 'space occupancy' (fig. 4.33). In this five-minute observation made on April 2, 2011 at 13:00 at level 1 in the west hallway we found a couple with children resting. The children were quite noisy and it was clear to see how other visitors and customers rerouted in order to get outside the 'interaction zone'. As the family occupies the furniture as an 'island in the stream', other people take explicit measure of the situation and make choices to avoid further interaction and close encounters. Like the situation before, this is among the standard repertoire of mobile urban interactions. However, in this specific situation, the spatial confinements of a narrow corridor within a building seem to make the 'risk' of interaction higher than if the situation had taken place out in the open in a more spacious urban arena (even though there need not be spatial confinements to actualize mobile interactional choices, which can be seen from observing people passing in wide open spaces such as a field or a large urban square).

ginatricot

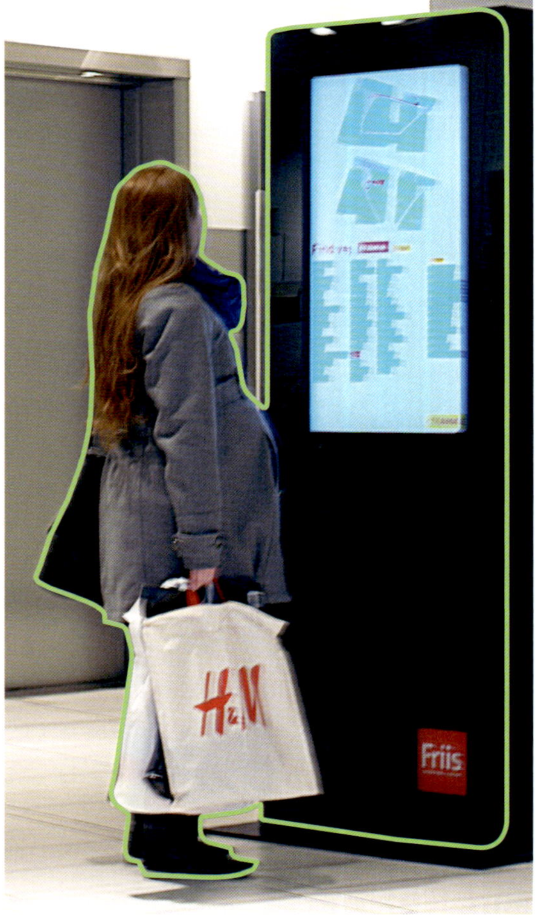
H&M
Friis

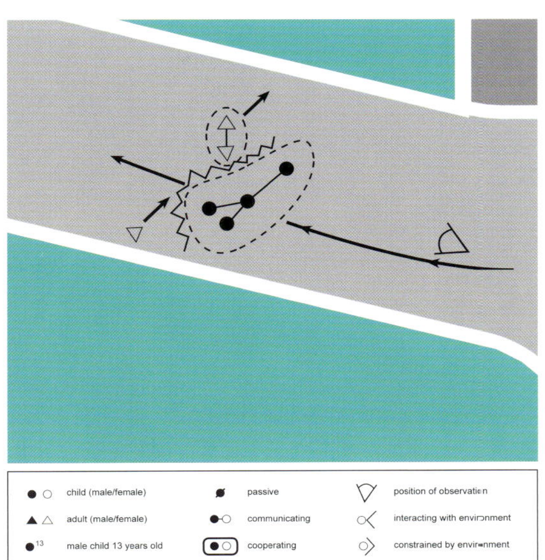

Fig. 4.25-4.31: Common mobile shopping mall practices

Fig. 4.32 : Collision

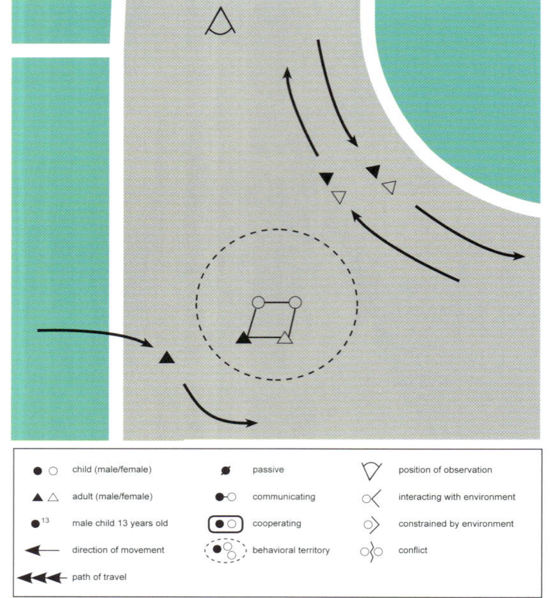

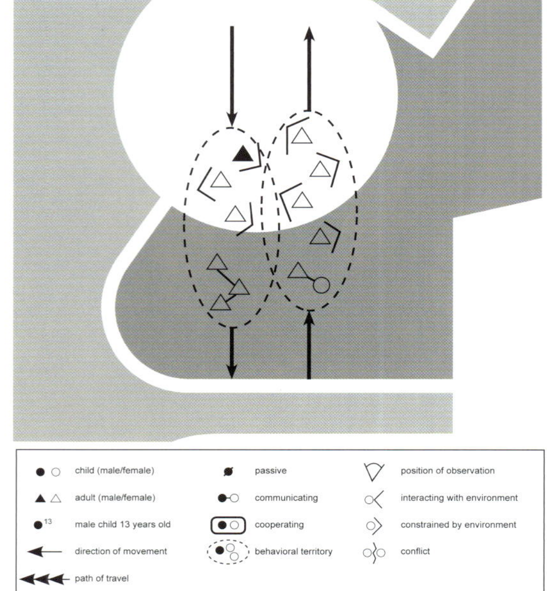

Figure 4.33: Occupying space

Figure 4.34: Cueing at the escalator

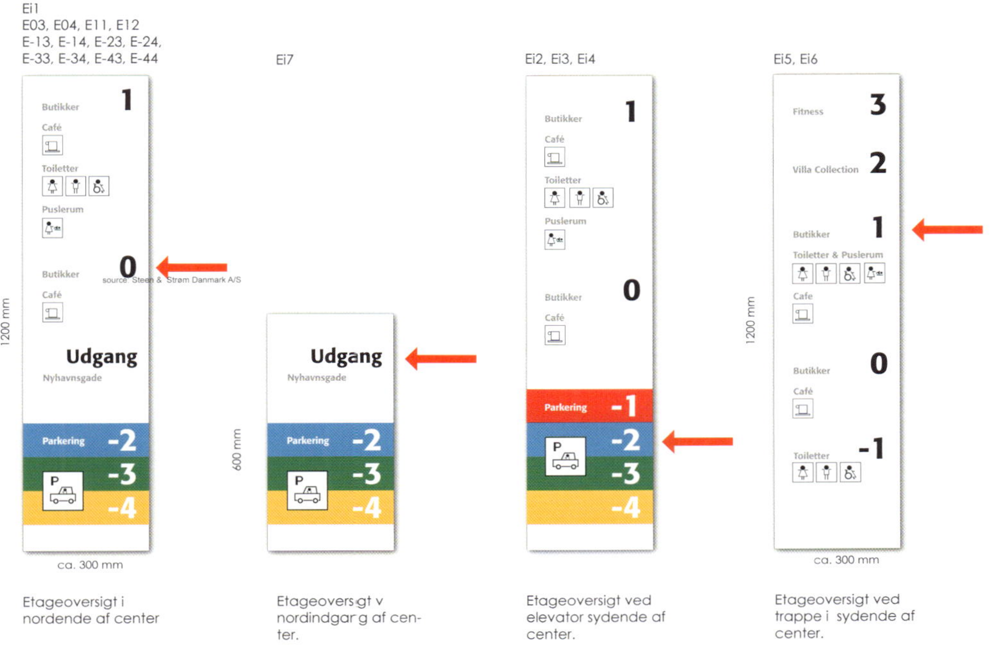
Ei1
E03, E04, E11, E12
E-13, E-14, E-23, E-24,
E-33, E-34, E-43, E-44
Butikker
Café
Toiletter
Puslerum
1
0
source: Steen & Strøm Danmark A/S
Udgang
Nyhavnsgade
Parkering
-2
-3
-4
1200 mm
ca. 300 mm
Etageoversigt i nordende af center
Ei7
Udgang
Nyhavnsgade
Parkering
-2
-3
-4
600 mm
Etageoversigt v nordindgang af center.
Ei2, Ei3, Ei4
Butikker
Café
Toiletter
Puslerum
1
0
Parkering
-1
-2
-3
-4
Etageoversigt ved elevator sydende af center.
Ei5, Ei6
Fitness
3
Villa Collection
2
Butikker
1
Toiletter & Puslerum
Cafe
Butikker
0
Café
Toiletter
-1
1200 mm
ca. 300 mm
Etageoversigt ved trappe i sydende af center.

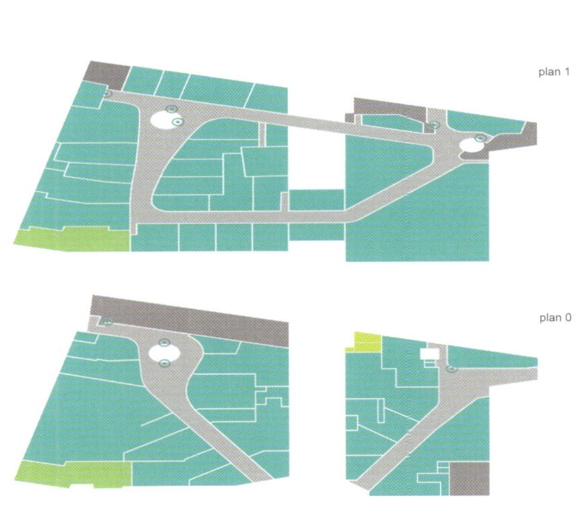
plan 1
plan 0

Friis

Fig. 4.35: Signage for level wayfinding

The third situation I want to present is the 'queuing at the escalator' (fig. 4.34). The observation was made on April 2, 2011 at 13:15 and lasted for about one minute at the level 0-1 south escalator. This is indeed a classic 'bottleneck' situation, where the capacity of the armature is surpassed by the volume of flow. However, as these are mobile subjects, much more is taking place. Queuing and the following escalator ride in close proximity offer many illustrations of 'negotiation in motion' and the fleeting interactions of 'mobile withs'. The tempo is slow but steady, laying bare various personalized expressions of identity and personality (from polite standing back to the less frequent cutting-in-front of other fellow moving subjects). As there is quite some traffic, the crossing gazes of the people going up and down are also key features of this situation. Mutual gazing and glancing over very short spans of time allow the up or down traveller to assess if there is anyone familiar riding the escalator as well as the myriad of other things mobile urbanites notice (albeit pretending not to with a 'blasé' attitude, Simmel 1903/50). So what takes place here is a complex dynamic and mobile situation of mutual interaction among people in the 'same lane' (e.g., 'going up') forming a 'mobile with' as well as the cross-lane interaction or awareness resembling what takes place in car infrastructures (to which I shall return to in chapter seven).

As mentioned we observed and mapped many more situations but space is a scarce commodity and here my main aim has been to show how mobile subjects are mediated by architecture and design, as well as how they interact in motion when they embark on the commercial flows in the XL building. Before reaching the concluding section I want to address wayfinding and semiotics as a separate theme.

Wayfinding and mobile semiotics

This is not so much subscribing to the idea that architecture (or any environmental ecology) is 'readable' as if it were signs and representations (even though this may carry some weight). Here I am concerned with the very explicit semiotic layer of signs and other communication vehicles added to the XL building in order to afford orientation and legibility. Large transit spaces such as airports, rail terminals, hospitals, and sports arenas almost always need to add some element of a designed wayfinding system (this goes for urban spaces and cities as well). In Friis we find signage systems that tell you at what level you are (fig. 4.35). The level wayfinding signs are situated at strategically important sites (creating CPCs between the two systems of customer flow and commercial activity).

Furthermore, there are a number of digital wayfinding stands in the building (fig. 4.36). These are of the sort where you operate a pressure sensitive screen and thus are able to locate any store you are seeking. Besides these semiotic devices, the whole centre is full of the internationally well-known and generic pictograms helping to find, for example, public toilets but also inscribing the centre regulation by signs about what is prohibited (for example, no skateboards or no smoking). Regulatory discourse and wayfinding systems mix with the rich semiotic environment of commercial signs where the senses are bombarded with many and strong visual impressions. At the end of the day all signs compete for attention and Friis is no exception to this.

As I mentioned, the legibility and wayfinding dimension is one of the challenges in Friis. One easily becomes at loss as to where one's actual location is, possibly due to the complex layout of layers and two buildings. Also the underground parking creates issues of disorientation that a wayfinding system must address. Much more detailed analysis could have been performed here. However, I mainly wish to state the point that the built environment in the urban XL building resembles other urban spaces where the need to get 'semiotic handles' is ever present. The mobile semiotics of Friis is distinct in terms of its own physical

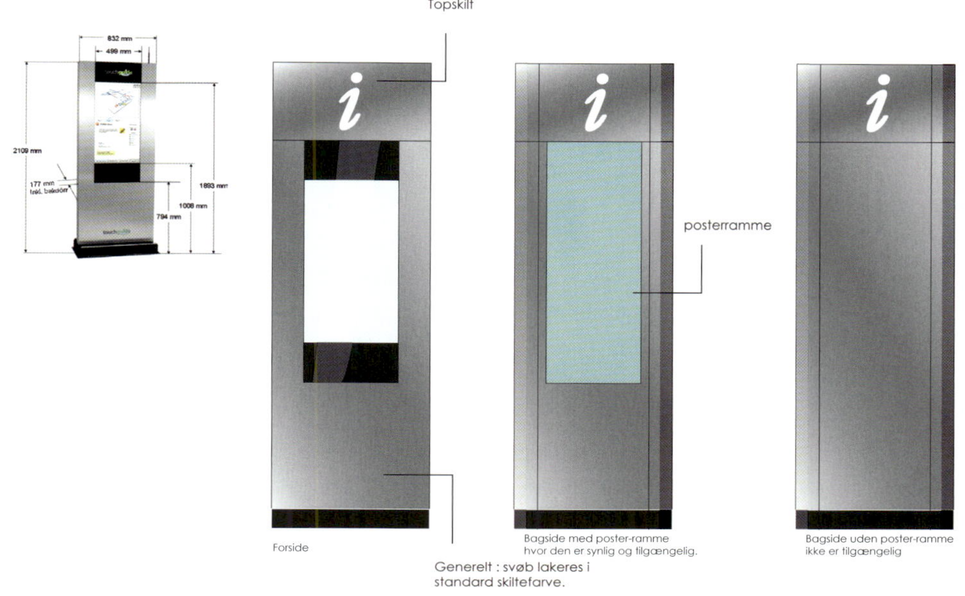

source: Steen & Strøm Danmark A/S

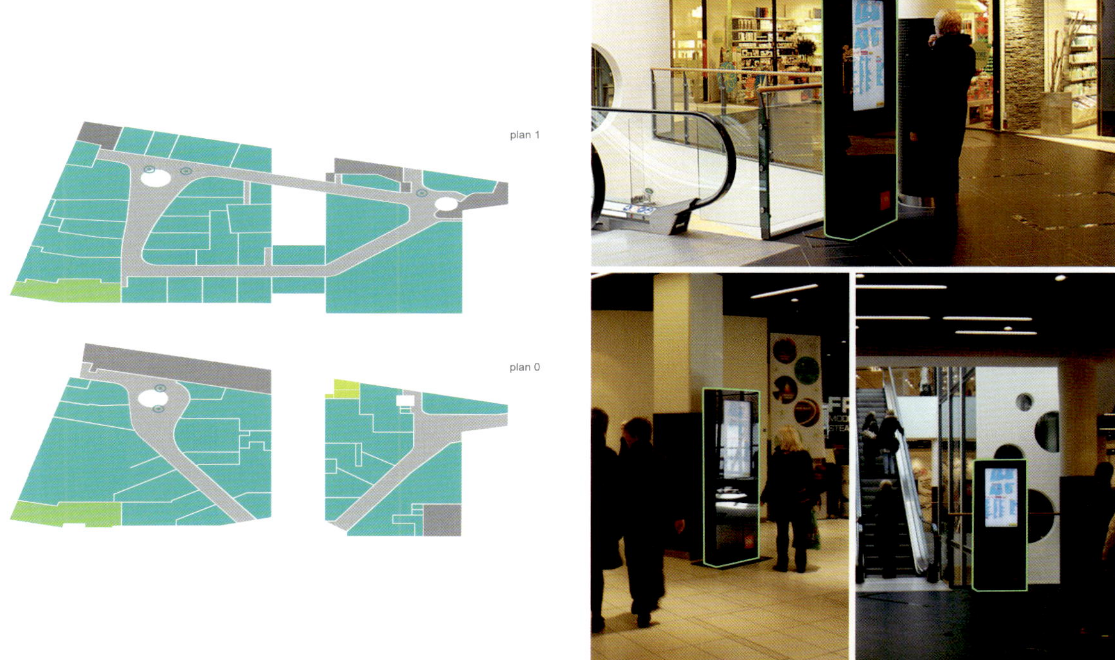

Figure 4.36: Digital wayfinding stands

properties and spatial layout; at the same time it is generic to the extent that mobile subjects need to be 'processed' by signs in order for the commercial flow to accommodate the intentions of the centre owner and designer (staging from above). Equally is the demand from people to actually make informed decisions about where to go (staging from below).

Concluding remarks

I trust that the reader senses that a much more detailed exploration could have been made. However, the case analysis needs to come to a close. I shall sum up and conclude by correlating the research questions presented in chapter one with the *Staging Mobilities* model, the key concepts presented in chapter three, and the empirical material from the case. The key issue is to look at the Friis case and explore how the design is affording and/or preventing particular mobile practices and cultures in everyday life. And from this general question, I engage with subthemes such as how design of various modes of mobilities and sites is hosting these mobile practices and affecting the mobile situations of everyday life. How does the design of mobility modes and sites of mobilities influence the social and cultural interactions and exchanges of the contemporary city? How does the design of mobility modes and sites of mobilities enact and engage with human embodied performances in the mobile situations of everyday life? And how may we, on the basis of the investigations and explorations carried out in this book, start to articulate a field of 'mobilities design'? When taking these questions as points of departure and exploring Friis through the analytical framework of *Staging Mobilities* applying the key words, a more fine-grained picture of Friis emerges. In general terms I would say that Friis is a 'gearbox full of speeds' (Graham and Marvin 2001), a layered machine of circulation, a transit space and 'hinge' between urban neighbourhoods, a critical point of contact that connects goods and experiences with mobile subjects, a horizontal and vertical arena for mobilities, and a vivid illustration of mobilities as both acts of physical displacement and production of culture. In order to reduce some of the complexity, I refer to the model and the diagrams corresponding to the selected key terms from the framework (fig. 3.14).

It should be clear now that Friis is a prime case for understanding and illustrating that situational mobilities are staged in complex material, social, and embodied processes 'from above' by means of planning, design, and regulations as well as 'from below' by mobile subjects. Being subject to an analysis nested within 'critical mobilities thinking', Friis must be understood both as a space of potential navigation loss and challenges to peaceful coexistence of user types, as well as having the potential for offering users new experiences and interaction opportunities. Friis is, seen through the double notion of 'problems and potentials' that grow out of 'critical mobilities thinking', a site and a phenomenon of great complexity. Friis surely epitomizes both the qualities of 'mobile sociopetals and sociofugals'. From the analysis we saw how sites and settings within Friis work particularly well in getting people to go there and conduct their activities. The shops are attracting and 'drawing in' people and things as if they were the epicentre of a magnetic field of gravity. Within the centre itself, zones are working as mobile sociofugals tending to 'push' people, goods, etc., away or distributing them from their centre of gravity. Examples are the flows distributed by elevators/lifts and escalators as well as the way the parking spaces distribute visitors and customers. In the analysis we saw how signs (in their broadest possible sense) afford, process, and coordinate (or obstruct) the physical circulation and movement of people, vehicles, and goods in a more or less codified system of infrastructure. In Friis, the semiotic systems modify and interact with the human body and sensations as the subject moves and thus afford particular motions, directions, speeds, modes, and routes. Through the wayfinding systems and the general signage we found illustrations of semiotic techniques, designs, media, symbols, and signs coming together in an emerging 'mobile semiotic grammar'. This may be one of the key challenges for Friis (next to the more commercial operation): to organize the flows of customers and visitors utilizing semiotic systems that are legible and readable. In the hallways of Friis we also saw the mobile body as a sign vehicle illustrated, for example, when visitors negotiated the relatively narrow hallways using quick gazes and visual encodings of their fellow mobile subjects. The centre has all the standardized signs of well-known regulatory discourses such as signs that say 'no smoking' as well as guiding signs leading visitors to their destinations (shops, toilets, cafes, or parking).

Together with the hard infrastructure and the technological networks, the signs and semiotics systems are elements of a larger system connecting bodies, money, goods, and experiences. Therefore Friis is a 'mobile assemblage' being 'host' to contemporary mobilities in a fairly complex and large material environment where technologies, humans, software, codes, semiotic and communicative systems, objects, and artefacts are assembled in a specific combination, facilitating and affording certain mobile practices and restricting or preventing others. Looking at Friis from the vantage point of a mobile assemblage, humans and non-human entities are circulated and connected by complicated scripts that both capture a staging from above by the centre management as well as a staging from below by mobile subjects. At times this mobile interaction takes place by detached individuals but even people entering Friis alone become members of various 'mobile withs' as, for, example when they take the elevator/lift or the escalator. Also many 'mobile withs' enter Friis, as when families or groups of friends are out shopping. These mobile social entities negotiate the spaces and flows with other similar entities or individuals in the centre.

In Friis I have not explored the technological and digital dimension of what I have termed the 'networked self' in much detail. During our observations we saw many instances of interaction and mobile coordination using mobile phones, and there are multiple examples of people reading and writing text messages while they are at Friis. However, due to the proximity and relatively small scale of spatial interaction, I have chosen to engage less with this dimension. But Friis is no exception to the rule of increased digital connectivity and mediated interaction within public and semipublic spaces. Also Friis is present on various social media such as Facebook, Twitter, etc., but this dimension of digital marketing and customer loyalty programs lies well outside the scope of this book. As we see visitors to Friis move through shops and hallways talking on phones or texting, we see also that within Friis the 'networked self' is 'linked-in-motion'. This, however, has less to do with the design and architecture of Friis than with the general social transformations of mediated interaction in urban spaces. Here Friis perhaps could work even in greater detail with digital customer interaction, for example, through experiments with Bluetooth technology interfaces with the centre users and visitors. Again, this is a potential that could be considered if Friis were to mirror the increased digitalization of urban spaces in general, but not something that I found present in the centre. The whole dimension of digital entertainment customized to Friis' visitors is a potential that may be explored in the future.

As we did see people 'linked in motion', the main focus of attention was their embodied presences in material space. Thus we found much evidence of 'negotiation in motion' among 'mobile withs' and across groups of strangers; at CPCs such as elevators/lifts or escalators many 'temporary congregations' emerged. A site that we have not mentioned in this respect, but which deserves to be mentioned, is the parking ticketing machine that is a vital CPC, negotiating the parking payment of customers. Around these machines rather large 'temporary congregations' emerge and from earlier visits I noticed quite a lot of verbal interaction between the strangers congregating around the ticket machine. Here people share everything from complaints over ticket prices to jokes about being 'caught in the system' of complexity or the ever-present discussion of timing in light of the time-zone pricing. Needless to say, more problematic issues such as conflicts over queue-jumping also surface at these strategic sites.

In Friis we found the mobility cultures related to the predominant mode of mobility: walking. So from our observations we saw the walking codes of close proximity interaction that we also have seen in many other urban spaces. The walking culture within Friis is staged from above by the layout of the armatures, in the form of signage instructing people how to behave and move. There is a staging from below in the ways centre visitors chose to interact as they move around in the centre on foot. Cars and bikes are also important elements; however, they are not moving inside the shopping area but are confined instead to the designated parking spaces out on the street (for bikes) and below in the underground parking space (for cars). In the latter space a whole set of car parking codes installed by the designers are present as the staging from above (e.g., 'one-way' signage and arrows directing the car flow); often, the conflict-ridden interactions between customers hunting for a free parking space expresses the aggressive car behaviour we know from the world outside Friis. Obviously, I have also witnessed polite gestures and interactions among more civil-minded fellow drivers in the parking garage.

On a whole I think the study of Friis confirms that we need to think about the body and the way embodied mobilities are tied into sensory experiences of moving across and within spaces. The surfaces, slopes, and gradients of armatures in the centre that all are experienced by bodies in motion open up to an understanding of a mobility aesthetics where the customer experiences of the centre are very closely tied to the feeling of flow and friction, of pavements and wideness of corridors and walkways. The embodied mobilities connected to the 'body work' of muscle-powered mobility are one set of issues for which the centre provides a particular experience. Similar to this is the fact that people are moving within a closed ecology with no wind and sparse daylight. But, additionally, the machine-powered forms of mobility such as elevators/lifts and escalators are significant to the mobile aesthetics at play in Friis. The 'mall experience' is a complex and situational engagement with the materiality of the centre, the various technologies and materials within, the commercial signage, and the other customers. The complexity of the shopping centre experience reaches far beyond the confinements of this analysis, but here by putting mobilities first, I illustrate that the way we move within such a designed environment is crucial for the way we experience it. Friis and the material layout and design of it afford certain experiences and practices and discourage others.

One thing we did not notice in the fieldwork in Friis was the very clear demarcation and illustration of 'mobility divides' or what I have termed 'segregated mobilities practices'. The centre management will not tolerate demonstrations and they would prefer not to have homeless people congregating in the centre, but we did not detect any such explicit segregation measures. However, the presence of cameras and security personnel is surely a designed element staged from above, where the effect is less presence of 'undesirables' and practices outside the control of the centre management. Here the staging of order within Friis lies very close to the mechanisms and design solutions we find, for example, in relation to metros and subways (which I shall return to in chapter six). In all fairness it should be noticed that we found no explicit and strong examples of 'mobilities divides' being created within Friis. This also applies to the accessibility dimension where the risk is that less able and handicapped people are divided by mobility design solutions of exclusion. Contemporary shopping centre design does seem to cater to open accessibility as a general norm. The closest we came to find indications of 'mobility divides' were in relation to the individual's competencies and skills for navigating and wayfinding. From observations it is clear that senior citizens often seem more bewildered as to where to go and how to find their way. But this phenomenon was only rudimentarily observed and would need more attention to be explored in more detail. However, we did see senior citizens as the largest group of people 'looking lost' in the centre.

From the analysis conducted, the applicability of the 'river' and the 'ballet' perspective should be clear. In Friis we have mapped the movements and flows of mobile subjects as if they were homogeneous elements of a uniform stream; we have also seen how the individual mobile subjects interact and encounter each other in the fleeting moments of mobile interaction within the centre. Moreover, the double gaze of 'river/ballet' corresponds to the basic distinction between staging from above and below. In Friis the staging from above is seen through the river metaphor and expresses the intentions and wishes from the centre management, the architects, and shop owners. The 'ballet' equally is a significant illustration of people's self-staging from below as they chose routes through the centre or when they perform mobilities, for example, in riding the escalator.

Friis is the first exploration in detail into how the *Staging Mobilities* framework may be utilized in an analysis pointing toward a new way of conducting empirical analysis within the wider 'mobilities turn'. The case analysis may be deepened, but enough has been said here to bring this forward as an illustration of the emerging research field I term 'mobilities design'. So rather than delving more deeply into Friis, I want to present more cases to show the applicability of the theoretical framework to other types of mobilities design. Therefore I now move from 'walk' to 'bike' and explore 'cycling assemblages' in Copenhagen, Aarhus, and Odense in chapter five.

TIVOLI
P
Zone

5 BIKE

CYCLING ASSEMBLAGES IN COPENHAGEN, ODENSE AND AARHUS

Travel by two human-powered wheels is an active choice to encounter urban elements that often go unnoticed and unappreciated by people of privilege. To commute by bicycle, for example, is a choice to breathe in the dangers of diesel pollution, which the city's poorest dwellers take in by design. But such a choice also, ten minute hence, gives access to a completely unfiltered and breathtaking view of a quintessential monument to modernity – the Brooklyn bridge – stretched out in masoned extravagance. And what is more precious than to be treated, on a late night ride along the Hudson River, to a private showing of lights reflecting in the water from tall buildings on the palisades of the opposite bank, while sailboats rock in the river's currents? Cycling also promises encounters with pedestrians and other cyclists. Greetings and reassurance, not glassed in by power windows or drowned by the noise of idling engines, can replace the sometimes violent spatial competition that plays out between travellers who move by other means.

Jen Petersen (2007) *Pedaling Hope*, p. 37-8

Cycle space is the organizing system an individual cyclist projects upon his or her city, in the sense that airspace is an imaginary system used to make sense of the sky.

Steven Flemming (2012) *Cycle Space*, p. 23

The bicycle, like the automobile, is an object that becomes meaningful through its relationship to an entire field of cultural practices, discourses, and social forces.

Zack Furness (2010) *One Car Less*, p. 9

Introduction

This chapter explores how cycling as a mobility mode is being designed in three Danish cities. The relationship between the moving body, the cycle as an artefact and material vehicle, and the wider system of cycle paths and traffic systems make up complex socio-technical assemblages that are designed with a clear agenda of trying to shift car users to bikes in inner cities. The empirical data is from the 'Bikeability' research project on which I worked; the material used in this chapter is some of the unused and less frequently published material as the project aims more at planning and policies than material design.

In this chapter I explore the relationships between the material spaces and infrastructure designs for bikes and the embodied mobile performances taking place within these sites. The embodied, material, effectual, and interaction-oriented dimension of cycling (Adey 2010, 159) is set centrally, and in accordance with the *Staging Mobilities* framing (Jensen 2013a). Thus I will not engage in the environmental issues that often are the key interest and motivation for research into cycling (for this, see e.g., Christensen et al. 2012; Gilbert and Perl 2010; Næss 2006). Nor shall I go deeper into one of the key dimensions relating to cycling, namely its 'war' against the car (or the reverse). As far as the material suggests, an involvement with the car and the 'politics of street scaping' will be touched upon, but not as a primary focus (see Bonham 2011; Furness 2010; Marshall 2005; Oldenziel and Bruhéze 2011; Peses 2010; Stoffers 2011). In relation to terminology I will be using 'cycling' and 'biking' interchangeably throughout the chapter. I have done earlier research on cycling in the United States and its differences with Denmark (Jensen 2007b). However, this material will only be mentioned here in passing as illustrative of how cycling in one context may be perceived as either recreational or political (United States) or as simply an everyday mode of transport (Denmark). So despite the fact that cycling is a worldwide phenomenon that these days seems to work as a 'travelling idea' (Tait and Jensen 2007) that any progressive city government must include in its urban planning, there are obviously rich cultural and contextual differences to understand when it comes to the specificity of urban cycling.

The structure of the chapter is the following: After the introduction I turn to theory as the second section inserts the biking issues into the *Staging Mobilities* frame but with extra attention to the potential of the 'assemblage' concept. In section three I present the general framework and the findings of parts of the 'Bikeability' project. In section four the empirical cases and the more detailed analysis of bike interventions in Copenhagen, Aarhus, and Odense will follow. The chapter ends with some concluding remarks and with a return to the overall analytical model of *Staging Mobilities* and the keywords developed in that context.

Cycling Assemblages - theorizing and conceptualizing biking

In this section I present the key idea related to looking at bikes through the lens of the 'assemblage'. However, this will be rather short since the main theory frame is the now well-presented perspective of *Staging Mobilities.*

As I have claimed elsewhere (Jensen 2013a), cars are understood in terms that are too simplistic when cars are seen as 'desensing' machines, detaching the user from the environment. Much more subtle 'filtering' and mediation take place than simply serving as a detached cocoon. However, as we approach the bicycle, we see why less sheltering and material around the vehicle-users may afford an interpretation that leans toward 'unfiltered' mobilities. So next to walking, cycling has the characteristic feature of being a seemingly neutral and simple mobility mode. Or put differently; '*Cyclists are guilty of simply looking like humans, rather than anonymous cars*' (Vanderbilt 2008, 36). This is, however, only partially true. The bike (as any other mobilities technology) is not particular interesting 'on its own'. In order to understand the bike and its way of working as a mobility mode, we need to appreciate how it is nested within social and cultural frameworks, how it depends on particular legal and economic systems, and not least how various material and physical infrastructures afford particular cycling practices. By putting the cycle's 'systemness' first, we start to appreciate that the 'staging' of mobilities in relation to the bicycle, of course, is dependent on a number of things, processes, and elements. To move toward such an understanding, I want to propose the notion of 'cycling assemblage'. The idea of applying the 'assemblage' notion is not something that should be seen as exclusive to cycling. My first attempts to apply such theoretical and conceptual thinking were in an analysis of metro (subway) mobilities (Jensen 2009, 2013a).

This notion of assemblage draws also on the concept of 'networked ecologies' which according to Varnelis is:

> A series of co-dependent systems of environmental mitigation, land-use organization, communication and service delivery ... [being] networked, hyper-complex systems produced by technology, laws, political pressures, disciplinary desires, environmental constraints and a myriad of other pressures, tied together with feedback mechanisms (Varnelis 2008, 15).

As Varnelis tries to capture the multiplicity and ecological perspectives of systems and infrastructures, the notion of cycling assemblages applied here furthermore links to the way Easterling understands infrastructures as moving beyond hardware and materiality to also include protocols and codes for action and interaction:

> While infrastructure typically conjures associations with physical networks for transportation, communication, or utilities, it also includes the countless shared protocols that format everything from technical objects to management styles of the spaces of urbanism – defining the world as it is clasped and engaged in the space of everyday life. Infrastructural space is, as the word suggests, customarily regarded as a hidden substrate – the binding medium or current between objects of positive consequence, shape, and law – yet it is also the point of contact and access, the spatial outcropping of underlying laws and logics (Easterling 2011, 10).

In my analysis of the Seattle Seawall project I, too, presented the notion of a large road infrastructure as an 'assemblage':

> ... One may understand infrastructure as a relational assemblage of 'hardware' (e.g., asphalt, concrete, columns, traffic lights, etc.) and 'software' (e.g., strategies, traffic codes, safety campaigns, etc.). It is this nexus of material and immaterial, human and non-human that needs to be understood in relation to the flow and friction it affords (Jensen 2012b, 74).

In order to facilitate the analysis of bike designs I lean on the definition of 'biking assemblage' that Mikkelsen et al. articulated as part of an analysis of cycling design and planning in Philadelphia. Accordingly a biking (or cycling) assemblage is:

> ... comprised of multiple social interactions, bodily sensations, material systems, solid objects, and infrastructural networks. Any given 'biking assemblage' is scalable from the local block up to the region ... It is important to understand that 'scale' is not an inherent and fixed dimension to a network, but a socially variable construction enforced by the various engagements that social agents afforded the system. This furthermore means that a 'biking assemblage' also includes cultures, values, and norms. This stretches from the way routing and rights of way negotiation engage with the political context of the given

> case, to the underpinning rationalities of what biking is all about, regardless of whether biking is seen as a mundane social practice, a recreational activity or a political manifestation. We claim that all three rationales are in play ... Here it is important for the point of defining 'biking assemblages' that it is not solely a material or physical entity. The values inscribed into the design and the materiality of the assemblage are as important as bike paths, curbs and wheels. The power issues and the attempts to enforce certain decisions and marginalize others also become part of the 'biking assemblage' as the making of cycling (as most other human practice) became a contested field from the very beginning. Most importantly perhaps is the understanding of how objects and subjects, society and technology, nature and culture cannot be kept separate in this perspective. If you take away my bike I cease to be a cyclist but I equally change as a cyclist if I have a predominantly recreational understanding of my practice as opposed to an everyday life mobility perspective or a political agenda (Mikkelsen et al. 2011, 6).

This attention to the 'systemness' and the nesting of the human subject into larger networks and technologies do, however, refer to only one dimension of the *Staging Mobilities* framework. Needless to say we need to keep the attention on the individual and the embodied practices related to cycling. As Patton argues:

> People's subject positions are mediated by their habitual activities in moving about the city. The common practices of walking, bicycling, bus-riding, or driving constitute distinctive forms of urban life, each with characteristic rhythms, concerns, and social interactions (Patton 2004, 21).

Biking is a unique bodily position: *'Faster than a walk, slower than a train, often slightly higher than a person'* (Byrne 2009, 2). The phenomenology of biking sensations and perceptions is a rich and deep topic that I cannot fully engage with here (see Jensen 2013a, chapter 5). One of the admittedly very positive accounts that resonates with the embodied affordances of biking is the one by Jen Petersen, who argues for exploring and experiencing (American) cities from the vantage point of the bike due to its sheer sensual and perceptual qualities:

> Bicycling provides us with an unbuffered range of sensory experiences of the monumental urbanity we have created, and a view into the spaces of hope in its cracks, fissures, and contradictions. To bicycle through frenetic and congested cities is a work of beauty, one that can redraw the often discriminatory boundaries of neighbourhoods, redeem strained social relations, and rehabilitate a suffocating natural environment, together with the ways urban inhabitants become crippled by it. Inherently human-scaled, it is one path to an alternative understanding of the urban ... Choosing to know a place differently, in ways more expressive of humanistic value, invites a different, clear-eyed urbanity to shape the individual ... Consciously seeking new perceptions of urban spaces literally changes our base of local knowledge, redirecting our attention to views not sanctioned by planners or cartographers of political and economic districts. Movement, after all, is a basic expression of freedom, and a deliberate modal choice is an essential way to claim that freedom – a basic right to the city (Petersen 2007, 37).

The 'view from the saddle' is precisely the perspective taken by Patton who (also with an American reference) regrets that this is not always the best and nicest view:

> Bicycling is a form of life in that the relations between the equipment, infrastructure, and people's practices shape what is socially

possible. Getting someone on a bicycle creates the possibility of that person seeing the city as a cyclist. Unfortunately, the 'view from the saddle' is often ugly: most city streets do not adequately support cycling and safety is the major obstacle for those who are otherwise willing to ride. While economically inexpensive, bike lanes are politically expensive because they require the reallocation of roadway capacity on streets with finite rights-of-way (Patton 2004, 18).

I need to bring this introductory conceptualization to a close. Hopefully enough has been said to illustrate that the situational mobilities of biking are very much a threefold phenomenon of material sites and design, social interaction between cyclists themselves and other modes of mobilities, as well as an embodied mobile performance that is dependent on how the human body operates and navigates the artefact and the 'system' within which it appears. Cycling is thus a situational practice staged from above through design, planning, and policy decision that shape the 'cycling assemblages' of the contemporary cities; it is also staged from below through the myriad of incremental decisions taken 'on the ground' in relation to everything from cycling equipment and route choice to cycling style.

From this conceptualization I to turn to some earlier research into cycling that partly covers the research project 'Bikeability' with which I was affiliated and partly draws on my research into cycling in the United States.

Bikeability - Notes from a Danish research project

In this section I briefly discuss cycling initiatives from earlier research into cycling in the United States (Jensen 2007b) and then I shall discuss the Danish Research Council funded project 'Bikeability', on which I was working in collaboration with colleagues a few years ago.

Bikeability is a National Research Council funded project aiming at exploring potentials for biking to increase and thus contribute to solving health and environmental issues. It is a cross-institutional set-up among several Danish universities, health NGOs and international partners (see more general information at the web site: http://www.bikeability.dk). From the project summary we learn the following about the overall aims and issues:

> Increased transition of person transport from automobiles to bicycles is generally regarded as a gain for society, most profoundly in terms of reduced emission and enhanced public health. However, the mode-share of cycling has decreased in recent years, leading to the conclusion by the Danish Government that the conditions for cycling must be enhanced to increase the use of the bicycle for transportation (Regeringen et al. 2009). This research project departs from this conclusion and focuses on the preconditions for cycling; the possible effects of changes of the urban environment and cycling infrastructure; and methodologies for assessment of changes to existing bicycling networks based on micro-level spatially explicit data. This way the strategic focus of the project is how to enhance *bike-ability* of urban areas. The project will investigate, analyse, and model cycling behaviour and motivation (http://www.bikeability.dk/summary/).

During my affiliation with the project, I was engaged with the 'work package' (WP) no. 4 on 'Interventions to the bicycling infrastructure'. This WP is of particular relevance to the theme of this book and I shall draw mainly on unpublished material here as well as inserting the existing data and material into new theoretical and analytical framings. From the Work Package 4 description we learn:

> The research approach will rely on a survey of Danish bicycle infrastructure cases/interventions in the period from 1978 to 2009, and a comparative case study of seven Danish cases of intervention to the bicycling infrastructure. WP4 incorporates a Dutch reference study analysing seven cases of intervention to the bicycling infrastructure, including new (to the Danish context) forms of interventions/projects – such as 'bicycle streets' – that [were not] implemented in any Danish municipality until 2009 (http://www.bikeability.dk/wps/wp4/).

I will not go deeper into the material from Bikeability here since it will be the key focus in the case exploration to follow. I mainly wanted to introduce the project and the conceptual thinking behind it. As an outcome of the Bikeability project a Dutch background report was made (Goverden and Godefroij 2011). The so-called 'Dutch Reference Study' explored three larger biking infrastructure projects in Holland where relatively detailed before-and-after evaluations were conducted. The report is fairly technical as well, as it orients itself toward planning and policy more than the everyday culture of urban mobilities. However, there are reflections on the notion of 'cycling culture' and how this may tie into policies and design:

> The interesting question of what preconditions are necessary for a cycling culture (as far as they are within the sphere of policy) cannot be answered fully by the reviewed studies. Certainly, the 'technical' requirements that a) the locations people visit generally are accessible by bicycle and b) there is an infrastructure for selling and repairing bicycles, are preconditions. We assume that a proper level of safety is another one. The strong decline of bicycle usage in some countries after the increase in car usage, leaving a marginal role for the bicycle, might be explained by the fact that cycling became too risky due to the increasing car volumes or that at least the perception of the risk discouraged people to continue cycling. In the Netherlands, generally five main requirements for a good bicycle network are considered: coherence, directness, attractiveness, safety, and comfort. These are directly derived from findings of the extensively evaluated projects in The Hague, Tilburg, and Delft (Goverden and Godefroij 2011, 86).

The Dutch reference study is, however, still more concerned with planning and policy making related to cycling than is the case in this book. Despite the success of the private automobile, there are so many different cycling schemes and policies across the globe that it would take a fully-fledged research project on its own to map and understand all these. Here I now turn to the empirical cases of bike system design and the 'cycling assemblages' materialising from them.

Cycling Assemblages in Aarhus, Copenhagen and Odense - case presentation

In Denmark the bike went from being an exotic upper class leisure time artefact to a working class mode of transportation for urban blue collar workers when many industrial workspaces still were in the city centres and then went on to become a cultural mass phenomenon (Bendtsen 2005). In the words of Thomsen:

> Bicycle riding represents a part of Danish transport culture that everybody might use. Still, compared to car usage, cycling symbolizes the limited financial means of the users and their greater awareness of an interest in their body, in exercise, and in nature (Thomsen 2001, 275, my translation).

The three cases that are described in the WP4 of the Bikeability project, which are the ones I shall analyse here (albeit in a very different manner and from a different theoretical perspective), are three cycling infrastructure projects in the cities of Copenhagen, Aarhus, and Odense in Denmark (fig. 5.1). In the

Fig. 5.1

descriptive paragraphs that lay out the context and the sites, I lean on the description we already made in the report (Andrade et al. 2012b), whereas the situational analysis is new and done specifically for this book. (I also utilize material and images not yet published.) The date differs slightly as the Copenhagen case officially was opened on September 14, 2006; the Aarhus case dates from July 15, 2010, and the Odense case from August 19, 2010. All cases are thus relatively new and they all are dedicated to bicycling as the single mode of transport. (Bryggebroen is in fact both for cyclists and pedestrians.) The architects are from within the three respective municipal departments and the engineering company is Grontmij in Copenhagen and Aarhus whereas it is Odense Municipality in Odense. The developer is Grontmij in both Copenhagen and Aarhus, and Odense Municipality in Odense. The daily operation is run and managed by the three municipalities. In terms of travellers per day, the project in Odense caters to approximately 7,000 people, the Aarhus project to approximately 1,250, and the Copenhagen project to approximately 7,400 people a day. The costs are very diverse as the Copenhagen project cost 47.6 million DKR, the Aarhus project 2.8 million DKR, and the Odense project only 800,000 DKR.

The three cities

Here I present briefly the three cities in their national context and with a focus on the political and planning context. The text here is based on the report 'Bike Infrastructures' by Andrade et al. (2012b).

Odense

Odense is the third largest Danish municipality and had a population of 188,777 inhabitants in 2010 (Statistikbanken 2010). The municipality is located on the island of Funen and it is part of the South Denmark Region (fig. 5.2).

In December 1993 the Danish government presented a strategic plan for sustainable transportation titled 'Traffic 2005', aiming to create a balance between economic development and environment based on principles of sustainable growth. One of the main objectives was to increase the share of cyclists in overall individual transportation in the country until 2005 (Trafikministeriet 2000). In order to achieve this objective, 4 percent of individual transportation was to be moved from private automobile to bicycle or walking. In practice, it meant that all trips shorter than three kilometres should begin to be made by healthier and environmentally friendly modes – cycling and walking. In this context, Odense was selected to function as a 'lab' for new solutions and became the 'National Bike City'. The main goal was to increase 2 percent of trips made by bike in the period from 1999 until 2002. At the international level, Odense municipality built its own exhibition at the 2010 Shanghai Expo, where the image of city is represented by both its bike infrastructure and cyclists and fellow-townsman Hans Christiansen Andersen (Odense Municipality 2010h). According to an interview with municipal employees working on urban design and traffic, one of the challenges that Odense municipality faces is to convince commuters living 5 kilometres away from the core of the city to use their bikes as main mode of transportation. Tackling this challenge, Odense Municipality launched a campaign in spring 2010 where it lent 100 electric bikes during a period of six months to car users living more than 5 kilometres away from the centre. A new phase of the campaign started in autumn 2010. Another strategic action toward enhancing cycling was to implement monitors in the main bike infrastructures of the municipality, counting and displaying the number of cyclists riding their bikes per day and per year (Odense municipality 2010e). This sort of public display of cycling volumes is now a very common dimension of many municipalities 'cycling assemblages'.

Aarhus

Aarhus is the second largest Danish municipality with a population of 307,119 inhabitants in 2010 (Statistikbanken 2010). The municipality is located on the east side of the peninsula named Jutland and is part of the Central Jutland Region (fig. 5.3).

In the Municipal Plan 2009 Aarhus municipality announced its new vision to become an environmentally and energy sustainable city. Within its vision, there is a goal to become carbon neutral by the year 2030 (Aarhus Municipality 2009). In order to achieve this goal, the Aarhus Traffic Plan articulates this year 2030 scenario: *'Aarhus Municipality's infrastructure offers optimal conditions for both cyclists and the public transportation. Moreover, Aarhus municipality is known internationally as a bicycle city'* (Aarhus Municipality 2009). 'Aarhus Bicycle City' functions as an umbrella for all the municipal initiatives with regard to cycling (e.g., city bikes, campaigns and events to promote a bicycle culture). The 'Aarhus Bicycle City' webpage (www.aarhuscykelby.dk) includes news about new bicycle projects, campaigns and a forum where people can make suggestions and proposals related to the Aarhus bike infrastructure. On April 10, 2010, the 'Aarhus Bicycle City' transformed the City Hall square in a 'bicycle's Mecca', where people could have diverse experiences with their bikes and also see different ways of experiencing cycling (Aarhus Cykelby 2010). Inspired by the zip code of central Aarhus (8000), another campaign launched by Aarhus municipality was the "8,000 benefits of cycling, where 8,000 citizens were asked about the benefits of cycling. The results of the campaign are posted on the 'Aarhus Bicycle City' webpage and there is also a movie on the Internet about the campaign. Aarhus municipality has implemented bicycle counting in the main bike corridors. The automatic cyclist counters and monitors are very informative and they are also used as an active element that inspires the population. In the most recent campaign, 'Aarhus Bicycle City' promoted a competition among every street with an automatic

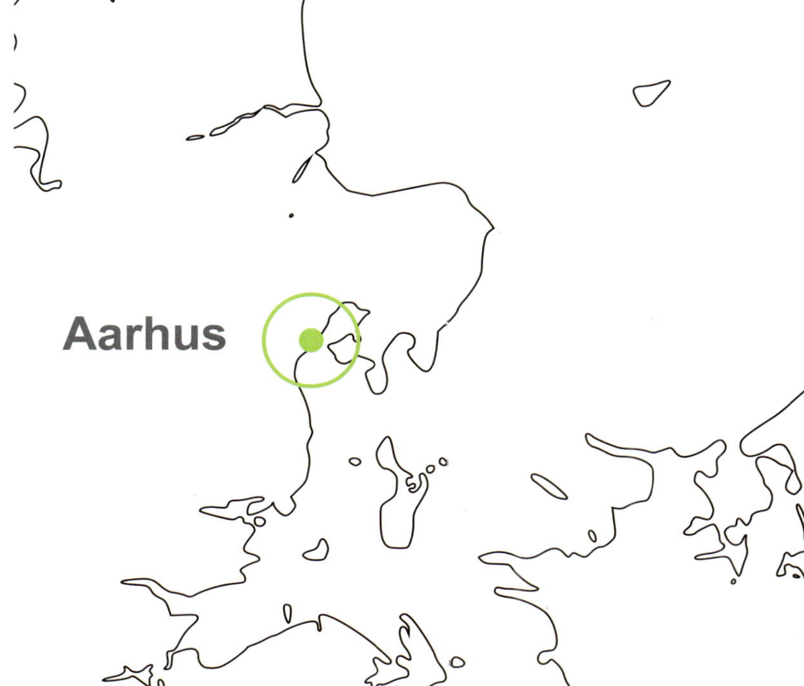

Fig. 5.2 and 5.3: The cities of Odense and Aarhus

bicycle count installed. The winner would be the street that most increased the number of cyclists. Using already installed automated counters in the different neighbourhoods, it was possible to register which of the neighbourhoods had the greatest increase. The winning street was Hans Broges Gade (the case I am about to explore here). The street won the competition with an increase of 41 percent in the number of bicycle rides during the two weeks of the competition (Aarhus Stiftstidende 2010).

Copenhagen

Copenhagen is the Danish national capital and the largest municipality of Denmark with a population of 503,699 inhabitants. The Copenhagen metropolitan area has a population of 1,901,789 inhabitants (Statistikbanken 2010). The municipality is located on the islands of Zealand and Amager (fig. 5.4).

Copenhagen's vision is to become the World's Eco-metropolis in year 2015 (Copenhagen Municipality 2009b) and a list of thirteen goals has been set up to achieve this objective. There are two goals directly related to cycling: to reduce carbon emissions by 20 percent from the amount emitted in 2005 and to become the world`s best city for cyclists. In order to become 'the world's best city for cyclists', Copenhagen municipality defined three main objectives to be achieved before 2050: to have more than 50 percent of its population riding their bikes to work or to school, to improve the cyclists' perception of safety in traffic, and to decrease the number of injuries by half from the year 2007 (Copenhagen Municipality 2009b). Currently 37 percent of Copenhageners working or studying commute by bike (Copenhagen Municipality 2010b). From this short account of the three cities and their cycling politics, I turn to the physical cycling system design projects.

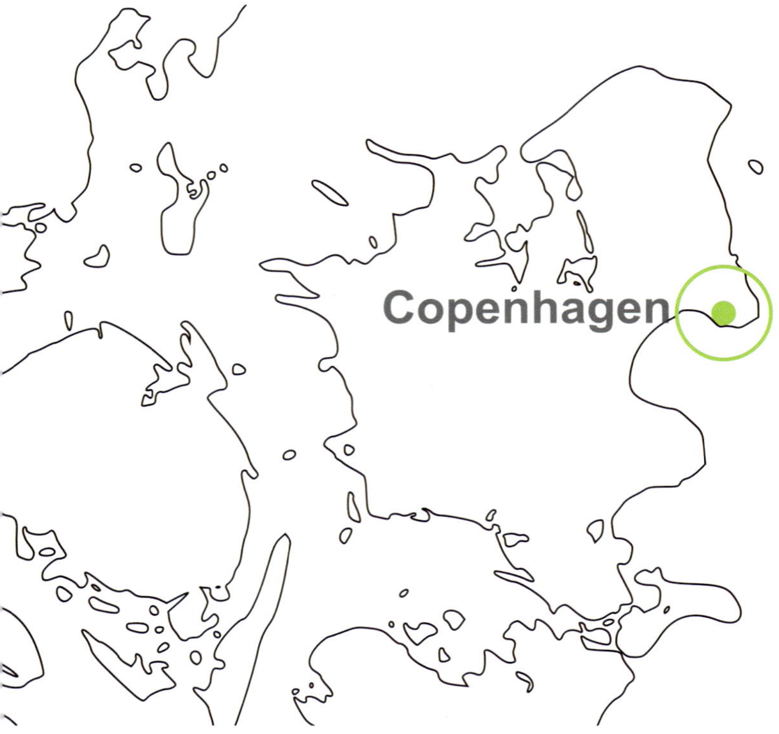

Fig. 5.4: The city of Copenhagen

The Streets - before and after

The intervention in Vestergade Vest and Mageløs (Odense) was completed on August 19, 2010. The former crowded street was transformed into a 'shared-used' space for pedestrians, cyclists, and a future central electrical bus ring. All the busses were rerouted to parallel streets nearby (Odense Municipality 2009i). The landscape architect from Odense Municipality who was responsible for the design solution at Vestergade Vest and Mageløs emphasized in our interview how important it is to improve urban life experience in the core of Odense. In relation to the intervention at Vestergade Vest and Mageløs, he said: *'I wanted to push the limits from what experiences people have in the public space and I also wanted to make them start to question and reflect about what a public space could be used for… It has been very provocative to put ping pong tables on the former motorized vehicle lanes… It has been a challenge to reinvent the former motorized vehicle lanes into a space for urban life, play and exercise'*. (Interview with Municipal landscape architect and planner, September 2, 2010). Since the opening of the new shared-use space, there has been quite some media attention. On September 13, 2010, the local newspaper (Fyens Stiftstidende) wrote an article with the headline *'Chaos plagues the new pedestrian street'* (Fyens Stiftstidende 2010b). During our registration we counted well above 600 bikes in the morning down to a low of just under 400 before noon and again after 6pm, but with a clear peak above 800 between 3-4pm. Formerly, Vestergade Vest and Mageløs had more than two hundred busses passing every day, causing noise pollution, air pollution, and discouraging a more friendly space for pedestrians, cyclists, and other potential activities. After the intervention, the public space changed its profile completely – enhancing walking, cycling, shopping, eating, playing, etc. According to the interview with the municipal planners, the intervention has stimulated a discussion about public domain and regenerated the image of Vestergade Vest and Mageløs as lively sites.

Hans Broges Gade is located in a dense neighbourhood in Aarhus composed by block structures up to five stories high built in the early twentieth century. The neighbourhood is on the edge of the city centre and the majority of its buildings are residential. However, some buildings are mixed use, with shops and offices on the ground floor. The street functions as an important link between the suburbs and the core of the city. Moreover there is quite a lot of pedestrian traffic from mostly local residents that use the local commerce. The purpose of the intervention at Hans Broges Gade was to improve a bicycle route connecting the southern suburbs of Holme to the centre of the city so that it would become one of seven main bicycle corridors of the bicycle network plan. In Hans Broges Gade we counted just above 120 bikes at the morning peak followed by a low down to the mid-forties, peaking again at 130 between 4-5pm. Hans Broges Gade used to be a street with broad lanes for motorized vehicles and car parking in both directions parallel to the sidewalks. There were bicycle lanes only at the beginning of the street for the first 100 metres on the side facing Marselis Boulevard. Along the rest of the street, cyclists had to ride their bikes on the outside of the rows of parked cars together with cars and busses. With long blocks of up to 150 metres, cyclists with their bikes parked on the sidewalk had difficulty accessing the road because of the parked cars. During the field observation several elderly residents mentioned that they found it unsafe to walk on the sidewalks because cyclists preferred to ride their bikes on them. In order to provide space to implement bicycle tracks in both directions of the street, one of the car parking rows was removed.

Bryggebroen was dedicated in 2006 as the first exclusively dedicated pedestrian and cycling bridge in Copenhagen. It is a 190-metre-long, six-and-a-half-metre-wide bridge, connecting Kalvebod Brygge over Havneholmen to Islands Brygge (CPHX 2009; Grontmij-Carlbro 2010). When opening Bryggebroen, the politician Klaus Bondam stated: *'To bridge the gap between the two wharfs is much more than the tangible construction; we use the term "to bridge the gap between" in many connections. To bridge a gap equals cooperation and dialogue, it equals overcoming gaps and obstacles – it is often about creating closeness and understanding between people.... It is my hope, that this new connection will give rise to new initiatives and that cooperation will occur – that this will also be a symbolic bridge between the two areas*'. During our field observations we counted a morning peak at 9am just below 1,200 bikes falling to a midday low around 350 and peaking at 1,100 between 4-5pm.

With the construction of Bryggebroen, the Copenhagen case is different from the two other cases because there was no connection prior to the intervention. The bridge improved the accessibility between the two sides of the Copenhagen Harbour; however, measuring the effect on the traffic patterns is a very complex issue since its 'effects' must be tracked into the wider bike system much further away. However, from our field work it is clear that many people are taking this new artefact on as a very positive intervention.

Methodological reflections

The data used in this chapter differ from the other cases in this book. This is mainly due to the fact that I have chosen to utilise existing data from the 'Bikeability' project on which I worked. This means that there are certain differences in how much situational detail I will be able to provide to the bike case. As we explored actual situations within bike infrastructure projects, the focus is still there; however, the registrations and data collections made in the biking project were of a slightly broader nature than the ethnographic account we saw in chapter four on Friis. Moreover, the data was provided by research assistants hired to do the job. Needless to say, this differs from personal data collection. But as with Friis a very through briefing was conducted before the actual data collection, ensuring that the research assistants knew precisely what to do and that they understood the theoretical perspectives underpinning the project.

In methodological terms we applied a number of methods in order to triangulate and ensure data validity. In the project both primary and secondary data were used, and here I relate mainly to the primary data. To create the primary data we used a questionnaire based on a web survey, manual counting, diary of daily flow, descriptions of atmosphere, image collection, interviews, and e-mails from key actors. For the secondary data, we used the municipal counting as well as planning documents, reports, newspaper articles, and press releases. Some bicycle counting was provided by the municipalities of Aarhus and Copenhagen so the counts we had to make ourselves were related to the Odense site. Here the manual count was made on September 12, 2010, over a 12-hour period from 7am to 7pm. The counts were conducted by a team of three research assistants. They divided the tasks so that one would count and monitor bikes going in one direction and one would count the opposite flow. In addition to this, the third observer was a backup for breaks and other observations. The counting techniques applied and the technical procedure all followed the standard recommendations of the Danish Road Directorate (Vejdirektoratet 2004).

The project provided much policy-relevant data such as how people assess the bicycle infrastructures and whether they have changed their mobility patterns and practices as a consequence of new or changed infrastructures. However, in this context I will not go into these dimensions of the material as my key concern is the relationship between the material design of the infrastructures and the situational actions taking place within them. I have, in other words, chosen a selective view of the material, knowing well that the research project offers a more detailed and rich pool of data and new knowledge. (One important dimension of the Bikeability study was the delicate 'before/and after' effect discussion that I will avoid in this chapter.) But for reasons of delimitation as well as because this book is dedicated to the relationship between 'staging mobilities' and 'designing mobilities' I will only 'carve out' selected elements of the project data. (For a more complete account of the material, see Andrade et al. 2012a, 2012b).

Bottom left page:
Fig. 5.5

Opposite page:
Fig. 5.6 and 5.7

PART I: Staging from above: Bike infrastructures of the Network City

I want to start the empirical exploration by applying the *Staging Mobilities* notion of staging 'from above'. Thus, the first dimension is the wider layout of the infrastructure systems and the specific place of the case interventions within. Common to all three cities is that they have well-developed bicycle networks and infrastructures. The staging of biking mobilities from above is therefore well established as a key priority

within the respective municipalities and their traffic planning and urban design.

The majority of streets in Odense accommodate the bike by reasonable infrastructures that facilitate biking (fig. 5.5). The entire system is comprised of 510 km of bike lanes and Odense is thus one of the most 'bike friendly' municipalities in Denmark, with 2.7 metres of bike lanes per inhabitant (superseding Copenhagen with its 0.77 metres and Aarhus with 1.46 metres per inhabitant; see Statistikbanken 2010). Odense has a long tradition of promoting bicycling and public campaigning in favour of cycling. More than 25 percent of all commuting trips are made on bicycles.

Due to the fact that the Odense project was rather low budget (compared to the other cases), there are no technical drawings from this project.

Aarhus municipality has 450 km of bicycle tracks and lanes (fig 5.6). The ratio of bike lanes per citizen is twice the number in Copenhagen and slightly less than in Odense. The structure mirrors the radiant system of road spaces connecting the hinterland of Aarhus to the bay of Aarhus. As in the other cases the city government of Aarhus prides itself on being a 'biking city'. The municipality has also, over the years, engaged in multiple forms of pro-bike public policy and campaigning. In the technical drawing of the Hans Broges Gade project (fig. 5.7), we see that the sidewalk has been divided into a 'shared space' between bike parking and a pedestrian path, and a grass-area separating the bike path from the road and the space for car parking. The length of the street is 430 metres and the area is predominantly residential with a few shops. The street has a light curvature and about midway there is a public square with grass and benches. The project was officially opened in 2010.

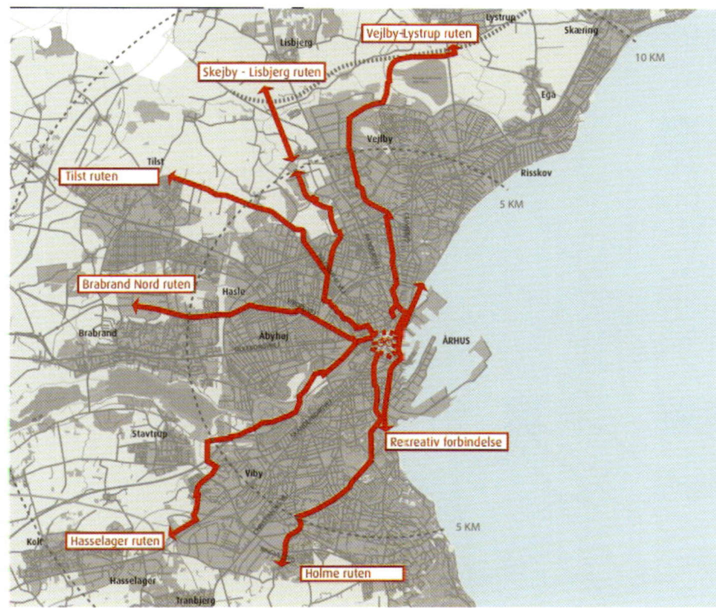

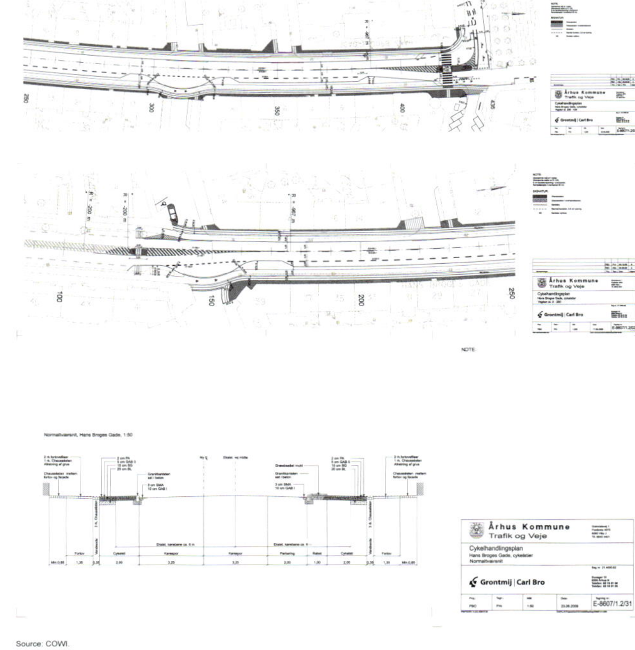

Source: COWI.

The section diagram illustrates the division of space between the modes of transport and is within the standard dimensioning of street layout in a Danish context.

Copenhagen is already well known internationally for its comparable high rates of bike cyclists (fig 5.8) with 37 percent of people working or studying in Copenhagen commuting by bike. The municipality plans to increase this number rather drastically to 50 percent by 2050. The city has become internationally known for what the outside world seems to think is a particular 'Copenhagen Style' type of bike infrastructure. This is not the least due to the tireless work of architect and urbanist Jan Gehl promoting 'Copenhagen style' bike lanes, leading CNN to shoot a feature in the city and labelling it 'Copenhagenisation'. Gehl Architects have taken ideas from Danish cycling culture and planning to New York, where they have revitalised the bike path system in Manhattan using a very successful plan (see www.gehlarchitects.com/#/378166). However, selling this as distinct 'Copenhagen style' seems to miss the point that cycling is a widespread cultural phenomenon across all major Danish cities (Jensen 2007b). On the other hand, nobody can claim that Copenhagen is not a cycling city, and the city government has been very active in various campaigns over the years. Compared to the other two case cities, Copenhagen has quite a strain on its bike infrastructure capacity that leads to regular traffic jams on the bike paths and multiple issues related to how cyclists behave in a crowded space such as the bike paths system. The case project chosen here is a bike and pedestrian bridge connecting two neighbourhoods divided by water and thus offering the cyclist the choice of a faster route through the city. Bryggebroen was the first bridge in Copenhagen exclusively dedicated to bikes and pedestrians and was officially opened in 2006. However due to construction at its site, there was only temporary access to the bridge until 2009. The bridge is 190 metres long (fig.

Bottom left page:
Fig. 5.8

Opposite page:
Fig. 5.9

5.9) and has an elegant and light design as it curves slightly, offering a steepness that most cyclists will be able to overcome. At night, the bridge is illuminated and stands out from its context as something rather spectacular. To both its users and visitors the bridge has become a landmark infrastructure.

In all three cases we see different approaches, locations, contexts, and designs as illustrations of how cycling mobilities are being staged from above through municipal planning, urban design, and architectural solutions. I want to address this staging from above theme-by-theme hereafter rather than look separately at each project. The aim of this study is not to make a comparative study of three bike system designs but rather to see them according to one perspective, the 'staging mobilities' framework.

Physical Settings: Pavement materials

The first level of staging I want to focus on is the pavement materials (figs. 5.10-5.15). In Odense at Vestergade Vest and Mageløs the pavement solution uses flagstone material. There is a colour difference between the middle track and the side tracks. In order to slow traffic, quite an unusual array of methods are used. So next to the ordinary speed bump that obviously lowers people's speed, there are ping pong tables and cafés suggesting an underlying design philosophy that sees a road space as much more than an armature for A to B movement. The bump is avoided with partial success in the morning hours when many cyclists manage to turn right around the bump, utilizing the lane dedicated for pedestrians. This tactic is of less use in the afternoon when more bikes as well as displays from the street's shops fill up the space used for this manoeuvre. The design code for the Odense project is clearly outside of the ordinary traffic design solutions. On the sidewalk blue plastic guides are integrated into the pavement, directing where shops may put goods and signs on display. Most shops seem to respect this rather clearly marked division line, whereas others constantly are pushing the boundary for space and customer attention. The stone surface is plain with no potholes, offering a smooth movement surface for the cyclists. The Odense project has an element of 'Shared Space' design influence as the paving (all at a similar level) illustrates a more subtle division of mobilities modes than the traditional elevated bike paths. Moreover, the pattern of stones and the clear but subtle colour distinctions are elements of the 'Shared Space' design doctrine (Shared Space 2005).

In Aarhus at Hans Broges Gade the flows of cyclists in opposite directions take place at each side of the road. The layout of the project is rather traditional in the sense that pedestrian pavements are closest to the adjacent buildings. Next come the dedicated bike lanes, then car parking and grass buffers, and finally the road space. The bike lanes are deliberately curved as they enter the crossings, making the cyclist pay more attention to the crossing traffic because they must slow down in

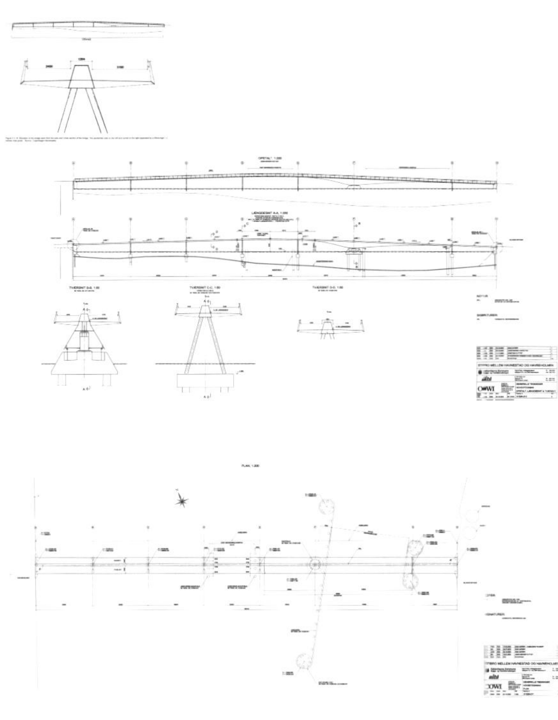

Source: Copenhagen Municipality

Opposite: Figs. 5.10 - 5.15

order to negotiate the curved path. The paving is rather traditional with concrete tiles, stone tiles, and asphalt. The bike lanes are provided with clear markings of mode dedication in terms of large, white bike icons laid down onto the path. The bike path is elevated from the road space, making small asphalt ramps necessary in order for bikes (and trolleys) to negotiate the height difference as smoothly as possible. This elevation then promotes the safety of the bikes and pedestrians since it forces diagonally crossing cars to slow down significantly. At Bryggebroen in Copenhagen the bridge is made in concrete and the pavement material is black asphalt. The lanes are separated by a rather solid concrete middle girder that supposedly keeps bikes on one side and pedestrians on the other. (In practice we often noticed bicyclists entering the pedestrian lane by mistake and then finding themselves without options other than jumping off the bike and becoming a pedestrian or quickly turning around and returning.) To guide the cyclist into the lane, there metal path guides have been laid down into the concrete; these, however, become rather slippery when it rains. In fact this seems to be Bryggebroen's largest problem: the conflict between pedestrians and bicyclists at the two landing areas. As soon as the modes have been separated no conflicts arise, but the complex and tight zone of negotiation at each entry point is a challenge and we saw many examples of conflicts and potentially dangerous situations during the observations. This is aggravated by the fact that bikes are able to pick up quite some speed due to the curvature of the bridge. As they move 'downhill' they approach the zone of negotiation and potential conflict with the pedestrians. The bike lane itself is divided into two lanes of opposite direction, indicated by a white dashed line down the middle. On the two landing areas on each side of the bridge there are rectangular granite areas. On the Brygge Islands side of the water there is a cobblestone road alongside the extensively used harbour promenade. Most people pick out the rectangular and larger stones set as two parallel lines in order to avoid the bumpier ride on the smaller cobblestones. The surface materials are thus utilized to guide and stage users about where to go.

Physical Settings: Bike Parking

The next theme I want to touch upon is bike parking (figs. 5.16-5.21). As anyone familiar with urban cycling knows, bike parking is a central issue and also often one of some dispute even though bikes take up a modest space for storage when not in use (compared with the car at least). Many places are flooded with bikes that, as soon as they are not in their 'proper' places in bike racks, are considered litter and obstacles. In Odense the bike parking racks have been given a very central location almost in the middle of the space. This is of course due to the fact that the design affords easy access to the adjacent shops when you arrive on bike. The outcome is, however, also that the space seems confusing at times as the centrally located bike racks both in a visual and a functional sense create obstacles at the centre of the space. As we observed, pedestrians often had to negotiate the parked bikes with some difficulty. In Aarhus at Hans Broges Gade the parking solution includes both bikes and cars. As this is a more traditional road design, the allocation of designated bike parking has been down prioritized whereas the cars have multiple designated parking spaces. As a consequence the bike parking practice is to put the bikes alongside the building envelope of the adjacent buildings. This, then, takes away space from the pedestrians moving on the sidewalk and it is a major problem for disabled and blind people. The parking situation is an altogether different matter in Copenhagen. At Bryggebroen there are no designated parking spaces. As the project is a transit connection between two separated neighbourhoods, one may argue that there is no need for parking spaces: people are moving through this space, not staying there. However, the field studies at the site tell a slightly different story about the need for parking spaces. Judging from the number of bikes parked either so that they can be locked directly to the fence of the bridge

Vestergade Vest and Mageløs

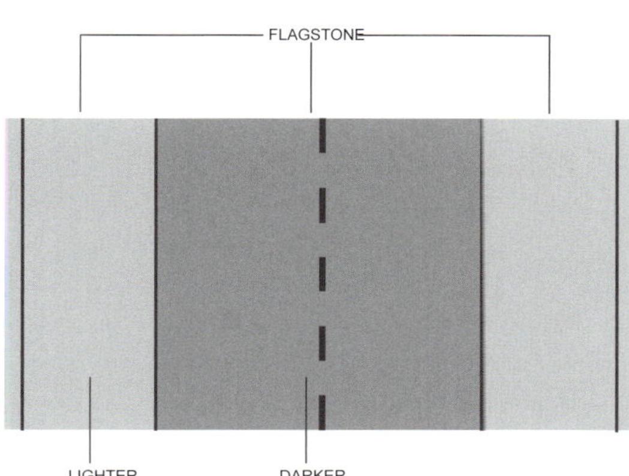

Hans Broges Gade

Bryggebroen

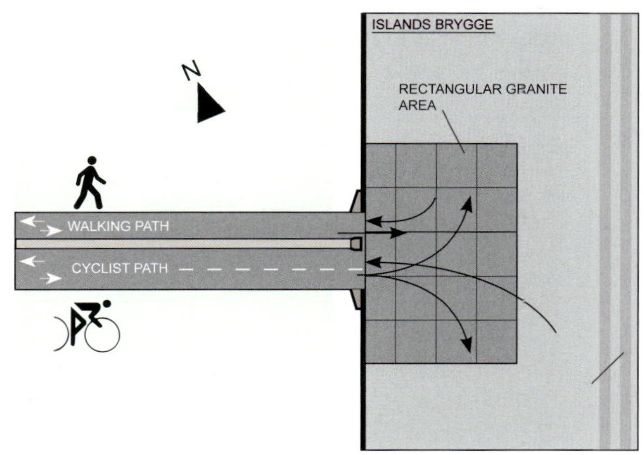

Vestergade Vest and Mageløs

Hans Broges Gade

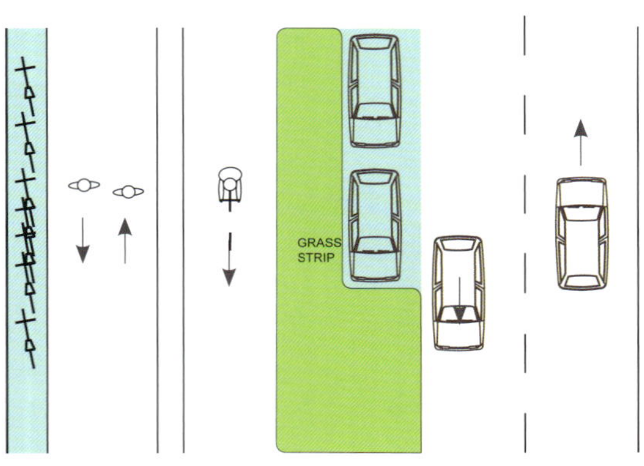

Bryggebroen

Figs. 5.16 - 5.21

or scattered in the adjacent area, some people find the place suitable for parking their bikes.

Physical Settings: Street Furniture

Even though I am mostly concerned with the traffic infrastructure we must pay attention to the part of the road that is occupied by various types of street furniture (figs. 5.22-5.27). In Odense the space is, as mentioned, rather untraditional. One of the more conspicuous pieces of street furniture or artefacts is the dark blue table tennis equipment set up alongside the central armature. The equipment is not completely tucked away into the sidewalk areas; instead, the tables are on the edge of the zone between the fast and the slow moving traffic, adding yet another practical example of the combination of 'Shared Space' philosophy and a mobilities design thinking that goes beyond simple A to B movement. This street is for moving as well as playing! This point is also illustrated by the fact that a letter game is painted onto the street surface inviting more play. Moreover, the Odense case also illustrates how café tables may be brought into the street in this edge zone. Needless to say, this type of road space design is only possible when dealing with the slower modes of bikes and pedestrians. (There are motor vehicles entering the streets but they are restricted to unloading goods for the shops). In Odense we also find the more traditional street furniture such as trash bins (in various sizes and shapes) and light poles. The street furniture in Aarhus at Hans Broges Gade is very traditional and includes light poles, trash bins, and benches. In particular there are many benches due to the public square in the area. The street furniture as such does not really engage with the flow and the movement patterns of the bike system. In Copenhagen we find no benches or similar items on the bridge itself as it is a confined space with neighbourhood connectivity as its prime goal. At the landings at each side, there are trash bins inviting the bikes riders and pedestrians to deposit litter here rather than on the bridge.

Physical Settings: Lighting

In every urban space the issue of light is crucial (figs. 5.28-5.33). The invention and presence of electrified lighting surely has changed urban spaces dramatically, not only in terms of usability -- where lighting in principle opens up spaces to 24/7 usage -- but also in terms of what sort of ambience and atmosphere the site creates. One might say that urban lighting has the potential for both creating more functional and safe spaces as well as the capacity to 'gestalt' spaces. For all its innovative dimensions the project in Odense is not particularly spectacular when it comes to the issue of lighting. There are street lamps hovering over the middle of the street and light poles along the sidewalk. Next to this the shops along the street light up the street, which obviously affects the ambience but not as a part of the mobilities design. In the same way, the lighting design in Hans Broges Gade in Aarhus is part of the standard urban lighting system of the city. The street is lit by lamps hanging at its centre over the road space. Around the public square additional light poles light the area. The Bryggebroen in Copenhagen has what the two former projects lack in innovative and creative potential for lighting. The bridge is illuminated by indirect lights placed both on the movement surfaces as well as on the railings and the fences. The light chosen on the bridge area is white but beneath the bridge a light design using different colours adds to the ambience. As one moves along the bridge, the lights secure good vision and a sense of safety, and seen from a distance the bridge stands out as an illuminated and glowing structure. This effect is accentuated by the mirror reflections of the light onto the water. At the landings, however, less white and directional light is found, potentially creating safety issues. This has been identified already as the critical point even in daylight.

Physical Settings: Semiotics

The projects are marked by all sorts of signage and semiotic tags since they are public space infrastructures (figs. 5.34-5.39). Here I will mainly touch upon the semiotics related to the official traffic

Vestergade Vest and Magelos

Hans Broges Gade

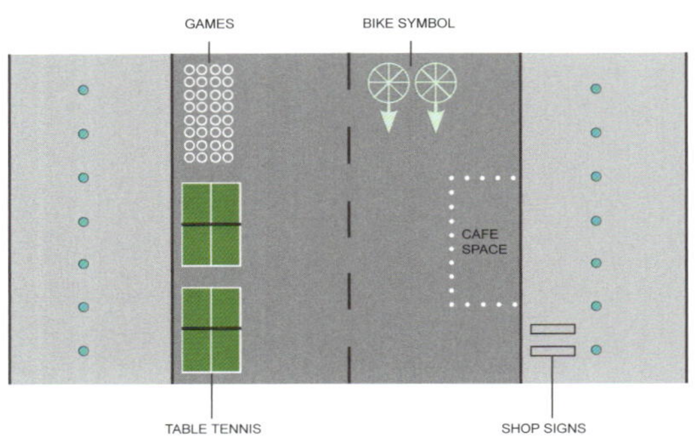

Bryggebroen

Figs. 5.22 - 5.27

Vestergade Vest and Mageløs

Hans Broges Gade

Bryggebroen

Figs. 5.28 - 5.33

Vestergade Vest and Mageløs

Bryggebroen

Hans Broges Gade

Figs. 5.34 - 5.39

design or 'regulatory discourses' (Scollon and Scollon 2003). The presence and importance of, for example, graffiti will not be dealt with in this analysis even though such 'transgressive' acts of semiotic tagging add to the site's identity. In Odense the most dominating signage (despite all the playful inventory) are the commercial signs on the shops, in large part because some of the shops exploit the opportunity to 'share' the space in such a way that their signs almost impinge upon the areas where bikes move. In the street there are also regulatory and directional signs pointing to destinations in the city; other signs proclaim the restrictions on usage and access to the street. Additionally, there are the very conspicuous drawings on the movement surface. These are the 'game board' drawings on the pavement, where symbols of feet and bike wheels on the surface invoke a sense of playful alertness to the mixed mobility modes present. At Hans Broges Gade in Aarhus we find the same types of signs as mentioned (regulatory, directional, etc.). In semiotic terms the most eye-catching elements in this space are the many white bikes drawn on the bike paths assuring the territorial 'ownership' and legitimate right to the bike path. Next to this, the bike counting poles are quite conspicuous. As has been done in many other cities, the municipality in Aarhus has erected a number of poles that show the number of bikes passing during the day. This is a rather simple technology and artefact, but one which on a more subtle level invokes a sense of 'community of practice' among people cycling by. As one is continually reminded of the many other cyclists, these bike counting devices work to construct a social identity among the cyclists passing. Bryggebroen also has official and regulatory signs attached to it. In particular the indications of lane separation between bikes and pedestrians is a key piece of information laid into the semiotic system. Even though I will not touch upon the transgressive semiotics of graffiti, the bridge is of course an obvious target since it represents a clean concrete canvas for tagging. Moreover, Bryggebroen has been a target of the subcultural practice of placing a small lock with names of lovers onto the bridge fence. This is a global trend (termed 'love padlocks') that I have witnessed many places around the world (from the Grand Canyon in the United States to Cinque Terra in Italy). The love padlocks add to the symbolic dimension of the bridge as it turns it into an evocative and emotional artefact next to a piece of traffic infrastructure.

Physical Settings: Intersections

As the various armatures nest and intersect into the urban fabric, it becomes very important to the general understanding of the materialities of mobilities (figs. 5.40-5.45) to understand the intersections (or Critical Points of Contact). In Odense the project street is nested within an inner city network of relatively small and narrow streets. The main street is crossed by dedicated pedestrian streets so the general pace of the area is on the slow end of the continuum. The main instrument for highlighting intersections in the Odense project is differences in the pavement materials (pavement stones in various materials and sizes). In the Aarhus project the numbers of intersections are few and legibility is generally good. One of the critical issues is when (and this is 'when' and not 'if') cars park across the exit and entry points for crossing bike traffic in such a way that physical movement is impaired and that the signs communicating the bike exit/entry points to the path are blocked by cars, obscuring the visual information. At Bryggebroen the key issue is, as mentioned before, the bridge landing itself. Negotiating relatively fast going bikes coming off the bridge with slower bikes entering and even slower pedestrians can make a difficult and at times dangerous mix. There is relatively good legibility, but a fair amount of 'facework' and 'negotiation-in-motion' takes place in order for Bryggebroen to fulfil its task as neighbourhood connecting infrastructure.

Physical Settings: Connection to adjacent infrastructures

Another dimension of the project sites' connectivity to their respective contexts is the issue of connection to adjacent infrastructures. In all three cases we are in the city centre and there is relatively good legibility and visibility (figs. 5.46-5.51). This means that 'understanding' how the project site is related to its context and how to get to and from the site is fairly easy. The situations do differ as the bikes in Aarhus at Hans Broges Gade are the ones closest to the cars and the ordinary road system. The connection to adjacent infrastructure in the Odense case is less an issue of cars and more a question of negotiating the how long visitors remain at the site (playing, shopping, etc.). The adjacent traffic system is rather tightly regulated as it comes into contact with the Vestergade and Mageløs area by means of both traditional regulatory practices (the application of standard right of way rules) as well as inspirations from the 'Shared Space' thinking. At Bryggebroen in Copenhagen there is, of course, a link to the wider urban traffic network, but the key challenge, as I already have mentioned, is the CPC of bikes and pedestrians at the two landing areas. Complex negotiations take place here and alertness to the mobile other is required.

Physical Settings: Mode divisions

Part of the connections to the wider system discussed here draw from various ways of thinking about mode coexistence or mode separation (Carmona et al. 2010; Gehl 2010; Jacobs 1961; Shane 2011). From the doctrines of modernist functionalist planning, we know mode separation is a must. More modern planning and design philosophies such as 'Shared Space' thinking challenge these design principles. However, given the difference in vulnerability between, for example, car drivers and pedestrians or cyclists, most planners and urban designers would probably agree that some level of mode separation is needed for the safety of the weaker parts. Studying both section and plan diagrams of the mode divisions (figs. 5.52-5.58) is key to grasping the underlying assumptions about mode division and thus also of mode hierarchies. Mode division and separation are often carried out to enhance traffic safety, but looking more closely at, for instance, the amount of space and level of detailing attached to the respective modes, indicates both political and economic priorities. In Odense the section and plan diagram clearly illustrates the mixing philosophy of 'Shared Space' but also the option for pedestrians to stay in their dedicated lane alongside the house facades. The street layout in the Aarhus case is, as mentioned, more traditional but also serves more variation in modes since there are faster moving vehicles (cars, busses, motorcycles, etc.). Therefore the mode division needs to be more strict and legible. Having said so, the curvature of the bike path at the junctions is an innovative design element that affords more careful practice from the cyclist's point of view. Moreover, this design detail actually adds a different ambience and is different from the aesthetic experience one ordinarily would get riding on the average bike path. Bryggebroen clearly stands out from the other two cases in its character and aim. As a bridge dedicated to bikes and pedestrians only, the design task is different and in some senses simpler. It is a very clear mobilities armature, where the division of modes is the most evident feature next to its iconic features as an artefact on its own. But as mentioned we witnessed quite some unintended mode mixing when cyclists by accident drove into the dedicated pedestrian lane.

In this section of the case analysis I wanted to address the staging taking place 'from above'. I have looked at the three cases from the point of view of the network city and partly with an interest in how they fit and blend into these larger scales of mobilities systems. In part, I have taken the analysis down scale to focus on the materialities of mobilities as they manifest themselves in surface materials, design guidelines, and mode division. As mentioned I do not aspire to do a cross-case comparison of these projects. Interesting as that may be, that would be another research project.

Vestergade Vest and Mageløs

Bryggebroen

Hans Broges Gade

Figs. 5.40 - 5.45

Vestergade Vest and Mageløs

Bryggebroen

Hans Broges Gade

Figs. 5.46 - 5.51

Vestergade Vest and Mageløs

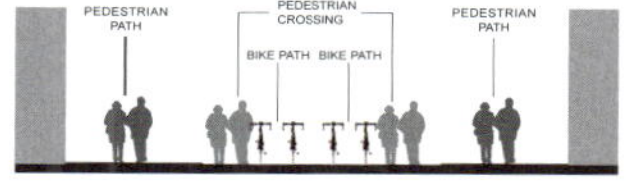

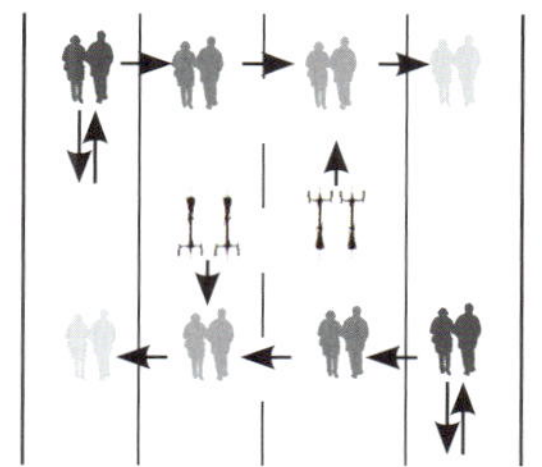

Hans Broges Gade

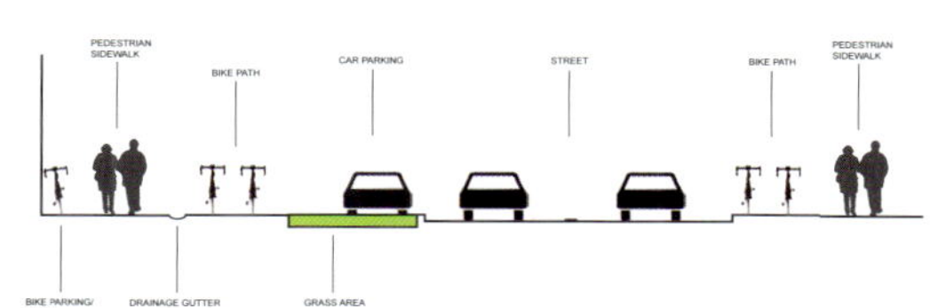

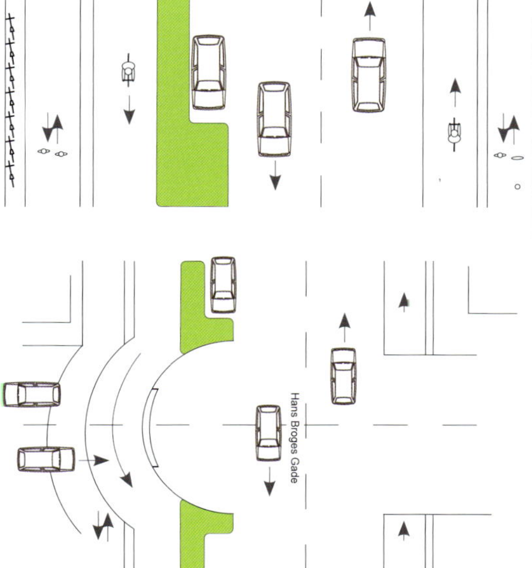

Bryggebroen

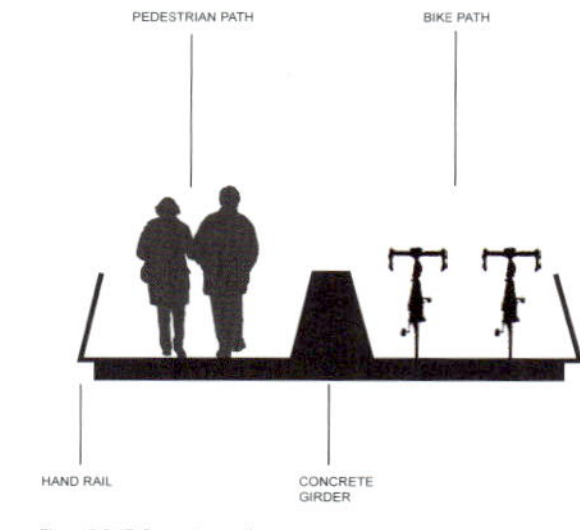

Figure 3.3.17: Bryggebro section.

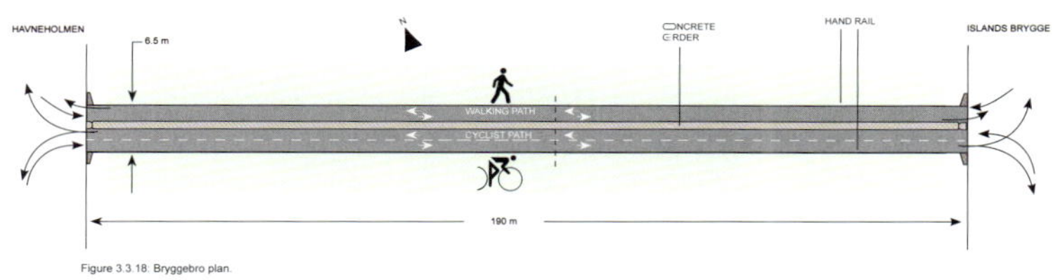

Figure 3.3.18: Bryggebro plan.

Here I wanted to use the empirical material from the 'Bikeability' project to illustrate how mobilities are being staged in a complex process of planning and regulatory frameworks, material conditions, and technological options and creative design solutions. But of course each project speaks to different dimensions of this analysis. I did, for example, explore the more playful and ludic dimension to the Odense project. I noted the special and rather compelling design features of the Copenhagen project (as well as the modal conflict), and the more traditional traffic design solution in Aarhus. So far I have kept to the 'from above' perspective and illustrated how the mobile situation is framed and afforded by these complex decisions. Having the analytical framing in mind, though, I want to 'zoom in' even closer and start exploring the embodied and social perspectives of the mobile interactions taking place in each of these sites. The staging 'from below' by mobile subjects and their interactional dynamics is the other half of the story to which I now turn.

Figs. 5.52 - 5.58

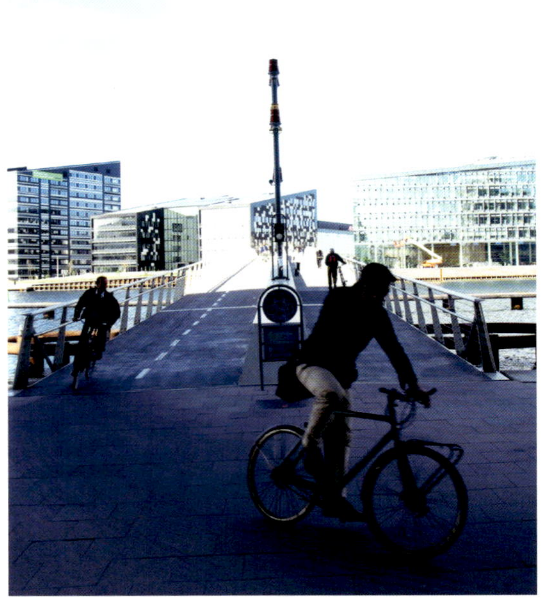

PART II: Staging from below: Bike assemblages

The 'from below' dimension of the 'Staging Mobilities' perspective to which I now turn has to include the embodied practices of the mobile situation as well as the interactional dynamics among mobile consociates (fig. 5.62). Therefore the level of situational detail will increase as I will be inferring more analytical and interpretative conclusions. As mentioned earlier in this book, the chosen method of field observation rather than interviews will only let me go so far in stipulating what people's motives, thoughts, and rationales are. Had the research question pointed in that direction, other methodologies should surely have been brought into play. However, here I want to keep a deliberate 'distance' from the inner life of our mobile subjects. This is important, certainly, but if the focus is on the situation as we may all observe and recognize it on the street, and observe how material space and physical design meld into the complex patterns of everyday life mobilities, the research strategy chosen is to stay at what I might call the mezzo level. This is not the abstract and general level or the psychological inner-world level, but the concrete, observable, and situational level.

User interaction and hierarchy

I want to address the issue of user hierarchy as a way into the perspective of staging from below, well aware that this dimension actually is laid out 'from above' as design decisions shape the hierarchy of mobile subjects on the street. This is part of the 'zooming in' process and will take us to the staging 'from below' perspective.

In Hans Broges Gade the bike is at the top of the hierarchy, followed by pedestrians; the car comes last. As we zoom in on a detail in the layout shown in figure 5.64, we see how the priority of bikes over cars has been materialised in the elevation of the bike path, which results in a bump-like effect for the crossing cars that will have to slow down in order not to damage the vehicle. At Bryggebroen in Copenhagen cars are not allowed and the mobility divide between cycles and pedestrians is equal.

As mentioned before, the landing area at Bryggebroen is where potential clashes between these two side-ordered mobility modes may arise. As we shall see later this area is particularly interesting as a site for studying negotiation-in-motion and the staging 'from below' made by the mobile subjects themselves. In Odense slower modes are given priority, which is seen both in the regulatory discourses banning ordinary car use and in the material design where various 'obstacles' create designed friction and thereby afford slower modes.

Paces

The pace (or speed) by which people can move within the specific case sites obviously differs. Here the situation at Vestergade in Odense is quite interesting since the 'shared space' philosophy has been

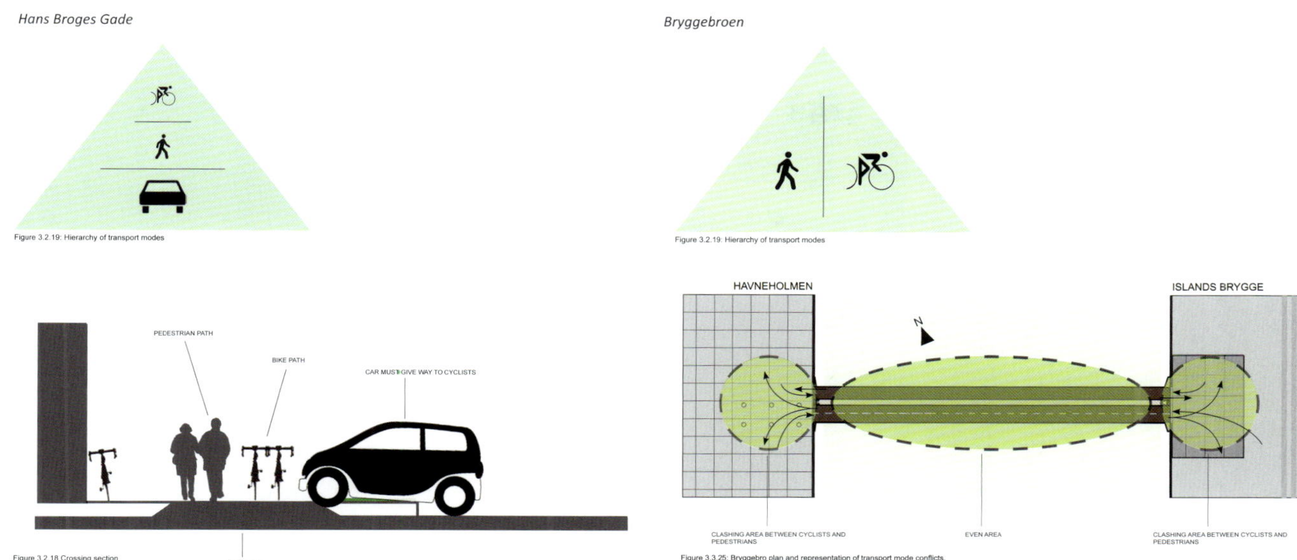

supplemented with a standard traffic bump solution in an attempt to minimize the speed at which bikes and cars move through the street. In figures 5.67 and 5.68 we see how the bicyclists negotiate the bump by simply going around the obstacle. As this takes place quite a lot of turning and swinging occur, leading to a 'conflict zone' between the cyclists and pedestrians in these zones parallel to the road space. (This can be seen in figure 5.67, where a cyclist and a pedestrian are very close to each other.)

At Hans Broges Gade in Aarhus (figs. 5.69-5.72), we see how cyclists appropriate the spaces and allow themselves to bike quite fast in their dedicated and prioritized environment. The crossings are, however, also intersections of pace reductions for the cyclists as the curved bike paths afford slower speed. But the design in Hans Broges Gade also allows for 'mobile withs' and their interaction. For instance this is seen in figure 5.72, where two cyclists (a child and an adult) are moving along the path in close proximity and interaction as they are having a conversation on the go. At Bryggebroen (figs. 5.73-5.75) the pace is indeed modified and mediated by the specific design of the bridge. So when people are moving 'uphill', so to speak, the pace is slower and as they progress 'downhill', speed increases. This is most common for the cyclists, offering them a different negotiation with the bridge and its topography. The dedicated pedestrian path is characterised mainly by two speeds: the walking pace of most pedestrians and the jogging speed of runners. Both groups seemed to be able to share the pedestrian space with no particular challenges.

Public Art: Facilitating interaction and reflection
As a more general trend in public space and traffic design, many sites are now being overlaid with some element of public art and semiotics that challenge the understanding of transit spaces as rational sites of movement only. In the case from Odense this is most

Opposite page:
Fig. 5.62

Right Page
Figs. 5.63 - 5.66

Vestergade Vest

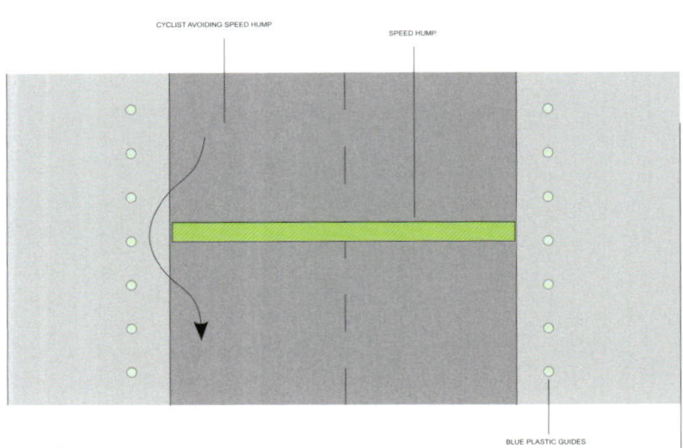

Figure 3.1.13: Cyclists avoiding speed hump.

Bryggebroen

Hans Broges Gade

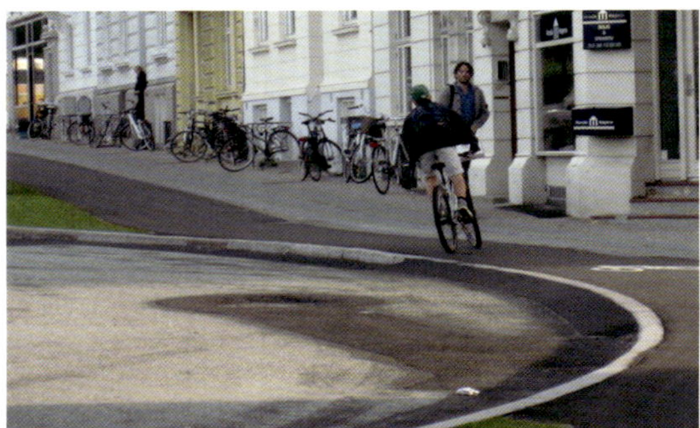

Figs. 5.67 - 5.75

Vestergade Vest and Mageløs

Words written on pavement

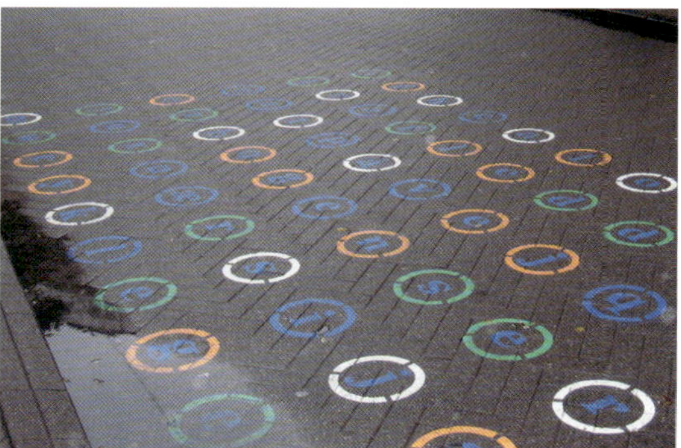

Painted game board in the pavement

Table tennis in the street

Marks inviting cyklists and pedestrians

Hans Broges Gade

Statue in memory of Hans Broge

Bryggebroen

Light installation marking the connection between two different parts of the city

Figs. 5.76 - 5.81

evident, and there are both written statements on the street as well as a painted game board and even table tennis equipment in the street space. In Hans Broges Gade the public art is more traditional and confined to a statue in memory of Hans Broge, after whom the street has been named. Bryggebroen with its light installation is particular at night time an artwork in and of itself. As mentioned before the way the illumination creates playful and aesthetic experiences for the user is quite outstanding.

Public Art: Consociates' stage modifications

In such public spaces the art may also be of a more bottom-up nature. In general we could talk about how mobile consociates are modifying the mobility stage of the street. In Odense this is not done so much by citizens and grassroots organizations, but perhaps more by the business community as in the case of the large advertising signs along the road (fig. 5.82). This is of course not art, but is an important modification

Vestergade Vest - An employee is placing a commercial on the street

Figs. 5.82 - 5.87

Bryggebroen - Habitating mobilities through street art

Bryggebroen - Habitating mobilities through commercial and political stickers

Bryggebroen - Technical installations are overtaken

Bryggebroen - Emotional mobilities: Lovers write names and through the keys in the habour

Bryggebroen - Emotional mobilities: Lovers write names and through the keys in the habour

of the semiotic properties at this particular site. At Bryggebroen in Copenhagen things are different and this is most striking in the graffiti and tagging by grassroots and local artists (figs. 5.83-5.85). And then there is the special situation of the emotional mobilities displayed by lovers' names on the locks alongside the fence (figs. 5.86-5.87). These so-called 'love padlocks' are illustrations of an appropriation of the infrastructure from below and a modification of the 'stage' for mobility.

Seen from the perspective of 'staging mobilities', some of the features staged from 'above' may be interpreted and negotiated with a specific outcome by the mobile subjects in the spaces. This is for example the case at Bryggebroen where the paving of the cobble stones have been intersected by two lines of larger stones in parallel. These two lines affords smoother and more high speed bike riding so there is a certain competition for riding in those lanes. If you want to overtake the other bikes you have to diverge from these two lanes, bringing you out into the more bumpy terrain. So even though there is plenty of space to accommodate more bikes side-by-side, the two parallel lanes of stone afford a particular set of practices and behaviours by the bicyclists. Rather than 'filling out', the space people stage themselves in long rows of cyclists that prioritize the smooth ride. Other details may be studied, as for example, how cars (that are at the low end of the hierarchy in the Hans Broges Gade case) neglect the signs and spaces dedicated for the bikes. In figure 5.92 we see how a car simply has parked across the bike sign communicating that this is a bike priority space. Equally, the bicyclists may stage themselves differently from what the traffic designers and engineers have in

Bryggebroen - two lines of smooth pavement are 'staged from above' and in a 'staging from below' consociates are either following the lines for a smoother ride or diverting from it.

Hans Broges gade - A car is parked in the bike crossing lane. A man is crossing the road in an illegal way.

Figs. 5.88 - 5.93

mind. In figure 5.93 we see a bicyclist crossing the road at a site he finds more attractive than the designated crossing areas.

Mobile situations: Crossing the road along the way

Now I have reached the most detailed level of the 'zooming in' and in the last section will focus on particular interactions and situations. If we start at Hans Broges Gade in Aarhus the situation I want to explore is this: a cyclist crosses the road by moving along the way rather than crossing the road orthogonally (figs. 5.94-5.101). The cyclist moves gradually into the car lane and moves along this path until she comes to the place where she wants to turn. This is a rather well-used practice for road-crossing that I also found in the analysis of the public transit space 'Nytorv' in Aalborg (see Jensen 2013a, chapter 7). Halfway through the chain of actions needed to make this turn, the bicyclist actually has positioned herself in the left of the two car lanes. Needless to say, this turning practice only works in a situation such as the one described here, where there is no or very little traffic. Even though Hans Broges Gade gives priority to bikes over cars, the situation changes when one moves into the dedicated car space on the road. The specific situation of crossing the road along the way would surely have been modified by the presence of heavy traffic. In that situation the cyclist would probably have followed the 'staging from above' much more strictly and bike along the bike path all the way up to the street into which she wanted to turn right. This crossing situation illustrates the staging 'from below' by a mobile subject taking into consideration the smallest microelements of the situation. If she had arrived, say, 30-45 seconds later, the car that is visible in the left lane (fig. 5.101) would have been closer and occupy the space in the lane the cyclist used for her turn. This is obviously a banal observation but it also is relevant to the point that a 'situational mobilities' perspective is sensitive to the micro acts and interactions that make up the mobilities practices of everyday life.

Mobile situations: Crossing road in front of car

The next situation is one where a female cyclist is crossing the road in a diagonal between connecting roads (figs. 5.102-5.109). At the same time she turns left onto the street, a car is making a right turn directly in front of her. The interactional proximity is very close and the speed slow, which makes this situation rather undramatic. As the two mobile subjects pass each other in each of their own vehicles, there is eye contact and the situation is thus a rather classic road interchange where the 'negotiation-in-motion' is played out by the standard gestures and gazes of mutual reinforcement. The simple road turn is a microcosm of the combination of formal traffic rules, social interaction according to social norms of the road, staged interaction from above through the material design of the site, and the individual's staging 'from below'. After the turn the bicyclist keeps on riding in the designated car space on the road. Presumably this would not have been the case if there were more traffic, but it again bears witness to the micropractices and decisions made 'on the fly'. Even though traffic planners and designers have created a safer and designated bike space, the mobile subjects of the situations only engage with the affordances and designs staged from above to the extent they find these pragmatically useful.

Mobile situations: Riding on sidewalk and avoiding obstacles

Here are two different situations starting from the same point: the mobile subject in question is staging an alternative practice in relation to the purpose for which something was designed. In the first situation the bicyclist finds it easier to ride on the sidewalk on the wrong side of the road than actually to cross the road to ride on the designated bike path in the direction he is heading (figs. 5.110-5.112). The second situation is one where a car has blocked the ramp from the bike path onto the street. Here the cyclist jumps off his bike and improvises by taking an alternative route for crossing the road (figs. 5.113-5.115). The two situations differ, however, in that the first cyclist is staging his mobility

A woman is crossing the road in a diagonal between connecting roads.

Figs. 5.94 - 5.101

A woman is crossing the road in a diagonal between connecting roads.

Figs. 5.102 - 5.109

A man is riding on the sidewalk in the wrong side of the road probably to avoid crossing the road to ride the bike lane in the other side of the road.

A car is parked in the bike crossing. The cyclist reacts by taking an alternative route over the road.

Figs. 5.110 - 5.115

according to some perceived advantage and thus violating some of the more commonly accepted rules of the road, such as not to ride bikes on the sidewalk and not to ride on the wrong side of the road. This is different from some of the international cases I have explored, where cyclists seem to have the (moral) right to ride, for example, on pavements and sidewalks simply because the infrastructures for bikes are so badly developed that they are very unsafe in the streets. In Denmark this is different and possibly this is due to the fact that there is a rather well-developed bike infrastructure network in most cities. This leads partly to less illegal cycling practice but also to less public acceptance of bending the rules. One exception seems to be if the cyclist is very young. Young children cycling on sidewalks do seem to be accepted, but only if they are in the company with adults and only up to a certain age (where this line of demarcation for public acceptance of children biking on the sidewalk actually is I cannot identify here). The second situation where the bicyclist is being blocked by the obstacle of a car is different since he presumably would have followed the designated route and thus staged himself within the logic of the general traffic design had someone not parked in the middle of the junction. The second situation also bears witness to the element of situational improvisations that make up everyday life mobilities conditions for millions of people. One has to improvise and negotiate the situations at hand in the best possible way, and in this situation we see how the cyclist simply jumps off the bike and moves into a space from which he can continue his journey.

Mobile situations: Negotiating crossing the road

The situation here is a road crossing where two bikes (one adult with a child on the back of the bike and one adult alone) negotiate the crossing (figs.5.116-5.122). We notice that there is also a car entering the road, but it awaits the result of the two bikes negotiating. In the background a man is crossing the street outside the zebra crossings. The main focus of attention for the two crossing bicyclists is, of course, any traffic on the road they are about to cross. We see the adult with child holding back for a car before entering the crossing. While being out on the street the two bikes are very close to one another and gazes and gestures illustrate that this crossing is negotiated. The two cyclists are clearly aware of each other's presence and are equally clear about the other's intention. Following this mutual 'body check' as Goffman termed it (1972), we see that both of the cyclists are looking and turning their heads to reassure themselves that the road space is still clear of cars. So even if this particular situation is very simple and without dense traffic and complex negotiations, we see how much interaction actually takes place in a very simple and mundane situation such as negotiating the crossing of the road by two bikes.

Mobile situations: Crossing the road without stopping

The following situation illustrates one of the key points about staging from below (figs. 5.123-5.129). The man who is crossing the street and making a left turn actually needs to await the clearance of the space since there are a couple of cars occupying it. 'Normally', or as it is described in the Danish traffic regulations, this person should get off his bike and await 'all clear'. Instead he is performing quite a bit of 'bodywork' and effort not to stop the bike. Eventually he needs to stop but he will surely not get off the bike. By appropriating the street spaces in this manner, he is actually exposing himself to some risk but he seems to be more interested in not having to dismount his vehicle. As he is in the middle of the road the only option for him is to put down his foot onto the street in order to keep his balance, but if he had been at a light crossing or closer to the curb he probably would have used these objects to stabilize and facilitate his temporary stop. (We often see cyclists grabbing onto light poles and other objects in order to prevent themselves from setting down a foot to keep their balance).

Two cyclists negotiate their way across the road, in the background a man is crossing the road outside zebra crossings.

Figs. 5.116 - 5.122

A man is crossing the road on the move without getting off his bike.

Figs. 5.123 - 5.129

Mobile withs are riding and talking on Hans Broges Gade.

Figs. 5.130 - 5.135

Mobile situations: Riding and socialising

Everyday life mobilities may be solitary practices performed in sites where few people go. However, as we are looking at inner cities and dense urban environments, very rarely are the mobilities practices carried out without any mobile consociates. We have seen a number of examples of how traffic is a complex order of social interaction. But often we also see people on the move as groups or what I term 'mobile withs' (figs. 5.130-5.135). One such case is this situation where the 'mobile withs' are occupying both the bike path and the sidewalk. The two people walking hand-in-hand on the very right-hand side of the images are performing the bodywork in close proximity while taking up the sidewalk space. The 'mobile with' of these two walking people obviously demands some level of mutual coordination and synchronization, but that is nothing compared to the other 'mobile with' made up by the two cyclists riding along the bike path and talking intensely. They are obviously engaged in a conversation but it is interesting to notice how they also are coordinating their body movements (actually to an impressive level of detail – notice how the pedals on the bikes are in almost perfect synchronization. I am sure this is not something of which they are even remotely aware. But often we find this sort of 'mirroring' effect between interacting people. Microcommunication studies, for example, also illustrate how two interacting individuals may 'mirror' each other's bodily gestures like shifting weight to another leg or touching one's ear or hair. (See Hall 1966; Whyte 1988.) What takes place as these two bicyclists are performing their practice as a 'mobile with' is thus very complex and speaks both to the work needed to maintain the mutual interaction and conversation as well as to move along the bike path without being exposed to dangerous situations. Furthermore, the precise location that is represented in these images is where the bike path bends just before the road intersection. Even in this place where attention is needed to steer the bike and ensure that no crossing or turning cars can create a dangerous situation, the 'mobile with' is in perfect sync and there is nothing that would disturb the conversation as it is being performed on the go. (Obviously a crossing car or a child running out on the bike path would change this dramatically.) The point about looking at the two bikes here is also that they reaffirm the more general assertion that mobilities is more than A to B. These moving cyclists are surely engaged in acts of physical displacement from one place to another, but, equally, they are performing sociality and using the road for more than just moving.

Mobile situations: Bike negotiations in motion

I have mentioned a few times that there is one critical point at Bryggebroen in Copenhagen (figs. 5.136-5.140). This is the landing area where bikes are both turning and crossing other bikes trajectories (some moving onto the bridge, others simply biking along the quay side). In this situation we furthermore see that not only is attention given to the bicyclist moving along the quay side, attention is also required for the mobile phone conversation in which one of the cyclists is engaged. Needless to say, texting and talking on mobile phones while one is driving creates a rather great safety risk. In Denmark it is illegal to talk on a mobile phone while driving a car unless a hands' free device is used. In cities biking and talking on the mobile phone at the same time is seen increasingly often. This is an illustration of the point that we are 'carrying networks' as we both move in time and space, as well as being engaged in communication transgressing the physical copresence. In this specific situation the presence of a mobile telephoning cyclists obviously adds to the complexity.

But even without the mobile phone the 'landing area' at Bryggebroen is a contested site and many 'negotiations-in-motion' takes place there during the day. As we can see from the images, some of the bikes ridging 'downhill' actually pick up some very decent speed, which adds a layer of complexity to the negotiation on the landing side. As a general rule, the lower speed, the more time to react and interact. Also the design of Bryggebroen with its two dedicated paths may create some confusion. We witnessed several situations where bikers came into the 'wrong path' and thus either had to turn back or jump off the bike. (Some also continued biking, but they were rather few.)

The examples chosen here have not covered completely the many situations we studied and documented throughout the Bikeability research project. However, a select number have been chosen for practical reasons and much more detailed analysis and exploration is possible. It should be remembered

Cyclists negotiating their way on and off Bryggebroen.

Figs. 5.136 - 5.140

that the cases presented in this book are explored mainly to illustrate how the 'staging mobilities' framing and conceptualisation may be used in analysing these empirical expressions of contemporary society. Furthermore, the aim is to point toward a new and emerging field of 'mobilities design'. In order to progress toward this discussion I move to the concluding remarks of this chapter.

Concluding remarks

From the outset of this book the key issue has been this question: *How is design affording and/or preventing particular mobile practices and cultures in everyday life?* The case material explored in this chapter has illustrated that contemporary bike infrastructure design is very complex and contains many layers, from performing as instrumental sites of physical displacement and movement from A to B toward being central elements of a city's public space and built environment. In this chapter I have argued that bikes and the design for them may be understood as 'cycling assemblages', which are comprised of multiple social interactions, bodily sensations, material systems, solid objects, and infrastructural networks. In accordance with the *Staging Mobilities* framework, I have shown how biking as a mobile practice is staged 'from above' in planning, design, and regulatory frameworks. I have also shown that the situational practices are illustrations of a staging 'from below' by mobile subjects performing a mobile presentation of self. As I study the bike designs in Aarhus, Copenhagen, and Odense, the specific situational mobilities lend themselves to be understood as materialising within the dimensions of their physical settings, material space, and design; we also saw how these elements are both social interactions and embodied performances. Overlaying the *Staging Mobilities* framework with the notion of cycling assemblages furthermore illustrates the complexity of these bike designs and how they rely on mobile subjects and planning guidance as well as on material artefacts and objects distributed into the urban fabric.

From the examples of situational mobilities and their material embedding put forward in this chapter, it becomes clear that biking is a complex and multidimensional practice that needs certain features in the built environment in order for it to become a mobility mode. Moreover, the mobile subjects practicing biking need also to make sense of the practice and imbue it with the values and interest springing from the desires and wishes of an everyday life practice. The cases explored all bear witness to the particular mobility affordances created by material design, social interaction, and embodied performances. The bike paths and their wider connections with urban traffic systems afford commuting practices and ways of organizing everyday life mobilities. As the material infrastructures looked at in this chapter all are inner city bike systems, we see that one of the key affordances of urban biking infrastructure is to enable alternative mobility forms to, for example, walking, driving, and mass transit. Moreover, the citywide biking systems afford a particular mode of orientation and navigation within the urban fabric. Quite often this has to be understood as a mixture of at least two different underpinning rationales. Either the bike infrastructure system affords rational and instrumental displacement of mobile subjects between A and B, or it offers aesthetic experiences or natural ambiences (as when the path system is routed along picturesque sights). The mobile aesthetics afforded by urban biking are rather different from, for example, driving a car or riding a bus. This obviously has to do with the embodied performances that are of a different nature since the cycle is a mobile technology that is muscle powered but at the same time affords the user the ability to cover much more ground than the pedestrian. On the other hand, the bike cannot cover ground, distances, or match the speed of the car. However, the cyclist perceives the environment in a very different manner. Not as 'unhindered versus cocooned' which some scholars seem to think (see Jensen 2013a, chapter five), but rather as two completely different body-technology nexuses. The car driver is not 'sealed off' from the materiality of the city but rather 'filtered' and senses the topography, sounds, and sights through the mediation of the vehicle. This is also the case for the cyclist but obviously in a different sense since the sounds, sights, and environmental characteristics are sensed much more directly. But this embodied performance of cycling is not unmediated since surface material of the bike paths, topographies of the infrastructure system, as well as the type of bike, the number of gears, and the quality of the tyres all contribute to particular and mediated embodied mobilities. The cycle offers a unique opportunity to experience and explore the city, and it has its own particular features of an 'aesthetic experience in motion'. The topography, climate, and immediacy of the sensed environments makes the view from the saddle' a special way of engaging with the city. As we have seen, some writers tend to romanticise this, and obviously the fantastic and deep sense-oriented mobile aesthetics of urban cycling should be countered with another dimension of the 'cycling reality' such as being exposed to rain, snow, wind, and perhaps most seriously, being very vulnerable to contact with, for example, cars.

I have explained that much of what may look simply like 'traffic' (i.e., physical displacement of a body) very often also is a series of complex social interactions. In the city bicyclists are constantly facing multiple mobile others representing various modes. The social interaction of everyday life mobilities affords a constant social mirroring and communicative practice that for most of the time is routine and goes on unreflected. As with other human practices this obviously changes when things go wrong (for example, if someone hits you when opening a car door or goes through a red light, causing you to brake dramatically). The biking practices in the city may therefore be understood as afforded by the 'hardware' of infrastructure and vehicle technology as well as they are shaped by the multiple mobile others of the urban interaction field we erroneously often think of as simply 'traffic'. As Conley argues with sociological sensitivity: 'It takes two to traffic' (Conley 2012, 222). Moreover, and this is the common denominator regardless of what kind of bike and style of riding, all are performing mobilities with their bodies. The mobility affordances of urban cycling are thus a complex and multi-layered phenomenon that reaches well beyond the widespread policy interest in shifting car drivers to cycling. This is all well and good, but urban biking is a rich, multisensorial and social phenomenon that influences understandings of self, other, and the built environment. This I argue justifies talking about mobility cultures and approaching cycling as a cultural phenomenon as much as a set of practices that afford movement about the city.

The complexity and intertwining of mobile bodies, social interaction, and material systems have been addressed through the notion of 'mobile assemblages'. As I have been looking at cycling in particular, I have offered the notion of 'cycling assemblages' precisely to capture that the staging 'from above' as well as the staging 'from below' is much more complicated that simply a reflection of individual transport preference or a city government's transport policy. These are vital elements of the complexity affording cycling, but by adding the notion of 'cycling assemblages' I wish to turn the spotlight on the importance of technologies, objects, and artefacts. The socio-technical systems of which cycling assemblages points beyond the omnipotent subject and into the messy world of traffic lights, bike path pavements, cycling technologies, curbs, light poles, traffic signs, and multiple other 'requisites' for the staging of situational biking mobilities. Moreover, even though most biking practices are done without the assistance of networked technologies -- those who track their routes on GPS and upload these to servers are still a minority -- it is no more exotic to see people biking at the same time as they are engaged in a mobile telephone conversation with some distant but situational copresent other. Even when we look at the rather simple and still very mechanically oriented technology as a bike, people riding bikes are often expressions of 'networked selves' that are 'linked-in-motion'.

Applying the metaphor of 'the river' to the bikescapes studied, we see how the flows of 'body-bike particles' are following the armatures and channels quite stringently (even though we did see examples of bikes transgressing their designated areas). The overall traffic system of the city and its accommodation of cycling in more or less generous ways are managed, designed, and installed from the top down. The width of the path affords certain volumes of cycles and the bending, curvature, and topography of the routes determine the speeds of travel. However, there are 'cracks in the foundation' when cyclists appropriate the systems and sites in their own manner, as in Odense where cyclists turn outside the speed-reducing devices. So as the 'river' metaphor tends to homogenize mobile subjects on the move as if they were large and often anonymous flows, I proposed to balance this perspective by adding the metaphor of the 'ballet' as indicative of the embodied interaction seen from the point of view of the situational participant. The bike design schemes explored here all have different interactional effects and thus afford different 'ballets'. Needless to say, they also have commonalities such as bike paths of approximately the same width although not in the Odense case, where the 'shared space' philosophy opens up the biking domain toward the wider street space.

The 'cycling assemblages' are managing and staging various relationships within the phenomenon I termed 'mobile sociopetals and mobile sociofugals'. The notion of mobile sociopetals refers to how some sites and settings are particularly well functioning in getting people to go there and conduct their activities. This is a well-known feature of public squares and plazas but differs slightly when we study 'cycling assemblages'. But the much discussed 'landing area' of Bryggebroen is an example of how the bridge 'draws in' cyclists in order for them to utilize the affordance created by the bridge (crossing the water at this particular site), thus working as a 'mobile sociopetal'. However, we may have to define this quality relative to the direction of the flow as the 'landing' functions as a mobile sociofugal when cycles and pedestrians are 'getting off'. The bridge dispenses its content and floods the surrounding area with pedestrians and bikes only to have them diffusing out in various directions and being absorbed into other parts of the city's 'cycling assemblage'. This is a dynamic and intricate play between the 'river' and 'ballet' perspective. It is a pulse and rhythm of 'ebb and flow' as it 'draws in' mobile subjects and 'pushes them out' into the city again.

The 'cycling assemblage' is both a traffic system of physical displacement of bikes and bodies from A to B, as well as an interactional and social space. This quality is highlighted by the notion of 'negotiation-in-motion' and is seen in all three cases. Cycling is a social and complex affair and even the smallest turn or rerouting calls for scanning of the environment and assessing relative speeds and positioning of other artefacts, objects, and mobile subjects. The microprocesses of situational negotiation increase in complexity as the mobile subjects do not just face each other at a static standstill but move instead with different speeds and trajectories. Often the bike paths are occupied with mobile subjects travelling together as 'mobile withs'. These may certainly challenge the dimensioning of the bike paths. In the Aarhus case we saw people biking and socialising, which was possible only because they were almost alone at the site. In dense and jammed systems, as in Copenhagen, these social dynamics are less easy to carry through. Nevertheless, 'mobile withs' are present even in these crowded systems as friends, families, and lovers take to the bike paths, carrying with them their social relationships and interactions. These will, however, often need to expose a certain level of 'stretchiness' (Jensen 2013a, 14). As part of a city's larger infrastructural system the 'cycling assemblages' are allocated a specific place in a wider mobility hierarchy. Thus the 'cycling assemblage' also contributes to the creation of 'mobility divides' as it offers certain opportunities and blocks off others. This is again, however, dependent on the dynamics of the situation rather than something to be deducted a priori. For example, even though cyclists are not able to cover as much distance as cars, they have immense advantages in speed when rush hour hits town. In such a situation, the 'cycling assemblage' affords a particularly generous mobility divide in favour of the bikes. Most of the time, though, the arrow points in the other direction, creating advantages for car that cloud cycling's positives (except to the really dedicated few). The point about the various mobilities divides and the affordances created in a 'cycling assemblage' leads me to press on toward a key point in the *Staging Mobilities* framework, namely the double-edged perspective of what I termed 'critical mobilities thinking'. Accordingly, we should be alert to the problems created by the way mobilities design is materialised (e.g., when a city-wide infrastructure system marginalizes weaker modes of mobilities). But we should also be sensitive to the potentials of such systems. In the case of a 'cycling assemblage', the potential to be more than an instrumental flow space is already realized by many users (e.g., the aesthetic and sensorial qualities of 'the view from the saddle'), but there are also underutilized or undiscovered potentials to be explored and experimented with (e.g., taking seriously that 'cycling assemblages' are public spaces full of social interaction and cultural meaning may challenge the existing bike system design). The field to explore and experiment with the potential dimension of 'critical mobilities thinking' is the emerging field I term 'mobilities design'.

Urban bike infrastructures are 'cycling assemblages' with a vital semiotic component. Traffic signs, painted pavements, and other traditional illustrations of mobile semiotics are evident. So is the fact that the cyclists themselves are 'signs' that need interpretation by other mobile subjects. In this chapter I have not gone into this, but the whole legal code related to how to signal your intentions with your body by applying highly standardised gestures and hand/body signalling adds considerably to the complexity of the mobile situations. (See the story about the 'highway code' in Jensen 2013a, 117-118.) As a matter of fact, the particular sites we studied in this chapter had a rather low frequency of 'hand signalling' cyclists. I consider this to be a result of the relatively confined nature of these spaces that expose cyclists mostly to other cyclists. Even though some cyclists do hand signal to other fellow cyclists (in particular on the clogged bikes paths of Copenhagen, where intention communication by hand signal may be crucial to avoid dangerous situations), the main situation of using hand signals occurs is when other modes of mobilities are present and, I suppose, in particular with cars as they inherently represent a physical threat to the cyclist.

I have cut across the three cases presented in this chapter. I realize this creates a slightly different balance and flavour of the chapter than, for example, the more ethnographic account of the mobilities within the Friis shopping centre in chapter five. But the nomenclature and theoretical conceptualization growing out of the *Staging Mobilities* framework is equally applicable to these three cases. The 'language' of *Staging Mobilities* affords new ways of talking and thinking about cycling and cycling infrastructure. Having said so, I must admit that much more thorough explorations need to be conducted to discover the more detailed situational dynamics of 'cycling assemblages'. Here I have tried to utilize the concepts and theories on existing material from an already conducted empirical research project. I chose to do this so that I could address cycling in this context even though I could have explored it more in depth and with only one site as the focus. This will change in chapter six where I explore one specific site, namely the 'metroscape' of Nørreport Station in Copenhagen.

6 TRAIN

METROSCAPES AND MOBILITIES – NØRREPORT STATION

For subway lines, like lifelines in the hand, meet and cross – not only on the map where the interlacing of their multicolor routes unwinds and is set in place, but in everyone's lives and minds.

Marc Augé (2002) *In the Metro*, p. 6

Urban railway stations are testing grounds for the borders between private and public, semi-public, semi-private. They represent a special kind of urban commons, a terraine vauge, neither inside nor outside. They are wide open, inviting and centrally located. Although designed as machines for the swift flow of travellers, they are used of other purposes as well. Very different kinds of people co-habits this transit space, long distance travellers, tourists, daily commuters, but also many kinds of non-travellers who for different reasons are attracted to the station: homeless searching shelter, bored teenagers looking for action, people out of work trying to pass the day. This mix makes it a special kind of urban common.

Orvar Löfgren (2014) *Sharing an atmosphere: spaces in urban commons*, p. 3 (italics in original)

In many ways the history of transport architecture with its interest in space, construction technology, light and social provision is the story of modernism itself … Nowhere is this more evident than in the transport interchange with its concentration right in the heart of cities of competing social, economic, engineering and design forces.

Brian Edwards (2011) *Sustainability and the Design of Transport Interchanges*, p. 23

Introduction

In this chapter I examine 'trains'. However, I keep focus on the city and the networks hereof so the theme is not the isolated train journey but rather the multimodal train station or urban transportation hub. In the chapter I explore the busiest of the train and metro stations in Copenhagen, Nørreport Station, as the case illustrated how 'metroscapes' are designing, hosting, and orchestrating mobilities. By looking in detail at how the Metro Company has approached the aim of almost 'pure circulation' and no public activities and programs next to the busy and more 'open-minded' (Walzer 1986) approach to the rest of Nørreport Station, the Metro is used to show the staging and designing of mobilities within complex assemblages of socio-technical infrastructure systems creating habitats of mobilities in urban everyday life. As with the other chapters I remind that the general issue is to explore: *'How is design affording and/or preventing particular mobile practices and cultures in everyday life?'* Here Nørreport Station offers itself as a particularly complex and interesting case for exploration.

This chapter is structured in the following manner. After a short introduction the theoretical and conceptual framing is introduced. Here I will call on the architect Brian Edwards and his fine book *Sustainability and the Design of Transport Interchanges* (Edwards 2011), as well as exploring the work of Norman Foster as one of the key influences on my thinking when it comes to the design- and architecturally oriented dimensions (Foster 2007). Hereafter the empirical field study is presented. First I focus on the context of Nørreport Station, then on the flows and movements within it. After this the analysis will shift toward focus exclusively to the Copenhagen Metro and its station within the Nørreport hub. I am doing this in two parts: first by looking at the material design and physical layout of the Metro Station and next by looking at the embodied performances of metro users. Finally the chapter ends with some concluding remarks.

Metroscapes – conceptual and theoretical framing

The urban railway and metro station must be understood as a place of transit, a dimension of the public realm, and a key driver of contemporary urban transformation strategies (Edwards 2011; Jones 2006; Powell 2000; Trip 2007; Zacharias et al. 2011; Xue et al. 2012). Often such strategies come along the lines of what is termed 'Transit Oriented Development' or TOD. Like Rem Koolhaas once pointed provocatively to the convergence of the city and the airport where the one has become conspicuously like the other (Koolhaas 1995), so have many larger urban train stations taken on 'urban properties' and complexity as they engage with urban programs such as shopping and leisure. This is, for example, the case in Berlin with the new central station (see the appendix on global references) or with Tokyo Station (Zacharias et al. 2011). Also 'subways' or 'metros' are rather complex socio-technical artefacts that are multilayered and vital for the wider circulation system of the city (Ascher 2005). The sites and places where the 'interface' between the metro/train systems and the city takes place are often complex and multilayered access points, or 'Critical Points of Contact' (Jensen and Morelli 2011; Jensen, Wind, and Lanng 2012). Such strategic sites are especially interesting since they combine proximity and accessibility (Trip 2007, 39). However, reminding ourselves of Latour's point that *'a technological project is not in a context, it gives itself a context'* (Latour 1996, 133), we should equally seek to understand the 'agency of the train station'. In relation to Nørreport Station this means that there is a more complex coupling and intertwinement than simply a 'dig out' of a train tunnel and the erection of a station building. The station is part of the larger system I term a 'metroscape' and the building complex itself becomes a socio-technical nodal point interfering, 'messing with', and disturbing the site rather than simply 'being put' there. Elsewhere I explored the notion of 'metroscape' as a way to comprehend the material and social complexity of metro mobilities and defined the notion of 'metroscape' as:

> … an umbrella term for the network structures and socio-technical systems which must be in place in order to orchestrate mobilities in the metro. A 'metroscape' is thus to be understood as a mobility 'landscape' consisting of everything from rails and (driverless) train cars to ticket machines and security cameras … This perspective defines urban metroscapes as physical mobility landscapes as well as the codes, rules, and cultural norms that create the active joining of technologies, infrastructures, and social practice … lived mobility in these metro systems are afforded by the assembling of trains, tracks, stations, platforms, elevators, subway personnel, travellers, signs, advertisements, musicians, homeless, police, tickets, ticket machines, power supplies, newsagents, coffee bars, customers, etc. in a complex socio-technical system that creates the lived metro mobility in … (Jensen 2013a, 155-156).

Also it is important not to make a sharp distinction by mode of transport here. The mobile subject moves through the city utilizing multiple modes and tries to construct a seamless route (if the daily commute is the case in point) or she may be off for a more exploratory trip across town. Either way from the point of view of the mobile body, the many systems may be negotiated and operated in different ways, but they all come together in the everyday life that is lived through myriads of interchanging 'mobile situations'. Put differently, people do not experience the city in academic disciplines or municipal jurisdictions. Rather, they move in a continuous series of situations. The metroscapes are in this sense not 'put into the context of the city' (to return to Latour) but they are the city! This point is very clearly understood by Norman Foster when he describes the experience of metro users in the following manner:

> A metro system is an excellent demonstration of how the built environment influences the quality of our lives. The building of tunnels of trains is usually seen in isolation from the provision of spaces for people – even though they are part of a continuous experience for the traveller, starting and ending at street level (Foster 2007, 484).

The way I want to approach the 'metroscapes' and Nørreport Station in particular is obviously in line with the earlier conceptualisation made in chapter five, where I used the notion 'cycling assemblages'. Therefore I will not repeat the theoretical framing of this concept too much here, but only note that the 'metroscape' of Nørreport Station also must be understood in the light of its capacity as a socio-technical system to circulate, filter, and block mobile subjects and artefacts in a complex relationship.

When the 'metroscape' function as a public domain, we may start to think of it as an 'urban commons' (Löfgren 2014) or a public space where multiple different groups meet and mingle. However, if we are facing '100 percent flow' and generic transit designs as in the Copenhagen Metro, then the 'urban' qualities start fading (Jensen 2013a, 161). What is truly interesting about Nørreport is that it works as both a traditional train station hosting all these different users and social groups, as well as containing the Metro with its pure flow design and its deliberate lack of urban programs. This connects to Walzer's distinction between 'open minded' and 'single minded' spaces where he speaks of:

> Single-minded space, designed by planners or entrepreneurs who have only one thing in mind, and used by similar single-minded citizens … open-minded space, designed for a variety of uses, including unforeseen and unforeseeable uses, and used by citizens who do different things … (Walzer 1986, 320).

Importantly the distinction does not simply refer to good or bad. However, if single-minded spaces proliferate, this will take cites on a trajectory that concerned Walzer:

> I don't mean to equate open-minded/single-minded with good/bad. Nothing is so simple: we need not be against airplanes or highways or even fast-food restaurants. Single-minded spaces are sometimes wonderfully convenient … but the reiteration of single-mindedness at one public site after another seems to me something that civilized societies should avoid … (Walzer 1995, 323).

I will use this distinction to point at the interesting mix and potential conflict between the Metro, which is a single-minded space throughout its stations and the wider system, and Nørreport Station, which is more 'messy' and in some respects an open-minded space. Intimately connected to the issue of single-minded or open-minded is the 'question of belonging'. When we look at train stations (or any other mobile site for that matter) we may ask ourselves 'who belongs here?' (Löfgren 2014). How one becomes a legitimate user of the space and its facilities is an interesting perspective and this may often be 'read off' from the materialities and designs at the site. For example, you need to be relatively able and fit to use the platform area of the Metro since there are no benches but only 'leaning devices'. Moreover, the lack of urban programs such as a newspaper stand suggests that you are not meant to go and read your paper on the platform (or at least the 'system' does not afford this by selling newspapers). This is an example of some of the 'mobilities affordances' inscribed into the materiality of the site. Obviously, you may also often find a written code of conduct or regulations physically attached to the station area and these normative pointers for 'correct train station behaviour' are also part of the enrolment into a 'metroscape' as much as are the small and detailed design solutions.

Löfgren conducts a thorough analysis of the Main Train Station of Copenhagen, and I am not able to go into detail about his ethnographically rich and sensitive account of that site. Instead, I borrow elements from his shrewd analysis as, for example, the notion of the 'station as a sensorium' (Löfgren 2014, 8). By this is meant that the train station must be experienced (as well as understood) as a multisensual event. Sight, smell, sound, and touch all come together in composing the 'metroscape' experience and need to be understood in order to explore the meaning of moving within these systems. Smell is, for example, often mentioned as one of the negative characteristics of Nørreport Station (I will return to this later), and leads to the notion of 'smellscape' (as an accompanying term to 'soundscapes' and other 'scapes'). The touch or the 'haptic' is obviously also a key element in the embodied mobilities unfolding in a 'metroscape', as it presents the '*ways people handle the material world of the station'* (Löfgren 2014, 10). Obviously this multisensorial jumble is lived in a holistic and embodied experience, leaving our analytical and theoretical concepts as merely faint shadows of the 'actual experience' but this is the condition of all theoretically informed mobile ethnography.

Edwards describes three spatial levels of transport interchanges: the urban, the building, and the interior. Inside the building envelope he further points at three types of spatial arrangement, namely that of rounded and enclosed spaces, directional but contained spaces, and finally open, linear spaces in direct contact with the mode of transport (Edwards 2011, 28-30). If we add to these categories the distinction Shane makes between the enclave and the armature (Shane 2005), we have a vocabulary for understanding that urban train stations must be understood in their relation to the wider urban fabric. They must be comprehended as architectural buildings that have highly dynamic interiors. As we 'move inside' so to speak, the 'metroscape' nodes may organize the flows of people in different ways according to waiting and staying versus fast transit. The 'metroscape' node thus may work both as an enclave and an armature feeding passengers into the wider system. This is precisely the point with the notion of 'mobile sociopetals' and 'mobile sociofugals' introduced in chapter three. Nørreport station 'draws in' thousands of passengers, visitors, and people occupying the space at the same time as it 'spreads out' these passengers into the wider infrastructural system within its various modes of mobilities. When many transport modes meet in a node, the designer needs to engage in 'three dimensional planning', coordinating and synchronizing the vertical and horizontal dimensions of the circulation systems (Edwards 2011, 51, 68). Edwards draws on a foundational historic reference within architecture in relation to this when he quotes Leon Alberti who, in 1486, allegedly stated that *'the order lies in the plan* [of the building], *but beauty and legibility in the cross-section'* (Edwards 2011, 68). The mobilities design thus needs to be comprehended both in 'plan and section' to account for the complexity of the site. In other words, there are rather large challenges awaiting the 'mobilities designer':

> Design [of interchanges] is, therefore not just a question of utility and function, but that of enhancing public amenity and social value through good-quality spaces, the use of attractive and durable materials, and attention to physical and psychological comfort in all the interchange areas (Edwards 2011, 65).

The contemporary urban train station is very often a multifunctional space with a number of programs (shops, cafés, ticket offices, travel agencies, etc). As Finizio argues: '*In the new planning philosophy, the railway station is a meeting place, a lung for the city, a plaza to stop and spend some time in the comfort of adequate structures, to then start moving again*' (Finizo 2006, 188). The functionality of the transport infrastructure is overlayered with sites and activities of leisure and consumption that create a new hybrid typology (Edwards 2011, 38-39), and which are key to understanding why they have become drivers in urban transformation as well as 'circulation machines'. Edwards sees these new hybrid spaces as 'scenes for the urban drama':

> What makes an interchange exciting is the way this fundamental *theatre* is amplified into ever greater *drama* as the number of connecting transport services increase and hence the flow of people is multiplied (Edwards 2011, 39, italics mine).

This is on par with the *Staging Mobilities* frame and spoken in the language of 'more than A to B'. In Edward's optics, interchanges have the potential to be exciting places of experience as well as mundane 'people movers'. Smith also points to the fact that the development of contemporary transport infrastructures and technologies leads to new architectural typologies as we move 'beyond big' with the new, complex, and hybrid mobility nodes (Smith 2003).

In terms of interesting designs of urban train stations and deeper reflections about the practices related hereto, I want to highlight the work of Sir Norman Foster. Throughout his career, Foster has had a very successful design practice reaching across many different transport modes and complex settings. Foster is interesting both from the point of view of his deep understanding of e.g., the potential of metro stations as social and urban places, but also because he seems to think in metaphors of the 'theatre' and the 'drama' when he 'stages' the flows through the terminals and transit buildings (Foster 2007, 56, 85). Good examples of this are the King's Cross Master Plan in London, the iconic 'tube' station at Canary Wharf in the London Docklands, the Metro of Bilbao, and the King's Cross International Terminal. All these are interesting design solutions catering to the transformative capacity of transit spaces and infrastructures as well as they are illustrative of a profound understanding of these sites as socially and culturally rich and not just instrumental, terminals and nodes (this is perhaps less the case at Canary Wharf). Foster articulates the underlying concepts in this manner:

> I think we [Foster + Partners] are unusual as architects in that we don't see a distinction between architecture and infrastructure, which has traditionally been the domain of the engineer. Given the move toward infrastructure that is more and more inhabited and more in the public domain, I would argue that *the quality of a city's infrastructure affects our lives to a greater extent than the quality of its individual buildings.* Infrastructure has a direct influence on the way that we experience mobility within a city and between cities. That might be the experience walking across a bridge or using a station; or moving from one terminal to another in an airport (Foster 2007, 168, italics mine).

This is precisely the understanding of design, architecture, mobilities, and the city for which I have been arguing from the *Staging Mobilities* perspective. Foster has a profound understanding of the importance of mobilities in a functional sense as well as articulating sensitivity to the culture and sociality that exist within these sites. For example, when Foster designed the Bilbao Metro system, he spoke of the 'poetry and excitement of travel' as a factor equally important to the functional properties of a metro system (Foster 2007, 492). Further, he noticed that *'the Bilbao Metro was conceived to demonstrate that infrastructure of communications has a symbolic importance beyond the function of simply moving people quickly form one place to another'* (Foster 2007, 507). In relation to the earlier discussion of what the 'analytical' disciplines such as sociology and mobilities theory might learn from the 'interventionist' disciplines such as architecture and urban design (Jensen 2013a, chapter nine) I believe Foster's works are a key case in point. Here we actually see the materialisation of mobilities as well as the underpinning concepts and values in a very clear form. It is well known that a sharply defined architectural competition entry actually is less complex than a holistic understanding of a city and its mobilities systems. But the statement on the Bilbao Metro point at the potentials for mobilities research if it engages with architecture and urban design as these disciplines creates 'experiments' on the scale of 1:1, so to speak.

In line with Foster's thinking is the fine and very design-oriented book *'In Search of New Public Domain'* by Hajer and Reijndorp, on which I have drawn from various places for its notion of 'public domain' and how this may come into being in all the 'non-places' and backside spaces of the contemporary city. The book was in fact written precisely to facilitate a discussion of high-speed train stations and their potential for creating new public domains (Hajer and Reijndorp 2001). The book itself is an empirical catalogue of examples of how alleged 'non-places' have the potential to become public domains. As such, their work aligns with the *Staging Mobilities* framing and the 'more than A to B' on a theoretical level; the notion of 'public domain' becomes a key question to explore when studying Nørreport Station.

Case – Nørreport Station

Historically Nørreport was the city gate ('Nørre' refers to 'North' and 'port' means 'gate). Before the city growth spread the urban fabric beyond the fortifications this was already a node and a CPC regulating the in- and out-flow of people and goods in the city. More recently, Nørreport has become one of the busiest train stations in the Greater Copenhagen area and is thus, in many ways, simply the historical prolongation of an already well-established trajectory. The red neon signs with the name 'Nørreport Station' are landmarks and their graphic qualities draw the spectator toward a particular 1940/50s Modernist and functionalist aesthetic.

The mapping at Nørreport Station was conducted by a research assistant on August 23-24, 2011. Maps and diagrams were produced in September 2011 based on accessed material and documentation. Prior to the mapping and field work, a thorough process of deliberation was conducted in order to ensure that the research assistant was in compliance with the theories, methods, and research questions underlying the *Staging Mobilities* framework. The research assistant is an urban designer by education and therefore very skilled in mapping and diagram making. Furthermore, this person was enrolled in the urban design program in the period during which I taught the 'Network City' studio on Nørreport in particular. He therefore had a very detailed insight into the site-specific issues related to the station as well as the architectural competition.

The 'old' Nørreport Station is being rebuilt and reworked by the Municipality of Copenhagen, Danish Rail (DSB), and Banedanmark. The transformation started in 2011 and will run until 2014. The redesign work takes place both on the surface level in the urban spaces as well as below ground. It is a comprehensive operation involving all modes of transport from walking and cycling to regional trains and Metro. The work is the result of the design competition from 2009 where the winning proposal was made by a team comprised of Public Arkitektur, Cobe, Grontmij, and Bartenbach Lichlabor. (For more information on the competition, see www.nynoerreport.dk).

Renovation of the station started after an architectural competition was launched in 2009 and terminates in 2014. My registrations and field work date prior to many of these changes and in this respect what I am looking at is 'old' Nørreport. Interestingly Nørreport Station has been subject to much criticism from its users over the years. Many have complained about smell, noise, and the lack of space, light, etc., in this station, one of the busiest in Denmark. The platform at Nørreport Station is in places very narrow and this, together with lack of space, light and high decible noise, contributes to the sense of confinement and insecurity that may be experienced on the platform. However, during the design competition, the site has had some almost nostalgic rehabilitation from artists, writers, and public intellectuals. It is as if the design competition unfolds a key dilemma where Nørreport Station is both a non-place full of noise, dirt, and confinement at the same time as it is a site of memory and everyday liveability. This is for example the case in the illustrated book '*Nørreport Station*', where the photographer Klaus Holsting has supplemented his many photos with poems and literature by authors, poets, and writers 'narrating Nørreport into existence', as it were (Holsting 2012). In the book, poet Søren Ulrik Thomsen writes:

> To me it is a reflection of Modernity and Western civilisation when I at Nørreport witness how people of any ethnicity mingle, how the impeccable civil servants on their way to the Ministries, busy lawyers and smart 'creatives' from publishing and media houses move frictionless between drug dealers, suburban housewives on shopping, loud drunken high school kinds and homeless hobos with 'fox tails', push carts and crazy dogs (Søren Ulrik Thomsen in Holsting 2012, 18, my translation).

In the book, Nørreport Station is labelled everything from a 'hole in the ground' to a 'dynamo' and a 'gateway' to the city and the world. Copenhageners' memories of childhood and coming of age with Nørreport Station as the 'stage' are plentiful in this book as are the bemoaning of the 'new' and the fear of losing an historic site. However, many authors also find this place intolerable in terms of noise, filth, smell, and diesel pollution. It is as if the plans for reinventing Nørreport Station have triggered all the ambivalences related to this mundane mobilities scene. Many contributions are reflections upon the 'invisibility' of mundane infrastructure spaces like Nørreport Station. The book by Holsting is aesthetically beautiful and full of portraits that cover the isolated commuter, the senseless drunk, as well as the many near-voyeuristic portraits where passengers 'pose' in front of the camera in a rather blunt and self-staged manner. Together with

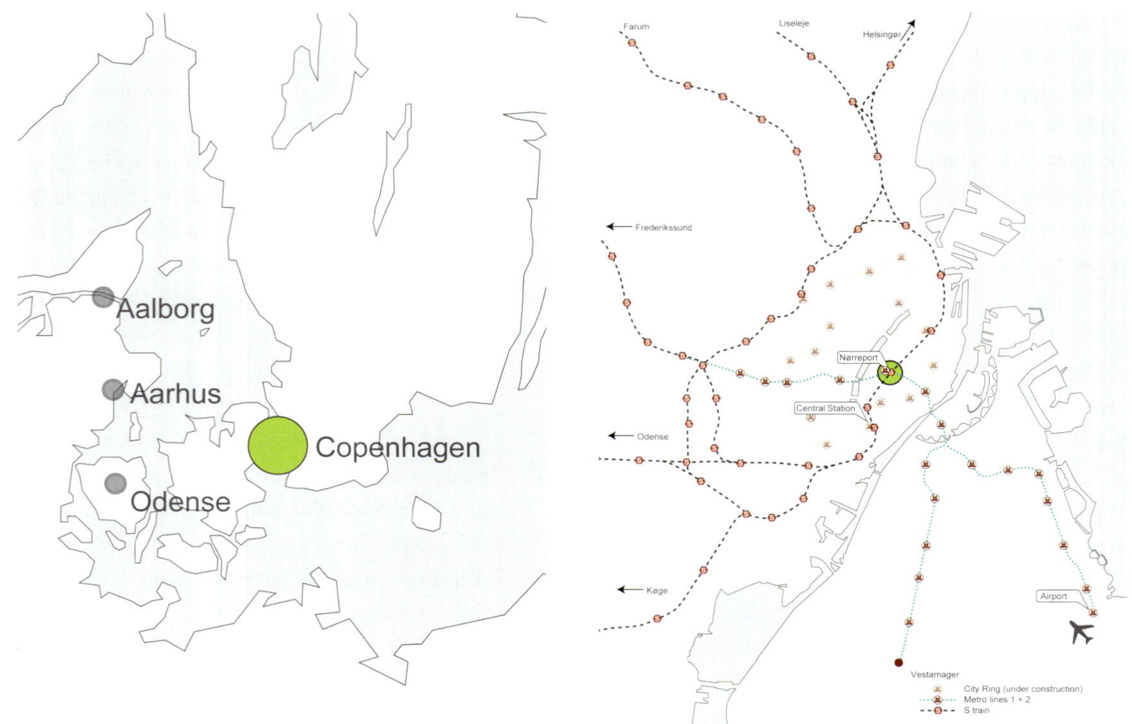

Left: Fig. 6.1: Nørreport and Denmark

Right: Fig. 6.2: Nørreport and Copenhagen

Bottom: Fig. 6.3: Nørreport from above

the concern for loss of 'the old', the book chimes in with the choir of critical voices about the generic design of the Copenhagen Metro that has one of its busiest stations build into Nørreport Station. One author contrasts the generic Metro with the Parisian 'Metro' and its distinct stations as well as its urban buzz. The book is an important artistic documentary on the 'spirit' of Nørreport Station before it changed.

PART 1: The Context

If we start by looking at Nørreport in its national context (fig. 6.1) we notice the centrality of its location in the capital city of Copenhagen. The connectivity of the station can be illustrated by the diagram that shows travel times from Nørreport Station to important nodes in the Copenhagen region as well as to the main cities of Denmark (measured by using the route planner 'Rejseplanen's' web site). The diagram also captures the multimodal character of Nørreport Station.

'Zooming in' we see that Nørreport Station is nested within the network of S-trains and Metro in Copenhagen (fig. 6.2.). In the diagram the S-train and Metro lines are pictured together with the three major nodes of the Central Train Station, Nørreport Station, and Kastrup Airport. Further, we see the planned extension of the Metro system termed the 'City Ring', which is currently under construction.

There are four layers to be taken into account in the analysis to follow: the surface/street level, the regional train platforms, the S-train platforms, and finally the Metro system. These all have their different identities and in particular the regional train platforms have a reputation for being dirty, very crowded, and not very habitable.

PART 2: Nørreport Station

As we get closer to the materiality of Nørreport Station we may start with the photographs of 'Nørreport from above' (fig. 6.3.). Utilizing Photoshop to stitch several images into one, we get a representation of Nørreport Station from the 'river' perspective. The images capture the complexity of the external urban space surrounding Nørreport station and the multimodal character of the site.

Moreover, a characteristic feature of the urban space of Nørreport Station is the relatively solid 'wall' of building facades on both sides of this rectangular urban plaza. Most of the buildings are 5-6 storey buildings with a rather homogeneous aesthetic expression facing the street. Nørreport is as mentioned so-named because it is the 'gate' to the city, and the site connects two rather different urban typologies: the medieval town with narrow streets on the one hand, and the modern city with its wider boulevards on the other. The rectangular square forming the immediate context of Nørreport Station is a busy urban space and very much defined by cars, busses, lorries, cyclists, and pedestrians. The cars are rather dominant even though the large number of people actually is 'handled' by the trains and Metro to which Nørreport is the gateway. The busses mostly run along the edges of the square but have the right to 'cut across' the middle in order to park and load/unload passengers. Given the volume of people moving through this space as pedestrians, cyclists, and drivers, there is a rather hectic atmosphere both at the surface square and in the 'subterranean world below'. A predominant feature of the train station building at Nørreport is that it has been confined to only one storey. Thereby the station is almost dwarfed by the adjacent building volumes, and its visual appearance from the surface level underestimates the huge numbers of transit passengers flowing through its gates on a daily basis.

A walk through Nørreport

As I showed in chapter four on Friis shopping centre, the method of 'serial vision' developed by Gordon Cullen (1996) is useful to get closer to the eye-height perspective of the human body on the move within the stages set for transit. The serial visions made here are illustrative of various routes through the station

Next page:
Fig. 6.4: Serial vision (foot)

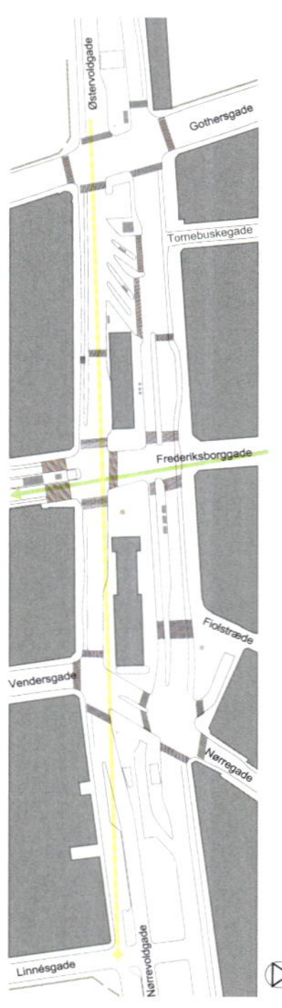
Østervoldgade
Gothersgade
Tornebuskegade
Frederiksborggade
Fiolstræde
Vendersgade
Nørregade
Linnésgade
Nørrevoldgade

8-20 9-18
8-20 8-17

40

area as one approaches it from the adjacent streets and illustrates the arrival to different entrances below street level. The route has been drawn on the plan drawings. The interval of taking photographs has been developed on a discretionary basis, trying in the best possible way to emulate the visual impressions one gets walking through these spaces. The serial visions are therefore examples of the 'ballet' perspective laid down over Nørreport Station. Several serial visions were conducted as part of this research, but due to space constraints I will not utilize here all the serial vision mappings we conducted at Nørreport station.

The first serial vision I present is where the route was made on an East-West axis starting at Østervoldgade at the Gothersgade end, moving alongside the rectangular space in parallel with the train terminal building and the streets, and from the crossing side starting out in Frederiksborggade and crossing the 'terminal island' in the middle (fig. 6.4.).

These two serial visions illustrate the many CPC's of street systems, bike paths, pavements, and various building entrances. Moreover we sense how there are multiple negotiations taking place as one moves through the sites. The street system design is relatively traditional, with a broad sidewalk adjacent to a bike path and then finally, for cars, two lanes of traffic separated in their directionality by the 'terminal island' in the middle. The situation where a person drags two suitcases on wheels out into the bike lane in order to pass by a group of people on the pavement is not unusual and shows quite clearly that this space is rather competitive for its appropriation. The many signs indicating construction work are obviously of a temporary nature, but from years of return visits to this site. In visual terms the legibility of the street space is rather difficult and one has to pay quite some attention to the multiple modes negotiating for passage as one walks through the site. There is a regulatory system imposed from above by the traffic lights that regulate the flow of the whole space, as well as various prohibitory signs that, for example, forbid right turns at certain streets. The speed limit of 40 km/hour is only reached outside the peak hours. Normally the speed of cars passing through this site is much lower than 40 km/h due to massive congestion in the space. As Nørreport Station is a very busy 'hinge' to the rest of the city, many 'mobile withs' are tourists trying to navigate their way through this rather complex space. As elsewhere in Copenhagen, the presence of parked bikes is felt clearly as one walks along the busy streets of the Nørreport Station area.

Opposite:
Fig. 6.5: Serial vision (foot)

Some of the buildings adjacent to the urban space 'reach out' over the pedestrian areas offering shelter but they also seem less secure. In a serial vision made toward the Metro entrance at Frederiksborggade, we see this 'tunnelling effect' of this building feature (fig. 6.5.).

Walking through this underpass and across the street at the pedestrian crossing we see how the stairs and entrance to the Metro are both a wide horizontal entrance space, but also a rather narrow vertical one. As one moves down the stairs it is actually not possible to see what sort of site one is walking into. As this is a daylight serial vision, the train station entrance to which we walk down seems like a 'black whole' in the ground. This is obviously different at night time due to the illumination of the subterranean spaces that gives much more visual information about the space below. The staircase on this serial vision is as mentioned fairly wide, but with the characteristic 'low ceiling entrance' that is less appealing and works against key principles and ideas of legibility. The staircase material is concrete as is the rest of the Metro system below; we find a two-lane separation by a fence in the middle almost intuitively leading people to walk down and up on the right-hand side. There are no signs specifying this as a regulated practice, but I assume that the 'walk to the right side' practice followed by many (not all) is due to the wider system of right-hand side driving of the national traffic systems in Denmark. During rush

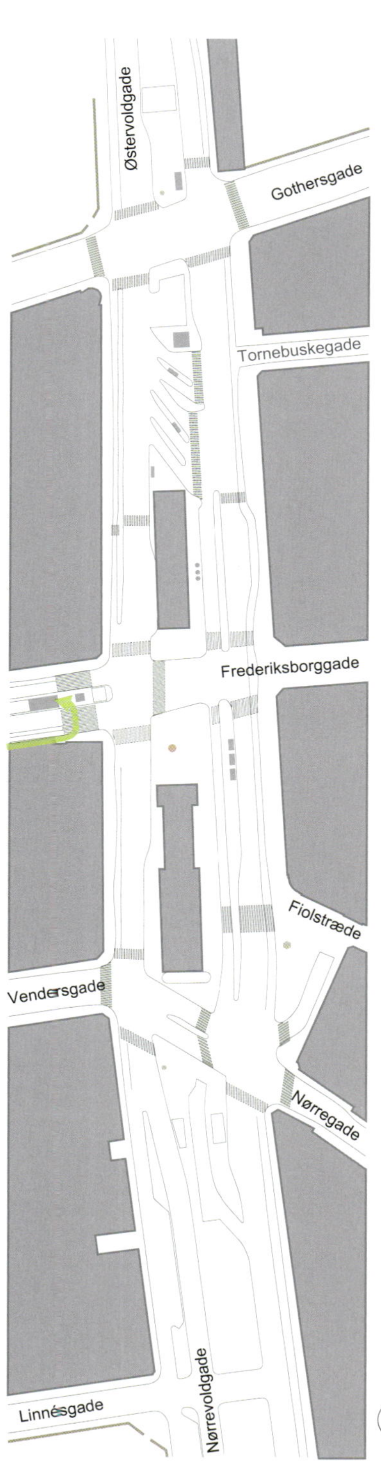

Østervoldgade
Gothersgade
Tornebuskegade
Frederiksborggade
Fiolstræde
Vendersgade
Nørregade
Linnésgade
Nørrevoldgade

LINNÉSGADE
18-14

EDC Poul Erik Bech
Nørreport
matas

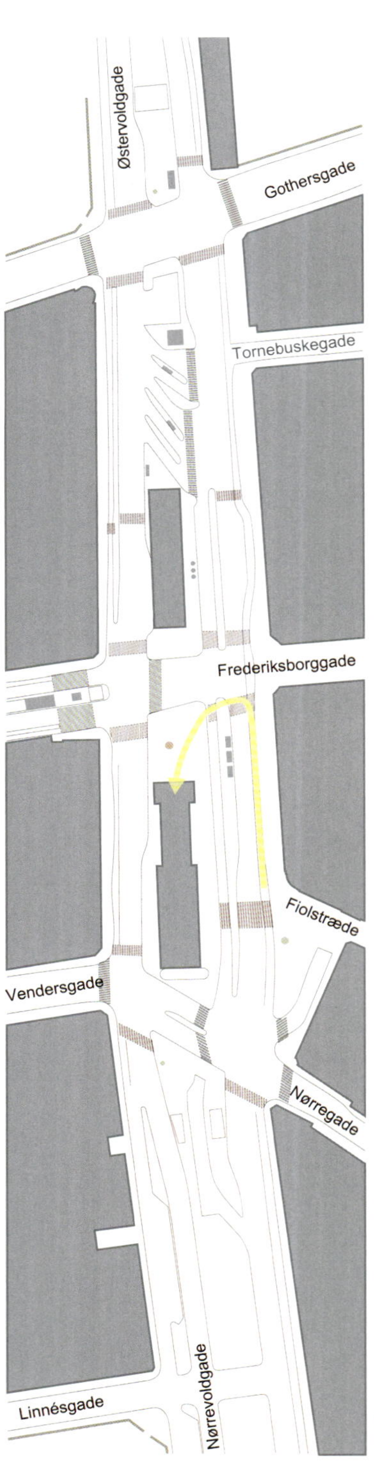
Østervoldgade
Gothersgade
Tornebuskegade
Frederiksborggade
Fiolstræde
Vendersgade
Nørregade
Linnésgade
Nørrevoldgade

Bank

FONA
FONA

Nørreport
Station

hour the divergence from this system by a few people puts the whole smooth operation in jeopardy. (Below in the Metro, there are signs directing passengers to stand to the right and walk to the left when using the escalators).

One serial vision on bike was conducted. The bike serial vision is made from Fiolstræde and onto the entrance of the train station at the centre of the 'terminal island' (fig. 6.6.). Several things spring to mind here. One is the complex and almost messy negotiation of various modes of mobilities: there is a car in the middle of a pedestrian crossing and a cyclist driving there as well (a very widespread but illegal biking practice in Denmark).

The serial vision also clearly illustrates the challenge posed to finding enough space for bike parking. (This was actually one of the key dimensions of the architectural competition for the 'new' Nørreport.) But what is evident from this serial vision is also the presence of commerce and consumption. Entering the train terminal under the big clock we pass a flower shop out in the open space as well as the 'Seven-Eleven' shop selling coffee, newspapers, and fast food. At the entrance we pass people 'hanging out' either in terms of what looks as though they are waiting for someone, or more idle types just watching the flow go by. Very often this is also the entrance where homeless people sell their magazine *Hus Forbi* (an equivalent to the *Big Issue* in the United Kingdom). At this entrance one find shelter from the rain when one is not 'below' in the system. The entrance is a key CPC and filters many people in transit. The paving in this area is also conspicuous as the choice of cobblestones in the pavement gives the station entrance a rather traditional ambience. Finally, when we move below the old stair entrance, the train station is very different from the one we saw in the previous serial vision (leading to the Metro). The dimensioning is much the same in width, but since it is shorter both the steepness and the legibility in terms of letting its users see 'what is at the end' are very different. Sheltered by a ceiling but with big transparent windows, the entrance to this part of the station building seems much more welcoming and light than the one we saw at the Metro entrance.

One serial vision was made by car, and this mainly illustrates the fact that the existing car spaces are rather dominant but also that the train station area I termed the 'terminal island' is relatively isolated from the 'sea of cars' surrounding it (fig. 6.7.).

There are of course lanes dedicated to dropping off and picking up passengers by cars, but the main interaction between the train station and motor vehicle is through the bus-train interface. In other words, Nørreport as an urban space is full of cars, but Nørreport Station is actually not interfacing with too many cars. The modal change is predominantly from bike, foot, and bus to train and vice versa.

The pedestrians fill up the space according to all indicators I have viewed. Here, for a start, I want to show one serial vision that visualizes a person coming out of the Metro and moving onward through the platform system (fig. 6.8.). In this very short sequence of images we get a sense of the 'space of processing' below ground level and in particular how this person is 'being processed' by the 'system'.

I have chosen to include this serial vision since the person being 'shadowed' actually is texting on a mobile phone while being processed. First of all this is by no means unusual, but is a very common sight in today's urban transit systems across the world. But what I find compelling about this short sequence is precisely the mundane and routine way in which the person inhabits the system. Clearly she notices other mobile subjects, the potential conflicts of intersecting trajectories, the door entrances, and the routes being 'carved out' for her either in the material layout of the platform widths or the multiple subtle openings and closings of 'routes' through the 'sea of people' through which this

Opposite:
Fig. 6.6: Serial vision (bike)

Next page:
Left: Fig. 6.7: Serial vision
Right: Fig. 6.8: Serial vision (train)

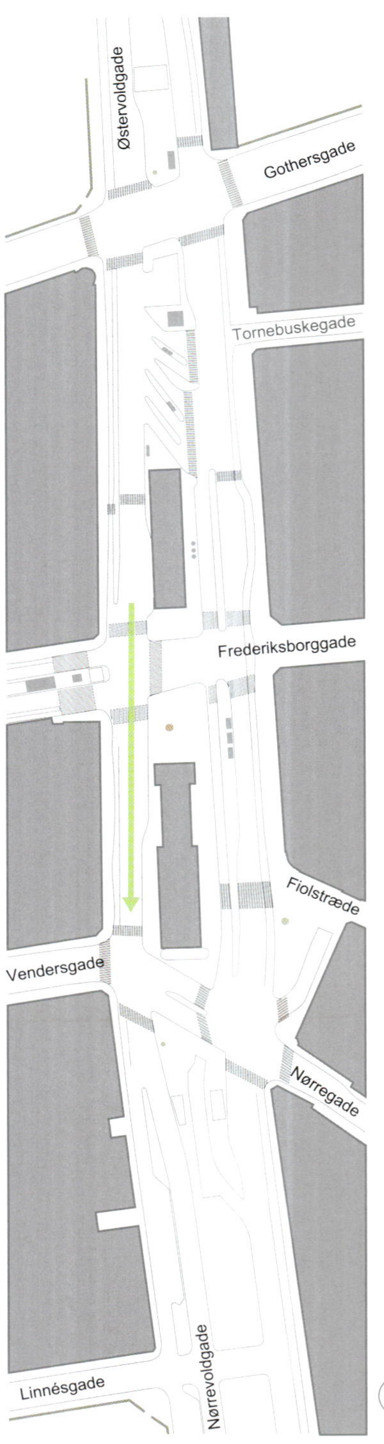
Østervoldgade
Gothersgade
Tornebuskegade
Frederiksborggade
Fiolstræde
Vendersgade
Nørregade
Linnésgade
Nørrevoldgade

Østervoldgade
Gothersgade
Tornebuskegade
Frederiksborggade
Fiolstræde
Vendersgade
Nørregade
Linnésgade
Nørrevoldgade
Udgang
Christianshavn

person seems to flow in a rather seamless manner. The presence of the mobile phone in this situation thus points at the way a transit interchange hosts many other practices than simply transport. (Whether she is working, organizing a night out with friends, or checking the stock market is unknown). The situation also speaks to the fact that as we move through the complex transport networks of the contemporary city, we 'carry networks' with us. In a complex manner we are both immersed in the transit network as well as carrying communications networks that challenge the simple distinctions between the material and the digital realm, and between and the near and far away. The small serial vision here gives clues to a new understanding of how the mobile subject inhabits transit spaces and what it means to be on the move in the city.

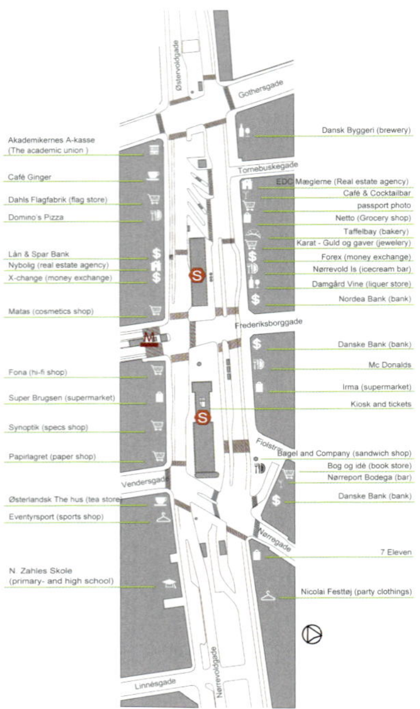

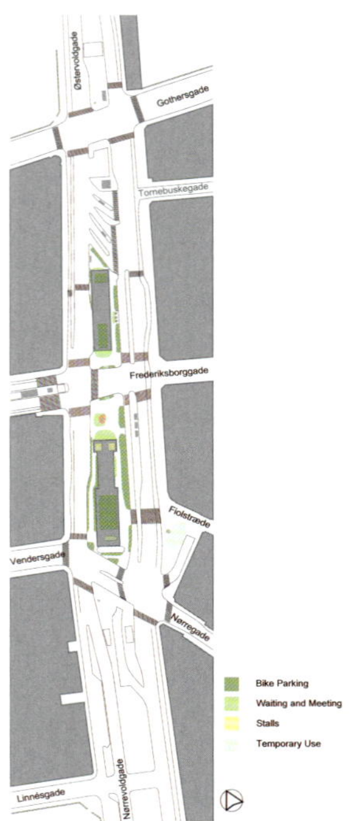

Top: Fig. 6.9: Functions

Bottom: Fig. 6.10: Zones of use

From these serial visions let me turn to the organization and functionality of Nørreport station or the 'programming of the site' as is the architectural and urban design nomenclature. A fine way of capturing the complexity of Nørreport Station and the area surrounding it is to show the various urban 'programs' of the site on a map (fig. 6.9.). From this diagram it becomes quite evident that we are in a complex setting in which we engage with many commercial and urban activities.

The diagrams illustrate why most people coming through Nørreport station experience this as busy and 'urban'. Moreover, when read in a barcode-like manner (i.e., reading all the programs and functions from top to bottom), the sense of diversity and multiplicity of the site also become tangible. Side-by-side are real estate agents, cafes, grocery stores, banks, old-fashioned bodegas, new cafes, bakeries and much, much more.

In addition to mapping the individual programs of the site, we may also take a look at the 'zones of use'. Here I am in particular thinking about the zones of use related to transit and mobilities. In figure 6.10 we see the four types of activities: bike parking, waiting and meeting stalls, and temporary use mapped onto the site map.

To add to this diagram's rather abstract representation, I propose the following photos illustrating precisely bike parking, waiting and meeting, the stalls, and various forms of temporary use (fig 6.11.). In particular I find the latter category important as a window into the multiplicity and multifunctionality of a public space such as Nørreport Station. The mobile subjects in these images utilize the sites and spaces for various activities and practices and thereby illustrate that they are 'dwelling-in-motion' as much as anything else. We see people meeting in face-to-face interaction, people talking on the phone while sitting on the curbs and edges that were not designed for this specific activity (in fact, not for any activity). Someone is eating, and there is a group of people waiting but also tending to a youngster and seemingly having a close small-group interaction within this buzzing and rather congested space.

Next to the zones of use and the practices, we note the entrances as a general category. These are of particular interest since they are the CPCs of the terminal building complex (fig. 6.12.). Here I have chosen entrances that all, furthermore, mediate surface and below-surface levels.

As mentioned before, the Metro entrances are distinctly different from the other entrances (the S-train platform and regional platform). They are smoother in their surfaces and there are no open gazes to other elements, urban furniture or objects as one moves up and down the stairs. (On the other hand, the entrances to the S-train and regional train with their transparent fences give the person visual clues as he/she rides up or a smoother transition descending to the system underground).

Right: Fig. 6.11: Zones of use

1 - Regional platform

2 - S-tog platform

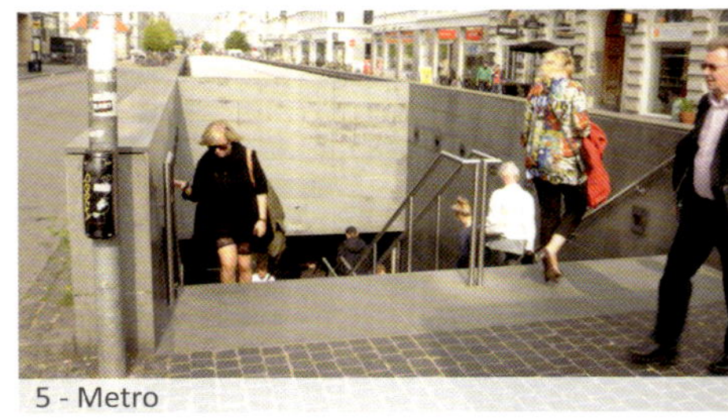
5 - Metro

3 - S-tog and regional platforms

4 - S-tog platform

5 - Metro

Fig. 6.12: Entrances

Before I move below ground and into the systems, I would like to point to another architectural and urban design tool and term, namely the 'spatial structure' diagram (fig. 6.13.). In technical terms the diagram shows a three-dimensional modelling of the station and train platforms. It is generated on the basis of technical drawings from Copenhagen Municipality and the model is made in '*SketchUp*' and thereafter exported into '*Illustrator*' to be collared. In the collage of diagrams we see the layered systems of S-train, regional trains, and Metro that are the key to the interchange and the CPC functionality of Nørreport Station. The diagram is deliberately kept at a rather simplistic level of detail. As such it is, of course, an abstraction. If I were to bring a diagram illustrating the 'true conditions' of this subterranean space, there would be so many cables, wires, tubes, and pipes that the overview of the station would vanish completely. The complex layered utility networks of power, water, sewers, gas and much else that exists below surface level in the contemporary city is truly amazing and merits a study of its own. (See Ascher 2005 for a beautiful story of this infrastructure complexity.)

What is immediately clear is the design decision to have the three trains systems linked but yet still clearly demarcated and separated. Perhaps it is too much of a birds-eye view abstraction to state that the systems are 'clearly demarcated and separated' since many users find the navigation within the station and, in particular, between the three train systems rather difficult and complicated. However, there is some truth to the claim that the three systems are demarcated and separated. If the diagram of the spatial structure is looked at carefully, we see that the regional trains move into the station at the mid-level with their own dedicated platforms. On top of this we find the S-train level with yet another dedicated platform level. Finally the late-coming Metro system is 'added on' orthogonally to the old S-train and regional train system and is placed at

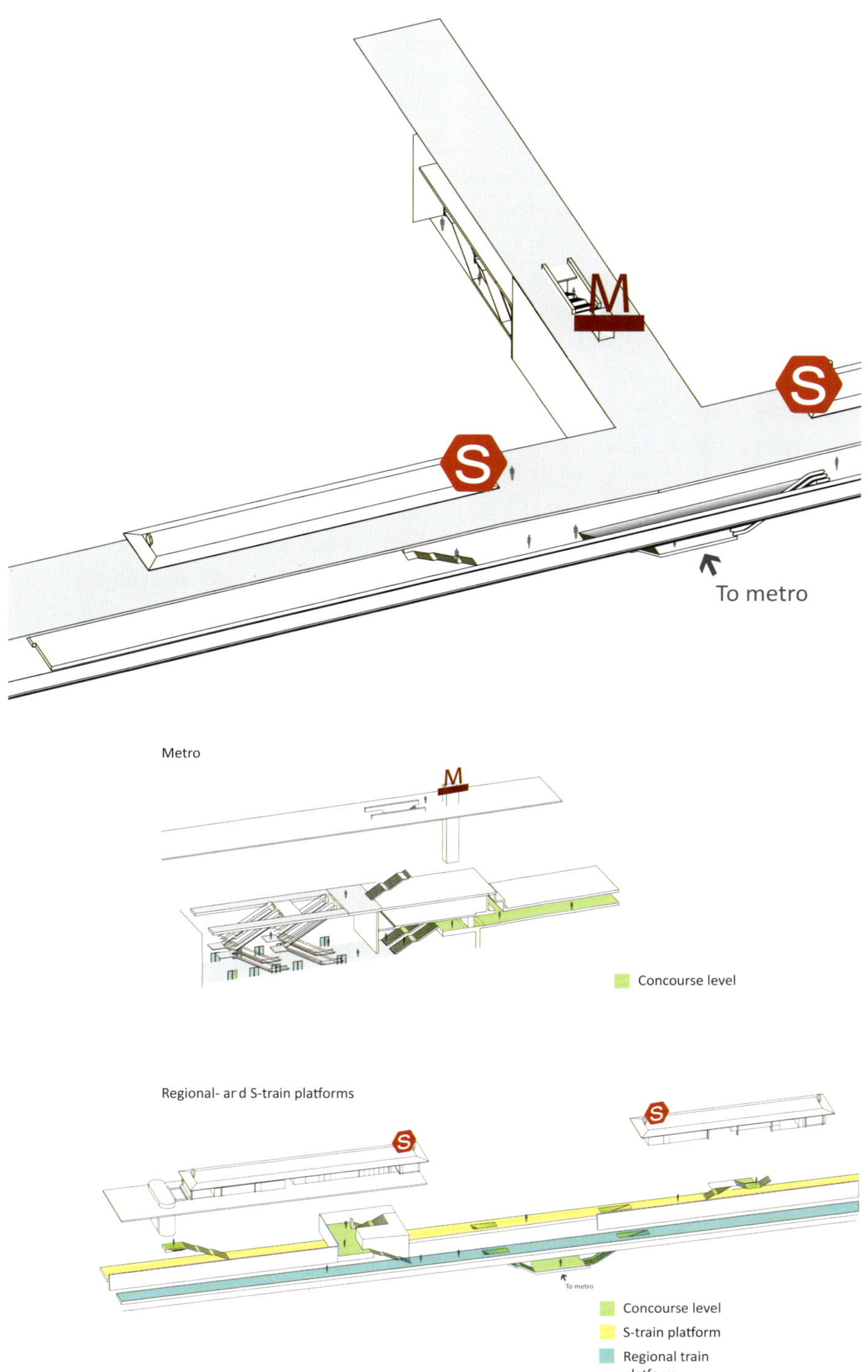

Fig 6.13: Spatial Structure

the lowest level of the three systems. This systematic should in principle give a clear sense of dedication and individuality to the three systems meeting in the CPC of Nørreport Station (and it is also an important functional requirement). The Metro furthermore has its own entrance from the street level and is coupled to the other systems below ground. This rational principle of organizing the station's functionality might be an adequate answer to the mobilities design challenge at Nørreport Station. (Merging a new mode into an existing station with two other train systems is a big challenge.) But the experience of the mobile subject moving within the system is much more tied to notions of chaos, confusion, disorientation, and lack of legibility.

Given the fact that the situational mobilities and the experiences of the mobile subject are central concerns, I want to turn to one of the absolute key issues: 'navigating Nørreport'. The following diagrams capturing the complexity of navigating Nørreport are a cross section of a large number of situational mappings and thus not a serial vision following one particular mobile subject (fig. 6.14.). Instead, what I have tried to capture with the series of images is the complexity of semiotic systems, material armatures (stairs, paths, and platforms), and different ambiences that meet the mobile subjects in the 'belly' of this huge machine for people processing.

Some of the images almost speak for themselves in terms of the dark, rather gloomy, and spatially confined character of the armature (a particular feature of the regional train platforms). Some illustrate the different processes of wayfinding and navigating, at times utilizing the signage systems and at other times the traffic information systems. The images illustrate the single mobile subject well aware of his or her route and trajectory through the system, as well as the many 'mobile withs' often deeply engaged in making sense of the system and figuring out where to go. Navigating Nørreport is a complex endeavour and the interlocking and interchange of three different systems into one CPC is a challenge, but is also a window into the fact that even within this rational machine of mobilities design much more than simple physical movement takes place.

As mentioned earlier, the metaphor of the 'river' is adequate for the analysis of larger flows of anonymous people. The images here are taken from above to illustrate the 'channelling capacity' of the armatures (fig. 6.15.). What we see here are the designed and dedicated flow channels in which people move by muscular power (walking) as well as by machine power (the escalator and the Metro itself). There are signs encouraging people to 'stand to the right, and walk to the left' in those cases where the speed of the escalator is not sufficient for busier mobile subjects. There are no scripted rules for the ordinary staircases specifying such a 'mobilities differential' based on speed, but in general people tend to walk on the right hand side as seen in the upper right image. This is probably due to the wider cultural context of 'right-hand side driving' and should actually be different given the fact that the Danish traffic regulations generally tell pedestrians to walk on the left-hand side in order for them to be able to see right-hand side vehicle drivers approaching them. However, the 'culture of right side movement' that, legally speaking, is for motor vehicles only seems to have a more hegemonic status and de facto also regulates the movement among pedestrians.

If we look more closely at the four images showing a stream of travellers entering a Metro compartment, we see explicitly one of the key CPCs of the Metro system, namely, the doors for entering and exiting the carriage. The doors are automatic and will only open when the train has come to a stop on the platform. Interestingly, though, it has been necessary to draw up lines of demarcation differentiating the entering passengers from the exiting, which will be seen as the white stripes on the pavement. Even though it is a general and global practice to let people out before new passengers can step in, it has been found necessary

Opposite:

Top and lower left:
Fig. 6.14: Navigating Nørreport

Lower right:
Fig. 6.15: The 'river' through Nørreport

1 2

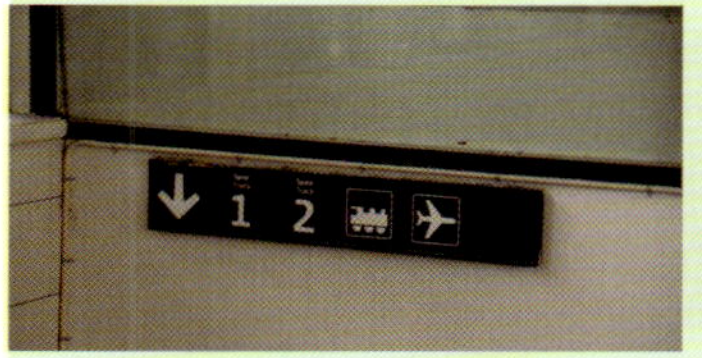
1 2

学丹麦语-选
Where you'll learn Danish
حتى تتعلم الدنماركية
ia

Metro
S 3 4

to inscribe the environment in semiotic terms in order to ensure that exiting travellers may have adequate space for exit before the inflow starts. From the images one can almost feel the pressure of the 'river' as the exiting people move out of the doorway and the stream starts to flow in.

The twin metaphor to the 'river' was the 'ballet' and in image 6.16. I shift to this perspective (fig. 6.16). The images have been recorded at a crucial intersection in the station building at its western main entrance. Here people walking down and up the Metro stairs have to negotiate the space with passengers from the S-train (the staircase with the posters). Due to the lack of visibility as well as the practice of 'cutting corners' in order to minimize the walking distance, many people have to stop and literally negotiate face-to-face in order to move through the space without physical interaction and touching. In particular this is noticeable with the male wearing a white shirt and dark coat. As he walks up the stairs we can see in frame three that he not only stops but also makes a slight rightwards sidestep (notice the outward pointing of his right foot) in order not to collide with the gentleman coming down the stairs.

Fig. 6.16: The 'ballet' at Nørreport

However, other techniques of the 'ballet' are present as well. This is the case with the man wearing a green cap. He seems deliberately to choose the 'long route' as opposed to the man 'cutting the corner'. The two persons are actually moving in the same direction from the surface level and further down, but the latter has chosen a technique that will lead him into fewer face-to-face negotiations than the former. It may be hard to tell from these images, but I would say that the 'corner cutting' person is in a greater hurry than the person taking the longer route. One dimension of the 'ballet' perspective that I have not looked at in much detail here is the swift and mutual 'read off' and social placing of the person one meets head on in this system. As I explained elsewhere (Jensen 2013a, chapter 7), it makes a big difference whether one meets a single woman, two big men, or someone with earplugs and a cap. Actually the gentleman with the green cap and earplugs seem to have chosen a technique for minimal involvement in general if we start to consider both the trajectory of his movement and the 'cocooning devices' (earplug and cap) that make a withdrawal from potential interaction more likely.

In a complex hub like Nørreport Station, signage in general and the theme of 'mobile semiotics' in more specific terms becomes inevitable. Nørreport Station is host to different mobility systems and is the facilitator of their intersection so the legibility of the environment is of course crucial (and is one of the key problems with the 'old' Nørreport Station). However, rarely is a complex infrastructure hub capable of communicating its functionality to the users without any signage, wayfinding, or traffic information system. And this is also the case for Nørreport Station where we find all sorts of signs and semiotic systems. (fig. 6.17).

On the semiotic sample of signs, the ones with green framing are from the S-train and regional train system whereas the images with the purple frame are from the Metro. One of the most iconic signs in the whole of Copenhagen's traffic system is the red hexagon with the white 'S' that is found in the public spaces wherever there is an S-train station. The sign is seen in the upper left image and is instantly recognizable and of an iconic status. Not being from Copenhagen I remember that, when I visited the city as a child, these signs were key markers and indicators of Copenhagen. (No other Danish town has this particular sign.) Additionally, the public space is marked by the traditional infrastructure timekeeper, the clock. Next to city halls and churches, train stations have always been marked by such timekeeping devices. This is partly as a service to the passengers in need of information about how they are doing on time in relation to particular journeys or itineraries. But as with churches and public buildings, a visible clock becomes a sign of centrality and wider urban coordination. This is also the case at Nørreport Station. The wayfinding system of the S-train and regional trains is of the general design code that Danish Rail (DSB) applies to all its stations. The icons of trains and planes as well as arrows and platform numbers seen in the upper right are all inscribed into the semiotic grammar and design manual of DSB. If we move toward the Metro this is slightly different. It is a much newer system that, despite its many intersection points with the wider transport system, has established its own design manual and signage system. Like the S-train sign the Metro has a red 'M' as the iconic landmark sign. This is placed mostly on large metal cylinders outside the stations but is also present within the stations as we see in the sign saying 'Nørreport' with the 'M' incorporated on top. The font of the travel information system and the signs are unique to the Metro and are consistently implemented into the semiotic environment, adding coherence and a sense of a comprehensive design philosophy. Real-

Fig. 6.17: Signage

time signage also informs travellers about the next departures of the Metro; the ticket machines, litter baskets, and maps all carry the unique logo of the Metro system. The underpinning philosophy seems to be that everything within the Metro is designed in accordance to the original design manual, but also that the stations and trains should look similar regardless of where one encounters them. (This principle is being challenged slightly with the new 'City Ring').

PART 3: The Metro

Now I 'zoom in' on the Metro in particular. I focus on the system and its design here since the most detailed of my mobile situation studies are conducted within the Metro (fig. 6.18).

As mentioned elsewhere (Jensen 2012a, 2013a) the Metro in Copenhagen is rather unique in its modernistic design and very coherent design code. The outcome is a 'circulation machine' with driverless train technology and identical station design that operates a high-frequency service. I am interested in the design issues so the more political and economic issues will be bypassed here. For a start we may note a little practical information on the Metro taken from the Metro Company's yearly report of 2009 (Metroselskabet 2009). The history of the Metro is connected to the development of the Ørestad project, which was a New Town development project at Amager in Copenhagen conceived in the late 1980s. Space prevents me from laying out the genealogy of the project, but the key idea was to sell land for urban development and thereby provide revenue for a metro to Copenhagen. This, however, did not happen in a straightforward manner and remains a major discussion in the history of Danish urban planning. (See the very positive account by City of Copenhagen 2003 or the highly critical account in Skovmand 2000). The Metro is co-owned by the Danish Government (41.7%), the Municipality of Copenhagen (50%), and the Municipality of Frederiksberg (8.3%).

At this writing, the Metro is facing a new development phase as the so-called 'City Ring' is being built, which adds coverage and capacity to the system (as well as engendering much criticism in relation to the construction sites and related impacts on the environment). The new 'City Ring' will open in 2018 so here I focus on the existing Metro system. The Metro system has a length of 21 km with 22 stations and 34 trains. It carries over 50 million passengers per year and runs as a completely driverless system on a 24-hour, 7 day-a-week basis. The average speed (including stops) is 40 km/h and the technical system is provided by the Italian train manufacturer Ansaldo. The architectural design was done by the Danish company KHR Architects. According to the Metro company itself, they have a 'timeless' and generic design for all stations and trains. The fact that many of the stations are designed with natural daylight is said to help make passengers feel more secure when the effect of daylight counteracts the feeling of being 20-30 feet below ground (fig. 6.19).

The Metro Company highlights the presence of daylight as a character trait that gives the Metro an atmosphere of an urban space. The Metro is, as mentioned, a driverless train system whose station design system is termed a 'cut and cover' system. In popular terms this means that a 'box' is dug out for and then submerged and covered. This has the obvious advantage that the Metro Company can operate with highly standardized and thus cost-effective solutions. This is also related to another general design principle, which is described as 'more of the same'. This means that all trains, stations, and platforms are identical in their construction, materials, and designs. This leads to a very cohesive and clear aesthetics and a rational management of resources (though it is also a point of criticism in connection with the discussion of identity-less and generic design).

One of the key features of the Metro design is its comprehensive and coherent design manual that takes

Above:
Fig. 6.18: The Metro

Below:
Fig. 6.19: Architecture and Design

into account accessibility for disabled passengers and the seamless operation of the system (fig. 6.20). The design solutions at the CPCs where passengers enter and exit the trains are provided with raised markings on the surface that help blind people to navigate and orient themselves. The system runs with a joint feature of lifts and escalators that providing accessibility to push carts and wheel chairs. It is also possible to bring a bike into the Metro but outside rush hour only. (The S-trains have dedicated bike compartments and offer a more fully developed service to cyclists.)

In general terms one might say that the various design solutions support the Metro Company's vision of merging functionality and simplicity with a mixture of Italian and Scandinavian design. Detailing in terms of aesthetics and materiality is, as mentioned, very coherent and all details are taken care of (fig. 6.21). The white lines of demarcation between entering and exiting passengers might be thought of as less aesthetic and more of a necessary functional solution, but, for example, the way daylight hits the angled hand rails, creating reflections of the 'upper world', speaks to a high degree of detail orientation and coherent design rationality.

Even though the Metro is a high-frequency train system, there needs to be space designed for staying and waiting. Here there is less help for the tired and disabled. The key feature for tired passengers is the 'leaning devices' that people lean against and which senior citizens often bemoan as poor substitutes for benches (fig. 6.22). Those able to do so might simply sit on surfaces not designed for resting or occupancy, such as the sides of the escalators.

The critique of not catering to those waiting is countered by the Metro Company with a reference to the fact that a new train will be arriving within a few minutes, thus deeming benches superfluous artefacts within this

Fig. 6.20: Accessibility

perfect circulation machine. I will return to the social stratifications and the exclusionary consequences of these design decisions when I look at the specific mobile situations in the next section. But suffice it to say that the lack of benches and other types of urban furniture is a reflection of a design rationale that aims at keeping people moving and not allowing people to occupy the Metro for more sedentary purposes such as hanging out, sleeping, or socializing (the case in many other metro systems all over the world).

PART 4: Metro Users

As part of this wider examination of how mobilities design affords particular practices and how mobile situations are acted out within systems, I want to turn to the Metro users (fig. 6.23). Here I explore how the mobile situations of the Metro are staged within the threefold analytical framework of material design, social interaction, and embodied performances from the *Staging Mobilities* model.

As I get closer to the staged mobile situations of the Metro users, I also need to balance what might be perceived as a very positive and uncritical analysis of the coherent Metro design that was discussed earlier. I do believe the design code is coherent and that nothing is left to chance in the design of the Copenhagen Metro, but this does not mean that social exclusion and 'mobility differentials' are not being made apparent. There is a clear tactic embedded into the design code to exclude 'unwanted' citizen groups (e.g., homeless people sleeping, drug dealers dealing, young people congregating, etc.). In addition to the 'standard' order-keeping technologies such as CCTV and 24/7 surveillance, the Metro manages the exclusion of such groups in a very subtle manner. A case in point is the so-called 'leaning devices' that substitute for the benches that otherwise would have afforded space for both sleeping and hanging out by various groups. The design manual and code thus embed both a functional rationale for maximum flow, as well as carrying a

Left:
Fig. 6.21: Aesthetics and materiality

Right:
Fig. 6.22: Design for Stay

value base of nonaffordance for 'unwanted' people and practices. The 'mobilities differentials' created by the Metro system thereby, in a rather subtle manner, connect the flow aspirations with the control and power interests of the Metro system. Also the '100 percent flow' design rationale means that the Metro as a 'single-minded space' underutilizes a number of potentials that could help it become a more urban and vibrant space (e.g., shops, staying areas, and public domain). These effects are by no means either neutral or coincidental. Rather they are manifestations of a particular way of staging mobilities from above that has very tangible results.

Here as elsewhere in any transit system there are people waiting. The practice of waiting might be thought of as 'wasted time', a necessary evil and second-order activity compared to the 'real reason' for being at a transit site. Needless to say, we do not find people in the Metro for the sheer joy of the architecture or the ambience of the environment. Having said that, however, practices such as waiting should not be neglected and underestimated when it comes to making sense of mobilities. We might not like waiting, but it is a significant practice that influences the way we understand ourselves and our environment (socially as well as physically). In other words, the mobile practice of waiting in transit is a fine illustration of the mantra said here quite often: there is more to mobilities than moving from A to B! So even though the individual traveller might prefer to move seamlessly from one mode of transport to another, the practice of waiting is a fact of life and influences the social fabric and the cultures of mobilities. Here I have chosen a small selection of waiting Metro travellers, and I want to make a point of observing these, dependent upon whether they are alone or in a group. The latter falls within the category of 'mobile withs'. As we see in the selection of individual waiting travellers (fig. 6.24) there are different ways to pass time. Reading a newspaper, a book, or looking at one's mobile phone are all rather common waiting practices. Second to these, the individual traveller seems occupied with what most people in public spaces hold to be the main interest: other people. From our observations it is clear that looking at other people and thus the 'small dramas of mobile everyday life' is one of the key activities of the waiting traveller. Even though the instrumental non-place discourse of transit spaces tries to lure us into thinking that 'nothing' happens here, quite a few things indeed take place in these everyday sites of mobile situations.

Opposite top page:
Fig. 6.23: Metro users

Opposite bottom page:
Fig. 6.24: Waiting (alone)

I mentioned that people waiting in the Metro did not go there to soak up the aesthetics or behold the beauty of the architecture. However, people do notice their environments (to various degrees) and an illustration of this is the woman in the image on the lower right hand side. Clearly she is gazing upwards toward the ceiling at the prisms catching and distributing the daylight. Gazing up gives the space a cathedral-like sensation and I think one clearly senses that from this image. Obviously, multiple other activities may be observed. But what I find of particular interest is the relationship between the waiting body and the material environment. Almost all the images illustrating the waiting individual passengers show bodies placed in close proximity to walls or other solid surfaces, creating the waiting behaviour of 'edging'. By this I mean the tendency for most waiting people to position themselves adjacent to physical objects and surfaces in order to get a sense of security and control that is a primal and unconscious concern for animals of all sorts (Hall 1966; Lawson 2001; Sommer 2007). There are, of course, individuals who position themselves in the middle of the platform space such as, for example, the woman gazing upward. In this particular case, that is explainable because there is a better view upward when moving a little away from the edges of the space. Normally the practice of positioning oneself in the middle of the platform space is reserved for peak travel times, when people simply have to utilize the surface space in the middle of the platform in order to find a space for waiting.

FULDKORN

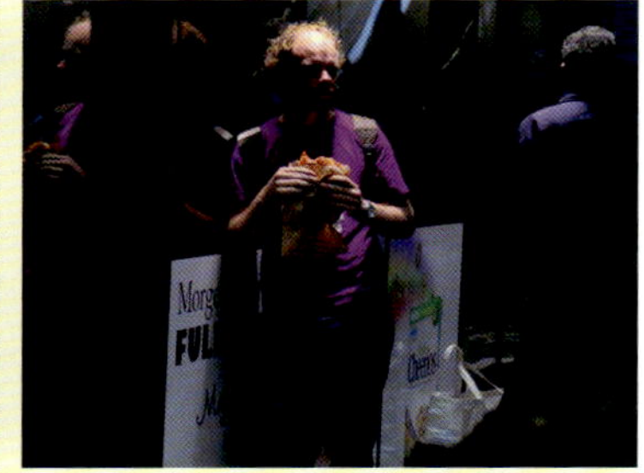

Cheerios

FULDKORN

If we extend the perspective from the waiting individual to the waiting group, we start to explore the more dynamic properties of situational mobilities of which a 'mobile with' is an expression. In the selection here we have both small groups in pairs as well as larger parties (fig. 6.25). There are also situations represented where the determination of the 'group boundary' and thus ultimately figuring out 'who belongs to the group?' might be hard to decide. For example, it seems as if the group in the lower left image may have some interactional dynamics, judging from their facial and bodily orientations. However, the distance between the bodies also indicates that this may not be a socially tight 'mobile with' but perhaps more likely one of ephemeral 'temporary congregations' where the people in question might simply be exchanging information about the destination of the next train or some other fleeting travel condition.

The same can be said about the people in the lower right image even though the bodily distance is more distinct and they are a 'temporary congregation' brought together by standing in front of the automatic doors around which they all gather. As mentioned before, the situations related to entering and exiting the train, and thus the functionality of the doors in assembling 'mobile withs' into 'temporary congregations', stand out quite clearly in these images. The close body proximity of the 'mobile with' in the upper left indicates two good friends or even family members as the distance of embodied encounter here crosses the line of intimacy. We also see by the facial orientation of this particular 'mobile with' that they are passing time by engaging in the popular activity of looking at other fellow travellers. Rather different is the 'mobile with' depicted in the image on the upper right. This is clearly not a standard commuting group, as the presence of luggage indicates travellers on some longer trip. These might be tourists or at least people less familiar with the Metro, as they seem to gaze slightly uneasily to the sides. The placement of this particular 'mobile with' is interesting because it is rather central at the platform level but also just below the escalators. This placement is not the most obvious choice for people very familiar with the Metro as it brings them out of the immediate reach of the train doors; it also seems to suggest that they are not only waiting but perhaps also trying to figure out more elaborate issues related to their journey.

Somewhat overlapping the theme and issue of waiting are the themes of staying and resting. The people in the following images may be said to be waiting as well (fig. 6.26). I have, however, singled these out since they appropriate the spaces and engage with the materiality of the design in more sedentary ways (or simply put, they sit or lean in order to relax).

The images of resting travellers are illustrations of the point discussed earlier about the lack of benches and other types of urban furniture. The Metro Company might not have designed many objects catering to the travellers' urge to rest, but nevertheless people seem to figure out solutions to this for themselves. Sitting on the edges of escalators is the most popular and obvious alternative to the so-called 'leaning devices'. There is actually one example of a rather rare resting position, which is the image at the lower left. Here a passenger has actually transformed the 'leaning device' into a bench proper by climbing up and sitting down completely. This is, however, a rather marginal practice of utilization and I seriously wonder about the comfort of sitting on top of this device! But it is just another illustration of how the mobilities design staged from above is modified by practitioner's staging from below. As we gaze across the images chosen here to represent resting travellers, we see the same practices as mentioned before: people resting are also reading, talking on phones, and looking at other mobile subjects.

The presence of Metro users with no or little advance knowledge about the system is another theme that deserves attention. Even though some seem to think that 'good architecture needs no explanation', one

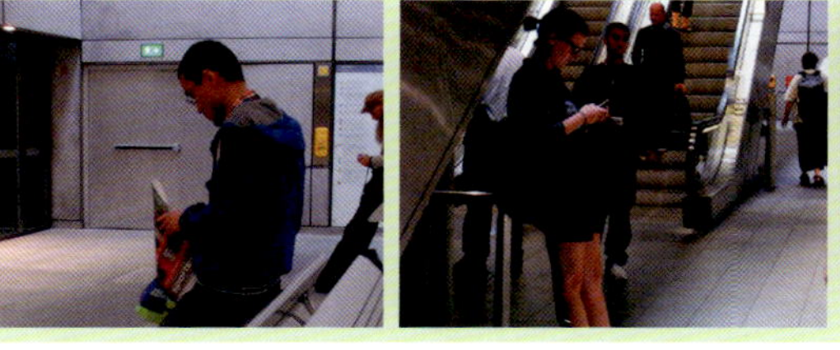

Left:
Fig. 6.25: Waiting 'mobile withs'

Right:
Fig. 6.26: Stay/rest

cannot design a well-functioning infrastructure and mobility system without some level of signage and wayfinding (fig. 6.27).

In the images chosen here to illustrate wayfinding, tourists are prevalent. The pictures show how portable maps, fixed maps on walls as well, and the zones for payment are scrutinized carefully by the passengers without detailed and contextual knowledge about the Copenhagen Metro. These wayfinding systems are mostly of a rather traditional type using posters and maps. But there are as mentioned also more dynamic signs, such as the ones with information about upcoming arrivals and train destinations. There is also an image of a wayfinding 'technology' not very predominant in the Metro, namely a train steward (i.e., an employee servicing the Metro users). In the lower right image we see the train steward who, besides keeping order and controlling tickets, serves the purpose of providing wayfinding information to the lost wayfarers on the Metro. The theme of wayfinding and the images presented here also illustrate that the mobile subject must obtain certain skills in order to navigate and operate within the system. The signs, hardware, and the mobile subjects thus all come together in a complex 'mobility assemblage' that partly requires context-specific knowledge and skills (e.g., geographic knowledge about Copenhagen) as well as generic capacities necessary to enroll in a 'mobility assemblage' (e.g., the ability to read the wayfinding information and orient oneself within complex systems).

It comes as no surprise that quite a few Metro passengers are in a hurry when they embark on a journey in the Metro. However, others utilize the Metro as a public meeting place before moving on. And there are also (despite the design rationale of a single-minded flow design) examples of Metro passengers playing games or at least having a ludic relationship

Fig. 6.27: Wayfinding

Opposite:

Top:
Fig. 6.28: In a rush, meeting and playing

Below:
Fig. 6.29: Mobile Situation 1

to the Metro. All three types of activities are only some of the many ways in which people behave in the Metro (fig. 6.28).

The many different ways of appropriating and inhabiting the Metro furthermore speak to the point that even within the Copenhagen Metro the staging of situational mobilities takes place at a nexus between staged conditions from above and embodied practices and choices from below.

Until now I have focused on people and their relations to the material environment of the Metro. But I zoom in on the last level of analysis in this case, namely the mobile situations and their social dynamics. The method used in analysing these situations is to study multiple picture frames closely and thereafter draw these onto a plan sketch of the Metro space. The pictures of the situations have been taken at two-second intervals.

For the sake of simplicity I term the first situation 'mobile situation 1'. The situation was recorded on August 24, 2011 at 12:24 on the eastern end of the platform and lasted 10 seconds (fig. 6.29).

What we see is that the person we might term 'actor one' (the woman carrying the white coat) sees that a train is about to depart. As she start to speeds up, she conflicts with 'actor two' (the woman standing in front of her on the escalator) who is in the projected path of the main actor. The main actor literally pushes aside actor two and rushes to the train. The timing is very tight and actor one barely makes it into the train compartment, where the automatic doors almost close on her as she enters the train. On the diagram the visual sightline of actor one is compared to the actual trajectory and distance she has to overcome in order to reach her destination. The situation is rather common and speaks to the way mobile subjects in general take fast decisions 'on the fly' as they suddenly realize that the train is about to depart. Moreover, the armature of the escalator as well as its relative placement in relation to the train door, creates the situational constraints where actor one has only the option of waiting or pushing the person aside if we disregard the logical option of jumping across the escalator edges. This is something not likely to be a modus operandi of this woman, but it can be observed when young people are 'playing' in the Metro in an almost 'parkour-like' fashion.

Mobile situation 2 also concerns the CPC of the train doors. The situation was recorded on August 24, 2011 at 12:07 on the western end of the platform and lasted 10 seconds (fig. 6.30).

What plays out here is a situation where actor one is standing in front of the door and thus not following the rules inscribed by the white stripes indicating the 'wait here' areas. Actor two (the young girl carrying a rucksack) has to turn and slightly reroute in order not to collide with actor one. Present in the situation are other mobile subjects who 'keep their place' in the waiting areas. The situation is interesting in illustrating how the staging from above by the Metro design code is challenged by the individual's decision to stage himself in the middle of the doorway, thus ignoring the rather explicit design message. Moreover, the situation is a reflection of the subtle mobile power plays that take place as mobile subjects move within the city. Clearly actor one is aware that he violates a general behavioural principle laid down by the Metro design code. It is hard to say whether this is a function of the age and gender relation between the exiting young girl and the entering man, but from earlier studies of people's mobile power plays in public spaces (Jensen 2010b), I think we could expect actor one to have behaved differently had the disembarking passenger been a large and seemingly violent character.

Date: Aug 24, 2011
Time: 12.24
Duration: 10 seconds
Location: Eastern end of platform

Actions:
- The main actor sees a train about to depart
- The second actor stands on the escalator in the path of the main actor
- The main actor push the second actor aside and runs to the train
- The main actor is close to getting squezed by the closing doors

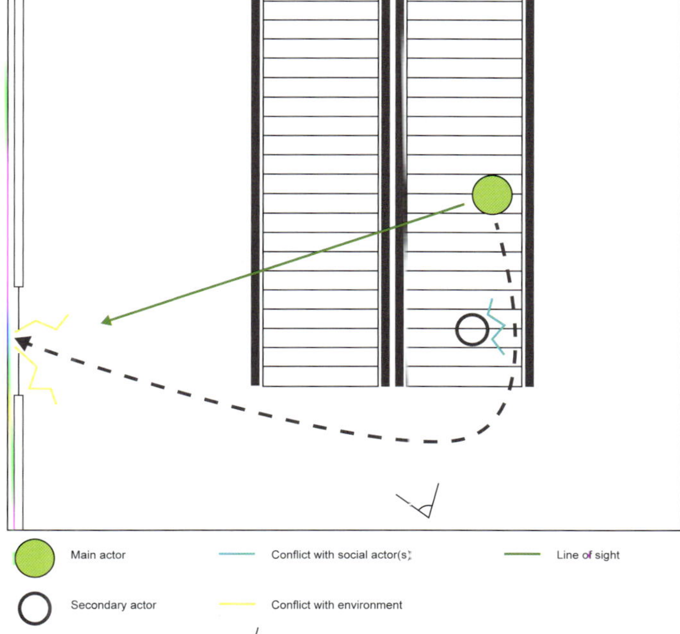

In mobile situation 3 we see more dynamic interaction as the number of mobile subjects is greater here. The situation was recorded on August 24, 2011 at 12:56 on the eastern end of the platform and lasted 20 seconds (fig. 6.31.).

The situation at hand is one where a ring of actors has assembled in close proximity to the door, blocking it. The incoming crowd pushes forward and actor two (which is here a group of disembarking passengers and thus essentially a 'mobile with' making a 'temporary congregation') is trying to push through in the opposite direction. Eventually the group of waiting passengers increases as more and more people join, leaving only a narrow corridor for the passengers leaving the train. The situation is an illustration of the mobile power plays and the 'mobilities differentials' being played out in an ephemeral situation. Moreover, the interesting thing here is that the material constraint exercised upon this 'temporary congregation' is made up by human bodies rather than the hard surfaces of the Metro. Of course this still creates a wider context for the situation, but the detailed mobile microinteraction is determined by the train doors and the crowd of people, creating a temporary armature in the guise of a small and narrow passage between bodies of mobile subjects. Furthermore, the situation 'spills out' and creates ripple effects out into the platform space. This can be seen by the number of waiting people who end up actually blocking the escalator down to the platform area.

The final situation is situation 4, where we see something rather important even though also unusual. The situation was recorded on August 24, 2011 at 11:40 on the eastern end of the platform and lasted for 10 seconds (fig. 6.32).

Opposite:

Top:
Fig. 6.30: Mobile Situation 2

Below:
Fig. 6.31: Mobile Situation 3

What takes place in this situation is that actor one is approaching the escalator but realizes that it is broken. She then tries the escalator on the right hand side, only to find that it moves in the wrong direction. She actually tries to use it but gives up and walks up the broken escalator. This situation is again evidence of the 'on the fly decisions' that the mobile subjects continually have to make. Also this speaks to the issue of systems failure and breakdown. As with most other technologies the conscious awareness of one's positions and horizons of actions only becomes clear when the subject finds him- or herself nested within a malfunctioning system. I am quite confident that actor one in this situation would have rejected the option of walking up a down escalator if this situation had been presented to her in the abstract. However, in the actual situation, she makes a swift decision to try walking up a down escalator. The situation thus explores the system's vulnerability and the creative and situational restaging made by the mobile subject from below as she moves along the transit systems of the network city.

Conclusion

I want to end this chapter as I ended the previous, namely by repeating the overarching question from the very start of this book. As one might recall, this was to engage with the question: *How is design affording and/ or preventing particular mobile practices and cultures in everyday life?* The particularities of the Nørreport Station have been dealt with in quite some detail but I would also argue that more general inferences are possible from the analysis. So I will sum up the findings but also relate these to the more general and theoretical concepts from the *Staging Mobilities* framework in order to test the applicability of the new 'vocabulary' as well as to point out more general areas of relevance than a train station in Copenhagen. This is done as in the other case conclusions by using the framework presented in the model at the end of chapter three, where the *Staging Mobilities* framework is overlaid with the diagrams that capture the more detailed conceptual tools.

The analysis of Nørreport Station clearly relates to the ideas of the *Staging Mobilities* framework in general and the idea of 'Critical Mobilities Thinking' in

Date: Aug 24, 2011
Time: 12.07
Duration: 10 seconds
Location: Western end of platform

Actions:
- The main actor is standing right infront of the door, not following rules set up by designers (passengers are meant to wait in the 'Wait Here' pitches)
- The secundary actor needs to avoid the main actor causing conflict
- Bystanders are standing in the pitches

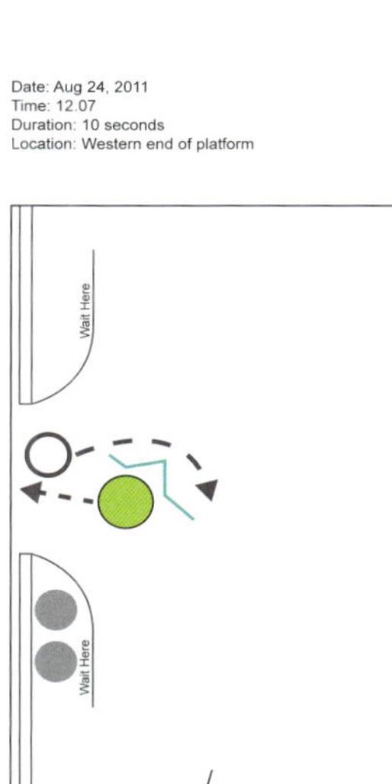

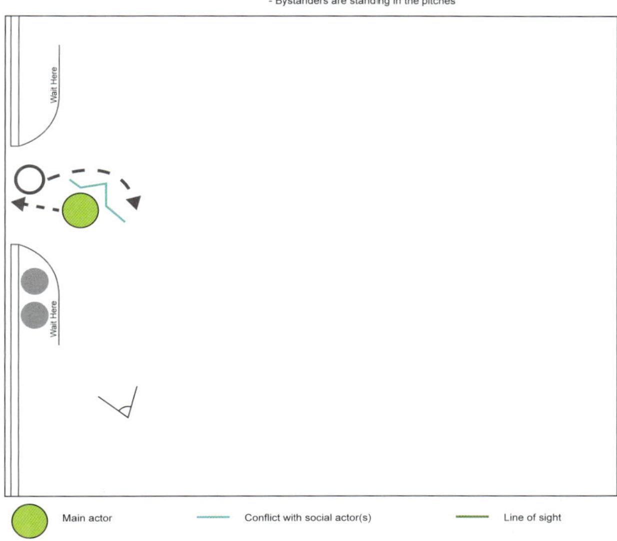

Date: Aug 24, 2011
Time: 12.56
Duration: 20 seconds
Location: Eastern end of platform

Actions:
- A ring of main actors has assembled close to the door blocking it
- The crowd pushes forward and the secondary actor is trying to push through
- Eventually the grouping of waiting passengers gets larger as more bypassers join, leaving only a narrow corridor for the passengers getting off the train

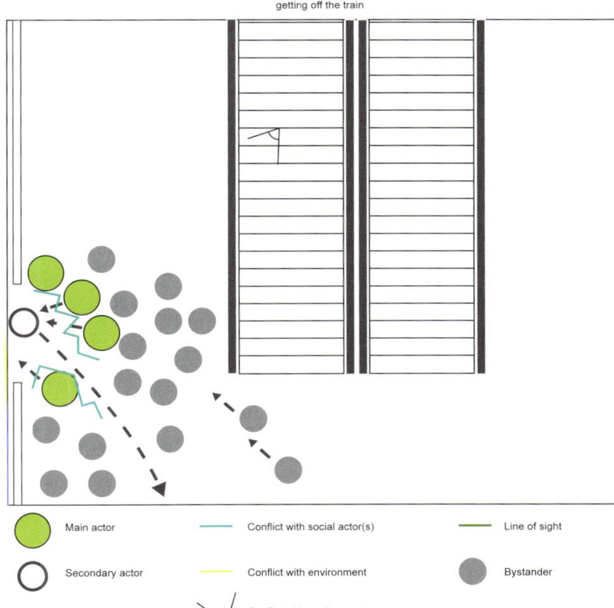

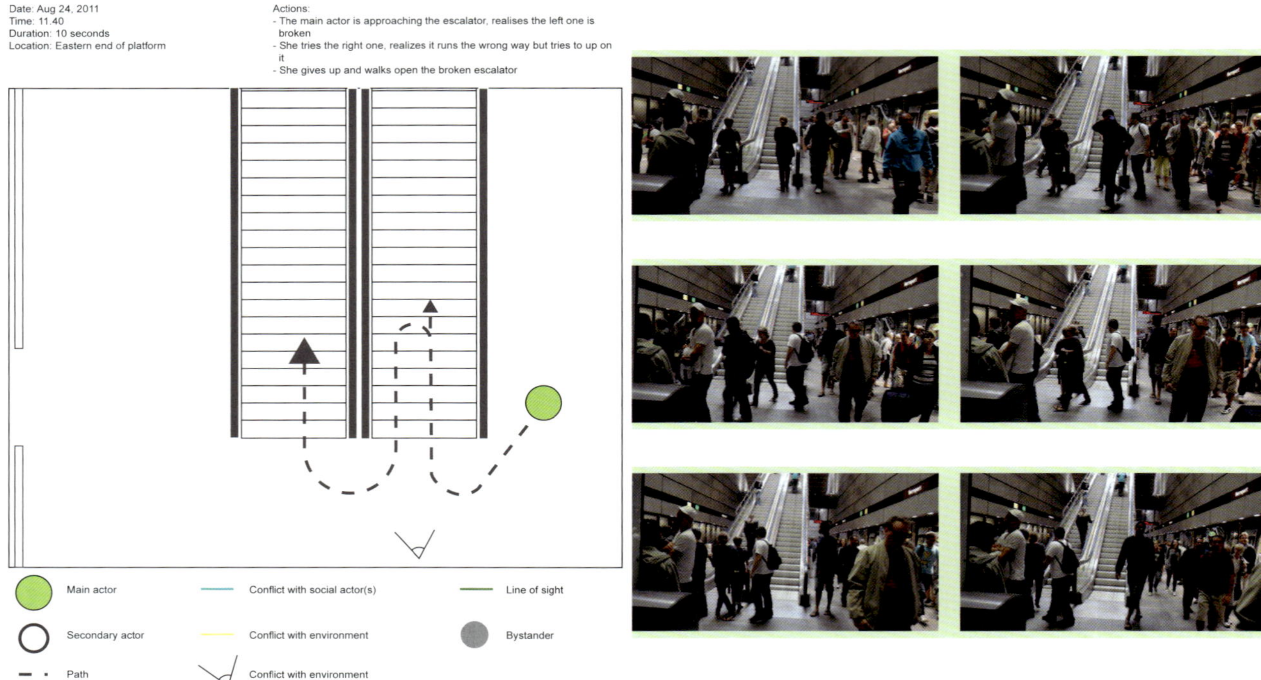

Date: Aug 24, 2011
Time: 11.40
Duration: 10 seconds
Location: Eastern end of platform
Actions:
- The main actor is approaching the escalator, realises the left one is broken
- She tries the right one, realizes it runs the wrong way but tries to up on it
- She gives up and walks open the broken escalator
Main actor
Conflict with social actor(s)
Line of sight
Secondary actor
Conflict with environment
Bystander
Path
Conflict with environment

Fig. 6.32: Mobile Situation 4

particular, as it aims to include both the 'problems' and 'potentials'. The analysis shows that there are a number of problems and issues related both to the environment and the socially exclusionary practices inscribed into the train station design. (This has in particular been illustrated with reference to the Metro). But Nørreport Station is also a public domain and a busy place that may open up even further to capitalize on its potential. The Metro has been the pivotal case in point when it comes to underutilizing a potential for increasing public interaction and affording urban interaction among socially diverse groups. The assumption that there is more to mobilities than instrumental movements indicates that a busy train hub like Nørreport Station also is host to innumerable everyday life practices and 'little social dramas' that risk being neglected if the notion of 'Critical Mobilities Thinking' is not applied to the understanding. The potential of adding commercial programs and public facilities is certainly underexplored, but so is the realization that people are interacting and relating in this 'metroscape' at various levels of engagement.

Nørreport Station creates particular 'mobility affordances' in different ways depending on the modes of mobilities we are exploring. There is a tight relationship with the 'single mindedness' of the Metro and the mobility affordances created. But even though the Metro performs as an almost 100 percent circulation machine, we saw 'cracks in the walls' when mobile subjects appropriated the systems in alternative (if nor subversive) ways. The idea of 'mobility affordance' in Nørreport Station is visible if we think about the mobile subjects being processed by platforms, paths, stairs, lifts, and escalators in horizontal and vertical flows. The way the system affords bodily movement is different depending of the capacities of the bodies in question, but generally the armatures of escalators and stairs affords rather serial and linear practices of movement through the system. However, at times these are challenged by busy travellers trying to bypass the slower flows of passengers. The Metro has been the focus in particular and here the system with automatic doors and the attempt to position mobile subjects in reasonable areas of the platform in order to optimize the passenger flows have been very conspicuous indeed. (In fact, the issue of doors and entering the regional trains is an altogether different story where manual doors often create their own affordances as well as the opposite.) The temporalities afforded by the intersecting train systems are as complex and as multifaceted as the various time tables and temporal logic of each of the systems. The temporal pulse of the Metro with its much more frequent operations is layered over the S-train and regional train systems operating at different time intervals. This affords a particular dynamic temporality of the station that creates very specific conditions for the mobile subjects moving within the station.

I used the notion of 'mobile assemblages' in the previous chapter to analyse the bike systems, but in this chapter the applicability of the term may be seen even more clearly. Nørreport Station is an example of a 'mobile assemblage' where the systems and socio-technical networks become the action surfaces for thousands of mobile subjects. At Nørreport Station we see the S-train, regional trains, and the Metro systems interact and blend with pedestrian flows from across the city, cyclists, and bus passengers. (There is much less interface with the car system as mentioned.) From platform design to escalators and ticket systems to entrances and wayfinding systems, we see how Nørreport Station assembles a multitude of agencies into a complex mobility nexus. People find themselves both 'being processed' by the 'systemness' staged from above; we also saw many examples of staging from below where the mobile subjects interact with other fellow mobile consociates as well as with the artefacts and objects expressing non-human agency (running from the driverless Metro to the ticket machine and the automatic doors).

The complexity of tasks to be performed by the 'metroscape' of Nørreport Station makes some sort of information system necessary. Very much in line with most other transport hubs, Nørreport Station relies predominantly on signage and wayfinding systems. So we saw how a notion of 'mobile semiotics' becomes instrumental to understanding the performance of Nørreport Station and how the design decisions informing the outline of the systems creates the interface with the mobile subjects travelling through Nørreport Station. In line with the earlier conceptualisation and analysis, the geo-semiotic component is crucial. In other words the very complex decision to put, for example, a platform sign in a particular spot or the route-directing set of signs for the visiting traveller to follow are parts of the particular 'mobile semiotic' of Nørreport Station. Many of the semiotic interventions we see at this site are of the global and generic type and often draw upon the iconic resemblance of the sign image and the corresponding object (e.g., the train or plane sign). But Nørreport Station is also inscribed into a more specific semiotic context as, for example, when the red hexagonal 'S' sign communicates the presence of a S-train station. This code needs to be learned on the more site-specific level of Copenhagen. Also Nørreport Station does have commercial programs and wherever there are commercial activities, there are semiotic systems and visually communicating platforms to go along with them. Moreover, the station buildings and platform areas themselves may also be 'read' in semiotic terms by the traveller. Obviously the signs are layered onto this materiality, but the spaces themselves are 'read' as people move through them. For instance, doors and escalators are decoded by mobile subjects based on an acquired set of mobile knowledge affording the individual the ability to conduct his or her mobile practices. What takes place in a busy mobile setting such as Nørreport Station is that the mobile subjects on the move 'read' each other in order to detect clues for potential movement patterns, trajectories, and collision avoidance. The many layers of vertical and horizontal movement within a relatively confined subterranean space force the mobile subjects at Nørreport Station to be alert continuously to the 'mobile signs' of their fellow passengers' bodies. The 'mobile body semiotics' is as seen relevant within all the cases studied in this work, but at Nørreport Station this dimension becomes even more pertinent due to the spatial confinement: we have more people moving through smaller spaces. Such mobile densification affords a continuing interaction pattern where 'reading' other moving bodies becomes a crucial skill to develop and practice.

The ability to 'read off' intentions of other mobile subjects or the staging rationale behind the wider system leads to the identification of 'mobility cultures'. Any site of mobile complexity such as Nørreport Station relies on a particular mixture of generic and site-specific knowledge. The various 'codes' for moving through the station complex are thus at times instantly recognisable by most international travellers whereas other require more local knowledge. The 'mobility cultures' surfacing at Nørreport Station are mediated by the various types of usages and functionality of the place. Thus busy commuters develop commonly identifiable practices that are in contrast to the tourist being processed in the system. Moreover, some of the codes of conduct that develop into solidified practices and 'ways of doing' are inscribed and staged 'from above' (such as the 'stand to the right, walk to the left' message at the Metro escalators) whereas others are developed in situ by mobile subjects taking swift, incremental, and situational decisions 'on the fly' (such as the person deciding to push a fellow passenger aside in order to reach the train on the platform). In a broader perspective the temporality of the site affects these 'mobility cultures'. Here I am thinking about the difference between the mobile interaction at rush hour and at times of the day where there fewer passengers in the 'metroscape'.

At Nørreport Station the embodied sensations and the 'aesthetic experience in motion' in which the mobile subject engages are obviously different compared to their sensorial and physical abilities (a blind passenger will experience the space differently from the seeing person). However, there are also huge differences within the various areas of the 'metroscape'. We saw how there has been much criticism of the regional train platforms in particular (they are small, noisy, smelly, dark, and often not very comfortable). So the particular aesthetic experience is differentiated at Nørreport Station depending on whether the mobile subject is moving into the cathedral-like Metro or taking the regional train. Most often people shift between modes and systems (that is the whole idea behind a transit hub) and thus experience very different atmospheres and ambiences as they move through the layers of the 'metroscape' at Nørreport. In prolongation of the 'differential mobilities' and the variety that mobile subjects may experience, Nørreport Station also affords 'mobility divides'. Clearly some relate to the ability to orient oneself and 'read' the place, whereas others are inscribed into the body-environment nexus giving the regular users a clear advantage over first-time tourists but also giving an advantage to the fit and able compared to physically challenged users. In general, Nørreport Station is accessible and there is a good amount of design intervention to diminish blatant 'mobility divides' when it comes to the physical abilities of the mobile subjects. In terms of the legibility of the place, it becomes more difficult for those passengers either not able to view complex settings and environments or first-time visitors and users. The complexity of Nørreport Station crates 'mobility divides' between those who are able to cope with stressful and dynamic environments and those who are not. Moreover, there are very specific issues around 'mobility divides' if we look at the Metro on its own. Since the design manual has dismissed, for example, benches we saw how people aren't afforded longer occupancy in the Metro space. As mentioned, this is not necessarily a bad thing provided one's declared goal is to 'move people'. However, if we think of the centrality of the place and the way other urban transit hubs across the world afford social interaction and public domain (which admittedly may often also mean 'hosting the unwanted'), the Metro by its staging from above clearly has created a 'mobility divide' on the 'rational grounds' of flow optimization. By virtue of being a major transit hub within the Copenhagen infrastructural network, Nørreport Station performs as both 'mobile sociofugal' and 'mobile sociopetal'. The hub 'draws in' huge masses of travellers from across the city and 'distributes them out' again. This is the nature of the hub and as such Nørreport Station works according to the underlying staging principles. But by virtue of its design it also works less as a public domain affording people the opportunity to stay and meet. There are meetings at Nørreport Station, but these are of a very brief nature where the people meeting 'join up and move on' rather than sit down and socialise.

As the users of a busy everyday transit hub, many passengers at Nørreport Station are, not surprisingly, illustrations of what I termed 'networked selves' who are 'linked-in-motion'. The most frequent waiting activity seems to be gazing at one's mobile phone and the system is designed in such a manner that there is wireless connection even below ground as people move through the subterranean armatures. Nørreport Station thus illustrates how the contemporary transit travellers stage themselves by using digital media on the go, as they expect the systems to be staged in such a manner that these practices are afforded. The system thus enables mobile practices of stretching the situational interaction across time and space, or what I termed the 'proximity-connectivity nexus'. Sites of public transit in general, and here Nørreport Station is no exception, are increasingly sites of mediated communication and digital connectivity. This has the advantage that people may work, be entertained, or sustain relationships as they move. However, much also seems to suggest that this has an impact on the 'mobility cultures' of public transit and the practices of social interaction. Whether people are 'cocooning' and thus withdrawing more in today's public transit, I am not sure. Despite moral condemnation in the public debate of people being 'insulated and inward looking' utilizing digital media, I think this was always an option as people simply hid themselves behind books and newspapers. But there may be an extra dimension of withdrawal since the use of earplugs seals off mobile subjects from one another in a more radical manner. Studies of what this means to 'mobility cultures' needs to be carried out in more detail, however, before clear judgment may be passed.

Nørreport Station is, as are the other cases analysed here, comprehensible both from the analytical point of view of 'the river' and 'the ballet'. The complexity of the site has required very detailed design and meticulous staging decisions from above. The interaction and coordination between various transit systems and the relationship to the wider city network means that the designers of Nørreport Station need to examine the homogeneous and aggregated flow of people. Whether we look at the S-train, the regional train, or the Metro, there are complex synchronization schemes of timetables as well as functional interaction (e.g., how to get from one system to another) to be made. The 'river' perspective on Nørreport Station also illustrates how mobile subjects are processed and moved by smaller design interventions such as the width of a staircase or the speed of an escalator. As we move down to this level of detail, we inevitably shift into the 'ballet' perspective as we start to see how the microinteractions between mobile subjects are functions of the presences of mobile others as well as of the materiality of the environment. Nørreport Station is a dynamic and complex space of social interaction and the detailed analysis of 'mobilities in situ' clearly substantiates that there is much more to mobilities than simple movements. I like to think of these mundane everyday practices of situational mobilities as 'little dramas'. What looks like 'nothing' on the surface or like the 'necessary evil of transport' open up through the 'ballet' perspective to become complex face-to-face interactions, mobile presentations of Self, and 'negotiation in motion'. This is the case regardless of whether we study the singular mobile subject or the 'mobile with' moving through the system. The individual and the 'mobile with' moves through the transit space of Nørreport Station in what might look like 'isolated serial patterns'. But what takes place, for example, through the multiple incremental making and breaking of 'temporary congregations' is actually the production of everyday life sociality and culture. Nørreport Station is a complex space of interaction and speed changes that filter, circulate, and distribute passengers in a functional way. But it is also a space of social and cultural differentiation and reproduction. In fact the 'ordinary' and mundane sites of such trivial acts as urban transit might be said to be the most important sites for studying social norms, cultural differentiation, and identity formation. I think critical social analysis may benefit as much from the study of the 'ordinary' as from the study of the 'extreme' when trying to explore the underlying grammar of social life.

From here a general summary must indicate that Nørreport Station contains both the 'staging from above' as we find it created by planning, design, regulations, and institutions. We have seen equally many examples of 'staging from below' by consociates interacting and individual performances of mobile self-presentation. So the station is ideal for studying what I have termed 'Mobilities in Situ' within the threefold division of physical settings, material spaces and design, social interactions, and embodied performances. The engagement of passengers in this 'metroscape' is more dramatic and more relevant to our understanding of the mobile everyday life than often claimed.

I have now reached the final case of this book, and do therefore turn to the much discussed mode of mobility: the car. The final case chapter before the conclusion will address the idea of 'carscapes' and interurban motorways as assemblages for social interaction.

7 CAR

MOTORWAY ASSEMBLAGES IN EASTERN JUTLAND

Roads are technologies that play a fundamental role in the system of automobility, both as material things that enable the circulation of auto traffic as well as ideological constructs that are consciously designed to encourage certain practices while inhibiting others.

Zack Furness (2010) *One Less Car*, p. 83

The city was here before the freeway system, no doubt, but it now looks as though the metropolis has actually been built around this arterial network.

Jean Baudrillard (1988) *America*, p. 55

The road, more than simply a system of regulations and designs, is a place where many millions of us, with only loose parameters for how to behave, are thrown together daily in a kind of massive petri dish in which all kinds of uncharted, little-understood dynamics are at work. There is no other place where so many people of different walks of life – different ages, races, classes, religions, genders, political preferences, life style choices, levels of psychological stability – mingle so freely.

Tom Vanderbilt (2008) *Traffic*, p. 6

Introduction

In this chapter the interurban motorway that shapes and affords a very large part of the contemporary urban development is explored. The key goals are to understand the (interurban) motorway as a space on its own, governed by both formal regulations (staging from above) as well as cultures on the move (staging from below). The case explored is the stretch of motorway from Vejle to Aarhus, Denmark, also dubbed 'the 100 km City'. The chapter investigates how material conditions of the motorway design such as off-ramps, gas stations, and the built environment along its path, together with the complex interactions among the mobile subjects occupying the 'motorway assemblage', illustrate the staging of mobilities. What used to be thought of as 'pure' mobility armatures between cities and often part of larger nation building projects have now become another twist in the long development path of urbanization and infrastructural development:

> The growth of car ownership has now led to the evolution of a car world along the motorways: roadside restaurants have for a long time been more than just a place for a quick snack on the road, and are developing into places of entertainment and meetings; malls and leisure facilities are appearing at a number of locations in the urban field, which for all intents and purposes are only accessible by car (Hajer and Reijndorp 2001, 131).

It is a widespread assumption that car traffic affords anonymity (e.g., Bollnow 1963/2011; Putnam 2000; Sennett 1994). There is some truth to this if we think of the difference between a close, face-to-face encounter on the street versus the seemingly homogeneous stream of cars flowing through a motorway system. But this only holds true for a 'river' gaze at the motorway. As soon as we 'zoom in', we find a myriad of dynamic interactions and underpinning rationalities reaching from indifference to rage to altruism. Traffic is thus a 'living laboratory of human interaction' (Vanderbilt 2008, 34). The fact that we have developed detailed and normative codes of conduct for road behaviour as found in formalized and official traffic rules and codes of conduct (Highway Code 2008; Jørgensen 2007; Seiler 2008) seems to suggest that this is a human interaction space even though its material and technological configuration is different from, for example, the pedestrian meetings in public spaces. The staging of mobilities on the motorway is no different from others because we are dealing with human interaction and communication based on a situational dynamics. But the conditions for social interaction surely are different when you are in a 'metal box doing 110 km/h' within a confined armature – and that is precisely the topic of this chapter.

The structure of the chapter is the following. After this introduction I address the discussion of urban form and city growth as a function of the automobile. Then I move on to discuss the potential of car spaces. Here I reference some influential studies that have offered inspiration for the analysis to follow. Before I reach the empirical analysis, I devote a section to a short definition and conceptualisation of the notion of 'motorway assemblage'. Hereafter follows the first part of the empirical analysis, starting out with contextualizing the Eastern Jutland motorway as well as the methodological reflections. Then a section containing an analysis of the 'staging from above', focusing on the broader planning perspective. The following section gets 'closer' to the detail, focusing on the architectural stages of the motorway. The final part of the case analysis is carried out in section nine where I explore mobile situations on the motorway. The chapter ends with a conclusion.

Cities, Sprawl and Cars – beyond the traditional notion of a 'city'

Not many technological inventions have gained as much attention within urban research as the advent of the private car and its revolutionary transformation of society at large, and of the urban fabric in particular. The postwar development of cities within the Western world is fairly synonymous with the history of the car, and today this intertwinement makes thinking of a society 'after the car' rather challenging (Dennis and Urry 2009). Notions of post-Fordism, postmodernism, privatisation, neo-liberalisation, and a new unbundling of infrastructures led to the erosion of the monocentric city and to the condition of 'splintering urbanism' (Graham and Marvin 2001, 8).

The list of relevant literature discussing these trends is massive and I can only touch upon a few selected spots in the scholarly discourse. (For one of many comprehensive stories of postwar urban development, see Shane 2011). The nomenclature trying to fix, represent, and give meaning to postwar urbanism is plentiful. A few of the keywords are: *sprawl, the postmetropolis, the network city, splintering urbanism, the shapeless city, exopolis, the edge city, the borderless city, cosmopolis, the multiplex city, the polycentric city, the generic city, the vehicular city, the urbanized territory, the megalopolis,* etc. Bergman argues that by and large the metaphors and concepts of the bounded and coherent city have vanished from the vocabulary of urban scholars (Bergman 2008, 216). There is obviously a very complex development process behind the postwar transformation of cities that reaches far beyond mobilities and the urban fabric and deeply into the production and consumption of contemporary global capitalism. However, for the sake of simplicity I focus on the emergence of car mobilities and road infrastructure. These development trends changed the morphology of the city from a relatively enclosed, mononuclear and bounded entity to a connected/disconnected node in a complex network, reconfiguring sites of production, play, recreation, residence, and consumption. My preferred terminology is (despite its shortcomings) the 'network city' and I connect this concept to the notion of relational place, mobilities, and assemblages in the following manner:

> Cities and urban spaces have for long been described and understood in terms of their form, structure, and morphology. However contemporary change in the socio-spatial relation has made it clear that urban analysts are in need of a new vocabulary and new concepts. Thus an increasing number of urban theorists are turning toward flows and mobilities as something that can no longer merely be seen as a 'side effect'. Contemporary cities and urban spaces are defined by their connectivity and their relationships to other nodes in a global network. There is a need to conceptualise and theorise the multiple and complex flows of images, signs, meanings, goods, vehicles, and people that not only move within urban and interurban infrastructures but which constitutes the contemporary city (Jensen 2013a, 19-20).

The one term that probably has captured most of the popular imagination is, however, the notion of 'sprawl'. In a Danish planning context this translates into something like 'uncontrolled urban growth' and is thus by definition renounced by planners and advocates of the strong planning order of Danish society. In other words, some people surely would claim that there is no such thing as sprawl in Denmark. However, one question is how to define the phenomenon and thus decide whether or not it exists; another method is to use the sprawl literature as a window into the huge complexities of infrastructural dynamics and pressure for urban centralism and growth that are also part of Danish society. American geographer Ed Soja explains that sprawl is a 'nasty term' and traces it back to the eighteenth century where it most commonly referred to an *'awkward or clumsy stretching out of the limbs of the body'* (Soja 2002, 76). Surely the negative connotations and unruliness still cling to the concept today. Even though we may say that the motorway of Eastern Jutland is not in a technical sense sprawl, I believe the literature on this topic will help us to understand some of the problems and issues related to this specific urban situation as well as how the phenomenon of motorway mobilities have come to be understood primarily in negative terms.

American sociologist Robert Putnam identified sprawl and mobility as some of the underlying causes of disintegration of American contemporary culture in his influential book '*Bowling Alone*' (Putnam 2000). The argument goes like this: '*Nevertheless* [despite identifying American culture as nomadic], *for people as for plants, frequent repotting disrupts root systems. It takes time for a mobile individual to put down new roots*' (Putnam 2000, 204). Aside from the nomenclature of nature and a metaphor of 'humans as plants', this point were made with explicit reference to the increasing residential mobility in America (which is much greater in the United States than in Europe). However, Putnam continues his analysis and argues that the construction of suburban America (totally dependent on the car) is the real problem as it has led to '*greater separation of workplace and residence and greater segregation by race and class*' (Putnam 2000, 208). This technological shift toward the private car has led to a morphological change of the urban networks that according to Putnam carry serious repercussions:

> One inevitable consequence of how we have come to organize our lives spatially is that we spend measurably more of every day shuttling alone in metal boxes among the vertices of our private triangles … In short, we are spending more and more time alone in the car … the car and the commute, however, are demonstrably bad for community life … commuting has negative externalities (Putnam 2000, 212-213).

I find it hard not to sympathize with Putnam's worry about social cohesion and the 'negative externalities' of such mobile life forms. However, I think we need to avoid falling into the trap of moral condemnation, clouding our understanding of what mobility means. Surely it means the negative things that I have lumped together under the heading of the 'dark side' of mobilities. But we need also to understand the finer points of a mobile everyday life and this is not done by morally dismissing all dimensions and practices relating to the car. I have not been able to do justice to the long list of critical scholarly work on the car here. Many of these works are in compliance with the 'dark side' dimension of 'critical mobilities thinking'. However, most of the critique is well known to society at large. Moreover, I think the 'potential' side of car mobilities has not been explored to the same extent, so I want to engage with that body of literature in order to balance the framing of motorway mobilities. This double perspective of 'problems and potentials' related to urban development and mobilities was actually identified already by Halprin in the 1960s and has served as a key inspiration for my own work:

> The city of the future must be conceived of as an enormous megastructure in which the landscape with its recreational and life-giving qualities becomes a part of the immense urban environment. The green open spaces will be within a structured complex. But the city of the future need not imply any diminution of the amenities of urban living - if we can only recognize its <u>potentials</u> as well as its <u>problems</u> (Halprin 1966,154, my emphasis).

So analysts like Putnam sees sprawl as the direct cause of the erosion of social cohesion (Putnam 2000) whereas others are much less convinced of such an interpretation. I will return to Putnam's argument but for the sake of juxtaposition I want to reference the (controversial) position of Robert Bruegmann in his book *Sprawl – A Compact History* (2005). According to Bruegmann, sprawl is neither recent nor American, but rather a logical and democratic consequence of contemporary society's development! I will not try to give a verdict on this debate (apart from noticing the large volume of well-substantiated research pointing at the clear negative environmental consequences of sprawl, e.g., Næss 2006). The position taken in this work, however, is closer to that of David Kolb, who argues on the basis of relational understanding of place and brings a critical perspective to the moralist discourse: there are negative things to say about the built environment but also any judgment of a place needs to be made on the basis of de facto actions and practices carried out there and not on the basis of moralising judgements (Kolb 2008). Thus, when cities are becoming networked and increasingly dependent on the mobilities of people, goods, and information within new relational geographies, we need to ask ourselves how life on such 'stages' feels, how social interaction changes, and how the multiple incremental situations of mobilities that make up everyday life actually are lived. So I take on the perspective of being critically aware, but also curious of the practices and actions of people within what some deem 'non-places' by virtue of post hoc definition.

As Ed Soja proclaims, 'Sprawl is no longer what it used to be' (Soja 2002) and thus indicates a need for rethinking the term and developing a focus on a 'post-metropolitan transition', spatial justice, and regional democracy (Soja 2002, 88). Ingersoll sees sprawl as a phenomenon related to mobilities as a precondition and argues that most of the thought about sprawl seems to fall into two camps: the 'little city' critique advocated by people such as Leon Krier versus the 'generic city' perspective launched by Rem Koolhaas (Ingersoll 2006, 17). Ingersoll points to a position where one should understand sprawl as a key contemporary condition as well as trying to redesign and challenge it within its limits. This discussion takes us in the direction of regional and urban planning and is too broad with which to engage here. But the notion of 'sprawl' should not be dismissed as a predominantly North American and Asian phenomenon with no value for an analysis conducted in a well-regulated Scandinavian context such as the Danish. Surely there is a difference between the American and European versions of sprawl (Ingersoll 2006, 10). Also, the sprawl discourse might be off the mark as a single-handed representation of what goes on at the motorway assemblage in Eastern Jutland. However, much of the theoretical and conceptual debate related to sprawl research is relevant as a pointer toward how to articulate the relationship between contemporary urban developments and mobilities. The notion of 'cities out of control' is not only highly challenging to the self-perception of Western urban planners in general, but it also suggests that the urban dynamics are of a different nature than what may be captured by rational models of linear projection and forecasting. Schwarzer suggest that what we are facing is a 'mutation' of urbanism:

> Reaching from the scattered points on a far periphery to the dense cross-hatchings of old downtowns and the megastructure of the malls, the vehicular city resembles and organism that grows, not through replication, but through mutation (Schwarzer 2004, 71).

And within such 'mutation', automobiles institute their own architectural vocabulary (Schwarzer 2004, 72), creating new urban forms that facilitate new ways of organizing everyday life but also requiring new concepts and urban models. Many dimensions of this transformation would be relevant to describe here, but I focus on the changed perception of the environment as it is experienced by a new type of mobile subject, namely the car driver. The car affords various sensations and different engagements with the environment that are much more complex than simply 'sealing off' the senses (see Jensen 2013a, 110-115). In this context I want to focus on the visual transformation that the car affords its operator. There is a 'cinematic' understanding of the perception of the environment from the vantage point of the car (see Ingersoll 2006; Schwarzer 2004). Ingersoll refers to the notion of 'kinopravda' and 'jump-cut urbanism' in his discussion of how the perception of the driving citizen has changed compared to the pedestrian citizen within the 'theatrical order' of the urban street:

> For a driver, buildings, signs, and background perspectives are arranged much like a sequence of shots assembled for a film, and when the driver uses the rear-view mirror, the extraordinary phenomena of seeing forward and backward simultaneously occurs just like the montage of a cinematic jump cut … With the advent of the automobile, the theatrical order of the urban street was converted into a cinematic one, composed of long shots, close-ups, pans, tracking shots, and above all, the accelerated montage of jump cuts (Ingersoll 2006, 75).

Actually the Danish public debate on motorway design in the 1960s also included the notion of cinema and Nørgård spoke explicit of 'the film on the windscreen' as a metaphor for the cinematic experience on the motorway (Hovgesen et al. 2005, 52). This connects to the 'mobilities aesthetics' discussed earlier and to new ways of sensing the city and its environment:

> The automobile's moving cityscape is also a frontier of personal discovery. In a car, drivers can concentrate on their zones of special interest. Indeed, they assemble what amounts to their own private version of a place … The automobile view carries with it innumerable editing options, ellipses past dull blocks, or deliberately slow crawls where the action gets thick (Schwarzer 2004, 95).

Spoken in the language of 'cinematic urbanism', the idea of 'innumerable editing options' is taken too far in the sense that this perspective seems oblivious to the social and environmental costs of urban design based on the car (and to which I am certainly also critical). But what is worth noticing in Schwarzer's analysis is that it is sensitive to the new body-technology affordances created by the automobile. The rich literature on the 'cyborg' nature of the car-driver or driver-car (Dant 2004) is of relevance here but needs to be omitted due to space constraints (see Jensen 2013a, chapter 5).

The critique of the car's impact on the city and the notion of 'non-place'

The case I am going to explore in this chapter is a stretch of motorway between cities and bypassing city centres so the discussion of the automobile's impact on dense urban fabrics need to be broadened up a little. But we cannot leave the urban aside, since the interurban motorway assemblages precisely are part of the huge transformation taking place within and between cities today. The interurban motorway is part of the city and the cities are linking up in these vast networks that challenge the traditional notion of mono-nuclear and fortified enclaves. Master critic of urbanism with cars, Jane Jacobs, put it as a moral imperative when she stated that '*today everyone who values cities is disturbed by automobiles*' (Jacobs 1961, 338). Classics texts of 'car critique' are (to mention but a few) Bacon 1967; Buchannan 1964; Gehl 1996; Jacobs 1961; and Mumford 1956. Urry is highly critical of the 'system of automobility' as well (2004, 2007) and Berman spoke of how the infrastructural transformations of the city created an 'expressway world' (Berman 1983). There is also a massive environmentalist critique of the car to be found (e.g., Næss 2006; Gilbert & Perl 2010; Whitelegg 1997). Given my interest in transit spaces and mobilities armatures as 'sites of ordinary life', I shall, however, turn to another critique that can inform the analytical discussion. Here I am thinking of the seminal text '*Non-place – An Introduction to an Anthropology of Supermodernity*' by French anthropologist Marc Augé, who has been very influential in setting up a moral matrix of interpretation (Augé 1995). I will not go deeply into the arguments here (see Kolb 2008 for a good and balanced critique), but the book is important to mention since one of Augé's examples of a 'non-place' precisely are the transit spaces, armatures, and vehicles of the network city (Augé 1995, 34-35). Augé defines the notion of 'non-place' in the following manner: '*If a place can be defined as relational, historical and concerned with identity, then a space which cannot be defined as relational, or historical, or concerned with identity will be a non-place*' (Augé 1995, 77-78).

The 'real non-places of supermodernity' are, accordingly, the motorway, the supermarket, and the airport lounge (Augé 1995, 96). Augé does present the 'non-place' idea as a hypothesis and argue that it never exists in its pure form. Also he cannot be held accountable for the many simplistic interpretations of the notion of 'non-place' that in public discourse seems to be up for grabs whenever someone needs an argument for a moral condemnation of a shopping mall, an airport space, or a parking garage. However, there is a dangerously persuasive and sedentary underpinning to Augé's term from which I will distance my position. In passing one might notice (with no small irony) that Augé has written a beautiful account of his own childhood and socializing process in relation to the Parisian Metro! (Augé 2002). Here Augé is much closer to the position of 'Staging Mobilities' when he describes how the experiences of a city by means of the Metro is foundational not only to an individual's sense of the city, but also to the sense of Self (see Jensen 2013a, 26-30 for a deeper discussion of the nomad/sedentary metaphysics into which the non-place concept is inscribed).

Christie uses the term 'limbo' to describe the motorway as a space supressing our '*awareness of what lies either side of the tarmac ribbon along which we are moving*' (Christie 2002, 3). There is some truth to this critique raised by Christie but only insofar that the motorway assemblages we are thinking of are the sorts with very little or no design effort put into the 'views and vistas' that may be seen along the route. Also the initial time saving afforded by the advent of the private car is now being 'eaten up' as it were in large traffic jams and congested arteries of the infrastructure systems. This is a prime example of the 'irrationality of rationality' to use Ritzer's concept (1999, 93) since what may be a rational decision at the individual level (e.g., taking the private car to work) may become highly irrational as we end up shoulder to shoulder with other 'rational mobile subjects' queuing up on the motorways. Research documents that the threshold of generally accepted communing time is fairly constant about one hour (Vanderbilt 2008, 131). This means that for every 'speed leap' forward in mobilities we seem to substitute this with further travel. Or in the words of Crozet, '*speed does not help us save time but instead consume space*' (Crozet 2011, 73). So there are ample reasons to be critical and to try to rethink automobility. But precisely therefore we also need to understand the full implication of this mode and how it has become much more than simply a means of transportation.

The key issue for practical motorway design is nailed down with precision by Maxwell Gordon Lay, an independent traffic engineer advisor, when he says that '*the core problem has been incompatibility of the high operating speeds and resulting large dimensions of motorways, with the human pace and scale of urban living*' (Lay 2012, 137). Also the more philosophical corners of contemplation also provide critique as in the words of German philosopher Peter Sloterdijk who suggests that the car is better understood from the point of view of narcotics theory or religious studies than in ergonomics or mobility history (Sloterdijk 2011, 18). And the list of criticism continues also to include critics that connect the democratic issues related to a particular hegemony of mobility to basic issues of anthropocentric domination of nature:

> Motorways are quintessential products of the strand of modernity that celebrates and promotes the domination of nature by humanity, the domination of local cultures by national ones, and the centrality of speed and mobility to industrial progress (Christie 2002, 2).

Here Christie surely is on par with Putnam when seeing the motorway (and the car) as the forces leading to deteriorating social cohesion (Christie 2002, 3; Putnam 2000). The Belgian philosopher Lieven De Cauter chimes in equally with criticism that sees the car as a socially isolating technology, or a capsule: '*We don't live in networks, we live in capsules*' (Cauter 2004, 85). This critique is paralleled by urban scholar and sociologist Richard Sennett, who also sees the car and automobility as a social pathology (Sennett 1994).

Surely the car and its infrastructures are contested. There are negative effects of this technology but also positives and even unfulfilled potentials. I now turn to a few specific inspirational studies that have guided the analysis to come.

Inspirational Studies

I end this section before the framing of 'motorway assemblages' by referring in more detail to a number of studies that have been inspirational to my thinking about the case analysis to follow. The first is the seminal study by Appleyard, Lynch, and Myer entitled *The View from the Road* (Appleyard et al. 1964). Also the study by Hovgesen and his colleagues, *Byen, vejen og landskabet* (Hovgesen et al. 2005), has been influential to my understanding, not only in general terms, but also in site-specific terms since Hovgesen et al. include the motorway in Eastern Jutland in their book. Further, Merriman's fine analysis of the history and social interaction space developed around the construction of the M1 motorway in England serves as an important source of inspiration (Merriman 2007). The Dutch architectural company 'Monolab' has also been engaged with a project about motorway development, in which they are 'programming the urban vacuums' as they explain in their project for urban densification alongside the Dutch A20 highway (Kuilenburg 2004, 130). The analysis by Brorman Jensen of the O2 ring road in Aarhus has also been inspirational for the following case study (B. B. Jensen 2004) as has the Swedish architect Bosse Bergman with his analysis of Stockholm that follows the development along the E4 road (Bergman 2008). Another project trying to explore the meaning of road spaces (but from an altogether different perspective) is that of the Danish landscape painter Steen Larsen, who in a series of naturalistic oil paintings has described both the car and the motorway as cultural artefacts. His 'ROAD' exhibition and the accompanying book (Larsen 2012) are beautiful examples of the arts and their potential for investigating the meaning of moving. Steen Larsen's next big project is to make a full-scale mapping of the A45 from northern Norway to southern Italy, utilizing time lapse photos and music to create a narrative of the transnational infrastructure.

I want to mention in more detail some other inspirational studies. For example, an interesting study was conducted in Belgium after the national road 'N4' was downgraded from a first priority road in the national system to a second-tier road as a function of a new motorway. The project investigates what the N4 was and what potentials it carried, and was conducted by collaborating architects and engineers (Artingeneering 2007). Elsewhere I did a study of the 'old highway' from Aalborg to Aarhus in Denmark much inspired by this 'parallel road' issue (Jensen 2009b). Here I want to draw upon the N4 case as one type of illustration of the 'potential exploration' as they saw 'a roadside village 180 km long' (Artingeneering 2007, 18). What I am interested here is the mind-expanding framing of the N4 as a 'roadside village 180 km long'. The N4 study does concern the built environment alongside the road and not the mobile microinteractions between drivers, but it is still inspirational as it is part of the denaturalization of infrastructure spaces that fit with the overall notion of 'critical mobilities thinking'. The N4 study furthermore opens up the discussion of infrastructures and roads as public spaces. We seem to be rather sedentary in our understanding of a 'true public space' as the Athenian agora where the free citizens met and deliberated in democratic dialogue about the future of the city state. However, the motorway is also a public space and we need therefore to think about it in such terms in order to 'politicise the armature' (Jensen 2013a, 203). Often there is a conceptual 'freshness' to such interventionist projects but perhaps also at times an aura of overenthusiasm that needs balancing from the 'analytical' disciplines (Jensen 2013a). But the method of registration with very detailed mappings and technical drawings of the sites along the route surely are stringent and objective, as the many diagrams in plan and section document the potential of this huge 'roadside village'. Also there are situational studies where the various situations of accessibility between the roadside lots and the road space are analysed rather carefully. In general the N4 study therefore has been very inspirational for the mappings and registrations that the case in this chapter will present.

I am inspired by these many investigations but I also find the key elements of situational and interaction perspectives of mobilities less frequently addressed by these studies. Most of these analytics focus on the material and built environment only. I want to include them, but only insofar as they become intertwined with the 'little dramas' of social interaction. For some reason this way of thinking seems self-evident when we talk about urban spaces on the small scale, but as we turn to the motorway the cocooned mobile subjects are seen as if they were not social agents in interaction. As states this quote from Featherstone:

> Unlike the everyday presentation of Self (Goffman 1971) where 'facework and bodily gestures can be potentially carefully scrutinized by co-present others in face-to-face interactions, the usual mode of automobile communication entails impaired or restricted communication. The human body is enclosed within a metal body and the spoken word, eye contact and facial expressions are usually difficult or impossible to establish (Featherstone 2004, 12).

I do not disagree that the embedding into a metal body changes the conditions for social interaction and communication. But I would rather like to speak of these communicative interaction conditions as transformed than simply nonexistent. This runs in parallel to the argument that the car is not a 100 percent desensing technology which is suggested by authors such as Urry (2004) and De Cauter (2004). I prefer to think of the car as a 'filtering' technology (Jensen 2013a, 112). As Votolato compellingly argue '*every vehicle in which people travel provides an interface with the natural, physical world*' (2007, 9). This also resonates with Edensor's point in his analysis of the British M6 Junction 19-16, in which he states that '*I prefer to regard car travel as redistributing sensual experience, for (particular) cars and journeys contain their own sensual capacities*' (Edensor 2003, 153). I want to propose the analytical point that a motorway is not just an assemblage of fast-moving cars but equally importantly a vast interaction space.

The now seminal analysis of Los Angeles made by British architect Reynar Banham is in particular worth dwelling upon even though many found it rather provocative (and some surely still do). Banham opened his book titled *Los Angeles – The Architecture of Four Ecologies* with this statement on 'learning the locale language' of Los Angeles:

> … the language of design, architecture, and urbanism in Los Angeles is the language of movement. Mobility outweighs monumentality there to a unique degree … the city will never be fully understood by those who cannot move fluently through its diffuse urban texture, cannot go with the flow of its unprecedented life. So, like earlier generations of English intellectuals who taught themselves Italian in order to read Dante in the original, I learned to drive in order to read Los Angeles in the original (Banham 1971/2009, 5).

There is an uneasy bypassing of social exclusion here as one wonders how the physically challenged and poor people may 'move fluently through its diffuse urban texture'. Having said so, I think the approach of Banham was unique, and in his time very provocative. Just as Venturi et al. provoked the architectural establishment by deeming the Las Vegas strip and its vernacular box architecture 'real architecture' (Venturi et al 1972), so did Banham upset those who partly held Los Angeles in lower esteem (as the peak of American popular culture) and partly thought of road spaces as no more than instrumental landscapes of physical displacement. If we add to this the fact that Banham was an English architect that went to the United States, most people would have expected a Eurocentric discourse of dismay. However, one might have expected the same when French philosopher Jean Baudrillard rented a car to make a coast-to-coast trip – and the exact opposite happened, as Baudrillard was mesmerized by the American frontier and the infrastructural landscape of the 'new world' in what he termed 'Astral America' (Baudrillard 1988). Such interpretation resonates with the wider set of 'road mythologies' within American popular culture begun by the novel *On the Road* by Jack Kerouac (1957) and carried on in 'road pictures' such as *Bonnie and Clyde* (1967), *Easy Rider* (1969), *Badlands* (1973), and *Thelma and Louise* (1991). All of these capture a peculiar sense of restlessness (Steinbeck 1961) and even 'road fever' (Schwarzer 2004, 116), which is a very powerful and influential cultural trope, but in all fairness is also a very American perspective that reinforces the general perception of the American folk psyche as one of mobile and nomadic lifestyles.

Schwarzer comments on Banham by saying that '*the Los Angeles freeways form a gigantic network that can feel oddly like home – a kind of residence in fluid movement'* (Schwarzer 2004, 110). This resonates with the idea of 'dwelling in motion' (Hannam et al. 2006) and very much with Banham's attempt to interpret the Los Angeles freeway as more than a movement space. Instead of referring to the freeways of Los Angeles as a modernizing feature, Banham refers to the classic European movement systems in his interpretation:

> The motor age, from the mid-twenties onwards, again tended to confirm the going pattern, and the freeway network that now traverses the city, which has since added major aerospace industries to its economic armoury, conspicuously parallels the five first railways out of the pueblo. Indeed the freeways seem to have fixed Los Angeles in canonical and monumental form, much as the great streets of Sixtus V fixed Baroque Rome, or the *Grands Travaux* of Baron Hausmann fixed the Paris of *la belle époque* (Banham 1971/2009,17, italics in original).

'Zooming in', Banham keeps the provocative tone and argues that '*the fact that these parking-lots, freeways, drive-ins, and other facilities have not wrecked the city-form is due chiefly to the fact that Los Angeles has no urban form at all in the commonly accepted sense'* (Banham 1971/2009, 57). But what is truly refreshing in Banham's analysis is his ability to see the motorway (the 'freeway') as a space of mobile everyday life that resonates with the basic statement that mobilities is more than simply movement from A to B (Banham 1971/2009, 195-196).

Ending this section on Banham I want to point at his final and provocative remarks on Los Angeles that could be seen as a premonition of the so-called 'Los Angeles School' in human geography that in the 1990s countered the monocentric and sedentary urban theory of the Chicago school precisely by referring to Los Angeles as a 'new urban model' (Dear 2002):

> Los Angeles threatens the intellectual repose and professional livelihood of many architects, artists, planners, and environmentalists because it breaks the rule of urban design that they promulgate in works and writings and teach to

> their students … all the most admired theorists of the present century, from the Futurists and Le Corbusier to Jane Jacobs and Sibyl Moholgy-Nagy, have been wrong. The belief that certain densities of population, and certain physical forms of structure are essential to the working of a great city, views shared by groups as diverse as the editors of *Architectural Review* and the members of Team Ten, must be to that same extent false. And the methods of design taught, for instance, by the Institute for Architecture and Urban Planning in New York and similar schools, must be to that extent irrelevant … Los Angeles emphatically suggests that there is no simple correlation between urban form and social form (Banham 1971/2009, 218-219).

The way Banham (and others) have tried to open up our understanding of freeways or motorways as social sites of interaction has to do with a profound issue within our cultural reservoir of concepts that we utilize to describe experiences of transport. The Danish sociologist Henrik Dahl argues in the book *Den Usynlige Verden* (*The Invisible World*, Dahl 2008) that we lack concepts and language for dealing sufficiently with trivial and mundane experiences such as driving on the motorway (as well as a host of other everyday experiences). To Dahl such lack of 'meta-treatments' means we are left with a vocabulary of only traffic jams, black spots, and car crashes. Surely these are important aspects but they are only some of the many complex dimensions of everyday life mobilities. So he argues that we should be occupied by the question 'what is the name of my mobility experience?' in relation to mundane everyday practices such as driving.

The rosy story of Banham has of course not been left as the only impression of his work. For instance we find that Gehl draws out Los Angeles as dystopian nightmare compared to his vision of pedestrian heaven in Venice (1996, 104). Enough have been said about Los Angeles and the American literature about it; now I turn to a short theoretical identification of the motorway assemblage in order to set up the analytical framework of the case study to follow.

Conceptualising motorway assemblages

I end this conceptual and theoretical framing of the motorway by explaining briefly the notion of 'motorway assemblage'. In accordance with the application of the notion of 'assemblage' used throughout this book, I lean on Easterling (2011), Farias and Bender (2010), Latour (2005), Seiler (2008), and Varnelis (2008) among others. Also the notion of cycling assemblage (see chapter five) from earlier work is inspirational (Mikkelsen et al. 2011) as well as the idea of 'metroscape' (see chapter six). However, I do not want to repeat all these theoretical building blocks here; rather, I want to state that I think of 'motorway assemblages' in a similar vein.

In chapter three I presented the term 'mobility assemblage' in order to capture the ways in which systems and socio-technical networks that 'host' contemporary mobilities are complex and large material environments where technologies, humans, software, codes, semiotic and communicative systems, objects, and artefacts are assembled in a specific combination facilitating and affording certain mobile practices and restricting or preventing others. The key issue is how systems and networks assemble humans and non-humans in an attempt to 'stage' mobilities. So outside these lines of thinking I am proposing that we look at the Eastern Jutland motorway stretch from Aarhus to Vejle in the light of how it affords particular practices, how it works as both a flow space for vehicles, goods and mobile subjects, as well as how it is nested into the physical environment that at points along the route may take on properties of pristine countryside and at other points the properties of dense, built-up urban environments. As this is explored under the auspices of the *Staging Mobilities* framework I ask the 'Goffman question' of 'what goes on here?' In other words, what kind of (social) space is the motorway?

Of course people are navigating and controlling their vehicles in an instrumental sense in order not to get hurt, but speeding, joyriding, looking at the landscape, communicating (carrying networks), discussing with passengers, listening to the radio or books, working (Hislop 2013; Laurier et al. 2012), coffee drinking, studying maps and GPS devices etc., are all among the many motorway practices. In the words of Merriman:

> … driving is a complex *social* practice and activity, and drivers do communicate and interact with people and all manner of things, inhabiting and consuming the spaces of the car and road in a myriad of distinctive ways (Merriman 2007, 11, italics in original).

I am interested in the motorway as an interaction space, but as already mentioned there is, of course, much to understand in the relation between the mobile subjects in their vehicles and the context alongside the route. I have tried to reference some of these ways of thinking about motorway spaces since the relation between the road and its surroundings is important. Also one should have to think about the inside of the car as an interaction space. In the case of the car hosting a 'mobile with', there is obviously some sort of communicative interaction taking place between the mobile subjects present within the car. Mobility scholar Eric Laurier has devoted much energy to understanding how people inhabit the interior of car spaces as they move along, and has documented how the car is a domesticated space, an office space, and how, for example, families on the move negotiate and interact in such a space either in wayfinding practices or simply in social interaction as they move along (Laurier 2004; Laurier et al. 2012). What happens inside cars on the motorway is of course a huge part of the motorway as an interaction space -- many people listen to the radio, talk on the phone and much more -- but I need to draw the line of limitation here. My focus is on the interaction between cars in general but I will of course bear in mind the microinteraction climates within cars, even though I cannot engage in an analysis of same in this work.

The case – its history and context

This section is the first part of the empirical analysis, starting with contextualizing the Eastern Jutland motorway and methodological reflections. Many explorations of this complex nexus have been carried out by various scholars nationally by, for example, Buchardt and Schønberg (2006), Clemmensen (2008a, 2008b), Grunfelder and Nielsen (2013), Humlum (1966), Jensen (1999), Jørgensen (2001), Kaufmann (1959), Madsen (2009), and internationally by, for example, Marshall (2005) and Shane (2005, 2011). In Denmark, as in much of the world, the process of urbanization and centralization has perhaps slowed down but certainly not stopped. In the words of Hans Mammen: '*From North to South, from East to West, Denmark appears as one big garden city, an urbanized landscape with what is equivalent to one metropolitan population settled within short distances*' (Mammen 1997, 270, my translation).

The coining of sweeping metaphors for the national development process dates back to the 1950s and the discussion of a decentralized 'star city sketch' versus a centralised development pattern alongside the national motorway arteries termed 'the big H' was one of the main public discussions; see Jensen 1999 for an elaborate discussion. The 'big H' became the dominant metaphor coined around the structure of the main north-south motorway structure in Jutland, the east-west connection across Fyn, and the final connection toward the north and the greater Copenhagen area. Nielsen and Hemmersam show how the notion of the 'big H' affords an even more radical imaginary, namely the idea of an 'H-city' (Nielsen and Hemmersam 2004, 153). The key point here is that these large scale metaphorical conceptualisations lend themselves to both policy making and new perspectives on the national landscape and on what 'urban Denmark' really looks like.

It is now well documented that two dominant functional regions are on the rise in Denmark (Hovgensen et al. 2005; Miljøministeriet 2006). The one is in the eastern part of the country with the point of gravity in Copenhagen and the other is the region emerging around the motorway in East Jutland with a linear shape but bipolar gravity in Aarhus and the 'Triangle Area' (Miljøministeriet 2006, 38). Those documents also illustrate the extensive urban densification process that has taken place alongside the motorway (predominantly as Municipalities have reserved land for industry and businesses assuming it enjoy a strategic location close to the motorway). The effect of the urban densification along the motorway structure is rather complex to analyse but Hovgesen et al. argue that the motorway changes its character from being a high-classed road net for people driving from region to region to being a 'traffic machine' supporting the larger urban communities (Hovgesen et al. 2005, 41), or what is termed the 'urbanisation of the motorway' (ibid., 72). One of the future consequences may thus be the emergent 'motorway city' which the National Planning Report also identifies but argues should be limited by more restrictive planning measures (Miljøministeriet 2006). In the report the mantra is that 'there must be a difference between the city and the country' and this dictum is nested firmly within a tradition of strong enforcement of the 'country zone division' principle of the Planning Act; it is also seen as the political answer to the pressing question about the issue of 'sprawl'. The 2006 National Planning Report describes the situation at the Easter Jutland Motorway as follows:

> Eastern Jutland is developing into one coherent area with large population growth and interurban division of labour in the city ribbon that stretches from Kolding to Randers. Yes, one might even see the contour of an emerging new million city in Denmark. It is of national interest to ensure that there will still be open and coherent landscapes between the cities within the city ribbon (Miljøministeriet 2006, 20, my translation).

And further on the development of the Eastern Jutland motorway:

> The motorway has attracted new businesses – partly reinforced by the municipal area reservation in areas of close motorway proximity. The many reserved business areas along the motorway give the landscape an all-together different character and in many instances the rural communities are influenced by the urban growth spread and business buildings. Municipal requirements for more business areas of close motorway proximity put pressure on the free landscapes and green interurban spaces left … the functionally coherent city ribbon between Randers and Kolding should not over time develop into a physically coherent ribbon city. The cities in the region and along the motorway must be separate and remain as nodes with open land in between (Miljøministeriet 2006, 55-56, my translation).

This is a close as we get to a diagnosis of urban sprawl in a Danish context with the description of the 'the spread urban growth and business buildings' alongside the motorways. Also we find here the clear urban/rural distinction from the Planning Act as a policy guideline. This principle has been codified into the world famous 'Finger Plan' of Copenhagen which (even though under pressure) at least places restrictions on urban development in the green spaces and thus keeps the urban/rural division alive. A similar planning doctrine for the East Jutland motorway corridor is nonexistent and this could prove to be a serious condition for future development in this region. The contemporary urban development model with the motorway in Eastern Jutland may even be said to resemble the notion of 'strip development' coined by Venturi et al. more than four decades ago in their analysis of the Las Vegas strip (Venturi et al. 1972). I will not go deeper into the policy remedy and counter measures of the State in this case, but I will keep this description in mind when we start looking at the material space in itself.

Not all analysts of contemporary development seem to agree that lack of distinction between the rural and urban belongs to a potential future:

> To an increasing degree, "The Big H" achieves the character of a long urban band without any clear distinction between the towns it passes through or between the town and the landscape. This creates the need to redefine the traditional conception of the town and the landscape as each other's antipoles and results in the recognition of the fact that highway planning is no longer the orchestration of the "journey" through the golden age landscape. The completed road is a deeply integrated part of the new city and its surrounding recreational landscape ...The highway is no longer something the city turns its back on. The road does not solely belong to the landscape space, but to a greater degree is perceived as part of the new town (Bjarum 2011, 3).

Increasingly the 'urban motorway' is becoming a planning challenge with, for instance, requirements for noise barriers (Egebjerg 2011, 25).

That there is a cultural context even for the generic artefact we call the motorway is illustrated by the fantastic story of the Chinese Princeton graduate and, later, major Hong Kong entrepreneur Gordon Wu, who in the 1950s saw the New Jersey Turnpike and decided to 'bring it home to China' (Campanella 2005), but obviously not in the physical sense. Wu saw the potential of the freeway which was unknown in his home country, and acted upon his entrepreneurial impulse and together with a hand-picked team of engineers (and after a lot of lobbying and softening up of the Chinese political climate toward such Western ideas), he completed the construction of the 'Guangzhou-Shenzhen Superhighway' in 22 months for its final opening in 1994 (Campanella 2005, 301). One problem was the staging 'from above' as it proved to be difficult 'import' a highway; another problem was the staging 'from below' where the cultural understanding for appropriating this new technology was lacking, to say the least. Horrible stories about people and animals filling up the motorway spaces or trying to cross across them with fatal consequences. These events are witness to the fact that a motorway is to be appropriated both in a technological as well as a cultural sense. Less dramatic was the creation of the Danish motorway system. However, I personally recall moving to Aalborg and thinking that the construction of the stretch from Aarhus (my home town) to Aalborg would be a simple story of progress and larger interurban interaction until fellow students with families in the countryside told stories about how old friends stopped seeing each other and children's playmates were sealed off from one another due to the barrier created by the new motorway. There is no doubt that people living in Denmark were ready to appropriate the motorways in relation to mobilities skills and safety, but I believe many were still unprepared for the social transformations that came in the wake of building of such large structures. However, the policy argument for building the motorway system has been one of rational and instrumental movement of people and goods from A to B. There could have been an element of nation-building had it not been the case that the old highway system had contributed to that centuries before. So the 'H-City' as it is dubbed has had many different effects on interurban dynamics and one of the most dynamic stretches of the system today is the one going from Aarhus down south to Vejle – the stretch I explore in the empirical case analysis.

In the book *Byen, vejen og landskabet,* Hovgesen et al. make a distinction between three types of motorways in Denmark; the 'golden age road', the urban motorway, and the 'trucker path' (2005, 86-87). At the stretch I am analysing, all three may be found even though I will put most focus on the urban motorway and the 'trucker path' (named after the massive handling of freight which also includes commuting practices). The former is named the 'golden age road' with a reference to historic Danish landscape paintings of scenic and 'authentic' landscapes as scenery from the age of the rise of a national romantic identity. Here the notion primarily is relevant when the stretch of motorway cuts through open landscapes with wide horizons and clear vistas. From the description of the Vejle-Aarhus stretch, it is clear that urban densification has taken place along the strip and this is in particular the case along the section from Horsens to Vejle (Hovgesen et al. 2005, 58).

The Danish Road Directorate published the book *Beautiful Roads. A Handbook of Road Architecture* in 2002 and therein they specified a number of design requirements and principles that we find influenced the motorway assemblage of East Jutland. They argue that:

> A characteristic feature of Danish freeways [motorways] is a careful treatment of the landscape and terrain that rarely produces stark contrasts. Signage and other equipment are kept at a minimum and the absence of billboards, art, and other distracting and defacing elements in the road's immediate vicinity emphasizes the desire for clarity and simplicity. Lighting fixtures illuminate feeder lanes and exits, but otherwise there is almost no artificial lighting in the open countryside … There is a firm tradition in Denmark of limiting the use of roadside equipment and the equipment used is standardized and simplified as far as possible. With design aimed at simple systematization and good readability, Danish road signs present clearly understandable messages. One special problem in the open countryside is the demand for readability at great distances and high speeds. Information signs are consequently often quite dominating and special attention must be paid to where the signs are placed. It is important for how we experience the landscape, the road, or a building that signs be located appropriately in relation to them. We rarely associate suburban roads with design, but they usually do have standardized equipment such as bus stops, benches, fences, lighting fixtures, and bicycle racks (Road Directorate 2002, 27, 48).

Many studies have conceptualized the car driver as the spectator of the environment and the vistas designed by motorway designers. Here I argue that car drivers are mobile performers and that the motorway is a complex assemblage of social interaction and materiality. I am interested in the interaction between motorway users as well as how the armature of the motorway with its immediate environment of either buildings and urban structures or landscapes becomes enrolled into the situational mobilities of motorway driving.

Before I move to the analysis I want very briefly to present a few 'facts of the road' I am going to explore in more detail. In terms of location I am studying the motorway between the cities of Aarhus and Vejle in the Eastern part of Jutland, Denmark (hereafter simply referred to as 'Aarhus-Vejle'). The stretch I have chosen to explore is approximately 70 km long and has been constructed in sections: 1994 (Aarhus Syd), 1990 (Hedensted), 1980 (Vejle Fjord Bridge), 1980 (Ejer Baunehøj), 1997 (Skanderborg). The architects on the projects were Vejdirektoratet (anlægskontoret), Jysk Motorvejskontor, Møller & Wichmann, Møller & Grønborg A/S, and P. Hvidt & O. Mølgård-Nielsen. The engineer and developer were Vejdirektoratet (anlægskontoret) and Jysk Motorvejskontor and the daily operator is Vejdirektoratet (in English, the Road

Directorate). The stretch has various numbers of daily travelers: 49,000 (Vejle Bridge), 42,000 (Hedensted), 37,000 (Skanderborg), 33,000 (Ejer Baunehøj), and 21,000 (Aarhus Syd). The cost of building the motorway was approx. 70 million DKR/per kilometre which is about 4.9 billion DKR in total.

The case study is divided into three parts: part one concerns the 'staging from above' perspective and is titled 'The motorway in a larger planning perspective'. Part two is termed 'Architectural stages of the motorway' and finally the third part is termed 'Mobile situations on the motorway'. The case is produced through the utilization of photography, video caption, mappings, and sketching.

Methodological reflections

The whole stretch was captured using two cameras. Camera one is a HD camera mounted on the passenger seat of the car used for the mapping. The camera filmed straight ahead in a fixed position for the whole stretch. The idea was to capture the route objectively and make it possible to extract still photos of the route from inside the car from the video file. Also video capturing creates possibilities of extracting a series of pictures, e.g., to capture a mobile situation. Camera two is a compact camera and was attached to the head of the driver to capture the mobility practices of driving on the motorway. The camera was fixed to the forehead, positioned as close to the driver's eyes as possible. The capturing focuses on driving-related actions of the driver, e.g., looking over his shoulder to check for cars in the adjacent lane. The video material captures the sense of involvement in the motorway assemblage from the perspective of the mobile subject. A detailed process of editing and choosing the stills that represent the issues took place. Also the sketches and drawings in the case material have been made using the photos as inspiration.

The field work not only concentrates on being on the motorway but also studies the practices of motorway access and exit as well as entering and leaving the adjacent spaces, which are either part of the motorway (lay-bys and picnic areas) or more or less detached from the motorway (crossings connecting to built-up areas). The registrations made at street level are complemented by mappings of the infrastructures seen from above. A research assistant with a background in urban design made all the registrations and diagrams as well as the sketches illustrating this analysis. Sketches have been utilized in particular where I wish to underline a set of more generic principles and thus want to explore sketching as a means of highlighting particularities. As in the other cases of this book the empirical field work has been based on a thorough dialogue and instruction, and the interpretation of the material has been subject to intensive deliberation. Moreover, I am very familiar with the specific motorway stretch from Aarhus to Vejle as I have driven it innumerous times. I have taken some of these trips as a reflective mobilities scholar, others simply as an ordinary motorway inhabitant going either to visit friends and family, on holiday, or to various meetings.

PART I: Staging form above - the motorway in a larger planning perspective

I start out by contextualizing the stretch of road chosen for this case study. As mentioned I am exploring the approximately 70 km long stretch from Aarhus to Vejle in the Eastern part of Jutland as a part of the main E45 motorway (fig. 7.1). The stretch is a small section of the large North-South motorway armature cutting through Europe from Norway in the North to Italy in the South. In relation to its Northern European context we see that the stretch is strategically located near Aarhus, which is not only the second largest city in Denmark but also one of the busiest container harbours in Northern Europe.

Furthermore, the city of Esbjerg is a large container and ferry harbour as well. On the North-East axis we find the ferry terminals of Frederikshavn north of Aalborg (the gateway to Sweden and Norway) and the large German urban nodes of Hamburg and Berlin in the South.

If we 'zoom in' on the stretch itself we see the two end nodes of Vejle and Aarhus (fig. 7.2). As mentioned the stretch was completed in different stages and it connects smaller cities such as Skanderborg, Horsens, and Hedensted that are located adjacent to the motorway. Moreover, it facilitates the 'Triangle Area' (the cities of Vejle, Kolding, and Frederica) which is one of the fastest growing freight and logistics nodes in Eastern Jutland.

The design of motorway spaces in Denmark is a discipline reaching back more than five decades. There are many different reasons why the underlying design rationales reach from aesthetics and landscape culture to traffic safety to instrumental calculations of interurban mobility. The difference translates into different layouts and designs that evolved over time. Inspired by the 1930s German building of the 'Autobahn', the first designs had a wide central reserve. Later in the 1970s the inspiration from American highway design led to wider cross- sections. The different design principles led to different driving experiences. A large scale and wide cross- section that cuts through the landscape will enhance the open character of the landscape and afford good orientation to the driver, whereas a narrow and closed cross-section will create a 'corridor' with limited field of vision and smaller spaces for signage and safety equipment (Hovgesen et al. 2005, 50). There are three main models of motorway construction based upon the width of the central reserves in Danish motorway design (fig. 7.3): the four-metre wide central reserve (dating to the 1950s and '60s); the six-metre wide central reserve (predominantly constructed in the

Left:
Fig. 7.1: Aarhus-Vejle in a northern Northern European context

Right:
Fig. 7.2: Aarhus-Vejle and East Jutland

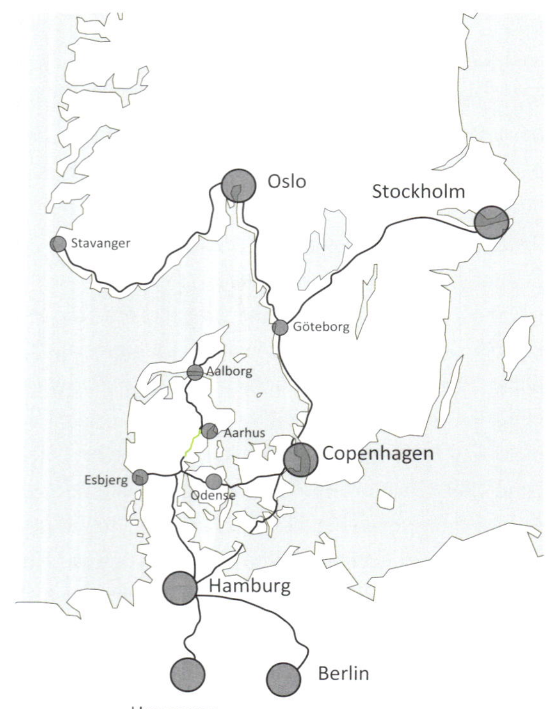

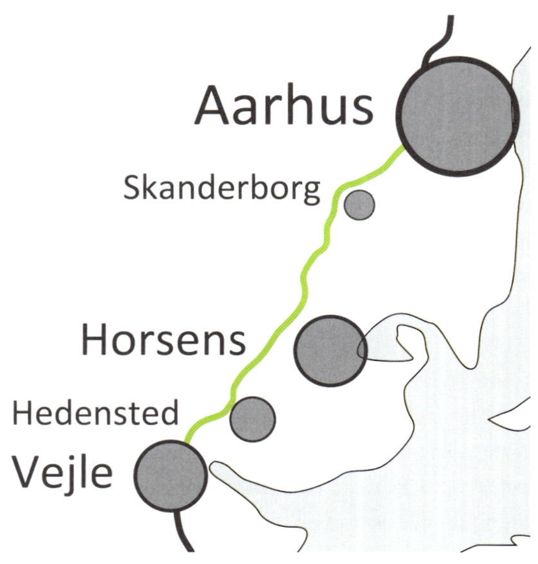

1960s and '70s); and the twelve-metre central reserve (built in the 1970s). In addition to these, a number of other designs are found for example, with plants and vegetation in the central reserve (Hovgesen et al. 2005).

Along the motorway, there is, of course, a difference between the rural and pastoral landscape and that of the urban motorway. There also may be all sorts of variations in the changing dynamics of motorway morphology. The urban character of the Aarhus-Vejle stretch speaks to this dynamic change along the route, where one will pass relatively dense and urbanized built-up areas as well as open landscape typologies. The creation of industrial development along the motorway also varies along the route. One example is at Hedensted (a small city between Vejle and Horsens). Until the advent of the motorway in 1992, the city was defined mainly by the presence of the railroad network and the old highway. Thereafter the stretch around Hedensted became a particularly fruitful illustration of the profound transformations taking place. The rapid urban densification along the motorway in Hedensted (fig. 7.4) illustrates the policy dilemma between the national planning policy of restricted urban development, with its respect of the 'country zone' planning doctrine, versus the interest in attracting companies and businesses to the local municipalities (Hedensted 2009). This pressure can be seen in the property prices, where the price of a lot facing the motorway is up to two and a half times the price of an area south of the city of Hedensted (web1, 2012).

From the diagram we see partly how the dual nodal structure based on highway and rail was transformed from 1972 through 2012. Also the diagram illustrates that the 'motorway densification' challenges the 'rail densification' and actually supersedes this by 2012.

As an attempt to analyse the motorway's staging from above, one may map the industry dwellings (built-up

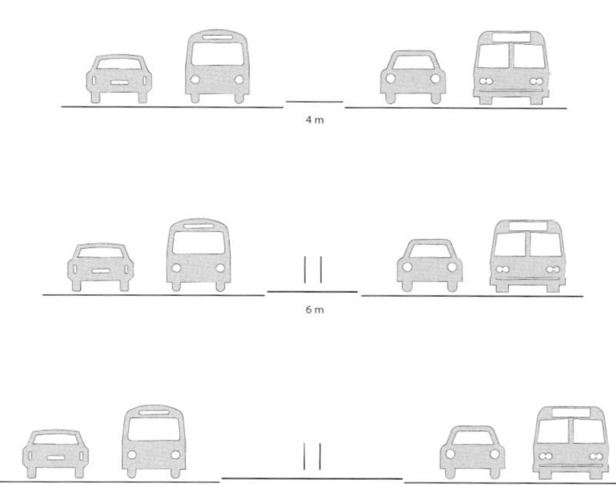

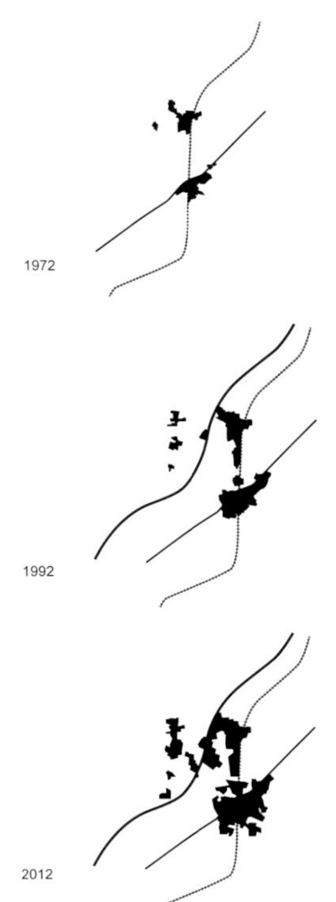

Top:
Fig. 7.3: Design principles

Bottom:
Fig. 7.4: Urban Morphology along Aarhus-Vejle

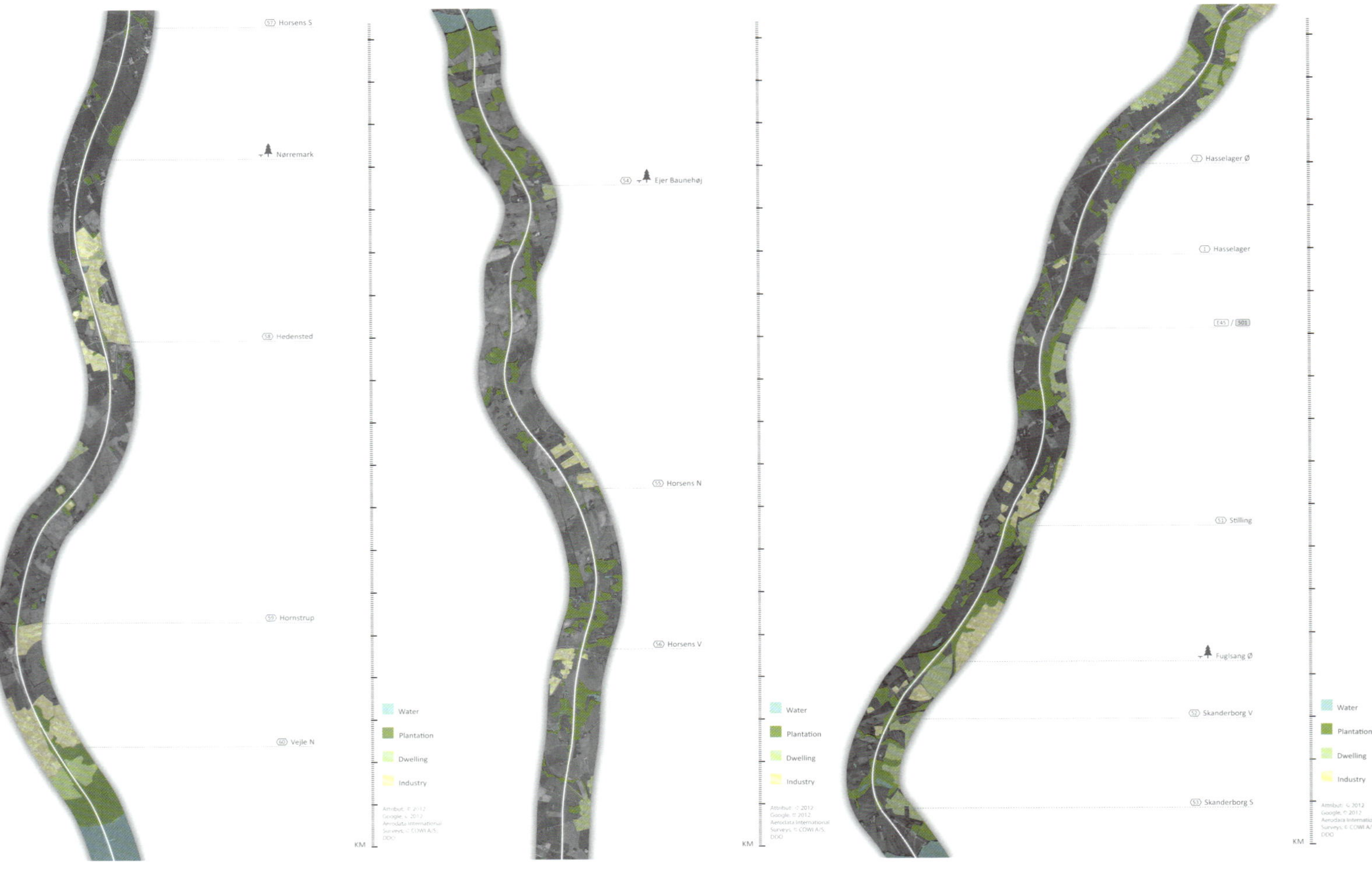

area) and the plantings and water (the landscape) along the stretch. If the stretch is divided into three parts (this is necessary in order to produce areal diagrams and maps large enough for analysis) and includes a 500- metre adjacent space ribbon, a rough impression of the programmed strip emerges (figs. 7.5).

By mapping the dimensions we start to understand rhythms, diversities, consequences of urban growth, as well as the fragmentary and clustered character of built-up areas en route. If we for instance study the 'water' category, two sections stand out. One is where Vejle Fjord meets the motorway and the other is where Skanderborg Lake meets the motorway. At these two intersections the landscape is divided and the 'blue structure' serves the purpose of being a landmark for the driver. If we look at plantings, they are present mainly as larger formations of forest intersected by the motorway (for example, at Ejer Baunehøj) or as more diffuse and scattered plantings in the open landscape and adjacent to smaller ponds (for example, at Fulgsang Ø) or buffers to 'backstage' the motorway in its relation to dwellings (for example, at Aarhus). Quite often plantings are utilized as a 'wall' for or buffer to the road space, either just to one side of the road

Fig. 7.5: Section 1: Vejle-Horsens

or as a more 'tunneling' model on both sides of the road. Such 'walls' may exhibit very different levels of visual transparency and, where there are gaps and open sections in the 'walls', these may frame objects and landscapes seen from the driver's perspective. The industrial areas are clustered mostly along the motorway adjacent to urban areas and cities. The morphology and shape of these industrial areas may, however, vary from enclaves relatively detached from the motorway (for example, Fulgsang Ø) to others developed in close proximity to the motorway as 'front stages' hereto (for example, at Hedensted). Finally, some built-up areas are reaching across the motorway (as is the case at Vejle N.). In general terms the motorway is staged as a 'backstage' to the dwellings alongside the stretch.

If we study the motorway from this 'staging from above' perspective, we see some of the traits and characters that will be revealed only at this level and scale. The programming dynamics along the stretch as it pertains to both landscape characteristics and urban features are being brought to life as we see the layout of these elements alongside the motorway's ribbon space. However, we may still study the staging from above in a closer 'zoom', which is what I propose with the next section on the 'architectural stages of the motorway'.

PART II: Architectural stages of the motorway

From the almost 'helicopter-like' perspective of the previous section I propose yet another 'zoom in' and will speak of the 'architectural stages' that the motorway design affords. In line with the tradition of architecture and urban design, I adhere to the notion of 'typologies' in order to create an overview of the differentiation in the design practices that materialise in the concrete design. First I will propose eight analytical spatial typologies of the motorway and then in the following exemplify them with reference to the Aarhus-Vejle stretch.

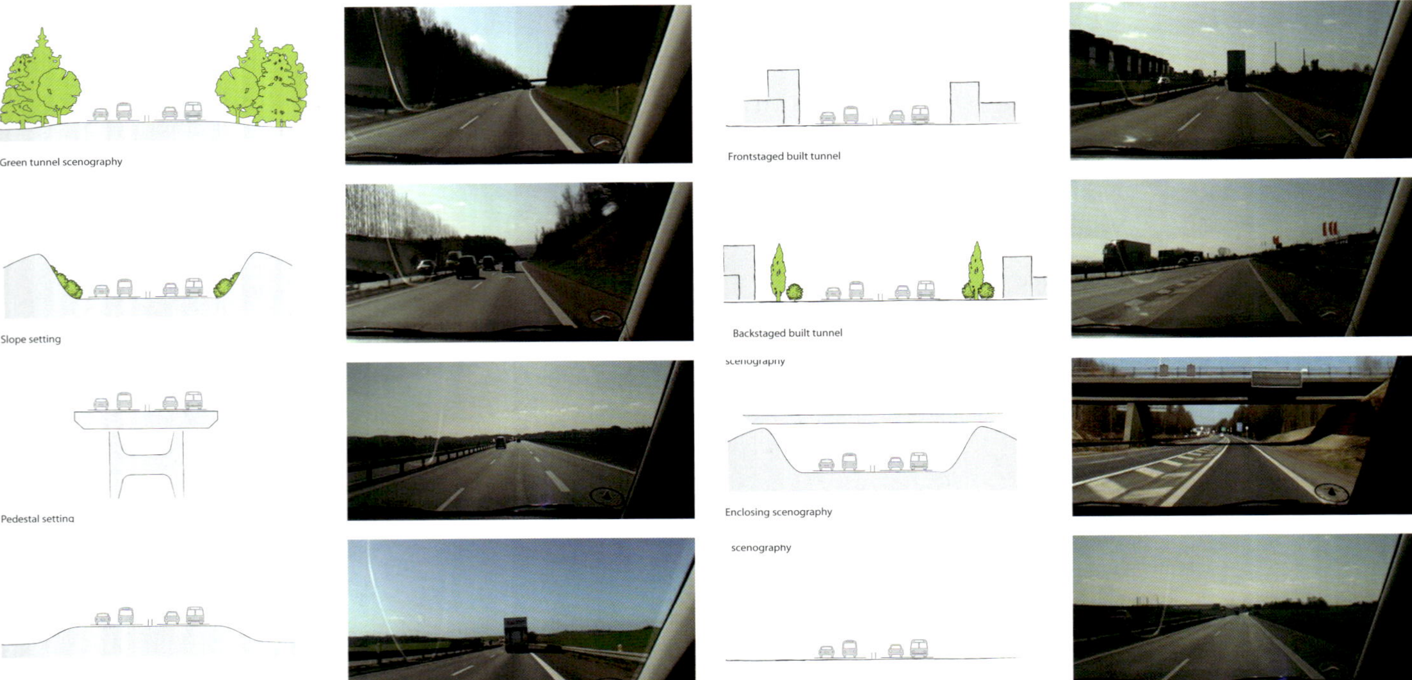

Fig. 7.6: Spatial typologies of the motorway

In creating the typologies the empirical material has been cross-referenced with the literature mentioned at the beginning of this chapter. The typologies proposed ranges from the open to the closed, as well as from a 'front stage' toward a 'backstage' perception. In the following diagrams the typologies are listed both in diagrammatic form as well as with a specific windscreen photo (fig. 7.6). The first typology is termed the 'green tunnel scenography' and this refers to the perception of plantings alongside the motorway armature as if it were a 'tunnel'. The transparency to the 'world beyond' depends on the thickness of the plantings and may vary from complete transparency to semi-open green stretches that gives 'framed visibility' to the landscape beyond.

The second typology is a variation of the first typology in the sense that we are looking at a model where the sides of the armature are bounded upwards and where the perception of the driver is framed by the upsloping sides of the motorway. The typology is termed 'slope setting' due to the framing created by slopes that delimit (or fully prevent) the driver to see beyond them. Such a typology is at times found in denser areas where the slopes act as active sound barriers. However, as the slopes open outward the sense of confinement is loosened up compared to the first typology. The height of the slopes obviously determines how much of the surrounding environment may be perceptible to the mobile subject.

The third typology is termed 'pedestal setting' and refers to the raising up of the road space, for example, to run over water or other types of natural environment that need to be passed over by the motorway. The Vejle Fjord Bridge is an example. The fourth typology is the 'open stage' (levelled), where we find many similar traits as in the former, but where the connection to the immediate landscape is closer and more integral to the motorway experience. The fifth typology is termed 'front stage built tunnel scenography' and as the name suggests this is one of the key typologies of urban motorways and is found with these many industrial and business developments alongside the motorway. Very often we see corporate architecture, signature buildings, and company logos, flags, banners, and billboards as the semiotic layer to this typology – hence the front staging of companies utilizing these spaces for massive commercial exposure. Typology number six is related to the former and termed 'back staged built tunnel scenography' and thus alludes to the application of some sort of barrier (either plantings and trees or sound barriers) creating a backstage feeling in the motorway space. The seventh typology is the 'enclosed scenography' and reassembles a tunnel dug underground but is mostly found at the critical points where bridges are crossing the motorway creating a 'tunnelling effect'. The eighth and final typology is termed the 'open stage' and is as the name suggests the situation where the motorway is at the same level as the surrounding landscape. This is fairly open and thus both transparent from the mobile subject's point of view while the mobilities taking place at the motorway are highly conspicuous from outside the motorway. To drive along a stretch of motorway like the Aarhus–Vejle strip is to become immersed into these various typologies at different temporalities (depending on one's speed) and at various rhythms (e.g., depending on whether one drives through during rush hour or late at night). Such motorway engagement within a dynamic and differentiated set of typologies offers multiple different experiences and views, some enclosing and turned inward, others open and having large vistas. Some afford the experience of travelling through an industrial corridor, others of sliding across green landscapes.

The perception of the architectural qualities of the motorway assemblage is obviously related to the speed of the travelling person (Jensen 2013a, 110-115). The mental capacities of the human perception of signs, information, and the environment in general are dependent on the speed of the mobile subject, which is why motorway signage conveys simple messages in large text or signage format. The readability of the environment is, however, also an issue for the buildings and other features of the environment. The businesses and companies that have built warehouses or domicile buildings alongside the motorway have accordingly created large building volumes, often with conspicuous signs or aesthetic features. If we think about the motorway assemblage as a semiotic armature offering potential commercial communication to the 'great moving public' of the road, the signs and buildings alongside need to capture the attention of the drivers. As mentioned before, the regulatory framework for motorway design in Denmark is fairly restrictive in this respect. This means that a company cannot build anything it pleases, and it can most certainly not erect objects or artefacts that the authorities deem to distract the driver's attentions and thus create hazards. (I will return to the case of placing an aircraft adjacent to the motorway shortly.) However, the interpretation of what may be done is still rather open, and the stretch between Aarhus and Vejle is actually one of the more 'colourful' of the Danish motorway stretches. On the sketch of the warehouse near Vejle N (fig. 7.7) we see the very simple principles of roadside communication at work. The building envelope is constructed as a 'screen' facing the motorway and the placing of the business logo on the upper right of the façade. Furthermore, the 'screen' and the 'frame' have been highlighted by the use of a lighter colour for the 'screen' and a darker one for the 'frame'.

The 'screen' captures the gaze of the mobile subject in a horizontal move from right to left simultaneously with the correspondent car movement that leads the viewer's gaze to stop at the corporate brand positioned at the upper right corner of the 'screen'. This is an example of the way that a motorway assemblage serves also as a space of communication and how this has been rather meticulously taken into consideration when locating, designing, and constructing adjacent buildings. Other examples of the relationship between speed and architectural perception are the office buildings at Hedensted (fig. 7.8). In this sketch we see four identical cubes sitting next to the roadside with a relative small distance between them. What is at work here is a playing with the notion of repetition and rhythm as the mobile subject, due to high speed travel, experiences the buildings as a unitary sign and not four separate entities, and thus ultimately an architectural expression of the unitary corporate brand.

The fact that these relatively smaller buildings are not just built into one big volume is the evidence of an underlying design principle of rhythm and repetition. Nothing could have been easier (and perhaps even cheaper) than to build these four boxes into one building. That four adjacent boxes stand on the roadside speaks to the motorway as a communication space. The last sketch I bring into this context is related to a warehouse near Aarhus (fig. 7.9). What we find here is very simple geometry and the use of one type of light metal material. The volume of the buildings is rather overwhelming (and some may say out of scale) and dwarfs the passing cars.

Top:
Fig. 7.7: Warehouse near Vejle N

Bottom:
Fig. 7.8: Office buildings at Hendensted

Opposite page:

Fig. 7.9. Warehouse near Aarhus

The geometry of the cubic architecture is instantly recognizable and placed so that it fills the horizon. This feature also provides the mobile subject with more time to observe and respond to the contrast between the soft hilly landscape and the box-like buildings as the landscape frames the buildings and thereby makes them stand out in stark contrast to their context.

From these sketches I have tried to tease out some of the underlying design principles that in very explicit terms take the particular motorway context into consideration. Obviously these are only very preliminary and superficial interpretations and I would need much more space for analysing the individual buildings. I would also have interviewed the owners, architects, and users had the goal been to make a detailed account of motorway architecture. However, I am more interested in how these elements are part of the larger assemblage that creates the experience of motorway driving and becomes the context for the situational mobilities that I end the chapter analysing. One dimension that this analysis does suggest for further exploration is the notion of 'design speed'. As I have progressed with the analysis of the architectural perception, the concept of 'design speed' keeps surfacing. The guidelines for designing motorways and other traffic infrastructures are often quite detailed and take into account speed as a functional requirement (Lynch and Hack 1984; Marshall 2005; Neufert and Neufert 2000; Road Directorate 2002). The *Design Speed, Operating Speed, and Posted Speed Practices* publication by the National Cooperative Highway Research Program (NCHRP) in the United States identifies no fewer than twelve different design speed definitions reaching back to 1936 and up to the present. As this is not an issue for a longer analysis, I merely present the revised definition of 1997 by Fambro et al. (a definition adapted in the so-called 'Green Book' of American highway design). The definition simply reads: *'The design speed is a selected speed used to determine the various geometric design features of the roadway'* (NCHRP 2003, 9). As Vanderbilt rightly argues, the notion of design speed is a 'confusing concept' and may also refer to the speed at which most people (dubbed the '85th percentile') generally like to travel (Vanderbilt 2008, 182). So the notion may both relate to an underlying design principle on the behalf of the designer as well refer to the pragmatic practices of mobile subjects in situational mobilities (which is termed the 'operating speed' as the nomenclature for the actual speed in NCHRP 2003, 9). Here I want to put emphasis on the speed for which the designer has designed the particular environment, realizing that this may partly be understood on a functional basis as, for example, how fast you may drive in order not to get involved in dangerous situations (either by the topography of the space like a sharp curvature or as a function of the local capacity as when the speed is lowered at the off-ramp stretches near larger cities due to congestion). But as mentioned we may also think of the speed affording particular perceptions of the site or experiences. We may even think of the design speed as a tool for controlling the mobile subjects as, for example, when smaller community roads are supplied with road bumps in order to slow down vehicular traffic. The notion of design speed seems to carry even greater analytical potential and will certainly be a topic for further research under the auspices of the emergent research field in 'mobilities design'.

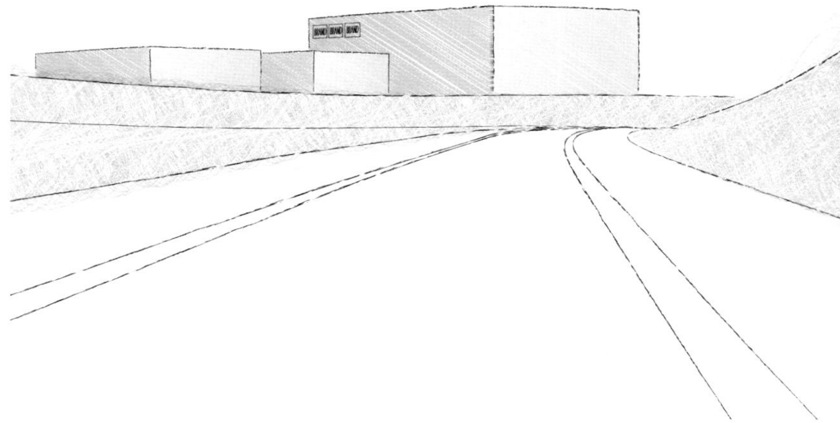

In direct prolongation of the discussion above of the motorway as a 'communication space' where we saw the commercial communication by roadside buildings, office spaces, business headquarters, and storage, we may also find the space utilized by cities and public authorities for city branding. Elsewhere I have described the nature of city branding as 'selective storytelling' and a phenomenon concerning both the communication in language (the 'word city') as well as that of the built environment (the 'stone city') (Jensen 2006c, 2007a). Here I focus on the materiality of artefacts and buildings erected alongside the motorway as a vehicle for representing the city and capturing the attention of passersby. Outside the city of Hedensted we find the very conspicuous 'HH' sculpture that is nested within a heavy industrial development along the motorway (fig. 7.10). Hedensted is a very active city in terms of self-promotion and staging along the motorway, and the stretch is one of the examples of a hybrid of the 'trucker path' and the urban motorway typologies mentioned earlier.

The HH landmark is designed by a local Danish designer named Asbjørn Lønvig and is created by two metal artefacts, one in blue and one in red that supposed to signify the capital letters of the city name. In fact there is a small business has grown up around the 'art piece' and you can, for example, buy HH logos and other HH merchandise products on the web at 'zazzle.com/lonvig' produced in Palo Alto, USA. (See http://www.lonvig.dk/hh.htm). This is probably rather extreme and to my knowledge the only story of a Danish motorway art work that has been commercialised to this degree.

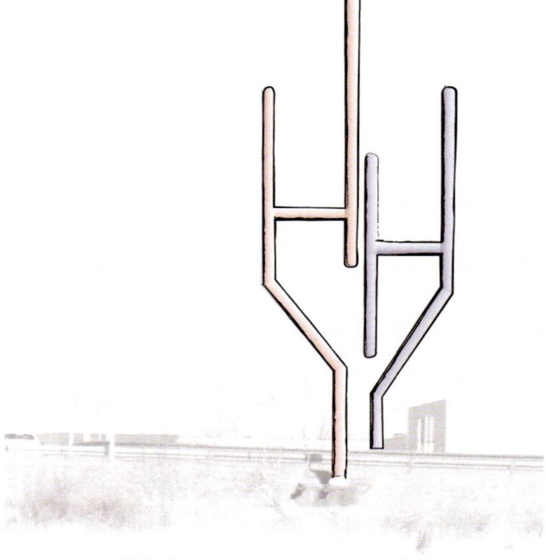

Fig. 7.10: The 'H' logo near Hedensted

Opposite page:

Fig. 7.11: The 'Wave' seen from the Vejle Fjord Bridge

Another example of roadside city branding is in Vejle, where the city has approved the construction of a very conspicuous building on the shore of the fjord. The bridge, with the motorway passing over the fjord, makes the view of Vejle to bypassing cars ideal and the shape of the building resembles waves hitting the shore (fig. 7.11 top). The wave-like building becomes a defining landmark of the city's silhouette seen from the motorway bridge above.

Vejle also planned to construct a set of buildings where each building would be the literal manifestation of the five letters in the city name. Spelling 'VEJLE' in real buildings was an idea that gained quite some media attention when the winning proposal of the architectural competition was announced, but the cost of construction proved to supersede the capacity of the developing agencies, so the project was abandoned. Had it become a reality it would have been the ultimate city logo with a name spelled out in real houses in scale 1:1 and widely open to the gazes from the motorway bridge.

From these branding perspectives I want to move closer into the motorway space itself. As the *Staging Mobilities* framework suggests, we may think of these sites in both a front- and a backstage perspective in order to understand their workings as motorway assemblages. If we take a section of the motorway north of the City of Skanderborg close to the smaller village of Stilling, we see the layout of a rather dense industrial buildup (fig. 7.12). As one drives through the section the ambience is urban and dense with no views of the landscape or nature. This particular stretch is probably the most famous in Denmark since it is here that the advertising company '727' in 2003 placed an old Boeing 727 airplane adjacent to its company headquarters at the motorway roadside (fig. 7.13).

Clearly the company is front staging its presences at this site, and the aircraft is one of the most conspicuous gimmicks to be seen in a Danish motorway context to date. The plane serves as a meeting facility and employee lounge as well as a roadside eye-catcher. The plane has gotten reactions of various kinds. There is, for example, a consultancy report made by the traffic engineering company 'Trafitec' on behalf of the Road Directorate with the title '*Investigation of car driver's behaviour passing a commercial aircraft at the motorway – distraction in traffic*' from 2004 (Trafitec 2004). The report is unique in its methodological approach by utilizing eye-tracking technology in order to establish whether the driver's attention is captured by the aircraft to such a degree that is constitutes a safety issue. The report concludes that the aircraft does capture the attention of the drivers to such a degree that it may at times during rush hour and congestion lead to increasing risks at the stretch (Trafitec 2004, 27). The plane is still there so somewhere in the process of discussing this, another conclusion obviously has been made. However, my point in referring to the report here has been more to illustrate this high degree of 'front stage' attention that this stretch of the motorway has had.

There has also been a lively public debate. During this Danish architect, Professor and Chair of the Danish Arts Council (Statens Kunstfond) Lars Juel Thiis said to TV2 in May 2013 that the presence of the airplane was a *'disaster'* and a '*ridicule to the Danish cultural landscape'* (http://www.tv2oj.dk/artikel/166889:Skanderborg--Duel-om-motorvejsfly). On July 25, 2013, the Danish newspaper Jyllandsposten published a longer exchange of viewpoints and reader opinions triggered by Thiis' statements. Among these are powerful critiques of

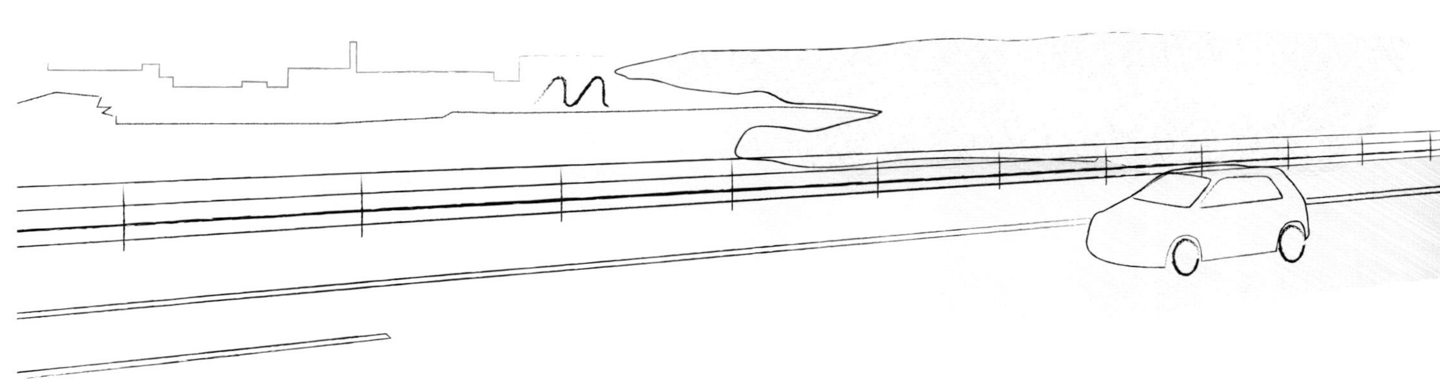

the aesthetic judgments made by the architecture professor. Here are a few examples taken from http://jyllands-posten.dk/indland/ECE5280065/laeserne-fri-os-for-smagsdommere/, my translation):

'We don't need more judges of taste. Let us have more Boeings' (Bjarne Rasmussen).

'We don't need more new rules as offspring from the public employees' urge to control the world. In my family we think of the infamous aircraft at the motorway as a fresh and brilliant event that makes us laugh and works as a landmark to assess how far we have travelled' (Marin Vestergaard).

In all fairness there are also critical voices to be found among the public, but suffice to say that the 727 has triggered emotions and attitudes. By virtue of its enrollment into the motorway assemblage, the aircraft has become a case in point for the argument that motorways are public spaces as well an example of how an armature may become politicized – event though I grant that more progressive messages could be addressed than simply branding an advertising company. Here the principles at work have, however, been the key point. But the stretch we see in the aerial photo contains many other buildings. The case of the aircraft suggests that what stands out in the public debate is the most conspicuous of artefacts rather than the general built-up environment. On the other hand, the discussion would have reached even higher levels of excitement had the aircraft been located in one of the pristine landscapes and not in this urbanized context. The whole environment is, however, indeed turning its front stage toward the drivers, offering an unusual (and perhaps also over-stimulating) semiotic environment.

I have mentioned the communication space of the motorway as one where architectural expressions,

Bottom: Fig. 7.12: Frontstage Skanderborg N

public messages, and commercial messages may proliferate. The strong regulatory framework keeping the general commercial semiotics at a comparable low level is found in the principles laid down in the aesthetic codes and road design (Road Directorate 2002). Despite the fact that Danish motorway spaces are rather modest when it comes to billboards, there are many examples of commercial discourse and commercial semiotics. Some, including the aforementioned architectural professor Lars Thiis, seem to think that this has reached a level of 'visual pollution' and commercial congestion. I am not so interested in passing aesthetic judgements, so I turn instead to the commercial semiotic elements in order to understand how the motorway assemblage is already performing as more than a simple 'people and goods mover'. The many commercial signs witness to a number of facilities that 'comes with the package' of creating a motorway system. As Merriman illustrates with the development of the M1 in England, the eating facilities and the gas stations are important infrastructural add-on typologies that need to be in place for the system to perform (Merriman 2007), and all of these come with a specific semiotic dimension.

In a contemporary motorway assemblage such as the one studied here, there are commercial signs in the built environment such as cafeterias and gas stations as well as on the vehicles themselves (fig. 7.13). As seen from the images here, both local companies and global brands are utilizing the motorway assemblage as a semiotic platform.

The semiotic landscape depicted here is, however, not easy to localize and connect to any particular place. Rather it is an illustration of the generic semiotic landscape of motorways that could be found practically anywhere. The signs are inscribed onto the pavements, on the cars, the house facades, on flags, as well as on various types of erected poles in the continuous semiotic battle for attention.

Before moving to the mobile situations, the final example of architectural stages I explore are the intersections (fig. 7.14). Seen from above, motorway intersections often make quite artful and conspicuous expressions of complex geometries in which the car driver perhaps has less sense of being involved. Gazing from the sky at the motorway intersections, we see different typologies that fit well with the international 'catalogue' of motorway intersections (Neufert and Neufert 2000, 220). The design of such intersections mixes instrumental rationales such as the 'design speed' recommended for negotiating the curvature of the intersection ramp with more aesthetic references to established typologies. (These even carry picturesquely resonating names such as the 'cloverleaf' of the Aarhus V intersection).

The intersection of the motorway assemblage is a 'Critical Point of Contact' (CPC) among different parts of the wider 'car system'. What takes places at the intersections is not just the practice of leaving the ordinary road system and entering the motorway system (or vice versa). It is also about 'mobilities differentials', and entering the high-speed zone of the motorway at intersections becomes a physical transition space where one has to navigate and increase speed, making the transition very tangible to the mobile subjects. In general terms we may discriminate between rather simple 'valves' to access and exit the motorway in an almost straight line (e.g., 51 Skanderborg N and 55 Horsens N) and spiral 'valves' in complex intersection with larger infrastructural landscapes (e.g., 46 Aarhus N). The intersection is also the critical site of one of the growing problems of motorway assemblages, namely what in Danish are termed 'ghost drivers'. This is the popular term for drivers accessing the motorway moving in the wrong direction. Given the speed at the motorway this is obviously a very dangerous practice and there have been a number of fatalities subscribed to 'ghost drivers' over the last years. The Road Directorate has been experimenting with different technical solutions to

51 Skanderborg N

1 Hasselager V

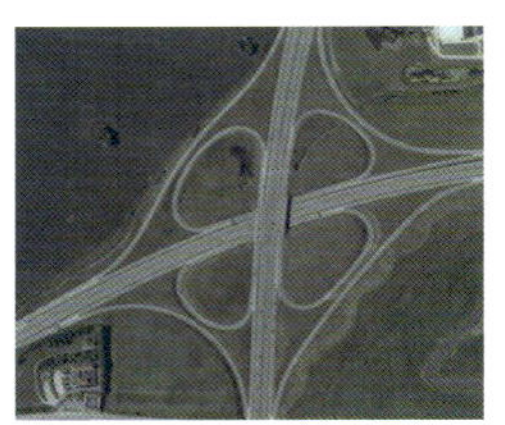

Aarhus V Motorway Intersection

47 Tilst

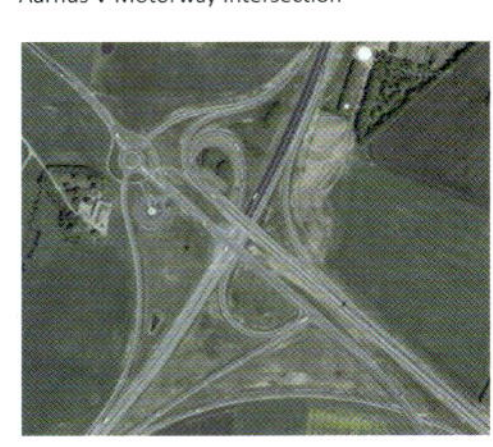

46 Aarhus N

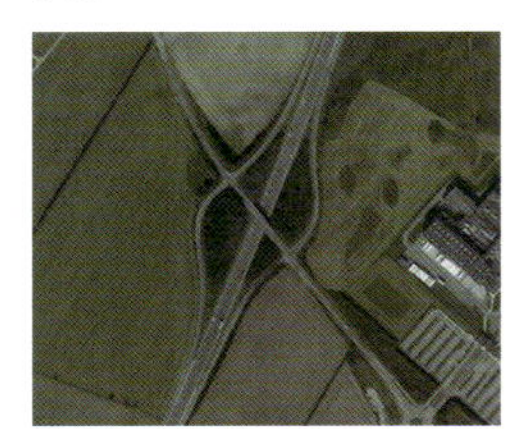

55 Horsens N

supplement the signage which obviously is inadequate in the case of 'ghost drivers'. But experiments with emerging spikes flattening the tires of cars moving against the driving direction have proved fallible. What is interesting is that the complexity of Danish motorway intersections, compared to, for example, the Los Angeles freeway, is rather simple. So explaining the 'ghost driving' phenomenon by citing the increasing complexity of the motorway assemblages in Denmark does not seem plausible. Rather, some have argued that the problem is an increasing number of senior citizens driving. This is obviously beyond the scope of this work to engage with, but the 'ghost driver' phenomenon is an interesting illustration of what happens when people's situational practices bring the trust of the whole motorway assemblage into jeopardy. A motorway assemblage is dependent on levels of mutual trust and respect for the regulatory and normative frameworks laid down as foundational 'rules of engagement'.

From this I want to 'zoom in' and discuss the mobile situations on the motorway in the final section of this case analysis.

PART III: Mobile situations on the motorway

In accordance with the *Staging Mobilities* framework I have now come to the level of small-scale practices in which the material environment, the embodied performances, and social interaction play out in de facto situations. However, I do need to make a disclaimer in relation to the reach of situational analysis within motorway assemblages. In opposition to, for example, the microsituational dynamics between passing pedestrians in the Friis mall in chapter four or interacting cyclists in chapter five, the motorway presents itself as an altogether less accessible environment. I explore the drivers' embodied and social interaction to a certain degree, but not to the extent I did when looking at pedestrians or bicyclists due to the simple fact that cars move very fast and I am therefore unable to 'read off' the embodied

semiotics and other microinteractional clues. So the 'situational' analysis in this chapter will be skewed toward the relationship between the mobile subject and the material environment and less oriented toward the social interactions. This is, of course, not due to a theoretical or analytical priority, but rather to methodological challenges. Had the social interactions between mobile subjects on the motorway been the sole focus of this book, I would have had a few options to expand that field as, for example, doing video or backseat studies of multiple drivers and their relations to other drivers; the research undertaken by Laurier (2004) or Jørgensen (2007) are examples hereof. So studying the interactional dimension of motorway assemblages is not considered impossible, but would probably have led to this being the only case of the book. In other words, I am aware that more 'motorway ethnography' is waiting to be undertaken.

Opposite page:

Top and bottom left:

Fig. 7.13: Commercial elements

Bottom right:

Fig. 7.14: Intersections

In methodological terms I already laid out the approach taken earlier. We used two cameras: one fixed and filming out the windscreen and another fixed to the driver's body (head). What we get from this methodology is a sense of the embodied perspective of the mobile subject (driver) and the relation to the material surroundings (something that is less developed in, for example, Laurier's and Jørgensen's studies mentioned above). What become clear from this 'dual image' of the situation are the abrupt and short glimpses of objects and landscapes that the motorway assemblage affords. So rather than experiencing the motorway as one smooth and continuous animation (which could be the interpretation if one only relies upon the 'cinematic' theories described above), the mobile subject is involved in multiple situations with different dynamics and variations (e.g., the difference between negotiating a situation of overtaking a large truck while being urged from behind by an aggressive driver versus a slow and smooth turn toward an uncongested off-ramp). The fragmentation of experienced situations may both be externally determined as when gazes are blocked due to plantings or buildings, or it may happen due to an event within the car (e.g., the ringing of a phone, the outbreak of a sibling quarrel in the backseat, or the accidental tilt of a coffee mug). The juxtaposition of the fixed, forward- looking camera and the mobile embodied camera shows quite clearly that situational mobilities within motorway assemblages are experienced in milliseconds as well as in longer stretches of time. This can be experienced, for example, both when a fast car suddenly appears in the rear mirror or someone in front of you drops luggage or other items requiring instant reaction, as well as when the gaze is at more distant objects such as a distant country church suddenly appearing between the trees in a wood.

Moreover, a more detailed ethnographic account may also have probed into the multiple non-driving practice that are taking place such as coffee drinking, talking on the phone, listening to the radio, conversations, daydreaming, life planning, GPS fiddling, putting on makeup, combing one's hair, singing, and whatever else takes place within cars on the motorway. So the complex time and space bundles created at the motorway are far from simply being understood by metal boxes moving between point A and B. Now I want to move toward some very specific situations taken from the rich empirical material. In practical terms I will partly be describing what you see on the photos, but I also offer a 'drivers interpretation' of the situation. This is, of course, an individual's interpretation that, in this case, has been subject to two different persons (my research assistant and I) making sense of the specific situations The 'drivers interpretations' of the following mobile situations are thus based upon two-person dialogues and one therefore easily could have imagined many different 'driver's interpretations'. This would have been a serious issue had the research task at hand been to investigate exactly the driver's experience. However, in this research I am as mentioned much more exploratory in my approach and see the various situational interpretations as illustrations of how we may learn to think about staged and situational mobilities.

The first situation I explore is the act of 'getting on' or entering the motorway (fig. 7.15). In this specific situation the car is slowly picking up speed as it is in the CPC zone of the access ramp, mediating the slower and the faster traffic systems. As the car enters the access ramp we notice a parked truck in the emergency lane at the curb. As this is not ordinary (but not completely extraordinary either) we ponder why the truck is parked there. Assuming that there must be some sort of unexpected reason for this (an assumption relying on car drivers to respect the law and not just park for fun in the emergency lane – an assumption that of course may be debateable), we may start to imagine what sorts of struggles the truck driver is facing. Is he (in this imaginary reflection my gendered language of male truck drivers also, of course, may be challenged) having vehicular and technical difficulties, or might he be lost? Has he been called to the side of the road by an urgent telephone call that he cannot ignore? Would that be from a boss or family member? These are enough 'imaginary driver' interpretations to illustrate the many different options for 'making sense of the situation'. Moreover, consider the fact that this is a situation within the timespan of few seconds – but surely reflections upon the situation may outlast the actual situational experiences which, for example, is the case if we pass a serious accident. In such cases the 'erasing of the situation' may take years or it may never disappear.

As the car continues its trajectory toward the motorway lanes via the access ramp, it enters a very important interaction zone as it has to merge into the existing traffic flows. In this case the situation is not very dramatic since the traffic density is rather low. So we see the phases of motorway engagement: progressing, checking in the rear mirror to observe an approaching van, orienting the car to the left to avoid hitting cars in the adjacent lane, and finally entering the motorway.

The second situation is on the motorway itself and probably one of the most generic and important of all motorway situations: the takeover (fig. 7.16). Due to the multiple and complex interchanges of 'mobilities differentials', a motorway assemblage is a very dynamic space full of 'negotiations-in-motion'. One such typical situation is the takeover, which in this example is initiated by the presence of a slower truck ahead. The situation here is also more dynamic than the latter since the specific site is busier and traffic is denser. This obviously means that the workload on the mobile subject in terms of orientation and checking the other mobile consociates is higher. So the first step is to realise that the truck ahead is going at a slower speed, and thus that passing or overtaking is what is preferred (one could of course choose to stay behind the truck). The next frame is more complex since what takes place here is an almost simultaneous act

Entering the entrance to the motorway

Observing a parked truck in the emergency lane, wondering why it is parked

Progressing...

Looking at the review mirror to observe van behind

Orientating to the right to avoid hitting cars on the adjecent lane

Entering the motorway

Getting ready to overtake the truck ahead

Looks to the left to observe car passing by, at the same time observing side-view mirror and side window for cars behind in the fast lane

Entering the fast lane

Overtaking truck

Orientating in the review mirror to avoid hitting truck

Entering lane and progressing

Top:
Fig. 7.15: Situation 1: Entering the motorway

Bottom:
Fig. 7.16: Situation 2: Takeover

of looking to the left to observe the car passing at the same time as checking the side view mirror and the side window for cars coming from behind in the fast lane.

As the adjacent fast lane is 'clear', we enter it and speed up to proceed overtaking the truck. After passing the truck there is another round of rear mirror orientation in order to make sure that the truck is not hit when re-entering the lane to proceed after overtaking it. In such a situation there are a number of interacting parties (from the few cars passing before overtaking is possible, to the truck driver, and then to the next set of passing cars) that can be viewed in the rear mirror in the last two frames. The practice of re-entering the 'slow lane' is something that seems to vary with the mobilities culture and the temper of the driver. So on Danish motorways people at times keep driving out in the fast lane despite the fact that faster vehicles are approaching from behind. My personal experience is that this does happen in Denmark but not to the same degree as, for example, in Germany, due to the much faster speeds and denser traffic on the German motorways. I assume that German motorway culture is more disciplined and strict precisely due to the fact that more negotiations at higher speed necessitate accuracy and 'getting out of the flow'. Moreover, it is only rather recently that giving signals for lane changes in Denmark has become mandatory in the traffic act. This has been the case in Germany for a long time. Such standardized semiotic practices may also explain why Germans seem more likely to re-enter the 'slower lane'. I did claim that this situation would be of greater complexity than the first one examined. However, this is obviously a relative term since what we have here is only two lanes of traffic. After having negotiated 2 x 13 lanes heading south of Los Angeles, I can say only that the complexity of overtaking a vehicle at the motorway indeed can increase! In many new cars there are multiple sensors and sophisticated technology to assist with driving, and one of the features relevant to this situation is the sensor often located in the side mirror and signalling with, for example, a small blinking light that there are objects to the right and left of the car.

The next situation is termed the 'mobile stage'. It actually resemble the previous in being an act of overtaking but what makes it special is the fact that the car overtakes a whole row of trucks that thus may be perceived as a local and mobile artefact or 'stage' in itself (fig 7.17). The presence of large and mobile truck groups form a 'mobile with' where the drivers are in communicative connection by means of radio communication (as in the Hollywood movie 'Convoy') or at least in contact by semiotic gestures such as flicking headlights or by the honking of horns. The sense of passing a 'mobile with' is furthermore sustained by this 'wall-like' quality of the row of trucks. Frame-by-frame the situation unfolds as follows; in the first frame the car is getting ready to overtake (with all the previously described orientations and acts of checking), then the first in the long row of trucks is overtaken.

As the car moves along and passes the truck convoy, it becomes clear that the vehicles create a 'mobile wall' which is dynamic, perforated, and diverse. This is so partly because the distance between the trucks varies and thus offers different intervals of the sight of and gazes toward the landscape to the right, partly because the trucks differ in size, material, and design. In this particular situation a tunnelling effect is created since the overtaking takes place as an overpass bridge is cleared. 'Coming out' again from the 'tunnel', the convoy continues and we notice different logos and paint jobs, representing company brands other the characteristic personalized truck driver's customization, and tagging with mural- or graffiti-like paintings on the trucks. Trucking communities constitute specific 'mobile withs' that to outsiders may seem macho and self-contained, which is too complex a phenomenon for me to engage with here. (See Evans 2000 for a piece of 'trucking ethnography'.) However, the material staging of such a massive mobile stage and 'mobile with' as seen in this situation only confirms to the car driver the stereotype of trucking as a closed world community. The sheer size and volume of the mobile stage passed may seem almost intimidating to a person within a much smaller vehicle. This experience of the situation may be reinforced by the specific phenomenon of turbulence that exists when a smaller vehicle is passing larger ones that create their own mobile microecology of turbulence. This may create a dynamic situation where the mobile subjects within the smaller car experience the push and pull effects of turbulence and wind that can be rather unpleasant and that are registered by the senses as a minor rollercoaster trip or at least sideways motions of the car.

The fourth situation to be explored here is passing a lake (fig. 7.18). As the car proceeds, the driver's attention is captured by an opening in the row of plantings alongside the motorway. Immediately thereafter, a flag indicates special side wind conditions due to a wider opening of the adjacent space. As the car comes into the 'clearing', a lake appears on the right hand side of the vehicle. After a quick gaze at the lake, the driver turns his/her head toward the left in order to see if the water continues one the other side, under the road. Immediately hereafter the 'clearing' disappears as another line of trees and plantings block the view.

That which happens in this situation is an example of a 'small discovery' of a landscape feature that triggers the curiosity of the mobile subject simultaneously with the process of driving and managing the safety observations of the lane conditions and the other co-present cars. The motorway designers clearly have meant that the drivers should be able to see the lake and enjoy this small vista of landscape as the roadside plantings deliberately have been 'punctuated' at the side of the lake. This is an illustration of the staging of a mobile situation from above and how it is being perceived from below by the mobile subject.

Getting ready to overtake a truck

The truck is the last in a long line of trucks

The line of trucks create a mobile wall, which is dynamic, perforated and diverse.

The truck convoy is flanked by a bridge and a safety fence on the left creating a tunnel for the driver

The wall contains different shapes and materials

The line of trucks end

Notice a pause in the plantation ahead

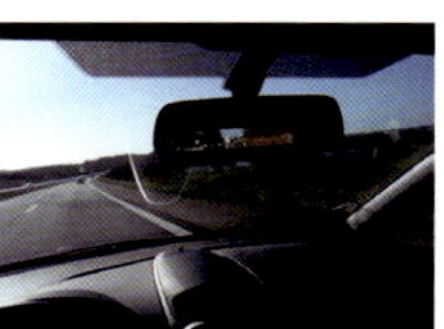
Sees a flag indicating wind signalling water surface ahead

Looks to the right to watch the lake

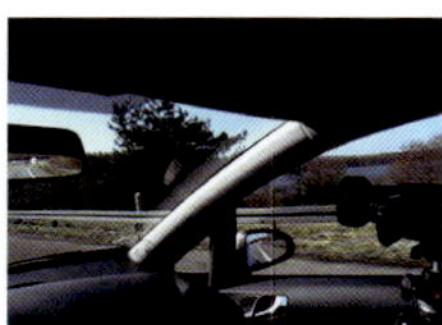
Turn head to see other side of the road

Looks in the other direction to see the water continue under the road

Proceeds into a tunnel of plantation

Left:
Fig. 7.17: Situation 3: Mobile stage

Right:
Fig. 7.18: Situation 4: Landscape

As mentioned before, the documentation of the interaction between mobile subjects in separate cars moving along a motorway at 110 km/h is a methodological challenge that lies somewhat outside the scope of this study. I have illustrated the driver's perspective and I have also shown situational readings of other drivers and the material environment. But the motorway assemblage is more than just the road space and tarmac. The assemblage includes resting areas, gas stations, and eating places alongside the road. Such lay-bys are important stages for the motorway mobilities as they offer pockets of relaxation and alternative practices to driving. In the following I explore small snap shots of social interaction in these 'edge spaces' of the motorway assemblage.

The first situation of social interaction is an illustration of the state of 'dwelling in mobilities' I have discussed to quite some extent (fig. 7.19). What takes place here is that a 'mobile with' containing two adults and a child has turned off the motorway at a resting area in order to take a break. The adult male and a young boy have gone off walking the dog while the adult female has taken a seat back in the car, with an open door enjoying the sun. Here motorway movement becomes entangled with other mundane practices such as dog-walking and sun-tanning.

The next situation is the 'stranger encountering' (fig. 7.20). Such situations are less common in these sites than they for example are in denser urban areas where encountering strangers is the order of the day. It is not possible for me to see precisely what is the nature of the topic, but the two mobile subjects that in no way seems acquainted to one another, passes at the car park having a short verbal exchange.

The topic of conversation could be anything from 'nice weather' to some more engaging comment. Either way it is an illustration of the swift and mobile encounters that are also part of the social interaction space of motorway assemblages.

The third social interaction is the meeting between two mobile subjects arriving at the resting area in separate vehicles (fig. 7.21). At a parking lot near Hedensted these two men met and discussed for a while.

The meeting might have been coordinated before the start of the journey or during the trip via communication devices. The situation is probably one where they are having a rest and stretching their legs before moving on to a common destination. Often various builders and construction workers were seen talking and interacting before taking up the journey again.

In situation 4, three men are having their lunch in an enclosed space between their cars, using tool boxes as improvised chairs (fig. 7.22). This illustrates nicely the complexity of a space such as this. One the one hand, it has been designed and laid out from above in terms of, for example, the spacing and dimensioning, but on the other hand, the space is constantly being

Top:
Fig. 7.19: Social interaction 1 – Dwelling in mobilities

Bottom:
Fig. 7.20: Social interaction 2 – Stranger encountering

inhabited by mobile subjects flowing in and for short periods of time, taking over with detailed and meticulous improvisations and appropriations.

In many of the resting areas alongside the Danish motorways, there are drive-in food shops where the mobile subject has no need to disembark the vehicle. This is the case in the situation here (fig. 7.23) where a car is coming around the corner of a fast food drive-in and approaches the counter in order to make payment.

There are many professional groups inhabiting the motorway assemblages such as delivery services, transportation firms, and other groups. One special community of mobile subjects inhabiting the motorway assemblages is made up of truck drivers (fig. 7.24). As mentioned, this group holds a public image of strong social cohesion and common identity.

In this situation one truck driver is having some kind of trouble with his truck and a fellow truck driver is giving him a helping hand. The helping out in situations of problems and difficulties is actually a quite common feature in sites like this, and here members of the same professions often seem prone to be the first to help out solidifying a sense of communal bonding. (I have never seen a truck driver asking help from a 'non-group' member on technical matters unless we are thinking of serious accidents)

The car is a specific technology that despite its many common features across various models and brands has the capacity to be customised and domesticated in different ways (from bumper stickers to the charms and 'fresh air' devices hanging from the rear mirror). The process of getting the car into the resting area and having the mobiles subjects within disembarking can be quite a show on its own. The 'unfolding of the car' in this situation is a good illustration (fig. 7.25). We see a 'mobile with' which presumably is a family on a trip disembark the vehicle in a process that almost resemble a 'spilling out' or 'floating out' of the content

From top:

Fig. 7.21: Social interaction 3 – Meeting

Fig. 7.22: Social situation 4 – Lunchtime

Fig. 7.23: Social interaction 5 – Buying food

Fig. 7.24: Social interaction 6 – a helping hand

of the car. As the car stops, doors are opened and mobile subjects as well as various artefacts spill out over the immediate surroundings, creating a small and temporary microecology of buzzing activity (and at times chaos).

The final small snapshot of social interaction I will mention is this situation where a young girl is sitting on the stairs resting (fig. 7.26). She clearly has found a nice, comfortable sunny spot as well as back support when an older man and a younger woman walk by, thus creating a small negotiation where the girl rises in order to let the mobile with pass.

This small negotiation is identical to the many similar situations we find in more dense and urban settings and again speaks to the micro-interactions taking place wherever there are mobile subjects to be found.

Top:
Fig. 7.25: Social interaction 7 – Unfolding car

Bottom:
Fig. 7.26: Social interaction 8 – negotiating the by-lay

Common to all of these illustrations of social interaction is the status of the resting areas as CPCs of the motorway assemblage. They are important safety features since people need rest in order to be able to drive safely on the motorway, but they are also commercial spaces as well as interaction sites illustrating that a motorway assemblage cannot be understood only as four (or more) lanes shifting vehicles among various points in a diverse geography. Motorway assemblages are social spaces full of interaction and human activity that require a more differentiated frame for understanding than simply a theory of instrumental movement. I want to round out this chapter on a theme and topic that have been much more challenging to study than the other cases in this book. To get closer to the microinteractions of fast moving human bodies in confined boxes of metal is not easy. However, I have strived to illustrate the key point of this approach to mobilities design, namely that even a site such as a motorway is rich in social interaction, identity building, and normative behaviours. Motorways assemble not only cars, goods and asphalt, but equally important routinized practices of embodied mobilities, experiences of the landscapes, and multiple other mundane practices.

Conclusion

Having reached this point, I will conclude the final case in this book by recapitulating the overall question that has been guiding the work from the outset, namely the issue of: *How is design affording and/or preventing particular mobile practices and cultures in everyday life?* The case studied in this chapter has differed from the others in this book because it is a more complicated issue of accessibility. Nevertheless, I have illustrated the general point about the motorway assemblages as both social spaces and sites of mobilities staged from above as well as from below.

Motorway assemblages are as important illustrations of the process of *Staging Mobilities* as any of the other cases in this book. I started out by looking at the motorway from above and how the planning and landscaping have created a huge stage for mobilities that in Denmark carries an important historical dimension. From the national physiognomy of the old highway structure (which again can be traced back in time to earlier days of human path building), today's motorway structure of the 'Big H' is a dominant and important 'skeleton' of the Danish infrastructure, as well as being a key dimension behind the functionality of the urban system on the national and regional scale. However, within this vast ecology of moving people and vehicles, millions of small-scale interactions and decisions are being made at the level of the individual, creating a living and mobile space of vast magnitude and high intensity. The mobile situations playing out in the motorway assemblages are all composites of complex relationships among material spaces and design, social interactions and embodied performances of the motorway inhabitants.

In relation to the perspective of 'critical mobilities thinking', one should address both the problems and the potentials of motorway assemblages. I believe that there are plenty of problematic issues to discuss in relation to motorway assemblages. These range from the environmental problems created by huge volumes of goods being transported on heavy trucks to the increasing commuting distances afforded by the upgrading of motorway infrastructures. Also there are issues of how the regional and local urban systems are affected by these vast corridors of movement that may threaten to bypass smaller towns and cities. I have chosen to engage with the more architectural and aesthetic dimension of the 'dark side'. I have done so partly since this is less explored in the general understanding of what motorways are and how they perform, but also because this is where we see an opening up to some of the 'potential' issues, such as the way these sites and spaces are layered with particular forms of communication and surface semiotics. I am not uncritically in favour of the way these roadsides appear, but their design and appearance needs to be explored according to a broader perspective than simple moral dismissal and judgment. These are sites of the mundane and mobile everyday life that hosts millions of people, and we must therefore explore how they are configured and how they work in more subtle ways. I have not gone deeply into the potential discussion with relation to motorways, but I think it is safe to say that many other types of programs and designs could be imagined than, for example, the relative generic office buildings and the warehouses that are mushrooming alongside the motorway these years. In particular the lay-bys or resting areas are sites of underused potential. Most of them facilitate a quick rest and break but not in a manner that affords social interaction and construction of public domain to a larger scale. Mobile subjects that actually are creating alternative ways of hanging out and resting as well as engaging in dialogue and interaction with other travellers are doing this almost in spite of the generic rest area designs. However, there is some focus on the potential of the resting areas and the lay-bys of motorway spaces in the more general discussion among planners and architects, so this is hopefully an area of increased activity in the future.

The motorway assemblages studied here are obviously illustrations of large linear armatures connecting across huge distances. In this capacity they work as 'mobile sociopetals' and 'mobile sociofugals' as they 'draw in' cars and vehicles from the hinterlands and redistribute them alongside the 'Critical Points of Contact' where the off-ramps 'spill' out vast numbers of exiting cars into the regions again. If looked at from above, this gigantic space has the important function of feeding cities with people and goods that mirror the cities' rhythms of contraction and expansion. The motorway assemblages are collecting and distributing flows in a complex but direct relationship to the rhythms and flows of the urban regions and cities connected by their armatures. We are looking at a special case of a 'mobile assemblage', which I defined as a socio-technical network hosting many different entities (technologies, humans, objects, and artefacts) in a specific combination facilitating and affording certain mobile practices and restricting or preventing others. In the motorway assemblage we clearly see how the situational mobilities are mediated and afforded by this vast network. As I chose a rather 'rural' stretch, the additional layer of, for example, 'intelligent' signage and traffic information systems (ITS) that are more prevalent, for example, in the greater Copenhagen area, slipped in 'under the radar'. Needless to say, within more dense urban areas even more complex technology would be added to the assemblage.

One of the methodological challenges was as mentioned that cars restrict our visual decoding of bodily interaction. We know that 'cars have drivers' and we may also see some indications of 'mobile body semiotics' (as when a fellow driver makes a gesture that can be polite or less than polite). But in general the 'capsuled driver-body' makes a semiotic decoding rather difficult. The semiotic dimension of the mobile interactions in the motorway assemblage is predominantly expressed by the sign-giving equipment of the car (head lights and flashing lights) as well as by the mobile positioning of the car; these are expressions of a geo-semiotic dimension (e.g., aggressive bumper-to-bumper positioning). All cars have the capacity to carry more than one mobile subject and we see many different social formations of the 'mobile with'. In general the family and friends leisure trip creates a very different form of 'mobile with' than trips made by those who are on the road as part of their professional work. The complex negotiations and interactions within the car have not been at the centre of this work, but I of course am aware that there is much interaction and communication taking place between the fellow mobile subjects within cars in the motorway assemblage. At particular critical moments the 'mobile with' of the car becomes conspicuous and clearly visible. This is, for example, the case when the car comes to a halt in the resting area and its contents 'spill out' over the adjacent surroundings or when we pass a wrecked vehicle parked in the roadside and the 'mobile with' is seen waiting for road assistance.

In the material enclosed here I have not presented much evidence of the fact that drivers are networked and connected by digital media. Many cars within the motorway assemblage carry GPS systems (built-in or mobile devices) which makes the motorway assemblage a vast 'datascape' receiving and transmitting location-based information. But the 'networked self' is also visible when we see people talking on mobile phones while driving. In Denmark the hand-held devices are not legal to use while driving and there is an increasing number of cars with Bluetooth technology affording hands-free interaction with mobile phone technology. Still we do, however, see people utilizing the hand-held phone with increased safety risks as repercussion (an even more dangerous practice than talking on the hand-held mobile telephone is the writing of text messages while driving!). The issue of 'networked self' would need more thorough research, but it is certain that a large number of drivers in the motorway assemblage are listening to various radio stations and thus become engaged in yet another layer of networked information (albeit one of one-way communication as opposed to the phone). The groupings of mobile subjects in the motorway assemblage may, however, also be one of physical copresence and proximity, which is the case when we see, for example, motorbike riders, truck convoys, or groups of mobile homes forming moving 'temporary congregations'. And likewise the queuing up for takeover of slower vehicles may create 'temporary congregations'; we may also experience driving next to a car for many kilometres only to become separated and then later 'reunited' since many drivers may speed up and slowdown in complex rhythmic formations (or we may find ourselves overtaking the same vehicles again when reentering the motorway after a rest).

Motorway assemblages are, as any other infrastructure armature and system, host to particular ways of performing mobilities and thus to different 'mobility cultures'. There are of course the legally sanctioned traffic rules which specify legitimate actions in addition to unwritten codes of conduct. As example is the practice of flashing the headlights at other drivers in order to give warning of an upcoming speed control by the police. Also the aforementioned 'mobile withs' may congregate in communities joined by particular normative codes; the code language and light signals of the trucker communities spring to mind (for example, the term '10-4' as a positive confirmation diffused from the closed trucker communities into daily language through the mediation of the Hollywood movie *Convoy*). The 'mobility cultures' may also be thought of in relation to particular driving styles, as, for example, the 'late lane merger' who often draws hostile attention from the drivers sitting patiently in the queue or the aggressive 'bumper-to-bumper' rider. 'Mobility cultures' are also seen in the motorway assemblages with respect to type of vehicle as, for example, the 'mobile homers' or the motor-bikers. Quite some attention was given in the theoretical section of this chapter to ideas on a different and specific 'mobility aesthetics' related to motorway assemblages. Here the key feature that sets the motorway apart from other car driving spaces is the increased level of speed. The high speed affords a very different set of sensorial responses and thus ultimately to the experience of the motorway. The whole design of the assemblage is coined around differentiated notions of 'design speed'. This means that the views and vistas are 'programmed' from above in the acts of motorway design. But the embodied experiences of high-speed areas and the perception of acceleration and deceleration becomes part of the particular 'mobility aesthetics'. In relation to the material design the 'mobility aesthetics' differ from the road and landscape interface and from the urbanized corridors to rest areas to the complex landscapes of access and exit ramps. The motorway assemblage has created its own typologies of built environment and material design, and this has often been ascribed to be an instrumental flow space only. However, many more things than physical displacement take place on these stages that are part of the particular 'mobility affordances' created by the motorway. The standard four-lane (or more) design of the motorway assemblage is not only created to create more carrying capacity. Rather the presences of parallel flow armatures (here in the guise of motorway lanes) create 'mobilities divides' as the slower traffic is thought to be moving in the far right side lane and the fast one taking the lanes to the left.

Motorways are connecting cities and regions, providing high-speed accessibility as seen. However, they also create massive barrier effects, for instance, in the countryside and villages they bypass. The 'segregated mobilities' practices growing out of such barrier effects are often understood as the necessary externalities of upper-class infrastructure provision. But of course these are mediated with underpasses and bridges at strategic sites (and the Danish Road Directorate actually spends substantial resources on dedicated armatures and passages for wildlife). Another dimension of the 'mobilities divides' afforded by motorway assemblages is the exclusion of particular modes of mobilities. Thus, pedestrians, bicyclists, and mopeds are not allowed to travel on the motorways due to safety issues. Such a 'high-speed regime' partly creates a segregated 'mobilities divide', but it also necessitates alternative routings in parallel to the high-speed armatures of the motorway if the areas crossed by the motorway assemblages are not to become completely sealed off and excluded.

In the analysis of this case I have, as in the previous cases, been shifting between the perspective of the 'river' and the 'ballet'. From the bird's-eye perspective of the 'river', we have seen how this huge infrastructural network has been born out of an agenda of 'nation building' and the creation of a large-scale urban system. Moreover, we saw how the design and the landscaping of motorway intersections carry their own aesthetics when viewed upon from the dizzying vantage point of the traffic engineer's 'helicopter view'. Most often motorway assemblages are discussed from this perspective and this may to a certain degree explain why such sites often are articulated as 'non-places' and sprawl agents. However, in the light of the *Staging Mobilities* framework, I have offered a different perspective by exploring the eye-level height of the mobile subjects, or what I term the 'ballet' perspective. As we move into the situational mobilities within the motorway assemblages, we see the dynamic and complex interactions that are expressions of the 'lived motorway life' and which transcends the instrumental movement between point A and B. What seems to be one large, instrumental flow space becomes in the framing of the 'ballet' something much more rich and complex – a nexus of cars, bodies, asphalt, gas stations, eating facilities, landscapes, off-ramps, and regulatory frameworks.

In returning to the general model of the *Staging Mobilities*' framework, we have seen how motorway assemblages stage situational mobilities from above by means of design, planning, and regulation as well as by mobile subjects in interaction. The three dimensions of material space, social interaction, and embodied performances are entering the understanding, albeit in various ways depending on the site of analysis as well as on the activities taking place. The journey thereby has come to an end, and I turn to the final chapter of general conclusions in relation to the issue of *Designing Mobilities*.

8 CONCLUSION

All the world is like a stage, and we do strut and fret our hour on it, and that is all the time we have.

Erving Goffman (1974) *Frame Analysis*, p. 124

The creative process of establishing a movement system is a difficult as, and perhaps even more difficult than, the process of composing a piece of music, writing a poem, or designing a building.

Edmund N. Bacon (1967) *Design of Cities*, p. 35

We must look at the performances of real places for the people who live there. No theory will be mature until it shows how performance tends to vary with the political and social context.

Kevin Lynch (1981) *Good City Form*, p. 323

Introduction

At this point, I conclude the general work carried out in this book by revisiting the individual cases and summarize their conclusions. Moreover, I address the issues of future research and challenges under the auspices of the new and emerging field of 'mobilities design'. The aim from the outset was to explore the following general research question: *How is design affording and/or preventing particular mobile practices in the everyday life?* As subthemes to this very general question I explored in more detail the following:

I. How is the design of various modes of mobilities and sites affecting the mobile situations of the everyday life?

II. How are mobilities represented and 'captured' in analytical and methodological terms?

III. How do the design of mobility modes and sites of mobilities influence the social and cultural interactions and exchanges of the contemporary city?

IV. How does the design of mobility modes and sites of mobilities enact and engage with the human embodied performances in the mobile situations of everyday life?

V. How can we, on the basis of the investigations and explorations carried out in this book,
start to articulate a field of 'mobilities design' and which theoretical, methodological, and disciplinary inputs may be needed?

In what follows I partly summarize the sub-conclusions of the book, and partly turn to a more general research agenda for the future.

Designing Mobilities – lesson learned

The first thing I need to highlight is the multiplicity of methods that are available to scholars of contemporary mobilities. Some of the new and very technologically led methods for mapping and 'capturing' mobilities may fade away as the technologies they rely on become outsmarted by new technologies. But this is no excuse for not exploring the potential of any new technology presenting itself to mobilities scholars as a potential tool. The second point is the complexity of diagrams and their potential for mobilities thinking and design. Across any selection of diagrams I believe we find examples of the complexity and the key features of any 'map': selection and choice. I see, as mentioned, the diagrams as 'vehicles for thinking'. I am not suggesting that all mobilities researchers should engage with such an exercise of diagrammatic thinking. But I do find the diagrams a viable route to reconnecting what needs to be connected: the analytical and theoretical sensibilities of the 'mobilities turn' with the material, physical, and interventionist awareness of design and architecture. The way I framed the notion of diagrams as 'vehicles for thoughts' speaks to a particular engagement with theoretical reflection and conceptual development that works with concrete, practical, and pragmatic situations and examples. Rarely will a concept or theoretical building block be of much value if it cannot be related to empirical real-life situations at some level. The theoretical framework developed in *Staging Mobilities* has been applied to empirical cases in this book. The way I illustrated this is by 'adding' diagrams to the *Staging Mobilities* diagram. I have been working with each of the concepts, exploring various diagrammatic expressions and the plotting of these onto the *Staging Mobilities* diagram is an expression of this effort.

In chapter four I identified the Friis shopping centre as a 'gearbox full of speeds'; a layered machine of circulation; a transit space and 'hinge' between urban neighbourhoods; a critical point of contact that connects goods and experiences with mobile subjects; and a horizontal and vertical arena for mobilities. Friis is a prime case for understanding and illustrating that situational mobilities are staged in complex material, social and embodied processes 'from above' by means of planning, design, and regulations as well as 'from below' by mobile subjects. Being subject to an analysis nested within 'critical mobilities thinking', Friis must both be understood as a space of navigation loss and challenges to peaceful coexistence of user types, as well as having the potential to offer users new experiences and interaction opportunities. Friis is a 'mobile assemblage' that 'hosts' contemporary mobilities in a fairly complex and large material environment where technologies, humans, software, codes, semiotic and communicative systems, objects, and artefacts are assembled in a specific combination facilitating and affording certain mobile practices and restricting or preventing others. Looking at Friis from the vantage point of a mobile assemblage, humans and non-human entities are circulated and connected by complicated scripts that both 'capture' a staging from above by the centre management as well as a staging from below by mobile subjects circulating as visitors. At times this mobile interaction takes place by detached individuals but even people entering Friis alone become members of various 'mobile withs' as, for example, when they embark on trips in the lift or on the escalator. Also many 'mobile withs' are entering Friis when families or groups of friends are out shopping. These mobile social entities negotiate the spaces and flows with other similar 'entities' or individuals in the centre. As we see visitors to Friis move through shops and hallways talking on phones or texting, we see also that within Friis the 'networked self' is 'linked-in-motion'. This, however, has less to do with the design and architecture of Friis than with the general social transformations of mediated interaction in urban spaces. I found much evidence of 'negotiation in motion' among 'mobile withs' and across groups of strangers; at CPCs such as lifts or escalators many 'temporary congregations' emerged. In Friis I found the mobility cultures related to the predominant mode of mobility: walking. So from the observations we saw the walking codes of close proximity interaction that we also have seen in many other urban spaces. The walking culture within Friis is also staged from above by the layout of the armatures as well as the signage that instructs people how to behave and move; it is also staged from below by the ways centre visitors choose to interact as they move around in the centre on foot. The cars and the bikes are also important elements, but they are not moving inside the shopping area but confined instead to the designated parking spaces out on the street (for bikes) and below in the underground parking space (for the cars).

The study of Friis confirms that we need to think about the body and the way embodied mobilities are tied into sense experiences of moving across and within spaces. The surfaces, slopes, and gradients of armatures in the centre that are experienced by bodies in motion open up to an understanding of a mobility aesthetics, where the customers' experiences of the centre are tied very closely to the feeling of flow and friction, of pavements and wideness of corridors and walkways. The embodied mobilities connected to the 'body work' of muscle-powered mobility is one set of issues for which the centre provides a particular experience. Similar is the fact that people are moving within a closed ecology with no wind and sparse daylight. But also the machine-powered forms of mobility such as riding lifts and escalators are significant to the mobile aesthetics at play in Friis. The 'mall experience' is a complex and situational engagement with the materiality of the centre, the various technologies and materials within, the commercial signage, and the other customers. From the analysis conducted, the applicability of the 'river' and the 'ballet' perspective should be clear. In Friis we mapped the movements and flows of mobile subjects as if they were homogeneous elements of a uniform stream, and we also have seen how the individual mobile subjects interact and encounter each other in the fleeting moments of mobile interaction within the centre. In Friis the staging from above is seen through the river metaphor and expresses the intentions and wishes from the centre management, the architects, and shop owners. The 'ballet' equally is a significant illustration of people's self-staging from below as they chose routes through the centre or when they perform mobilities, for example, in riding the escalator.

In chapter five I applied the notion of 'cycling assemblage' to cases of bike designs in Aarhus, Copenhagen, and Odense to illustrate the complexity of these bike designs and how they rely on mobile subjects and planning guidance as well as material artefacts and objects distributed throughout the urban fabric. Biking is a complex and multidimensional practice that needs certain features in the built environment in order for it to become a mobility mode. Moreover, the mobile subjects practicing biking need also to make sense of the practice and imbue it with the values and interest springing from the desires and wishes of everyday urban life. The cases explored all bear witness to the particular mobility affordances created by material design, social interaction, and embodied performances. The embodied performance of cycling is not unmediated since surface material of the bike paths, topographies of the infrastructure system as well as the type of bike, the number of gears, and the quality of the tyres all contribute to particular and mediated embodied mobilities. The cycle offers a unique opportunity to experience and explore the city, and it has its own particular features of an 'aesthetic experience in motion'. The socio-technical systems of which cycling assemblages are a part points beyond the omnipotent subject and into the 'messy world' of traffic lights, bike path pavements, cycling technologies, curbs, light poles, traffic signs, and multiple other 'requisites' for the staging of situational biking.

Applying the metaphor of 'the river' to the bikescapes studied, we saw how the flows of 'body-bike particles' follow the armatures and channels quite stringently (even though we did see examples of bikes transgressing their designated areas). The overall traffic system of the city and its accommodation of cycling in more or less generous ways are managed, designed, and installed 'from above'. The width of the path affords a certain volume of cycles and the bending, curvature, and topography of the routes determine travelling speeds. The 'cycling assemblage' is both a traffic system of physical displacement of bikes and bodies from A to B as well as an interactional and social space. This quality is highlighted by the notion of 'negotiation-in-motion' and is seen in all three cases. Cycling is a social affair and even the smallest turn or rerouting calls for scanning of the environment and assessing relative speeds and positioning of other artefacts, objects, and mobile subjects. The microprocesses of situational negotiation increase in complexity as the mobile subjects are not just facing each other at a static standstill but rather move at different speeds and trajectories. Often the bike paths are occupied by mobile subjects travelling together as 'mobile withs'. As part of a city's larger infrastructural system, the 'cycling assemblages' are allocated a specific place in a wider mobility hierarchy. Thus the 'cycling assemblage' also contributes to the creation of 'mobility divides' as it offers certain opportunities and blocks off others. This is again, however, dependent on the dynamics of the situation rather than something to be deducted a priori. For example, even though cyclists are not able to cover as much distance, they have immense advantages in speed when rush hour hits town. In such a situation the 'cycling assemblage' affords a particular generous mobility difference in favour of the bikes; most of the time, though, the arrow points in the other direction, creating car-advantages clouding cycling's positives (except to the few really dedicated).

From the analysis of Nørreport Station in chapter six I showed how it created particular 'mobility affordances' in different ways depending on the modes of mobilities. The idea of 'mobility affordance' of Nørreport Station comes alive if we think about the mobile subjects being processed by platforms, paths, stairs, lifts, and escalators in horizontal and vertical flows. The way the system affords bodily movement is different depending on the capacities of the bodies in question, but generally the armatures of escalators and stairs affords rather serial and linear practices of movement through the system. However, at times these are challenged by busy travellers trying to bypass the slower flows of passengers. The Metro has been the focus in particular and here the system with automatic doors and the attempt to position mobile subjects rationally in order to optimize the passenger flows has been very conspicuous indeed. The temporalities afforded by the intersecting train systems are as complex and multifaceted as the various time tables and temporal logics of each of the systems. The temporal pulse of the Metro with its much more frequent operations is 'layered over' the S-train and regional train systems operating at different time intervals. This affords a particular dynamic temporality of the station that creates very specific conditions for the mobile subjects moving within the station. Nørreport Station is an example of a 'mobile assemblage' where the systems and socio-technical networks become the action surfaces to thousands of mobile subjects. At Nørreport Station we see the S-train, regional trains, and the Metro systems interact and blend with pedestrian flows from across the city, cyclists, and bus passengers. (There is much less interface with the car system as mentioned.)

At Nørreport Station the embodied sensations and the 'aesthetic experience in motion' in which the mobile subjects engage are obviously different compared to their sensorial and physical abilities (a blind passenger will experience the space differently from the seeing person). However, there are also huge differences within the various areas of the 'metroscape'. We saw how there has been much criticism of the regional train platforms in particular (they are small, noisy, smelly, dark, and often not very comfortable). So the more general point of the mobile subject having a particular aesthetic experience is differentiated at Nørreport Station depending on whether the mobile subject is moving into the cathedral-like Metro or taking the regional train. In prolongation of the 'differential mobilities' and the variety that mobile subjects may experience, Nørreport Station also affords 'mobility divides'. Clearly some relate to the ability to orient oneself and 'read' the place, whereas others are inscribed into the body-environment nexus giving the regular users a clear advantage over first-time tourists but also favouring the fit and able over physically challenged users. In general Nørreport Station is accessible and there a fair amount of design intervention diminishes overly outspoken 'mobility divides' when it comes to the physical abilities of the mobile subjects. In terms of the legibility of the place, it becomes more difficult for first-time passengers to perceive the complex setting and environment. Nørreport Station is, as seen in the other cases analysed here, comprehensible both from the analytical point of view of 'the river' and 'the ballet'. The complexity of the site requires very detailed design and meticulous staging decisions from above. The interaction and coordination among various transit systems and their relationship to the wider city network means that the designers of Nørreport Station need to take a view of the homogeneous and aggregated flow of people. The 'river' perspective on Nørreport Station illustrates how mobile subjects are processed and moved by smaller design interventions such as the width of a staircase or the speed of an escalator. As we move down to this level of detail, we inevitably shift into the 'ballet' perspective as we start to see how the microinteractions between mobile subjects are functions of the presences of mobile others as well as of the materiality of the environment. Nørreport Station is a dynamic and complex space of social interaction and the detailed analysis of 'mobilities in situ' clearly substantiates that there is much more to mobilities than simple movements. What looks like 'nothing' on the surface or like the 'necessary evil of transport' opens up through the 'ballet' perspective to be complex face-to-face interactions, mobile presentations of Self, and 'negotiation in motion'.

In chapter seven I explored the case of the '100 km City' or the motorway stretch from Aarhus to Vejle and how planning and landscaping has created a huge 'stage' for mobilities that in Denmark carries an important historical dimension. From the national physiognomy of the old highway structure (which again can be traced back in time to earlier days of human path building), today's motorway structure of the 'Big H' is a dominant and important skeleton of the Danish infrastructure, as well as a key dimension behind the functionality of the urban system at the national and regional scale. However, within this vast ecology of moving people and vehicles, millions of small-scale interactions and decisions are being made at the level of the individual, creating a lively and mobile space of vast magnitude and high intensity. The mobile situations playing out in the motorway assemblages are all composites of complex relationships among the material spaces and design, the social interactions and embodied performances of the motorway inhabitants. The motorway assemblages studied here are obviously illustrations of large linear armatures connecting across huge distances. In this capacity they work as 'mobile sociopetals' and 'mobile sociofugals' as they 'draw in' cars and vehicles from their hinterlands and redistribute them again alongside the critical points of contact where the off-ramps 'spill' vast numbers of exiting cars out in the regions.

Motorway assemblages are, as any other infrastructure armature and system, host to particular ways of performing mobilities and thus to different 'mobility cultures'. There are of course the legally sanctioned traffic rules that specify legitimate actions as well as more unwritten codes of conduct. One example is the practice of flashing the headlights to warn drivers of an upcoming speed check by the police. Also the aforementioned 'mobile withs' may congregate in communities held together by particular normative codes. The 'mobility cultures' may also be thought of in relation to particular driving styles – from the late lane merger who often draws hostile attention from drivers sitting patiently in the queue to the aggressive tailgater. 'Mobility cultures' are also seen in the motorway assemblages with respect to type of vehicle as, for example, the 'mobile homers' or the motor-bikers. High speed affords a very different set of sensorial responses and thus ultimately the experience of the motorway. The whole design of the assemblage is formed around differentiated notions of 'design speed'. This means that the views and vistas are 'programmed' from above in the acts of motorway design. The embodied experiences of high-speed areas and the perception of acceleration and deceleration becomes part of the particular 'mobility aesthetics'. The motorway assemblage has created its own typologies of built environment and material design, and this has often been ascribed to be only an instrumental flow space. However, many more things than physical displacement take place on these stages, which are part of the particular 'mobility affordances' created by the motorway. Motorways connect cities and regions, providing high-speed accessibility as seen. However, they also create massive barrier effects, for instance, in the countryside via the bypass. The 'segregated mobilities practices' growing out of such barrier effects are often understood as the necessary externalities. But of course these are mediated with underpasses and bridges on strategic sites. Another dimension of the 'mobilities divides' afforded by motorway assemblages is the exclusion of particular modes of mobilities. Thus, pedestrians, bicyclists, and mopeds are not allowed to travel on the motorways due to safety issues. Such a 'high-speed regime' creates partly a segregated 'mobilities divide' but it also necessitates alternative routings in parallel to the high-speed armatures of the motorway if the areas crossed by the motorway assemblages are not to become completely sealed off and excluded. From the bird's-eye perspective of the 'river', we have seen how this huge infrastructural network has been born out of an agenda of 'nation building' and the creation of a large-scale urban system. Moreover, we saw how the design and the landscaping of motorway intersections carry their own aesthetics when viewed from the dizzying vantage point of the traffic engineer's 'helicopter view'. Most often motorway assemblages are discussed from this perspective and this may to a certain degree explain why such sites often are articulated as 'non-places' and sprawl agents. However, I have offered a different perspective by exploring the eye level of the mobile subjects in the 'ballet' perspective. As we move into the situational mobilities within the motorway assemblages we see the dynamic and complex interactions that are expressions of the 'lived motorway life' and which transcend the instrumental movement between point A and B. What seems as one big and instrumental flow space becomes in the framing of the 'ballet' something much more rich and complex – a nexus of cars, bodies, asphalt, gas stations, eating facilities, landscapes, off-ramps, and regulatory frameworks.

'Mobilities Design' as an emerging research field

From the discussion so far it should be clear that I consider the notion of 'mobilities design' and its accompanying research as an emerging field. I think the lessons learned from Friis, the bikes paths of Aarhus, Copenhagen and Odense, Nørreport Station, and the '100 km city' speak to the fact that regardless of their mode and scale, explorations that engage with the materialities of mobilities are needed. I propose, therefore, 'mobilities design' as a new 'material turn' within the already established field of mobilities research. There is a need for research targeting the material, physical, and design-oriented dimensions of the multiple mobilities from the local to the global. Despite its cross-disciplinary identity, the 'mobilities turn' has not capitalized on the potential to explore issues of material design and physical form. The way I think of the 'material' in this context resonate with Ingold when he argues that we should move from talking about the 'materiality' of objects to the properties of 'materials' (Ingold 2011:26). It is precisely the qualitative, pragmatic, and situational properties of things and objects rather than some abstract notion of the material that should be our concern. I am thinking of 'stuff' and how it shapes situational mobilities. So I propose that we need a new mobilities analysis of the design and politics of 'stuff', as well as the embodied and interactional dynamics of mobile humans and 'stuff'.

The exchange value with design is twofold; first, this means getting closer to the 'material', which is needed if mobilities research can claim to have understood contemporary mobilities. Second, it means that the creative, explorative, and experimental approaches of the design world become within reach to mobilities research, offering new potentials for innovative research. Design research, on the other hand, might enter into a fruitful relationship with mobilities research, taking in a 'mobile' perspective on design objects and issues, including methodological insights, concepts of space and place, and relations between fixities and flows. The term covering this new research field is 'mobilities design' and this is the second iteration of the mindset, concepts, theories, methods, and cases within this emerging field (see Jensen 2013a, chapter nine for an opening of this discussion). Also, we may learn a thing or two from a parallel discussion taking place at the nexus of design and anthropology (Gunn et al. 2013). Years of research into this relationship has led to the coining of the concept and discipline of 'design anthropology', from which the mutual learning potential from the two interconnected research and design fields is emerging.

Research into 'mobilities design' depart from the pragmatic question: *What makes mobile situations possible?* Therefore, research in 'mobilities design' explores the affordances created by material design in general, but also by other types of design decisions and interventions of a less material/physical form. Thus, design decisions and interventions within systems design and service design that create various user-interfaces may have to be included into the analysis of 'mobilities design'. A research strategy for mobilities design is focused on understanding how decisions and interventions within as such diverse fields as architecture, urban design, product design, planning, traffic engineering, software design, and interaction design enable particular mobile practices while supressing others. A research program for 'mobilities design' must be based on the notion of 'critical mobilities thinking' with its double focus on problems and potentials. Thus the emerging research area of 'mobilities design' should explore how decisions and interventions affecting concrete and specific mobile situations may be related both to 'dark side' issues such as power, social exclusion, marginalisation, environmental degradation, risk, failure, vulnerability, and breakdown as well as to potentials for new experiences, inclusive social engagements, new business models and opportunities.

A future research agenda for 'mobilities design' embrace a number of issues coming out of the merging of 'critical mobilities thinking' and design, such as exploring how mobility systems of the future might become: more socially inclusive; less environmentally restraining; more resilient and risk adverse; more flexible and less vulnerable; more inspiring and attractive; and more open-minded and fun. I cannot claim to have a fixed agenda for focus areas, methods, and theories. This would not only supersede my own capacity as a scholar, but also be highly inappropriate for the invitation to think across areas of research and disciplines of thinking. However, as a start, I would point to the foci of studies targeting situated practices, material doings, social acts and interactions. Studies that engage with the intertwinement of objects, artefacts, systems, technologies, spaces, and the human/non-human relationship should be particularly promising, as would studies focusing on the sensed and embodied practices and kinetic 'being in the world'. In terms of methods I would welcome more experimental creative and performative approaches. Regardless of the theme of study I find the situated and empirical very important and will keep insisting on emphasizing the material dimension in a rather literal sense. As the field is potentially very wide, this listing of foci and methods is obviously only my own proposal for a continuation of this line of work. But my own interest point in the direction of exploring relationships between post-phenomenology, various strands of "non-representational" thinking, and pragmatism. In particular I believe the latter to be an underdeveloped perspective. Pragmatist thinking from Peirce, Dewey, and James (the classic American position) seems to have been overlooked as a relevant epistemological source of inspiration to social science studies within the 'mobilities turn'. From the exploration into the design world, however, I have come to the see that various elements of classic pragmatist thinking may work as part of an underlying frame of reflection for the nexus of mobilities research and 'mobilities design'. This, however, is more of a hypothesis and something I will devote my energy to explore in the years to come.

I am interested in thinking further about theories, methods, and disciplinary input. The establishment of a situational and real-life sensitive theoretical conceptualization is the core theoretical contribution. Methodologically this work points forward toward even more empirical field studies applying various dimensions of mobile and ethnographic methods. As I have argued throughout, the exploration of mobilities in general and 'mobilities design' in particular need to move beyond singular disciplines. There will be a need to engage a new and cross-disciplinary multiplicity drawing on fields from sociology, geography, and anthropology to architecture, urban design, and planning and then toward more technical perspectives within engineering, computer science, and interaction design. Certainly, more work is to be done, but here the aim has been to explore a new 'material turn' to the mobilities research in order to argue for the importance of seeing the emerging field of 'mobilities design' as a new direction for the future. It is a 'turn' that orients itself toward design, space, and 'materialities of mobilities' much more than earlier research has done. This work was started with the publication of the two books *Staging Mobilities* and *Designing Mobilities* and has been further articulated in conference papers and talks (Jensen 2013b, 2013c) as the beginning of an effort to bridge mobilities theory and material design.

To state this briefly: *the staging of mobilities materialises within mobilities design!*

APPENDIX: GLOBAL REFERENCES

Air transport in a very short period of time has moved from being the prerogative of an elite minority to being a cheap method of travel for everybody. But it's very popularity presents problems. Design criteria for airports are usually stated in terms of passengers, per hour, per year. But you might take a different stance and suggest that the real challenge is how you make an airport a calm place.

Sir Norman Foster (2007) *Norman Foster Works III*, p. 108

When the quantity of flow is more than insignificant, it must be placed in defined channels, with terminals and interchanges. These channels are organized into networks, which distribute the flows over large areas ... The greater the flow, the greater the necessary definition, control, and specialization of the channel, with more elaborate terminals and interchanges.

Kevin Lynch and Gary Hack (1984) *Site Planning*, p.195

Transport architecture is torn between the utilitarian, the pressures of economic sustainability and the romantic. For many, the station or terminal is a functional building that provides the connection to train, bus or plane. For others, it is a place to welcome friends and lovers – the backcloth to more emotional moments. For others, too, it provides an alternative vision of a public realm where shared values and collective movement matter more than being cocooned in private vehicles.

Brian Edwards (2011) *Sustainability and the Design of Transport Interchanges*, p. 38

Dubai Metro
Photo: olekvi

Introduction

In this appendix I shall conduct a general and global review of references illustrating material designs of mobilities. The references serve as illustrative background for the more detailed case studies in the book. In contrast to the cases all the global references are from non-Danish contexts in order to present a global background perspective for the deeper analysis of the cases. I will be using the *Staging Mobilities* framework model as the guideline for briefly exploring how the reference projects are performing in terms of the model's three key variables; material spaces, social interaction, and embodied performances.

The High Line

Architects: James Corner Field Operations with Diller Scofidio and planting design by Piet Oudolf | Place: West Side of Manhattan, New York City | Built: 2009 (part 1) and 2011 (part 2)

The project is a conversion of an old elevated train line from the 1930s into a public space. Initially the old train line running 10 meters above ground was to be demolished but was saved by community groups and the site is now both an officially recognized public park and a very popular destination.

The project is an example of the new understanding of 'landscape' as it is seen in 'Landscape Urbanism' with its focus on the blurring of the city/landscape concepts (Waldheim 2006, 11). The project transforms an instrumental (infra)structure into a landscape merging with the urban fabric. The key functionality is now recreational with many references to old design and aesthetics as for example in the benches and seats of the site. The project stages new types of situational mobilities and it connects to historical forms of mobilities.

Physical Settings, Material Spaces and Design

The material design utilises old remains of the freight trains and the usage of materials such as gravel and concrete points back in time. Green and gray structures mix with the urban fabric as mediating context.

Social Interactions

The park encourages social interaction by offering new common sights and vistas of the well known urban context through a cinematic staging. Often a playful and open minded interaction amongst the users is found.

Embodied Performances

The physical settings are staging an interactional space where seating, walking and running is afforded. People inhabit the space in a contemplative and relaxed manner.

Bands guide the flow of people and mobilities are staged. Photos: Bottom left: Jacob Bjerre Mikkelsen, top and bottom right: Robb1e

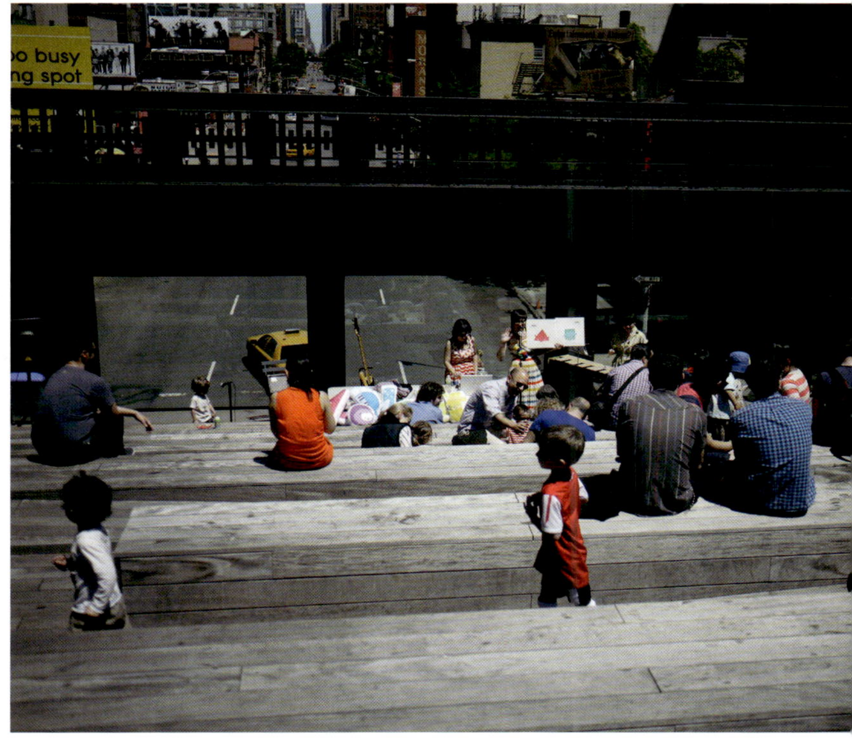

Longchamp Store

Architect: Heatherwick Studio | Place: SoHo, New York City, United States | Built: 2006

Bands stretch from the entrance to a light well in the ceiling. Photos: suwatch and Dogears

This project is actually the interior of a shop, but it is interesting in the way it utilizes the landscape and lights to afford the interaction visually as well as physically between three floors.

The project creates a new landscape of mobilities where layers and flows are working to erode steps and plateaus. Conceptually the project is inspired by a 'hillside' connecting the street to the top floor.

It is an interesting play with two directions of flows: the visual sight lines from the street and upwards and the flow of people walking up the stairs.

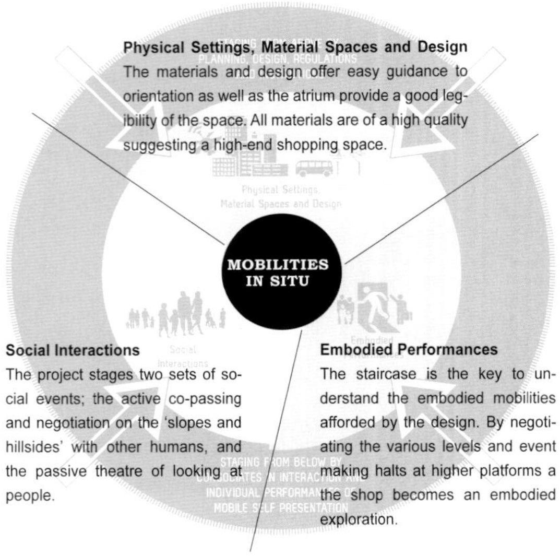

Physical Settings, Material Spaces and Design
The materials and design offer easy guidance to orientation as well as the atrium provide a good legibility of the space. All materials are of a high quality suggesting a high-end shopping space.

MOBILITIES IN SITU

Social Interactions
The project stages two sets of social events; the active co-passing and negotiation on the 'slopes and hillsides' with other humans, and the passive theatre of looking at people.

Embodied Performances
The staircase is the key to understand the embodied mobilities afforded by the design. By negotiating the various levels and event making halts at higher platforms a the shop becomes an embodied exploration.

Måløv Axis

Architects: LiW Planning (Landscape architecture) and Adept | Place: Måløv, Ballerup Municipality, Denmark | Built: 2010

The Måløv Axis breaks with the typical design code of the suburbs and adds experience to the routes of the suburb. Photo: Kaare Viemose (copyright Adept Architects)

The project targets the in-between public transit spaces of suburban Denmark and converts a dark tunnel and adjacent public spaces into a layered morphology of terraced paths and platforms. Combined with a conspicuous lighting design the site invites to a reinterpretation of suburban public space. The axis connects the old part of Måløv to the new neighbourhood of Søndergård. The key aspects of the project are partly the transformation of a 'non-place' transit area into a playful scene for public display, and partly the challenging of the barrier comprised of a massive road space and a rail track separating the community into two areas.

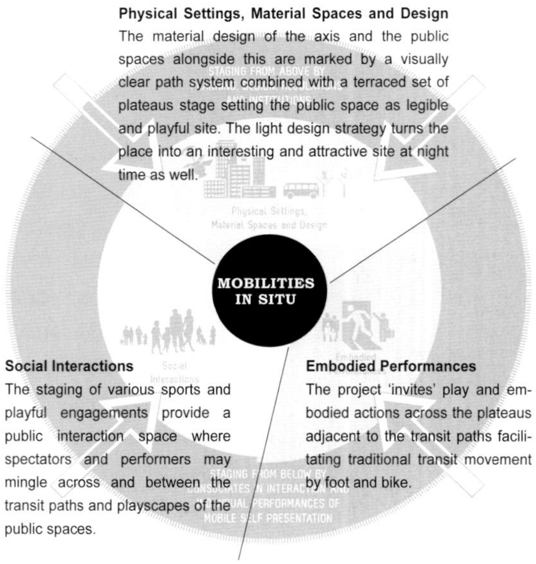

Physical Settings, Material Spaces and Design
The material design of the axis and the public spaces alongside this are marked by a visually clear path system combined with a terraced set of plateaus stage setting the public space as legible and playful site. The light design strategy turns the place into an interesting and attractive site at night time as well.

MOBILITIES IN SITU

Social Interactions
The staging of various sports and playful engagements provide a public interaction space where spectators and performers may mingle across and between the transit paths and playscapes of the public spaces.

Embodied Performances
The project 'invites' play and embodied actions across the plateaus adjacent to the transit paths facilitating traditional transit movement by foot and bike.

The shared space relies on negotiations in motion between consociates rather than traffic regulations. Photo: moonhouse

Skvallertorget

Architect: City of Norrköping | Place: Norrköping, Sweden | Built: 2006

The Swedish project 'Skvallertorget' (literally meaning the 'Gossip Square') is a traffic junction transformed in accordance with 'shared space' principles.

The old junction suffered from high accident frequencies so the new scheme was to improve safety as well as the urban ambience. There is only one level of pavement and all traditional urban furniture, traffic lights, pedestrian crossings are removed, making one continuous surface for all modes of traffic.

The number of accidents has decreased significantly and urban life has picked up. The lack of clear guidance has 'pushed' people into becoming more alert to one another and has reduced the average speed significantly. In quantitative terms the redesign has increased safety and decreased traffic efficiency.

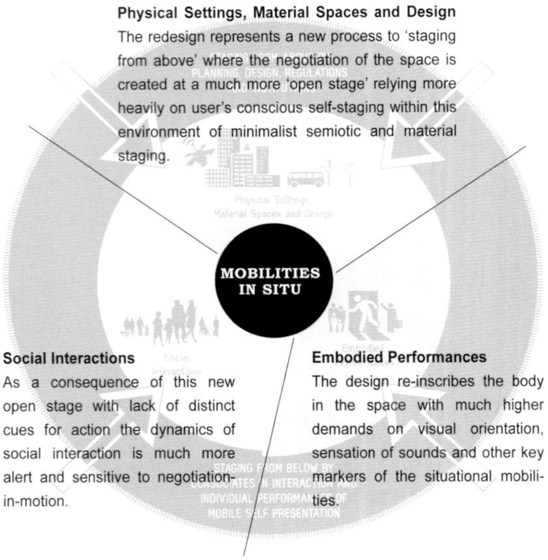

Physical Settings, Material Spaces and Design
The redesign represents a new process to 'staging from above' where the negotiation of the space is created at a much more 'open stage' relying more heavily on user's conscious self-staging within this environment of minimalist semiotic and material staging.

MOBILITIES IN SITU

Social Interactions
As a consequence of this new open stage with lack of distinct cues for action the dynamics of social interaction is much more alert and sensitive to negotiation-in-motion.

Embodied Performances
The design re-inscribes the body in the space with much higher demands on visual orientation, sensation of sounds and other key markers of the situational mobilities.

The Bike Hanger

Architect: MANIFESTO Architecture | Place: Seoul, South Korea and London, UK | Built: Design Proposal

With the increasing awareness of bike schemes and cycling as solutions to urban transportation the issue of upgraded bike parking infrastructure has becomes more pertinent than ever.

The project uses less ground surface space than other bike parking schemes and creates an innovative solution and stands out as an unconventional project requiring a certain amount of user activity that stimulates the urban environment. The bike hanger can store 15 bikes and is set in motion by the user pedaling to get the bike down from the storage setting. The small footprint on the area surface makes the project implementable in small and less utilized spaces like alleys.

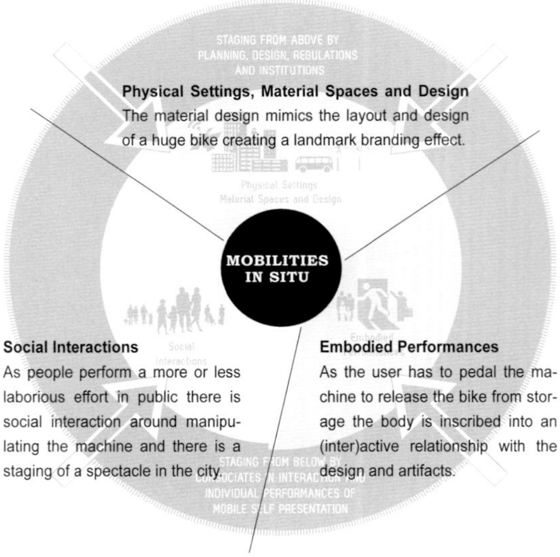

STAGING FROM ABOVE BY PLANNING, DESIGN, REGULATIONS AND INSTITUTIONS

Physical Settings, Material Spaces and Design
The material design mimics the layout and design of a huge bike creating a landmark branding effect.

MOBILITIES IN SITU

Social Interactions
As people perform a more or less laborious effort in public there is social interaction around manipulating the machine and there is a staging of a spectacle in the city.

Embodied Performances
As the user has to pedal the machine to release the bike from storage the body is inscribed into an (inter)active relationship with the design and artifacts.

STAGING FROM BELOW BY CONSOCIATES IN INTERACTIONS AND INDIVIDUAL PERFORMANCES OF MOBILE SELF PRESENTATION

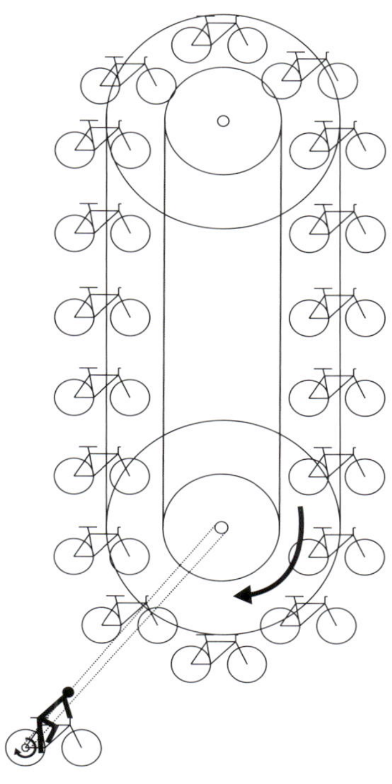

An interactive bike parking system brands bicycling and adds an experience to urban transportation.
Photo: Jacob Bjerre Mikkelsen
(sketch of working principle)

McDonald's Cycle Center

The bike community promotes biking as an alternative mode and creates fellowship around biking. Photo: bkusler

Architect: MULLER + MULLER | Place: Millennium Park, Chicago | Built: 2006

The project affords commuter biking by offering 300 secured bike parking spaces, day lockers, shower facilities, bicycle rental as well as bicycle maintenance facilities.

Furthermore, it contains a police patrol station for Millennium Park. The project works to encourage cycling within a distinct non-cycling context of a larger American city. Also the project affords explorations of the adjacent park and works to brand cycling as an environmentally responsible mobility form.

Physical Settings, Material Spaces and Design
Besides containing parking, maintenance, and a safety facility the projects merges with the parks incorporating green elements creating a symbolic symbiotic relationship between biking and the green parks.

MOBILITIES IN SITU

Social Interactions
By offering all sorts of biking amenities the project affords the creation of a biking community and social interactions amongst citizens of Chicago.

Embodied Performances
The project invites bodily engagement from the low key placing of a cycle in the rack, over repair and to showering as a hygienic practice.

Bicycle Transit Center

By designing a bike shelter of high architectural quality the project aims at improving the status of cycling. Photo: thisisbossi

Architect: KGP Design Studio | Place: Washington DC, USA | Built: 2005

This project encourages biking as alternative means of transportation by contributing to the public space with a very eye-catching design in a central urban location. Next to historic landmarks of the city the project advertizes cycling and offers parking spaces for 200 cycles, changing rooms, and a small commercial program.

By mimicing of the material bike design elements the projects aims at making cycling attractive to the solution of the 'last mile problem' (i.e. the challenge of having people close the gap between public transport and their workplace location).

Physical Settings, Material Spaces and Design
The material and physical design emulate the aesthetics of biking artifacts as well as it is an open and flexible structure.

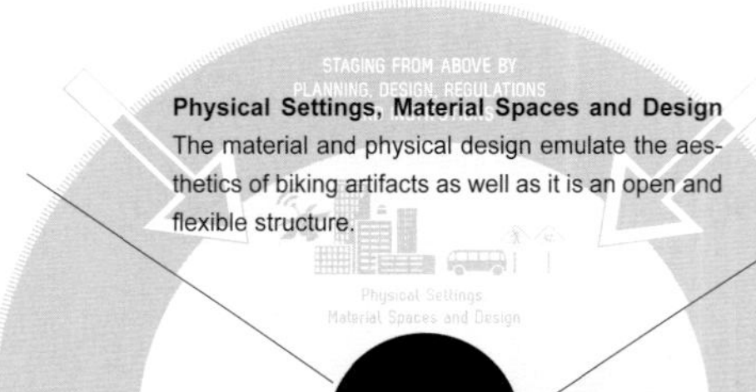

Social Interactions
The project is one of many encouraging social interaction and community building around biking practices as alternative for commuters.

Embodied Performances
The project affords easy access and modal shifts as well as it offering changing rooms catering to the user's need to remedy bodily performances resulting in high pulse and body heat.

The Citadel

Architect: Christian De Portzamparc | Place: Almere, the Netherlands | Built: 2006

Carparking is placed directly under commerce and dwellings - layers of everyday life are bundled and accessible through elevators. Photos: Left: stipo team, Right: Jacob Bjerre Mikkelsen

The master plan is made by Rem Koolhaas and prescribes multiple layers of mobilities incorporating thoroughfares for cars and pedestrians as well as layers of parking, commercial programs, and housing.

At the horizontal level mobilties are separated into dedicated layers for cars and pedestrians. Vertical elevators (lifts) connect the layers and afford easy access to the car park for residents. The division of the project into four blocks and its layered internal logic is illustrative of a 'XL' project where the flows have been instrumental in carving out the design.

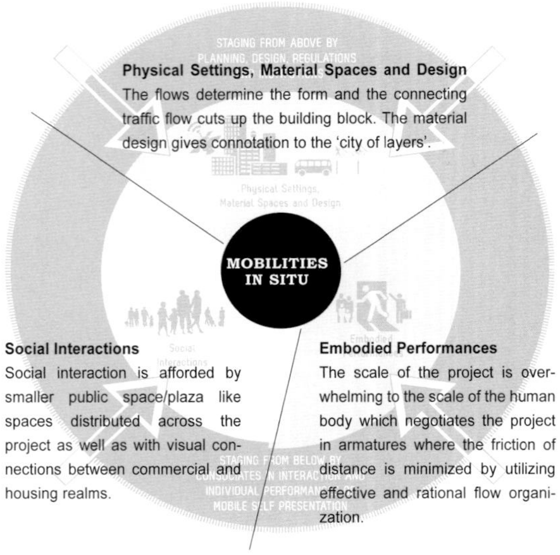

Physical Settings, Material Spaces and Design
The flows determine the form and the connecting traffic flow cuts up the building block. The material design gives connotation to the 'city of layers'.

MOBILITIES IN SITU

Social Interactions
Social interaction is afforded by smaller public space/plaza like spaces distributed across the project as well as with visual connections between commercial and housing realms.

Embodied Performances
The scale of the project is overwhelming to the scale of the human body which negotiates the project in armatures where the friction of distance is minimized by utilizing effective and rational flow organization.

Stockholm City Gate

Architects: BIG and Spacescape | Place: Hjulsta close to Stockholm, Sweden | Built: In progress

The sphere serves as a landmark and a screen displaying the mobilites surrounding it. Photos: BIG and Glessner

This project is the largest infrastructure project of its kind in Sweden. The project is basically a huge junction and its surrounding context is turned into a green landscape.

The junction is thought to become a functional entrance to Stockholm and it has the symbolic property of a key landmark with a reflective sphere hovering over the junction. The project works on mediating the disconnection of traditional highway junctions. The programs are reconnecting public buildings and functions with leisure, shopping, and a mosque.

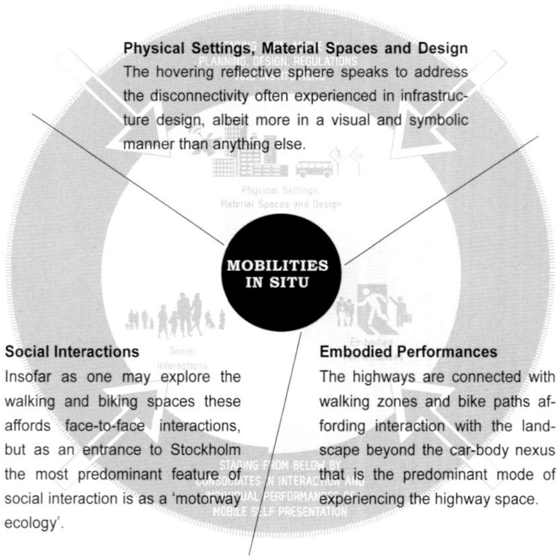

Physical Settings, Material Spaces and Design
The hovering reflective sphere speaks to address the disconnectivity often experienced in infrastructure design, albeit more in a visual and symbolic manner than anything else.

MOBILITIES IN SITU

Social Interactions
Insofar as one may explore the walking and biking spaces these affords face-to-face interactions, but as an entrance to Stockholm the most predominant feature of social interaction is as a 'motorway ecology'.

Embodied Performances
The highways are connected with walking zones and bike paths affording interaction with the landscape beyond the car-body nexus that is the predominant mode of experiencing the highway space.

The project presents 60 seconds of architecture: an animation experienced on the move. Photos and drawings: ONL [Oosterhuis_Lénárd]

Hessing Cockpit

Architect: Kas Oosterhuis (ONL Architects) | Place: Utrecht Leidsche Rijn, The Netherlands | Built: 2005

This project is an acoustic sound barrier combined with a car showroom along the A2 highway from Amsterdam to Maastricht. It is labeled '60 seconds of architecture' since the design takes point of departure in the view from a car doing 120 km/h.

The project is a dynamic salute to speed and evokes very different perceptions of the architecture depending on the actual speed of travel. The form language is one of smooth, waving lines resembling an animation movie as one moves along the 1.5 km stretch.

Physical Settings, Material Spaces and Design
The long, transparent and gridded structure offers a special spectacle as seen from the inside of a traveling car. The materiality of the design draws on aircraft and airport typologies recontextualizing this form language in a motorway space.

MOBILITIES IN SITU

Social Interactions
The design stages serial perceptions rather than social interaction. However, as groups of mobile withs are passing along the structure a joint theatrical spectacle is engaged.

Embodied Performances
The design explores the embodied perception at high speed as the key rationale, and offers a new aesthetic sensation of the motorway ecology.

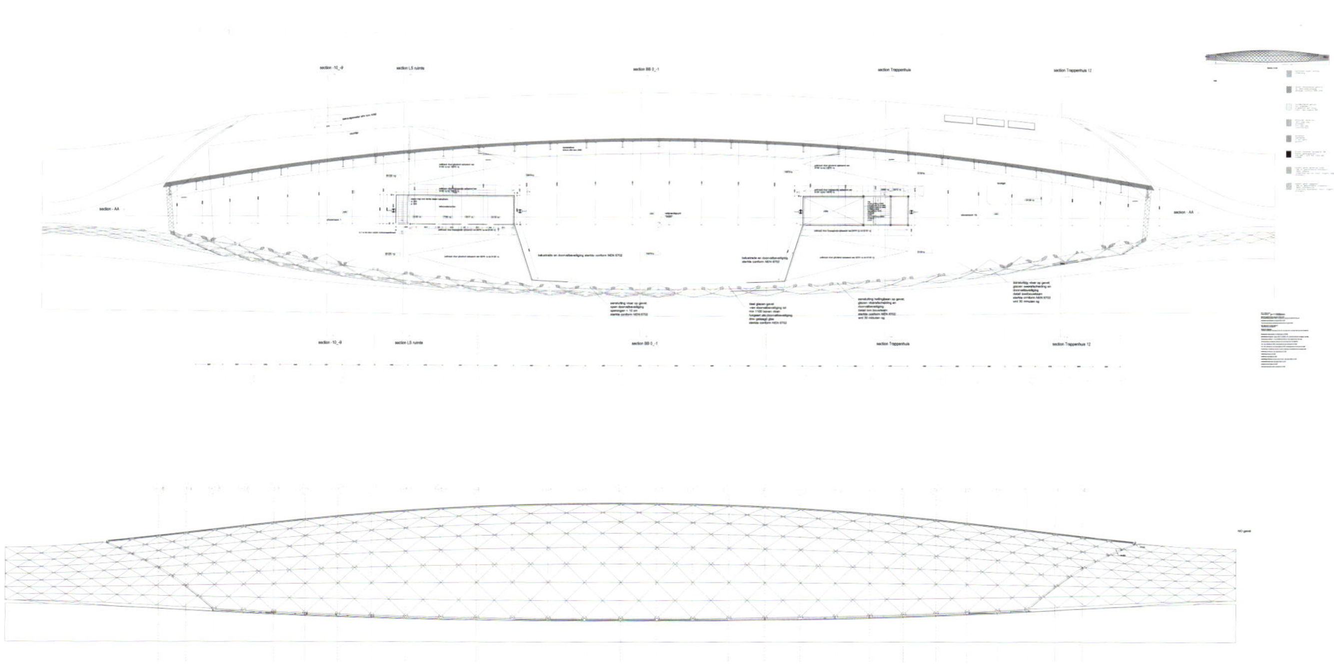

The Autostadt is an experience park revolving around car retail. Photo: ilovebutter

Autostadt

Architects: (Various architects) | Place: Wolfburg, Germany| Built: 1998

Autostadt in Wolfburg is an event center/park space for car buyers and car lovers. Build around car retail as the key program, the two 48 metre high glass towers containing 400 new vehicles each make a very special spectacle of mobilities artifacts.

The facility contains exhibition spaces, arts, and a restaurant all working to stage auto-culture as a cultural experience and as an aesthetic act of consumption. This staging recontextualises and ritualizes the mundane act of buying a car, offering costumers membership in a symbolic community.

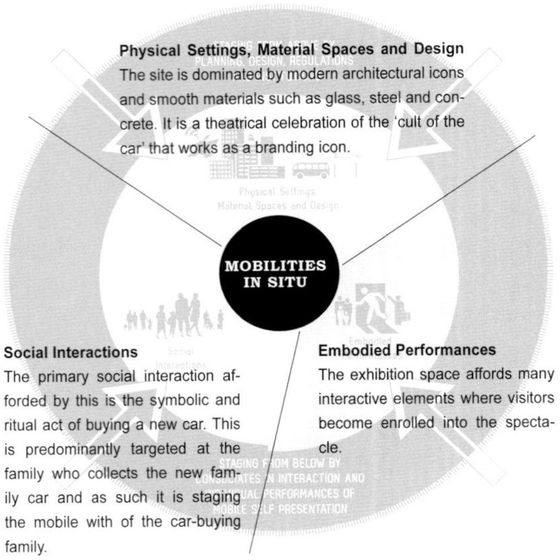

Physical Settings, Material Spaces and Design
The site is dominated by modern architectural icons and smooth materials such as glass, steel and concrete. It is a theatrical celebration of the 'cult of the car' that works as a branding icon.

MOBILITIES IN SITU

Social Interactions
The primary social interaction afforded by this is the symbolic and ritual act of buying a new car. This is predominantly targeted at the family who collects the new family car and as such it is staging the mobile with of the car-buying family.

Embodied Performances
The exhibition space affords many interactive elements where visitors become enrolled into the spectacle.

The Bus Rapid Transit system in Curitiba is used by 70 % of commuters in the city making it a profound part of the mobility culture of the city. Photos: xander76 and Thomas Locke Hobbs

Curitiba BRT

Architects: Lucio Costa and Oscar Niemeyer | Place: Curitiba, Brazil | Built: 1956

The Bus Rapid Transit system in Curitiba has become a global reference for BRT systems. The system carries 2 million people on a daily basis on its 60 kilometers of dedicated lanes with an average speed of 20-30 km/h.

The system has contributed to developing denser urban development and has been illustrative of innovative urban mobility design in relation to accessibility, efficiency, and aesthetics.

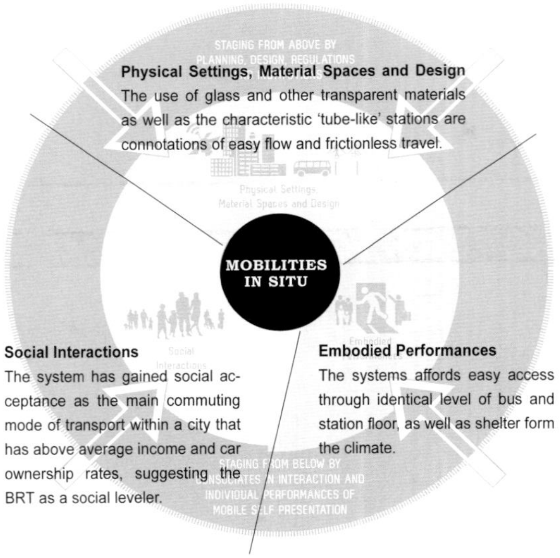

Physical Settings, Material Spaces and Design
The use of glass and other transparent materials as well as the characteristic 'tube-like' stations are connotations of easy flow and frictionless travel.

MOBILITIES IN SITU

Social Interactions
The system has gained social acceptance as the main commuting mode of transport within a city that has above average income and car ownership rates, suggesting the BRT as a social leveler.

Embodied Performances
The systems affords easy access through identical level of bus and station floor, as well as shelter form the climate.

cidade de curitiba

New Bus for London

Architect: Heatherwick Studio | Place: London, United Kingdom | Built: 2012

Being the first bus design project in London for more than five decades, the New Bus for London balances elements of the legendary 'Routemaster' from the 1950s with contemporary transport technology.

Thus the well-known 'hop-on hop-off' service is combined with a new glazing panel offering outside spectators a view of people moving up and down between the levels in the bus. Conversely the new glass section offers the bus riders new views over London. The New Bus for London is an example of a delicate balancing of a classic transport design icon with more contemporary design features and aesthetic solutions.

MOBILITIES IN SITU

Physical Settings, Material Spaces and Design
The new glass design reconfigures the inside/outside relationship between the bus and the city. The bus is an updated contemporary urban bus with for example LED front lights and a new design line.

Social Interactions
The increased transparency between inside the bus and the city's urban spaces invites more social interaction throughout the bus journey.

Embodied Performances
The new bus design affords a different experience of the city predominantly by catering to new visual sights as the passengers are seeing new views of the city.

The wrapped glazings ensure a constant contact between the passenger and the city. Photos: tompagenet

Innovative strategies to solve China's growing congestion problems are motivating this bus design. Photo: Jacob Bjerre Mikkelsen

The Straddling Bus

Architect: Shenzhen Huashi Future Parking Equipment | Place: Shenzhen, China | Built: 2010 (Pilot project in Beijing scheduled for 2011)

This bus runs partly on solar power and has a rather bold and futuristic design with the bus travelling above the cars driving on the road beneath it.

The Straddling bus has a capacity equivalent to 40 conventional busses, which should offer substantial savings in relation to CO_2 emission. Moreover the design and its capacity should contribute to a more efficient traffic solution decreasing the risk of congestion. In terms of comparable costs to a subway or metro system, the Straddling bus operates at only about 10 percent of the cost of a subway system.

Physical Settings, Material Spaces and Design
The bold and daring aesthetic design proposal draws upon a futuristic notion of mobility design that might help repositioning bus solutions versus for example light rail and subway systems.

MOBILITIES IN SITU

Social Interactions
The passengers on the Straddling bus may start to perceive themselves as being parts of a new type of commuters and thus members of a more innovative and future-oriented group of mobile subjects.

Embodied Performances
The design stages a different experience of the bus drive with a spectacle of watching car drivers 'below'. The design is a symbolic challenge of the supremacy of the car.

Art and mobilities merge in the Stockholm Metro. Photo: Francesco Rachello and Tobias Lindman

The Stockholm Metro

Architect: Greater Stockholm Local Transit Company | Place: Stockholm, Sweden | Built: 1950 - Now

Stockholm's metro system stations are literally carved out of the bedrock adding a very distinct atmosphere and identity to the individual stations.

Amongst the 100 stations about 90 of them has art installations made by more than 150 artists. The art installations include sculpture, murals, digital arts and more. The metro has earned a reputation as the longest art exhibition in the world with its 110 kilometre gallery. The Greater Stockholm Local Transit Company organizes guided tours to see the art installations and thus contributes to the illustration of public transit infrastructure's potential to become more than instrumental transport handling.

Physical Settings, Material Spaces and Design
The rough cave-like stations carved out in solid rock combined with the many art installations offer easy legibility and station identification and it give the whole systems its unique character.

MOBILITIES IN SITU

Social Interactions
The rather unique design with its many interactive installations and art artefacts offer the users potential for engaging in mutual aesthetic experiences as well as the social practice of transit.

Embodied Performances
The mobile subject is staged in a very different setting even though the ordinary everyday commute is performed. The ambience and aesthetic engagements with the senses offer a different metro experience.

Dubai Metro

Architect: Aedas | Place: Dubai, United Emirates | Built: Under development

Dubai City is facing severe congestion problems. Due to extreme population increase and tourism expansion, the city plans to construct a new metro system combining underground and elevated rails with stations adapting to the architecture of the city.

The underlying design doctrine is in line with the other iconic landmarks of Dubai such as the Burj Kalifa and the Burj Al Arab projects.

MOBILITIES IN SITU

Physical Settings, Material Spaces and Design
The design doctrine is one of smoothness and modernist form language combined with high-tech aesthetics staging the frictionless mobility of the 21st Century.

Social Interactions
As a key global tourist destination combined with a predominantly car-based mobility system the new metro affords social interactions across various groups in the city even though the segregated society may prevail.

Embodied Performances
The mobile subject is staged within a smooth metro system where legibility and easy orientation are the key to the embodied engagements.

This project draws the transportation system of Dubai into the iconic architectural discourse which has been the driving force in Dubai.
Photos: Left: Shahroozporia
Right: olekvi, Wajahat Mahmood and george shahda

Metro in Bilbao

Architect: Forster + Partners | Place: Bilbao, Spain | Built: 1995

The project challenges the traditional separation of metro space and ground level urban space enforcing a hallmark principle of Sir Norman Foster in infrastructure design, namely to take point of departure in the continuous experience of travelling through a series of transit sites and space.

The station design is in itself an attempt to increase the legibility of the system, creating a one-to-one relationship between the buildings and their semiotic properties.

MOBILITIES IN SITU

Physical Settings, Material Spaces and Design
The systems has a relatively sparse level of way-finding and semiotics as it rather works to create legibility and orientation by very simple architectural designs, simple engineering solutions and choice of materials.

Social Interactions
Within these clear and legible spaces people may easily orientate themselves, however not necessarily with any need to engage with cotravellers.

Embodied Performances
The design of the system is very much taking point of departure in the traveller's experience with moving within systems of mobilities. The design affords an engagement based on the perspective from a subject in motion.

A tube in the street leads the passenger onto an open concourse level and furter down to the platform in one continous space.
Photos: Left: Lauren Manning
Right: kurtxio, hesdes and Javi S&M

Southwark Station

Architect: MJP Architects | Place: London, Great Britain | Built: 1999

The station design relates to the increasing number of global projects utilizing the same types of tiles, materials, and signage.

As such it is an easily negotiated space that aims to provide a frictionless experience to its users. With the use of both artificial and natural lights the project does, however, challenge the global generic of transit design.

Physical Settings, Material Spaces and Design
The station appears as a 'flow machine' with little or no indication of alternative usages of the spaces. The choice of materials and design are of clean simplicity.

MOBILITIES IN SITU

Social Interactions
The station invites very few social interactions as the key rationale of 'putting flow first' is trickling down to the level of the users.

Embodied Performances
The station stages a sense of seamless travel with clear orientation and wayfinding affording the mobile bodies to move through the systems as effortlessly as possible.

Shanghai South Station

Architect: AREP | Place: Shanghai, China | Built: 2003

This station is one of the largest transit interchange stations in the world and has an iconic status as symbol of modern mobility. It services long distance train and local busses, metro systems and taxis under one circular roof structure enclosing 60,000 square meters.

The key design feature is the large glazed circular roof structure which is close to 300 meters in diameter and let light into the system. The waiting area of the station provides seating for more than 10,000 persons and offer spectacular views of the mobile scenery. The station marks a shift in design doctrine from automobility towards more public transit.

Physical Settings, Material Spaces and Design
The station's size along makes this a unique setting both for people in transit and people waiting. The light materials and the transparent roof give a certain lightness to the otherwise rather overwhelming structure.

MOBILITIES IN SITU

Social Interactions
The station does afford certain social interactions alone due to its huge dimensioning offering commercial programs next to the instrumental transport features.

Embodied Performances
People negotiating this busy transit hub are engaging in a complex systems of filtering and ordering bodies on the move, and with a particular sense of busyness due to the large and dense flows of people.

The station focuses on seamless travel presenting a frictionless design.
Photo: pixelthing

The station design presents an open layout with reference to the Chinese shaded gardens.
Photo: Gary Soup

Berlin Central Station

Architect: Meinhard von Gerkan and Jürgen Hillmer, gmp – Architekten von Gerkan, Marg and Partner (Hamburg) | Place: Tiergarten district, Berlin | Built: 2006

This station is the largest transport station in Europe. The building contains 100,000 square metres with five different transport levels. There is an unusually high mix of commercial programs combined with transit facilities and office spaces turning this into a huge layered circulation machine. The station connects both long distance train operations as well as local metro (U-bahn).

There are three key levels for transport: underground for long distance, regional lines and metro line; a ground level for local public transportation, bicycles, pedestrians, car parking and tourism transport; and the upper level for long-distance train and urban rail connections. The design is utilizing glass and many open sight lines for visual connection and legibility.

Physical Settings, Material Spaces and Design
Despite its large scale the station is reasonably negotiable and legible which is contributed to by the use of glass and an openness between various layers offering visual connectivity across layers and systems.

MOBILITIES IN SITU

Social Interactions
The station contains many waiting areas and commercial programs suggesting that this is more than an ordinary train station. The volume and density of programs are urban in their typology and invites public space interaction.

Embodied Performances
Moving across the spaces and both the horizontal and vertical layers combined with the many visual imprints makes the station at one and the same time easy to operate but also almost overwhelming in sense stimulus.

The largest train station in Europe resembles a modern mobility cathedral.
Photos: Jacob Bjerre Mikkelsen and dieter_titz (lower left corner)

Southern Cross Station

Architects: Grimshaw Architects and Jackson Architecture | Place: Melbourne, Australia | Built: 2007

This station takes up the space of a full block and links a regenerated area (Docklands) with the commercial centre of Melbourne. There is a train station at the lower level and a bus station at street level.

The station design utilizes light materials and glass to enforce legibility. The station's very characteristic roof structure resembles the 'dunes' and; it offers both shelter and easy-to-navigate architectural qualities.

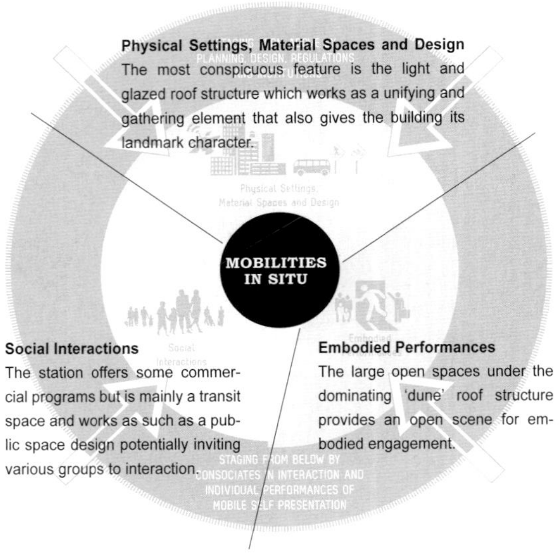

Physical Settings, Material Spaces and Design
The most conspicuous feature is the light and glazed roof structure which works as a unifying and gathering element that also gives the building its landmark character.
MOBILITIES IN SITU
Social Interactions
The station offers some commercial programs but is mainly a transit space and works as such as a public space design potentially inviting various groups to interaction.
Embodied Performances
The large open spaces under the dominating 'dune' roof structure provides an open scene for embodied engagement.
STAGING FROM BELOW BY CONSOCIATES IN INTERACTION AND INDIVIDUAL PERFORMANCES OF MOBILE SELF PRESENTATION

Lyon Airport Railway Station

Architect: Santiago Calatrava | Place: Lyon, France | Built: 1994

This station works as a regional connecting station between Lyon airport and the wider city region and is emblematic to the very distinct architecture and design of Calatrava.

The structure resembles a bird in flight. By connecting of the air travel, with rail travel the 'bird' symbolizes a intermodal shift and has an almost iconic quality to it that makes the traveler recognize it as a landmark. The structure is characteristically light and the structural engineering principles sustaining the building are very transparent and visible.

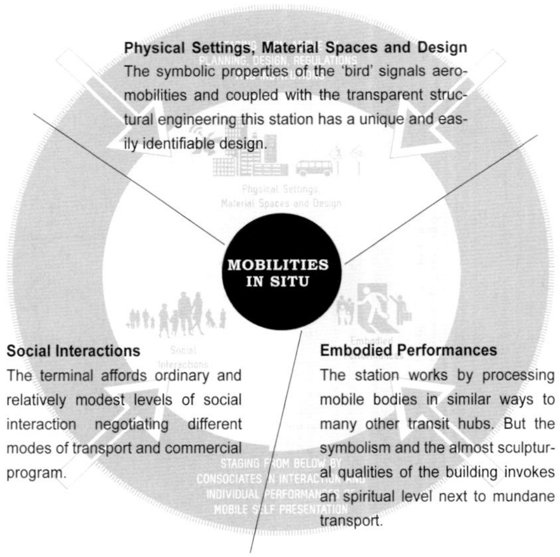

Physical Settings, Material Spaces and Design
The symbolic properties of the 'bird' signals aeromobilities and coupled with the transparent structural engineering this station has a unique and easily identifiable design.
MOBILITIES IN SITU
Social Interactions
The terminal affords ordinary and relatively modest levels of social interaction negotiating different modes of transport and commercial program.
Embodied Performances
The station works by processing mobile bodies in similar ways to many other transit hubs. But the symbolism and the almost sculptural qualities of the building invokes an spiritual level next to mundane transport.

The dune-like roof adds an experience for the passenger moving through the station.
Photo: 4nitsirk

The station constitutes a symbol of mobility and an abstraction of the action of travelling.
Photo: Bicycle Bob

The project uses public realm as approach to airport design. Photo: Jacob Bjerre Mikkelsen

Heathrow Terminal 5

Architects: Rogers Stirk Harbour + Partners | Place: London, Great Britain | Built: 2008

This project is globally known due to its centrality to one of the world's most busy airports. With an annual passenger capacity of 30 million and multiple commercial programs as well as public waiting facilities, the terminal is a buzzing hub.

Large roof glass structures provide an ample supply of daylight for the sections of the building where the layers are cut through. Two satellite buildings flank the main structure providing connection via rapid transit system. The terminal is connected to central London via a trains operating form deeper tunnels. The structure is fairly open and with transparent designs that create a legible terminal with easy to navigate properties.

Physical Settings, Material Spaces and Design
The open design stages an efficient flow of passengers through the system. The commercial programs have open shop facades erasing borders and inviting more flows of passengers into the commercial networks

Social Interactions
The terminal has a number of public seating areas where social interaction may be afforded

Embodied Performances
The many travelers and the high density combined with the open shopping spaces and the public seating areas create a busy airport space where people negotiate in motion

The demand for Thai culture in the airport resulted in a re-staging of the building. Photos: travelourplanet.com and Rev Stan

Suvarnabuhmi Airport

Architect: Murphy/Jahn Arcitects | Place: Bangkok, Thailand | Built: 2005

This project illustrates the dilemma between catering to international and global flows of capital while seeking to highlight national culture.

The project has attempted to balance this tightrope by adding local Thai furniture and art to what must best be described as a piece of generic transport architecture. Also the project is a window into a specific understanding of the importance of nesting transport infrastructure into a symbolic and cultural context where explicit connection between infrastructure and local culture is deemed of high importance.

Physical Settings, Material Spaces and Design
The project represents a global generic infrastructure design with an ad-on layer of local culture and art. The materials used are glass, marble, steel and concrete.

MOBILITIES IN SITU

Social Interactions
Being a prime Western tourist destination the airport hosts both Thai travellers and global leisure travellers without any particular form of interaction and engagement between these user groups.

Embodied Performances
The global/local competing semiotic systems are creating the underpinning and hybrid staging of mobile bodies in this fairly traditional airport design.

Departures
worlddutyfree

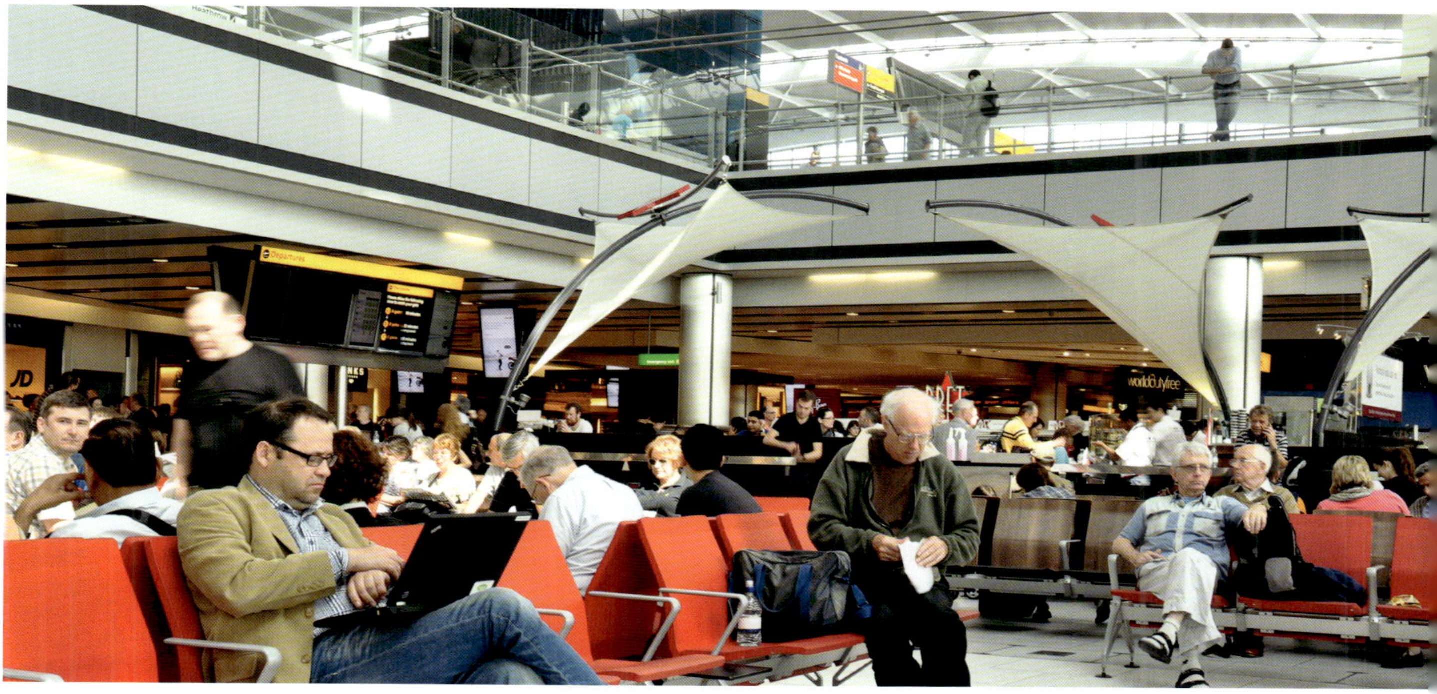

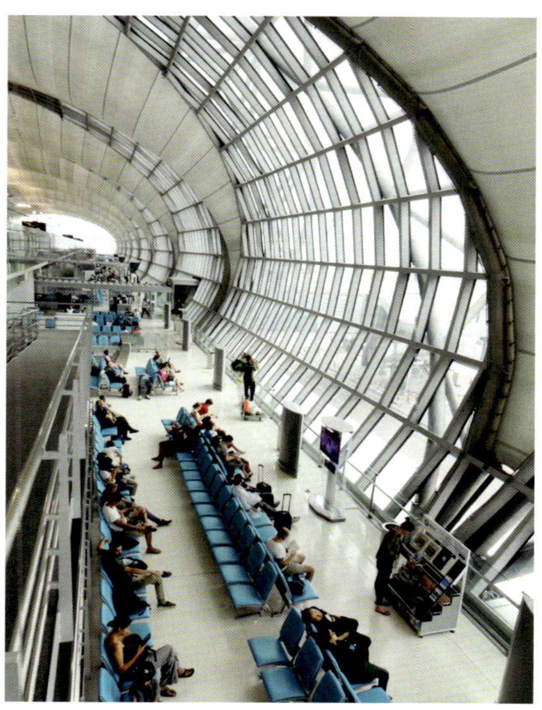

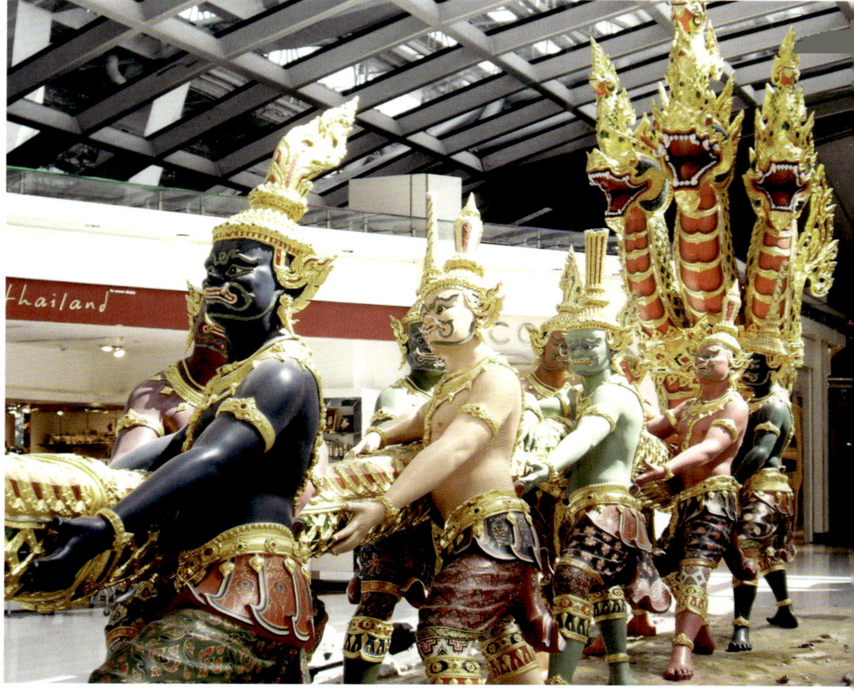

thailand

Madrid Barajas Airport

Architect: Richard Rogers Partnership and Estudio Lamela | Place: Madrid-Barajas, Spain | Built: 2010

The project's key feature is an open floor plan concept connected by light-filled 'canyons' filtering the sunlight to the lower levels of the airport. The large atriums are connected by walking bridges and act as landmarks providing further legibility.

The transparent materials and open floor concept facilitate a wayfinding system where smaller details like changing coloured columns are designed to facilitate orientation.

Physical Settings, Material Spaces and Design
The design of this airport is rather simple and easy to understand as the transparent and open spaces facilitate flow. The focus is on movement and the material design is legible.

MOBILITIES IN SITU

Social Interactions
The calmness of the airport design is in principle an opportunity to engage across user groups.

Embodied Performances
The visual senses are catered to with the design principle and the moving body through the 'canyons' of light and openness. They add an almost playful experience to moving through this transit space.

Jeddah International Airport

Arrival and departure areas are merged and added a contrast between the desolate desert surrounding the building and the grenery in the core of it. Photo: Image courtesy OMA

Architect: Office for Metropolitan Architecture | Place: Jeddah, Saudi Arabia | Built: 2005 (not built)

This airport has to accommodate two million Muslim pilgrims six weeks each year in the Hajj period who are visiting the Saudi Arabian city of Mecca. The airport becomes a gateway to one of the most iconic places on the face of the Earth and will thus also receive a fair amount of international attention.

The designers have deliberately explored a reversal of departure and arrival experiences. Departure halls tend to have better architectural qualities than arrival halls though the traveller's expectation are highest at arrival. The project accommodates arrival and departure sections at the same level and aims to stage the travel experience by adding a green oasis in the middle of the structure in stark contrast to the contextual environment of the surrounding desert.

Physical Settings, Material Spaces and Design
The circular design proposal offer an open and flexible space which should be able to accommodate the huge volume of travellers for a confined time period each year. The design is open and works as an oasis in the desert.

MOBILITIES IN SITU

Social Interactions
The busy Hajj season will offer a melting pot of pilgrims entering the country through this access point, and the open design of arrival and departure may facilitate more interaction between groups that normally are strictly separated.

Embodied Performances
The staging of high quality environments for both arrival and departure coupled with the sense of an 'oasis in the desert' give this airport a different potential for embodied airport experiences.

A waving roof covers a clear progression of spaces from arrival to departure areas. Photo: dalbera

The sleek design of the terminal offers a fast and frictionless connection between ferry and city. Photo: Stefan Ertmann

DFDS Ferry Terminal

Architect: 3xn Architects | Place: Nordhavn, Copenhagen | Built: 2004

The terminal serves large passenger ferries form Poland and Norway and has a capacity of 3 ferries, 2,000 passengers and 400 cars/130 trucks. The building stands elevated over the pier upon black concrete pillars making a stark contrast to its glass surfaces and transparent appearance. At night time the expression of the building changes rather dramatically. The interior of the terminal consists of one large space with functional programs in free standing boxes.

The building will become a landmark of the Nordhavn harbor standing on the border between free and custom regulated zones. Its relatively simple design is chosen to accommodate for a rather large of people within a short time span.

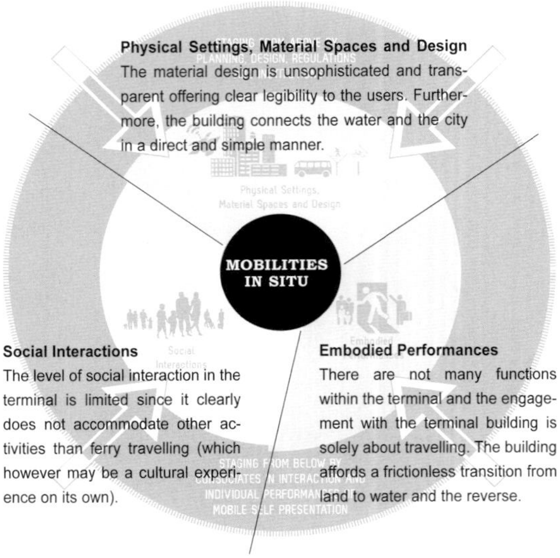

Physical Settings, Material Spaces and Design
The material design is unsophisticated and transparent offering clear legibility to the users. Furthermore, the building connects the water and the city in a direct and simple manner.

MOBILITIES IN SITU

Social Interactions
The level of social interaction in the terminal is limited since it clearly does not accommodate other activities than ferry travelling (which however may be a cultural experience on its own).

Embodied Performances
There are not many functions within the terminal and the engagement with the terminal building is solely about travelling. The building affords a frictionless transition from land to water and the reverse.

The project stages the transport hub and creates a landmark for international container trading. Photo: BIG

Superharbour

Architect: BIG | Place: Femern Belt, Denmark | Built: 2003 (In progress with small changes as 'Red Star Harbour', Guangxi, China)

This project originated in a thought experiment of reflection upon what would happen if all harbours in Denmark were assembled into one 'Superharbour'.

In the project the superstructure is located in the Southeastern part of Denmark close to Germany and the new Femern Belt Bridge, with good connections to the rest of the East European parts of the EU. The project would partly create a global logistic node, partly free a large number of city centre sites that now are occupied by more or less well-functioning traffic harbours in the cities across Denmark. A huge operation releasing real estate values estimated to reach 20 billion Euros. The project links city centre sites potentials of the old harbours with a new agglomeration of sea mobility.

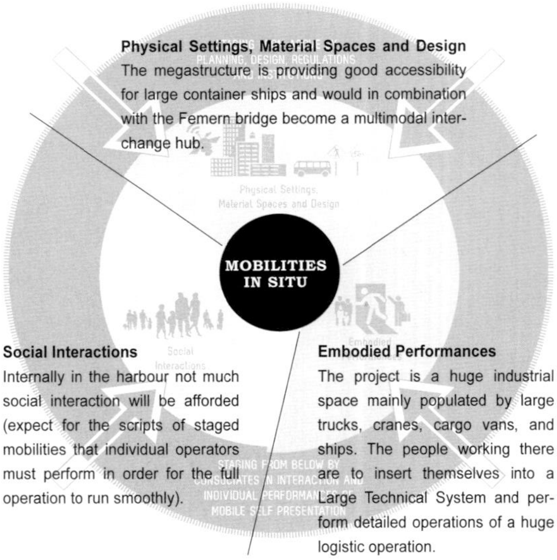

Physical Settings, Material Spaces and Design
The megastructure is providing good accessibility for large container ships and would in combination with the Femern bridge become a multimodal interchange hub.

MOBILITIES IN SITU

Social Interactions
Internally in the harbour not much social interaction will be afforded (expect for the scripts of staged mobilities that individual operators must perform in order for the full operation to run smoothly).

Embodied Performances
The project is a huge industrial space mainly populated by large trucks, cranes, cargo vans, and ships. The people working there are to insert themselves into a Large Technical System and perform detailed operations of a huge logistic operation.

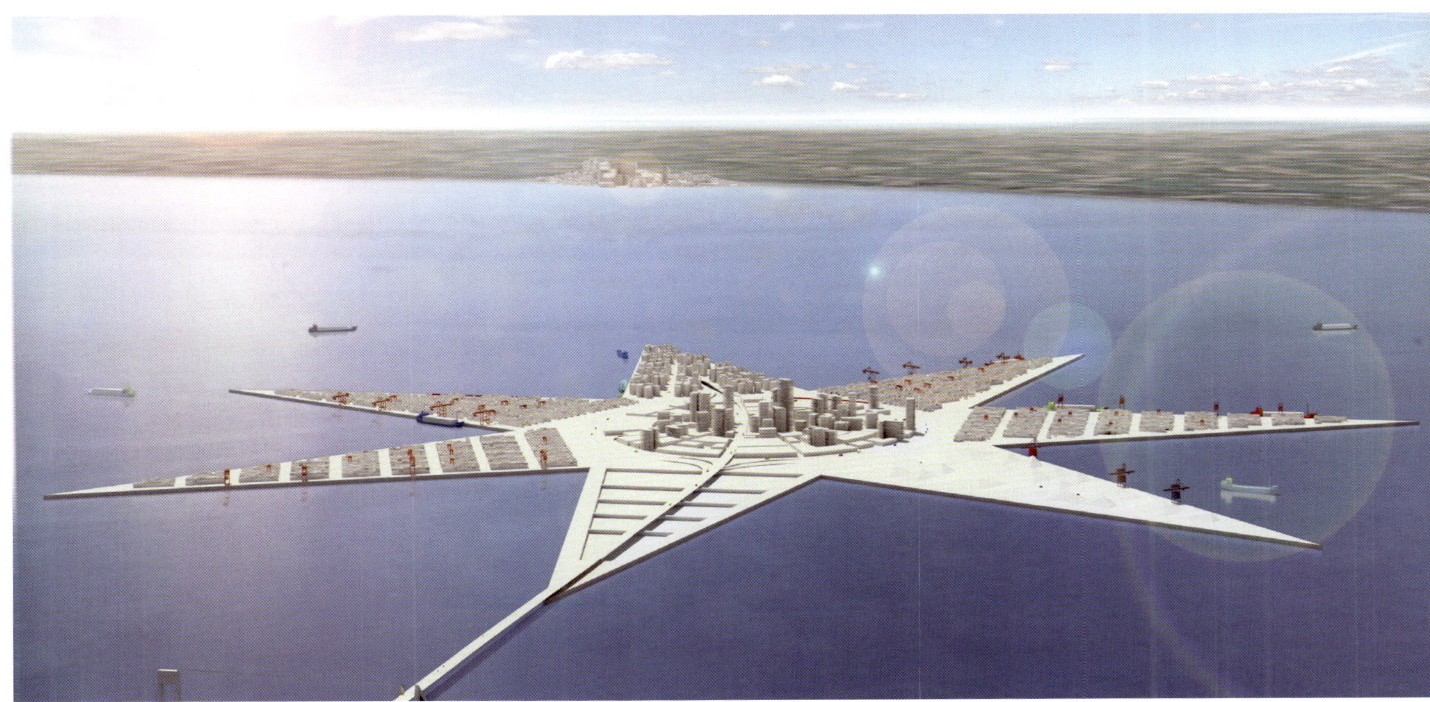

Värtaterminalen

Architect: C.F. Moller Architects | Place: Värtaterminalen, Stockholm | Built: Under development

This project will work as a hub for ferry passengers to and from Finland and the Baltics. The terminals are designed to resemble a moving vessel and the architecture draws on typologies from the history of ports (large cranes and warehouses).

The terminal design seeks to open up the space and draw in urban life to the new area at the harbour, reconnecting the city and the harbour. The terminal building itself is a hybrid of large scale architecture and the city drawing on landscape typologies and exploring inside/outside relations through transparent architecture and sloping flows of pedestrians. The building offers a number of new connections to the city centre of Stockholm.

Physical Settings, Material Spaces and Design
The design is an attempt to costage urban public space and transit flows and creating new mobility patterns in the city of Stockholm. The terminal area is designed as a vast landscape of flow lines and paths.

Social Interactions
The design facilitate infrastructural mobilities as well as it mimics the urban spaces of the adjacent city and thus offering public vistas and spaces for exchange.

Embodied Performances
The terminal offers a new perspective on the city and the sea, and furthermore the slopes of the paths may be explored by pedestrians in a walking landscape.

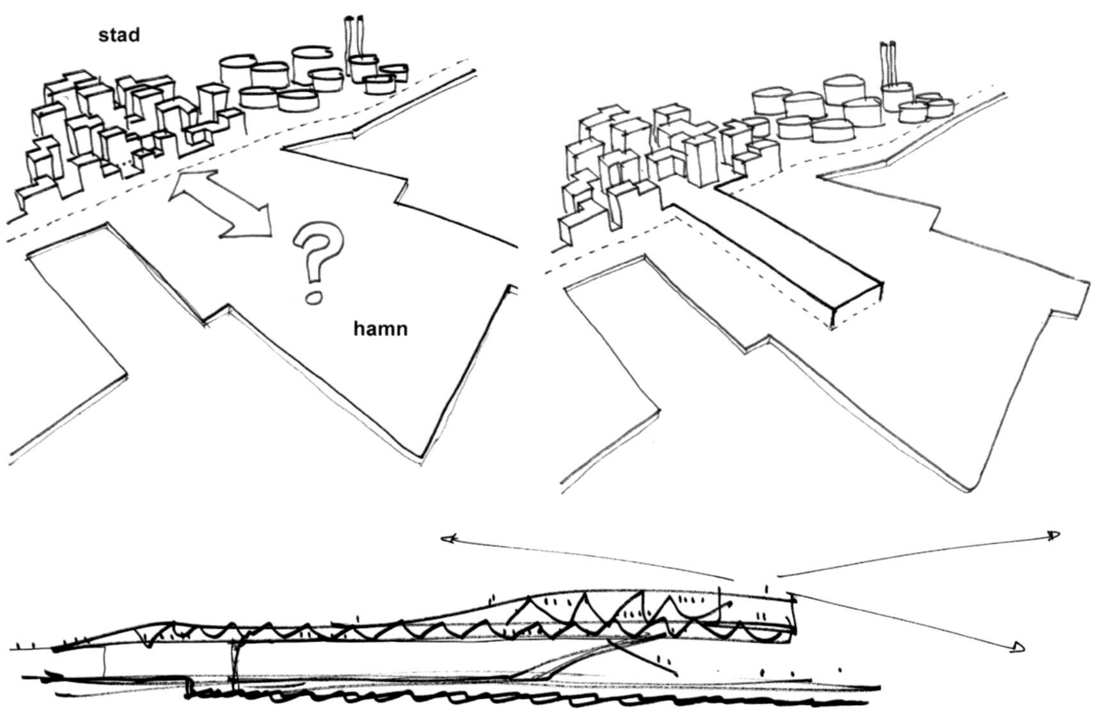

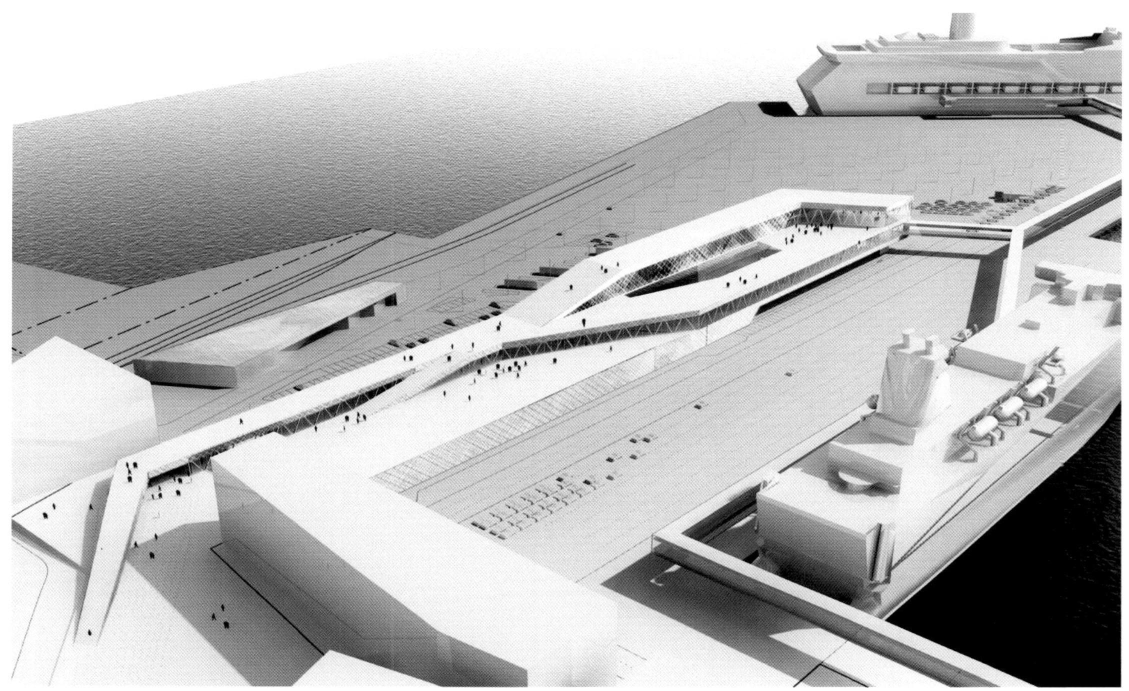

The terminal creates a new connection between city and water.
Photos and sketches: C.F. Møller Architects

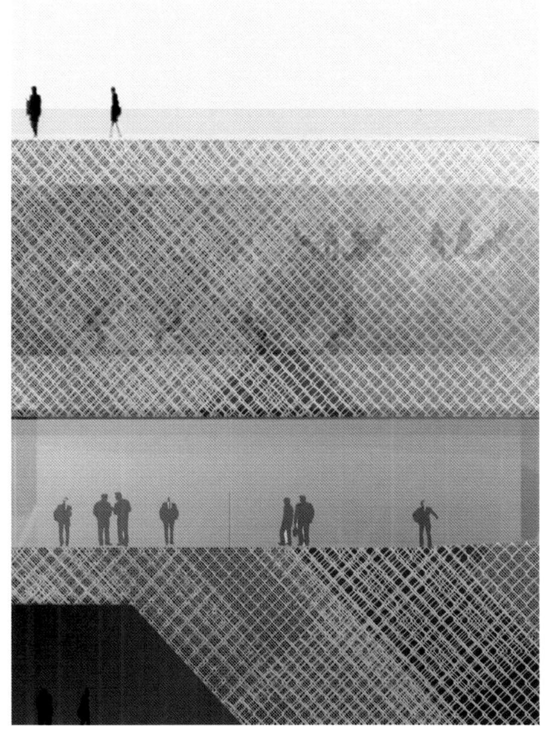

Yokohama Ferry Terminal

Architect: Foreign Office Architects | Place: Yokohama, Japan | Built: 2002

This ferry terminal design has become a global icon and reference. The roof of the terminal creates a platform for social gathering as well as a long promenade along the harbour. The mobile landscape connects to other parts of the city and acts as a recreational area with a view to the harbour and the sea.

The terminal is designed in smooth lines and gently sloping floors to guide people in the direction of the ferries or the city. The design of the terminal explores the borders of outside/ inside, public/private, city/terminal in an innovative reinvention of the ferry terminal as a infrastructure typology.

Physical Settings, Material Spaces and Design
The most predominant feature of this terminal is the way the landscape affords a horizontal park-like surface linking up to vertical movement layers. The wooden materials and the grass provide the design with an organic dimension rarely experienced in infrastructure design.

MOBILITIES IN SITU

Social Interactions
Since the terminal design is as much a leisure or recreational landscape, the potential for social interaction amongst various groups (passenger and urban dwellers) is large and there are multiple smaller sites where interaction may occur.

Embodied Performances
The landscape affords walking and exploring as well as options for recreational activities (these being static or mobile).

The design let spaces float into each other without strict borders to separate them. Photos: Janni Nesager Toft

Bibliography & List of Illustrations

Aalborg Municipality (2008) *Lokalplan 1-1-102. Butikker, Erhverv MV., Fjordgade. Aalborg Midtby. Tillæg til lokalplan 10-005*, Aalborg: Aalborg Municipality.

Aarhus Municipality (2009) *Kommuneplan 2009. Hovedstruktur*, Aarhus.

Aarhus Municipality (2010) Cykelhandlingsplan – En plan for fremtidens cyklist forhold i Århus Kommune. In: http://www.aarhuskommune.dk/borger/trafik/Trafik--og-anlaegsplaner/Cykelhandlingsplan.aspx

Aarhus Stiftstidende (2010) Det cykler for Hans Broges Gade. In: http://stiften.dk/article/20101012/AAS/710129950.

Adam, H. C. (ed.) (2010) *Eadweard Muybridge. The Human and Animal Locomotion Photographs*, Köln: Taschen.

Adey, P. (2010) *Mobility*, London: Routledge.

Alexander, C. (1964) *Notes on the Synthesis of Form*, Cambridge, Mass.: Harvard University Press.

Allingham, P. (2006) Oplevelsescentre: Transit og Shopping, in A. S. Sørensen & M. Zerlang (red.) (2006) *Kultur uden centre*, Århus: Klim, pp.108-130.

Amin, A. & N. Thrift (2002) *Cities. Reimagining the urban*, Cambridge: Polity.

Amoroso, N. (2010) *The Exposed City. Mapping the Urban Invisible*s, London: Routledge.

Anderson, B. & P. Harrison (eds.) (2010) *Taking-Place: 'Nonrepresentational' Theories and Geography*, Aldershot: Ashgate.

Andrade, V., O. B. Jensen, H. Harder & J. C .O. Madsen (2011) Bike Infrastructures and Design Qualities: Enhancing Cycling, *Danish Journal of Geoinformatics and Land Management*, vol. 46, no.1, pp. 65-80.

Andrade, V., O. B. Jensen, H. Harder & J. C. O. Madsen (2012a) *Transforming Vestergade Vest into a Ludic and Shared-Use Space*, in Andrade, V., S. Smith & D. B. Lanng (eds.) (2012) Musings – An Urban Design Anthology, Aalborg: Aalborg University Press, pp. 94-101.

Andrade, V., H. Harder, O. B. Jensen & J. Madsen (2012b) *Bike Infrastructures*, Department Working Paper series, Aalborg: Department of Architecture, Design and Media Technology, Aalborg University, vol. 69.

Appleyard, D., Lynch, K. and Myer, J. R. (1964) *The View from the Road*, Cambridge, Mass.: MIT Press.

Artingeneering (2007) *N4. Toward a Living Infrastructure!*, Brussels: A16

Ascher, K. (2005) *The Works. Anatomy of a City*, New York: The Penguin Press.

Associated Press (2007) Judge says that NYC can continue to regulate mass bike rides, *Associated Press*, April 18, 2007, article written by Larry Neumeister.

Austin, J. L. (1962/75) *How to do Things with Words*, Oxford: Oxford University Press.

Augé, M. (1995) *Non-places. Introduction to an anthropology of supermodernity*. London: Verso.

Augé, M. (2002) *In the Metro*, Minneapolis: University of Minnesota Press.

Bacon, E. N. (1967) *Design of Cities*, London: Penguin.

Banham, R. (1971/2009) *Los Angeles. The Architecture of Four Ecologies*, Berkeley: University of California Press.

Baudrillard, J. (1988) *America*, New York: Verso.

Ben-Joseph, E. (2012) *Rethinking a Lot. The Design and Culture of Parking*, Cambridge, Mass.: MIT Press.

Bendtsen, L. (2005) Cykling, markedsføring og fartkonsum I København ca. 1880-1900, *Den Jyske Historiker*, nr. 108, juni 2005, pp. 59-77.

Benjamin, W. (2002) *The Arcades Project*, Cambridge, Mass: The Harvard University Press.

Bergman, B. (2008) *E4 Staden. Det trafikala Stadslandskabet längs E4 gennom Stockholm*: Stockholm: Stockholmia Förlag.

Berman, M. (1983) *All That Is Solid Melts Into Air. The Experience of Modernity*, New York: Verso.

Berkel, B. & C. Bos (2010) Diagrams, in Garcia, M. (ed.) (2008) *The Diagrams of Architecture*, Chichester: Wiley, pp. 222-227.

BIG (2009) *Yes Is More. An Archicomic on Architectural Evolution*, Copenhagen: BIG ApS.

Bjarrum, C. (2011) Merværdi og Identiet/Added Value and Identity, *Arkitektur DK,* 2/2011, pp. 2-10.

Bollnow, O. F. (1963/2011) *Human Space*, London: Hyphen Press.

Bonham, J. (2011) Bicycle Politics: Review Essay, *Transfers* 1(1), spring 2011: 137-146.

Bosselman, P. (1998) Images in motion (in Carmona urban design reader, pp 267-292).

Bowring, J. & S. Swaffield (2010) Diagrams in Landscape Architecture, in Garcia, M. (ed.) (2010) *The Diagrams of Architecture*, Chichester: Wiley, pp. 142-151.

Buchannan, C. (1964) *Traffic in Towns*, Harmondsworth: Penguin.

Buchardt, J. & M. Schønberg (2006) *Lige ud ad landevejen. Med hestevogn og bil på amternes veje 1886-2006*, Danmarks Vej- & Bromuseum, Odense: Syddansk Universitetsforlag.

Burgess, R. G. (1991) *In the Field. An introduction to field research*, London: Routledge.

Byrne, D. (2009) *Bicycle Diaries*, New York: Viking.

Büsher, M., J. Urry & K. Witchger (eds.) (2011) *Mobile Methods*, London: Routledge.

Cage, J. (1969) *Notations*, New York: Something Else Press.

Caliskan, O. (2012) Design Thinking in urbanism: Learning from the designers, *Urban Design International*, vol. 17, no. 4, pp. 272-296.

Campanella, T. J. (2005) Transplanting the New Jersey Turnpike to China, in J. Rykwert & T. Atkin (Eds). Structure and Meaning in Human Settlement, Philadelphia: University of Pennsylvania Press, pp. 293-306.

Carmona, M., Tiesdell, S., Heath, T. and Oc, T. (2010) *Public Places. Urban Spaces. The Dimensions of Urban Design*, Oxford: Architectural Press, 2 Ed.

Cauter, L. D. (2004) *The Capsular Civilization. On the City in the Age of Fear*, Rotterdam: NAi Publishers.

Chianchi, M. (1984) *Leonardo's Machines*, Florence: Becocci Editore.

Christiansen, J., Chatterjee, K, Marsh, S., Sherwin, H. and Jain, J. (2012) *Evaluation of the Cycling City and Towns Programme: Qualitative research with residents*, August 2012, Report to Department for Transport by AECOM, Centre for Transport & Society and the Tavistock Institute.

Christie, I. (2002) *Motorway Culture and its discontents*, http://www.opendemocracy.net/globalization-transport/article_466.jsp.

Chung, C. J., J. Inaba, R. Koolhaas & S. T. Leong (eds.) (2001) *Project on the City 2. Harvard Design School Guide to Shopping*, Köln: Taschen.

CIAM (1933) Charter of Athens, *Congrès Internationaux d'Architecture Moderne*, accessed at http://www.getty.edu/conservation/research_resources/charters/charter04.html, on July 18 2013.

City of Copenhagen (2003) Ørestad, Copenhagen: City of Copenhagen.

Clarke, D. B. (2003) *The Consumer Society and the Postmodern City*, London: Routledge.

Clemmensen, T. J. (2008a) *Vejnettet og det Urban-Rurale Landskab*, Aarhus: Aarhus Arkitektskole, Ph.D. Afhandling.

Clemmensen, T. J. (2008b) Det oversete vejnet, *Nordisk Arkitekturforskning*, 3-2008, pp. 88- 97.

Clemmensen, T. (red.) (2011) *Grænseløse Byer. Nye Perspektiver for By- og Landskabsarkitekturen*, Aarhus: Arkitektskolens Forlag.

Conley, S. (2012) 'A Sociology of Traffic: Driving, Cycling, Walking', in P. Vannini, L. Budd, O. B. Jensen, C. Fisker and P. Jiron (Eds.)*Technologies of Mobility of the Americas*, New York: Peter Lang, pp. 219-236.

Cook, P. (2008) *Drawing – the motive force of architecture*, Chichester: Wiley.

Copenhagen Municipality (2009a) Samfundsøkonomiske analyser af cykeltiltag - metode og cases.

Copenhagen Municipality (2009b) COPENHAGEN'S GREEN ACCOUNTS.

Copenhagen Municipality (2010a) Grønne cykelruter. In: http://kk.dk/Borger/ByOgTrafik/CyklernesBy/KonkreteProjekter/OevrigeProjekter/GroenneCykelruter.aspx

Copenhagen Municipality (2010b) Cykeltal. In: http://kk.dk/Borger/ByOgTrafik/CyklernesBy/VidenOgTal/Cykeltal.aspx.

Copenhagen Municipality (2010c) Målsætning. In: http://kk.dk/Borger/ByOgTrafik/CyklernesBy/PolitikOgStrategi/Maalsaetning.aspx.

Copenhagen Municipality (2010d) Bryggebroen. In: http://www.kk.dk/Borger/ByOgTrafik/Anlaegsprojekter/UdfoerteProjekter/Bryggebroen.aspx.

Copenhagen Municipality (2010e) Indvielse. In: http://www.kk.dk/Borger/ByOgTrafik/Anlaegsprojekter/UdfoerteProjekter/Bryggebroen/Indvielse.aspx.

Corner, J. (1999) The Agency of Mapping: Speculation, Critique, and Invention, in D. Cosgrove (ed.) (1999) *Mappings*, London: Reaktion Books, pp. 213-252.

Cosgrove, D. (1999) Introduction, in D. Cosgrove (ed.) (1999) *Mappings*, London: Reaktion Books, pp. 1-23.

Cox, P. (2012) Cycling: Image or Imagining in the Cultural Turn, *Transfers* 2(1), spring 2012: 159-164.

CPHX (2009) FIRST BRIDGE IN 50 YEARS. In:http://www.cphx.dk/index.php?language=uk#/29190/.

Cresswell, T. (2006) *On the Move. Mobility in the Modern Western World*, London: Routledge.

Crozet, Y. (2011) Mobility: Time Savings aren't What They Used to Be ..., in Gay, C., V. Kaufmann, S. Landriéve & S. Vincent-Gelsin (Eds.) (2011) *Mobile/Immobile. Choices and Rights for 2030*, Paris: Forum Vies Mobiles, pp. 68-79.

Cullen, G. (1996) *The Concise Townscape*, Oxford: Architectural Press.

Dahl, H. (2008) *Den usynlige verden*, København: Gyldendal.

Dalkakoglou, D. & P. Harvey (2012) Roads and Anthropology: Ethnographic Perspectives on Space, Time and (Im)Mobility, *Mobilities*, vol. 7, no. 4, 1-7.

Dant, T. (2004) The Driver-car, *Theory, Culture & Society*, vol. 21 (4/5): 61-79.

Davies, M. (1992) Fortress Los Angeles: The Militarization of Urban Space, in Sorokin, M. (ed.) (1992) *Variations on a Theme Park. The New American City and the End of Public Space*, New York: Hill and Wang, pp. 154-180.

Davies, M. (2008) Why Do we need doctoral study in design?, *International Journal of Design*, vol. 2, No. 3, 2008, pp. 71-79.

Dean, W. & V. Garritzman (2010) Designing the Contemporary. OMA's little helper in the quest for the New, in Garcia, M. (ed.) (2008) *The Diagrams of Architecture*, Chichester: Wiley, pp. 228-236.

Dear, M. J. (Ed.) (2002) *From Chicago to L.A. Making sense of Urban Theory*, London: Sage.

De Boeck, L. (2002) After-Sprawl, in Xaveer De Geyter Architects: *After-Sprawl. Research for the contemporary city*, Rotterdam: Nai Publishers, pp. 19-32.
De Geyter, X. (2002) *After-Sprawl. Research for the Contemporary City*, Rotterdam: NAi Publishers .
Degen, M., C. DeSilvey &. G. Rose (2008) Experiencing visualities in designed urban environments: learning from Milton Keynes, *Environment and Planning A*, 2008, vol. 40, pp. 1901-1920.
De Landa, M. (2006) *A New Philosophy of Society. Assemblage Theory and Social Complexity*, New York: Continuum.
Deleuze, G. & F. Guattari (1997) City/State, in N. Leach (ed.) (1997) *Rethinking Architecture – A Reader in Cultural Theory*, London: Routledge, pp. 313-316.
Deleuze, G. & F. Guattari (2003) *A Thousand Plateaus. Capitalism and Schizophrenia*, London: Continuum.
Dennis, K. & J. Urry (2009) *After the Car*, Cambridge: Polity.
Dovey, K. (2010) *Becoming Places. Urbanism/Architecture/Identity/Power*, London: Routledge.
Dreyfus, H. & S. Dreyfus (1986) *Mind over Machine: The Power of Human Intuition and Expertise in the Era of the Computer,* New York: Free Press.
Easterling, K. (2011) Fresh Field, in N. Bhatia, M. Przybylski, L. Sheppeard & M. White (2011) *Coupling. Strategies for Infrastructural Opportunism*, New York: Princeton Architectural Press, pp. 10-13.
Edensor, T. (2003) M6-Junction 19-16. Defamiliarizing the Mundane Roadscape, *Space & Culture*, vol. 6, no. 2 may 2003, 151-168.
Edwards, B. (2011) *Sustainability and the Design of Transport Interchanges*, London: Routledge.
Egebjerg, U. (2011) Idéudveksling/Exchange of Ideas, Interview by Martin Keiding in *Arkitektur DK*, 2/2011, pp. 24-27.
Eisenman, P. (2010) Diagram. An Original Scene of Writing, in in Garcia, M. (ed.) (2008) *The Diagrams of Architecture*, Chichester: Wiley, pp. 92-103.
Elliott, A. & J. Urry (2010) *Mobile Lives*, London: Routledge.
Erlhoff, M., P. Heidkamp & I. Utikal (eds.) (2008) *Designing Public. Perspectives for the public*, Basel: Birkhäuser.
Evans, R. (2000) *You Questioning my Manhood Boy? Masculine Identity, Work performance and performativity in a rural staples economy*, Aberdeen: University of Aberdeen, The Arkleton Centre for Rural Development Research, Research Paper No. 4.
Fallan, K. (2010) *Design History. Understanding Theory and Method*, Oxford: Berg.
Farias, I. & Bender, T. (Eds.) (2010) *Urban Assemblages. How Actor-Network Theory changes urban studies*, London: Routledge.
Farias, I. (2010a) Interview with Nigel Thrift, in Farias, I. & Bender, T. (Eds.) (2010) *Urban Assemblages. How Actor-Network Theory changes urban studies*, London: Routledge, pp. 109-119.
Farias, I. (2010b) Interview with Rob Shields, in Farias, I. & Bender, T. (Eds.) (2010) *Urban Assemblages. How Actor-Network Theory changes urban studies*, London: Routledge, pp. 291-301.
Farman, J. (2012) *Mobile Interface Theory*, London: Routledge.
Featherstone, M. (2004) Automobilities. An Introduction, *Theory, Culture & Society*, vol. 21 (4/5): 1-24
Flemming, S. (2012) *Cycle Space. Architecture & Urban Design in the Age of the Bicycle*, Rotterdam: NAi010 Publishers.

Fincham, B. (2006) Bicycle messengers and the road to freedom, in Böhm, S, C. Jones, C. Land & M. Paterson (eds.) (2006) *Against Automobility*, Oxford: Blackwell, pp. 208-222.

Finizo, G. (2006) *Architecture & Mobility*. Tradition and Innovatio, Milan: Sikra Editore .

Forrester, J. (2004) Reflections on Trying to Teach Planning Theory, *Planning Theory and Practice*, vol. 5, no. 2, June 2004, pp. 242-251.

Foster, N. (2007) *Norman Foster Works 3*, Munich: Prestel.

Fraser, N. (1990) Rethinking the Public Sphere: A contribution to the Critique of Actually Existing Democracy, *Social Text*, no. 25/26, pp. 56-80.

Frers, L. (2009) Pacification by Design. An ethnography of normalization techniques, in Berking, H., S. Frank & L. Frers (eds). (2009) *Negotiating urban conflicts: Interaction, space and control*, Series: Materialities, Vol. 1, Bielefeld: Transcript Verlag, pp. 249-262.

Fuller, G. (2002) 'The Arrow – Directional Semiotics: Wayfinding in Transit', *Social Semiotics*, vol. 12, no. 3, pp. 231-244.

Fuller, G. and Harley, R. (2004) *Aviopolis. A book about Airports*, London: Black Dog Publishing.

Furness, Z. (2010) *One Less Car: Bicycling and the Politics of Automobility*, Philadelphia: Temple University Press.

Fyens stiftstidende (2010a) 200 busser forsvinder søndag fra centrum – Karsten Hüttel – Fyens Stiftstidende 30.07.2010.

Fyens Stiftstidende (2010b) Kaos plager ny gågade – Rune H. Blickfeldt – Fyens Stiftstidende 13.09.2010.

Fyens Stiftstidende (2010c) Cyklerne Skal ud af gågaden – Esben Seerup - Fyens Stiftstidende 15.09.2010.

Garcia, M. (ed.) (2008) *The Diagrams of Architecture*, Chichester: Wiley.

Gehl, J. (1996) *Livet mellem husene. Udeaktiviteter of udemiljøer*, København: Arkitektens Forlag

Gehl, J. (2010) *Cities for people*, Washington DC: Island Press.

Gibson, D. (2009) *The Wayfinding Handbook. Information Design for Public Spaces*, New York: Princeton Architectural Press.

Giedion, S. (1948) *Mechanization Takes Command. A contribution to anonymous history*, Oxford: Oxford University Press.

Gilbert, R. & A. Perl (2010), *Transport Revolutions. Moving People and Freight Without Oil*, Gabriola Island: New Society Publishers.

Girot, C. (2011) Landskabelige Udenomsværker/Landscape Peripherals, *Arkitektur DK*, 2/2011, pp. 34-39.

Goeverden, K. & T. Godefrooji (2011) *The Dutch Reference Study. Cases of interventions in bicycle infrastructure reviewed in the framework of Bikeability*, Delft: Delft University of Technology, Department of Transport & Planning.

Goffman, E. (1963) *Behaviour in Public Places. Notes on the Social Organisation of Gatherings*, New York: The Free Press.

Goffman, E. (1972) *Relations in Public. Micro Studies of the Public Order*, New York: Harper & Row.

Goffman, E. (1974) *Frame Analysis. An Essay on the Organization of Experience*, Boston: Northeastern University Press.

Gordon, E. & A. S. Silva (2011) *NetLocality. Why location matters in a networked world*; Chichester: Wiley-Blackwell.

Graham, S. (2011) *Cities under Siege. The New Military Urbanism*, London: Verso.

Graham, S. & Marvin, S. (2001) *Splintering Urbanism. Networked infrastructures, technological mobilities and the urban condition,* London: Routledge.

Grontmij- Carlbro (2010) BRYGGEBRO OVER SYDHAVNEN KLAR TIL BRUG. In: http://www.grontmij-carlbro.com/da/Menu/Aktuelt/Nyheder/BryggebroSydhavnen.htm.
Grunfelder, J. & T. A. S. Nielsen (2013) Det Østjyske Bybånd, in Albertsen, N., G. Jørgensen & L. Winther (red.) (2013) *Den Grænseløse By*, København: Københavns Universitet, pp. 43-46.
Guest, A. H. (2005) *Labanotaion. The System of Analyzing and Recording Movement*, London: Routledge, 4th Edition.
Gunn, W., T. Otto & R. C. Smith (eds.) (2013) *Design Anthropology – Theory and Practice*, London: Bloomsbury Academic.
Gänshirt, C. (2007) *Tools for Ideas. An Introduction to Architectural Design*, Basel: Birkhäuser.
Habermas, J. (1962/2009) *Borgerlig Offentlighed. Offentlighedens strukturændring. Undersøgelser af en kategori i det borgerlige samfund*, København: Informations Forlag.
Hajer, M. & Reijndorp, A. (2001) *In search of New Public Domain*, Rotterdam: Nai Publishers.
Hall, E.T. (1966) *The Hidden Dimension*. New York: Anchor Books Doubleday.
Halprin, L. (1963) *Cities*, New York: Reinhold Publishing Corporation.
Halprin, L. (1966) *Freeways*, New York: Reinhold Publishing Corporation.
Halsall, F. (2012) An Aesthetics of proof: A conversation between Bruno Latour and Francis Halsall on Art and Inquiry, *Environment and Planning D: Society & Space,* 2012, vol. 30, pp. 963-970.
Hamid, S. A., O. B. Jensen & V. Andrade (2012) Signs in Place: Choreographing Travel Flow in Urban Spaces, *Spaces & Flows: An International Conference on Urban and ExtraUrban Studies*, vol. 2. No. 3, pp. 115-128.
Hannam, K., M. Sheller & J. Urry (2006) Editorial: Mobilities, Immobilities and Moorings, *Mobilities*, Vol. 1, No. 1, pp. 1-22, March 2006.
Harper, D. (2012) *Visual Sociology*, London: Routledge.
Harvey, D. (1989) *The Urban Experience*, Oxford: Blackwell.
Hedensted (2009) *Kommuneplan*, Hedensted: Hedensted Kommune.
Herman, D. (2001) Mall, in Chung, C. J. J. Inaba, R. Koolhaas & S. T. Leong (eds.) (2001) *Project on the City 2. Harvard Design School Guide to Shopping*, Köln: Taschen, pp. 460-475.
Highway Code (2008) *The Original Highway Code. Reproductions of the Highway Code Booklets from the Thirties, Forties and Fifties*, London: Michael O'Mara Books Limited.
Hislop, D. (2013) Driving, Communicating and Working: Understanding the work-related Communication Behaviours of Business Travellers on Work-related Car journeys, *Mobilities*, vol. 8, no. 2, 220-237.
Hovgesen, H. H., J. B. Nielsen & U. Egebjerg (2005) *Byen, Vejen, Landskabet – motorveje til fremtiden*, Aalborg: Aalborg Universitet, KVL & Vejdirektoratet.
Hommels, A. (2006) *Unbuilding Cities. Obduracy in Urban Socio-Technical Change*, Cambridge, Mass.: MIT Press.
Hoete, A. (ed.) (2003) *ROAM. Reader on the Aesthetic of Mobility*, London: Black Dog Publishing.
Houben, F & L. M. Calabrese (eds.) *Mobility: A room with a view*, Rotterdam: NAi Publishers.
Houben, F. (2003) *A Room With A View*, in in Houben, F. & L. M. Calabrese (eds.) (2003) *Mobility: A room with a view*, Rotterdam: NAi Publishers, pp. 22-77.
Humlum, J. (1966) *Landsplanlægnings problemer. Med skitse til en landsplanlægning i Danmark*, København: Munksgaards Forlag.
Hård, M. & T. J. Misa (Eds.) (2008) *Urban Machinery. Inside Modern European Cities*, Cambridge, Mass.: MIT Press.

Ingersoll, R. (2006) *Sprawltown. Looking for the City on its Edge*, New York: Princeton Architectural Press.
Ingledew, J. (2011) *The A-Z of Visual Ideas. How to solve any creative brief*, London: Laurence King Publishers.
Ingold, T. (2007) *Lines. A brief history*, London: Routledge.
Ingold, T. (2011) *Being Alive. Essays on Movement, Knowledge, Description*, London: Routledge.
Isin, E. F. (2002) Ways of Being Political, *Distinktion*, Nr. 4, 2002, pp. 7-28.
Jacobs, J. (1961) *The Death and Life of Great American Cities*, New York: Vintage Books.
Jensen, B. B. (2004) *Byen Genopdaget – på sporet af den nutidige by*, Aalborg: Aalborg Universitet, Ph.D. Afhandling.
Jensen, O. B. (1999) *At ville noget med rummet - diskurs & rationalitet i Danmarks og den Europæiske Unions planlægning af byernes rumlige udvikling*. Ph.D.-afhandling, Institut for Samfundsudvikling & Planlægning, Aalborg Universitet 1999.
Jensen, O.B. (2004a) There is nothing as practical as a good theory, *Planning, Theory and Practice*, vol. 5, no. 2, June 2004, pp. 254-255.
Jensen, O. B. (2004b) *Byen, magten og netvæket – mod en reaktualiseret kritisk byteori*, Aalborg: Department of Architecture and Design, Department Working Paper Series, *AD-Files* no. 3, 2004.
Jensen, O. B. (2006a) Facework, Flow and the City. Simmel, Goffman and Mobility in the Contemporary City, *Mobilities*, Vol. 2, No. 2, July 2006, pp. 143-165.
Jensen, O. B. (2006b) *Thinking Mobilities – Crossing Disciplinary Boundaries*, Paper for the 'Sustainability and Landscapes of Mobility Problems and potentials in an urban architectural perspective' Conference, School of Architecture, May 22-23, 2006.
Jensen, O. B. (2006c) *Urban Branding, Imagebildung und regionales Wachstum/Urban Branding, Image Formation and Regional Growth*, in R. Sonnabend & R. Stein (eds.) (2006) Die anderen Städte/The other cities, Dessau: Stiftung Bauhaus, pp. 78-89.
Jensen, O. B. (2007a) Culture Stories: Understanding Cultural Urban Branding, *Planning Theory*, vol. 6(3), pp. 211-236.
Jensen, O. B. (2007b) *Biking in the Land of the Car – clashes of mobility cultures in the USA*, paper for the conference Trafikdage, Aalborg, August 27-28, 2007.
Jensen, O. B. (2007c) City of layers. Bangkok's Sky Train and How It Works in Socially Segregating Mobility Patterns, *Swiss Journal of Sociology*, vol. 33, no. 3, pp. 387-405.
Jensen, O. B. (2008) *European Metroscapes - the production of lived mobilities within the socio-technical Metro systems in Copenhagen, London and Paris*, paper for the 'Mobility, the City and STS' conference, The Technical University of Denmark (DTU), Copenhagen, November 20-22, 2008.
Jensen, O. B. (2009a) Flows of Meaning, cultures of Movement – urban mobility as meaningful everyday life practice, *Mobilities*, Vol. 4, No. 1, March 2009, pp. 139-158.
Jensen, O. B. (2009b) *Den Gamle Landevej – en undersøgelse af hovedvejes betydning og potentialer efter motorvejsnetværkets sejr*, Paper til Konferencen Trafikdage, Aalborg, August 24-25, 2009.
Jensen, O. B. (2010a) *Erving Goffman and Everyday Life Mobility*, in Hviid Jacobsen, M. (ed.) (2010) The Contemporary Goffman, New York: Routledge, pp. 333-351.
Jensen, O. B. (2010b) Negotiation in Motion: Unpacking a Geography of Mobility, *Space and Culture*, vol. 13 (4), pp. 389-402.
Jensen, O. B. (2010c) Langsom by – progressivt byudviklingskoncept eller rendyrket nostalgi?, in H.J. Kristensen,

J. N. Frandsen & J. Møller (eds.) (2010) *Citta Slow. Byudvikling med udsyn og omtanke?,* Odense: Syddansk Universitetsforlag, pp. 51-63.

Jensen, O. B. (Ed.) (2010) *Design Research Epistemologies I – Research in Architectural Design*, Aalborg: Departmental Working Paper Series, Department of Architecture, Design and Media Technology, Aalborg University.

Jensen, O. B. (2012a) Metroens Arkitektur og Bevægelser, in J. Andersen, M. Freudendal-Pedersen, L. Koefoed & J. Larsen (red.) (2012) *Byen i Bevægelse. Mobilitet – Politik – Performativitet*, Frederiksberg: Roskilde Universitetsforlag, pp. 40-60.

Jensen, O. B. (2012b) *If Only it Could Speak: Narrative Explorations of Mobility and Place in Seattle*, in Vannini, P., L. Budd, O. B. Jensen, C. Fisker & P. Jirón (Eds.) (2012) Technologies of Mobility in the Americas, New York: Peter Lang, pp. 59-77.

Jensen, O. B. (2013a) *Staging Mobilities*, London: Routledge.

Jensen, O. B. (2013b) *Mobility* Divides – 'Staging' differential Mobilities', Keynote paper for the 4th PanAmerican Mobilities Network Conference 'Different al Mobilities', Concordia University, Montreal, May 8-13, 2013.

Jensen, O. B. (2013c) *Designing Mobilities – Staging Materialities of Mobilities*, Paper for the Danish Sociology Congress 'Mobilitet & By', Roskilde University, Denmark, January 24-25, 2013.

Jensen, O. B. & M. Freudendal-Pedersen (2012) Utopias of Mobilities, in M. H. Jacobsen & K. Tester (eds.) (2012) *Utopia: Social Theory and the Future*, Farnham: Ashgate, pp. 197-217.

Jensen, O. B. & N. Morelli (2011) Critical Points of Contact: Exploring networked relations in urban mobility and service design, *Danish Journal of Geoinformatics and Land Management*, vol. 46, no.1, pp. 36-49

Jensen, O. B. & T. Richardson (2003) Being on the map: The new Iconographies of Power over European Space, *International Planning Studies*, Vol. 8, No. 1, pp. 9-34, 2003.

Jensen, O. B. & T. Richardson (2004) *Making European Space. Mobility, Power and territorial Identity*, London: Routledge.

Jensen, O. B. & B. S. Thomsen (2008) *Performative Urban Environments: Increasing Media Connectivity*, in F. Eckardt et al. (eds.) (2008) Mediacity: Situations, Practices and Encounters, Berlin: Frank & Timme, pp. 407-429.

Jensen, O. B., S. Wind & D. B. Lanng (2012) Critical Points of Contact – between urban networks and flows, in Andrade, V., S. Smith & D. B. Lanng (eds.) (2012) *Musings – An Urban Design Anthology*, Aalborg: Aalborg University Press, pp. 66-73.

Jiron, P. (2011) Becoming 'la sombra/the shadow', in Büsher, M., J. Urry & K. Witchger (eds.) (2011) *Mobile Methods*, London: Routledge, pp. 36-53..

Jones, W. (2006) *New Transport Architecture*, London: Michell Beazley.

Jørgensen, A. J. (2007) *Trafikkultur*, Aalborg: Aalborg Universitetsforlag.

Jørgensen, S. E. (2001) *Fra chaussé til motorvej – det overordnede danske vejnets udvikling fra 1761*, Dansk Vejhistorisk Selskab, Odense: Odense Universitetsforlag.

Kaufmann, E. (1959) En landsplan-hypotese, *BYPLAN* nr. 63, 11. årgang 1959, pp. 124-128.

Kellerman, A. (2006) *Personal Mobilities*, London: Routledge.

Kitchin, R. and Dodge, M. (2011) *Code/Space. Software and Everyday Life*, Cambridge, Mass.: MIT Press.

Kjærsdam, F. (1995) *Byplanlægningens Historie*, Aalborg: Aalborg Universitetsforlag.

Knudsen, A-M. S., Harder, H., Simonsen, A. K. and Stigsen, T. K. (2011) 'Employing smart phones as a planning tool: The Vollsmose case', Paper for the *4th Nordic Geographers Meeting*, Roskilde, May 24-27, 2011.

Kolb, D. (2008) *Sprawling Places*, Athens: The University of Georgia Press.

Koolhaas, R. (2004) *Content. Triumph of Realization*, Köln: Taschen.
Koolhaas, R. & B. Mau (1995) S, M, L, XL, New York: The Monacelli Press.
Krange, O. & Å. Strandbu (1996) *Kjøpesenteret. Handlemaskin og fornøyelsespark*, Oslo: Pax Forlag.
Krieger, A. and Saunders, W. S. (Eds.) (2009) *Urban Design*, Minneapolis: University of Minnesota Press.
Kuilenburg, J.W. (2004) Trigger-Happy Urbanism, in Nielsen, T., N. Albertsen & P. Hemmersam (eds.) (2004) *Urban Mutations – periodization, scale and mobility*, Aarhus: Arkitektskolens Forlag, pp. 126-147.
Kwinter, S. (2010) The Hammer and the Song, in Garcia, M. (ed.) (2008) *The Diagrams of Architecture*, Chichester: Wiley, pp. 122-127.
Lang, J. (2005) *Urban Design. A Typology of Procedures and Products*, Oxford: Architectural Press.
Lanng, D. B., H. Harder & O. B. Jensen (2012) *Toward urban mobility designs: en route in the functional city*, Paper for the conference Trafikdage, Aalborg, August 27-28, 2012.
Larsen, S. (2012) *Road*, Aarhus: Steen Larsen.
Latour, B. (1996) *Aramis or the love of Technology*, Cambridge, Mass.: Harvard University Press.
Latour, B. (2005) *Reassembling the social*, Oxford: Oxford University Press.
Latour, B. (2009) *En ny sociologi for et nyt samfund. Introduktion til Aktør-Netværk-Teori*, København: Akademisk Forlag.
Latour, B. & A. Yaneva (2008) "Give me a gun and I will make all buildings move": An ANT's vies of Architecture, in Geiser, R. (Ed.) (2008) *Explorations in Architecture: Teaching, Design, Research*, Basel: Birkhäuser, pp. 80-89.
Laurier, E. (2004) Doing office work on the Motorway, *Theory, Culture & Society*, vol. 21 (4/5): 261-277.
Laurier, E., B. Brown & H. Lorimer (2012) What it means to change lanes: Actions, Emotions and wayfinding in the family car, *Semiotica* 191 – 1/4 (2012), 117-135.
Lay, M. G. (2012) How Were Motorways Specified? A Comment on the Special Section on Roads, Transfers 2(1), spring 2012:134-140.
Lawson, B. (2001) *The language of Space*, Oxford: Architectural Press.
Lawson, B. (2004) *What designers know*, London: Architectural Press.
Lawson, B. (2006) *How designers think. The design process demystified,* London: Architectural Press, 4th Edition.
Le Corbusier (1929) *The City of To-Morrow and its Planning*, New York: Dover Publications.
Lefebvre, H. (1974/90) *The production of space*, Oxford: Blackwell.
Lund, A. (2011) Terrain Vague, *Arkitektur DK*, 2/2011, pp. 28-33.
Lynch, K. (1960) *The Image of The City*, Cambridge, Mass.: MIT Press.
Lynch, K. (1981) *Good City Form*, Cambridge, Mass.: MIT Press.
Lynch, K. (1990) *City Sense and City Design*, Cambridge, Mass.: MIT Press (ed. by Tridib Banjeree and Michael Southworth).
Lynch, K. and G. Hack (1984) *Site Planning*, Cambridge, Mass.: MIT Press.
Lyon, P. (2011) *Design Education. Learning, Teaching and Researching Through Design*, Farnham: Gower.
Löfgren, O. (2014) *Sharing an Atmosphere: Spaces in Urban Commons*, in C. Borch, E. Barinaga & M. Koruberger (2014) (Eds.) Urban Commons: rethinking the city, London: Routledge.
Maas, V. (2003) *Five Minutes City. Architecture and [Im]mobility,* Rotterdam: Episode Publishers.
Maas, V. (2010) *Metacity/Datatown*, in Garcia, M. (ed.) (2010) *The Diagrams of Architecture*, Chichester: Wiley, pp. 244-249.
Maas, V. & G. La (eds.) (2007) *Skycar City. A pre-emptive History,* Barcelona: Acta.
Madanipour, A. (2003) *Public and Private Spaces of the City*, London: Routledge.

Madsen, H. H. (2009) *Skæv og national. Dansk byplanlægning 1830-1938*, København: Bogværket.

Malnar, J. M. & F. Vodvarka (2010) Diagrams in Multisensory and Phenomenological Architecture, in Garcia, M. (ed.) (2008) *The Diagrams of Architecture*, Chichester: Wiley, pp. 112-121.

Mammen, H. (1997) Et dejligt skævt Danmark – de kulturelle forskelles dynamik, *BYPLAN*, nr. 6, december 1997, pp. 269-277.

Marling, G. (2003) *Urban Songlines. Hverdagslivets drømmespor*, Aalborg: Aalborg Universitetsforlag.

Marling, G. (2013) *Urban Bike Scapes in New York*, Aalborg: Department of Architecture, Design and Media Technology, Working Paper no. 64.

Marling, G., H. Kiib & O. B. Jensen (2009) *Experience City.DK*, Aalborg: Aalborg University Press.

Marshall, S. (2005) *Street Patterns*, London: SPON Press.

Marx, K. (1887/1972) 'Capital', in R. C. Tucker (ed.) (1972) *The Marx-Engels Reader*, New York: W. W. Norton & Company, pp. 191-318.

Massey, D. (2005) *For Space*, London: Sage.

McCormack, D. P. (2010) Thinking in Transition: The Affirmative Refrain of Experience/experiment, in Anderson, B. & P. Harrison (eds.) (2010) *Taking-Place: 'nonrepresentational' Theories and Geography*, Aldershot: Ashgate, pp. 201-220.

McCullough, M. (2004) *Digital Ground. Architecture, Pervasive Computing, and Environmental Knowing*, Cambridge, Mass.: MIT Press.

Merriman, P. (2006) 'Mirror, Signal, Manoeuvre': assembling and governing the motorway driver in the late 1950s Britain, in S. Böhn, C. Jones, C. Land & M. Paterson (eds.) (2006) *Against Automobility*, Oxford: Blackwell, pp. 75-92.

Merriman, P. (2007) *Driving Spaces. A Cultural-Historic Geography of England's M1 Motorway*, Oxford: Blackwell.

Merriman, P. (2011) Roads: Lawrence Halprin, Modern Dance and the American Freeway Landscape, in Cresswell, T. & P. Merriman (eds.) (2011) *Geographies of Mobilities: Practices, Spaces, Subjects*, Farnham: Ashgate, pp. 99-117.

Merriman, P., T. Cresswell, C. Divall, G. Mom, M. Sheller & J. Urry (2013) Ideas in Motion. Mobility: Geographies, Histories, Sociologies, *Transfers* 3(1), spring 2013:147-165.

Metroselskabet (2009) Årsrapport *2009*, http://www.m.dk/~/media/Metro/PDF/PDF%202010/aarsrapport_2009.ashx; accessed July 9, 2013.

Mikkelsen, J. B., S. Smith & O. B. Jensen (2011) *Challenging the 'King of the Road' – exploring mobility battles between cars and bikes in the USA*, Paper for the 4th Nordic Geographers Meeting, Roskilde, May 24-27, 2011.

Miljøministeriet (2006) *Det Nye Danmarkskort – planlægning under nye vilkår*, Landsplaneredegørelsen, København: Miljøministeriet.

Moeslund, T. B., A. Hilton, V. Krüger & L. Sigal (eds.) (2011) *Visual Analysis of Humans. Looking at People*, Heidelberg: Springer.

Molotch, H. (2005) *Where Stuff Comes from. How Toasters, Toilets, Cars, Computers, and Many Other Things Come to be as they Are*, New York: Routledge.

Moudon, A. V. (1992) A Catholic Approach to Organizing what Urban Designers Should Know, in A.R. Cuthbert (ed.) (2003) *Designing Cities. Critical Readings in Urban Design*, Oxford: Blackwell, pp. 362-382.

MVDRV (2003) *The Region Maker. RheinRuhr City*, Düsseldorf: NRW-Forum Kultur und Wissenschaft.

Mumford, L. (1956) *From the Ground Up. Observations on contemporary Architecture, Housing, Highway Building and Civic Design*, New York: Harvest/HBJ.

NCHRP (2003) *Design Speed, Operating Speed and Posted Speed Practices*, Washington DC: National Cooperative for Highway Research Program (NCHRP), Report no. 504.

Nielsen, J. B., Schultz, A. T., Nielsen, T. A. S. and Harder, H. (2005) *Byen, vejen og landskabet – Motorveje til fremtiden*, Frederiksberg: KVL, Center for Skov, Landskab og Planlægning

Nielsen, T. (2001) *Formløs. Den moderne bys overskudslandskaber*, Aarhus: Arkitektskolens Forlag.

Nielsen, T. (2009) *Det urbaniserede territorium. Østjylland under forandring*, Aarhus: Arkitektskolens Forlag.

Nielsen, T. & P. Hemmersam (2004) Imagining H-city: Denmark as and Urban Field, in Nielsen, T., N. Albertsen & P. Hemmersam (eds.) (2004) *Urban Mutations – periodization, scale and mobility*, Aarhus: Arkitektskolens Forlag, pp. 148-161.

Neufert, E. & P. Neufert (2000) *Architect's Data*, 3. Ed., Oxford: Blackwell.

Nold, C., O. B. Jensen & H. Harder (2008) *Mapping the City - reflections on urban mapping methodologies from GPS to Community Dialogue*, Aalborg: Department of Architecture and Design, Department Working Paper Series no. 25, December 2008.

Norman, D. (2007) *The Design of Future Things*, New York: Basic Books.

Næss, P. (2006) *Urban Structure Matters. Residential location, car dependence and travel behaviour*, London: Routledge.

Odense Municipality (2010a) Cyklisternes By - Cykelstier. In: http://www.odense.dk/web4/cyklisternesby/service/cykelstier.aspx .

Odense Municipality (2010b) Odense modtager Vejprisen 2010. In: http://www.odense.dk/home/Presse/Pressemeddelelser/Pressemeddelelser/Pressemeddelelser%202010/Odense%20modtager%20Vejprisen%202010.aspx.

Odense Municipality (2010c) Cyklisternes By – Odense. In: http://www.odense.dk/web4/cyklisternesby/~/media/BKF/Bymiljø/Cykelby/Strategi%20maj.ashx.

Odense Municipality (2010d) City of Odense at EXPO 2010 in Shanghai. In:http://www.odense.dk/web4/cyklisternesby/cycle%20city%20odense/expo%202010.aspx.

Odense Municipality (2010e) Flere cykeltællere i Odense. In: http://www.odense.dk/WEB4/CyklisternesBy/Det%20sker/NyhederNy/Flere%20cykeltaellere%20i%20Odense.aspx.

Odense Municipality (2010f) Cyklisternes By - Mål for Cylisternes By. In: http://www.odense.dk/web4/cyklisternesby/vision%20og%20maal.aspx.

Odense Municipality (2010g) Cyklisternes By – Klummer. In: http://www.odense.dk/home/WEB4/CyklisternesBy/Det%20sker/Klummer.aspx.

Odense Municipality (2010h) EXPO 2010. In: http://www.odense.dk/home/Topmenu/Borger/ByMiljoe/EXPO%202010.aspx.

Odense Municipality (2009i) Trafik og mobilitetsplan. In: http://www.odense.dk/Topmenu/Borger/ByMiljoe/Planlaegning/Trafikplan.aspx.

Oldenziel, R. & A. A. de la Bruhèze (2011) Contested Spaces. Bicycle Lanes in Urban Europe, 1900-1995, *Transfers* 2(1), Summer 2011: 29-49.

Olesen, M. & C. Lassen (2012) Restricted Mobilities: Access to and Activities in, Public and Private Spaces, *International Planning Studies*, vol. 17, no. 3, pp. 215-232, August 2012.

Patteeuw, V. (Ed.) (2004) *Considering Rem Koolhaas and the Office for Metropolitan Architecture. What is OMA*, Rotterdam: Nai Publishers.

Patton, J. W. (2004) *Transportation Worlds: Designing Infrastructures and forms of Urban Life*, Ph.D. Thesis submitted to Rensselaer Polytechnic Institute, New York: Troy.

Patton, J. W. (2007) A pedestrian world: competing rationalities and the calculation of transport change, *Environment and Planning A*, 2007, vol. 39, pp. 928-944.

Pesses, M. W. (2007) *Do Two Wheels make it more Authentic than Four? Spaces of Bicycle Tourism*, Paper for the Annual Meeting of the Association of American Geographers, San Francisco, April 17-21, 2007.

Pesses, M. W. (2010) Automobility, Vélomobility, American Mobility: An Exploration of the Bicycle Tour, *Mobilities*, vol. 5, no. 1, February 2010, pp. 1-24.

Petersen, J. (2007) Pedaling Hope, *Magazine on Urbanism*, no. 6, 2007, pp. 36-39.

Poulsen, E. S., H. J. Andersen, R. Gade, O. B. Jensen & T. Moeslund (2012a) *Using Human Motion Intensity as Input for Urban Design*, Paper for The International Conference on Ambient Intelligence, 16-18 November 2011, CCIS 277, Eds. R. Wichert, K. van Laerhoven & J. Gelissen, Berlin Heidelberg: Springer-Verlag, pp. 128-136.

Poulsen, E. S., H. J. Andersen & O. B. Jensen (2012b) *Full Scale Experiment with Interactive Urban Lighting*, Paper for the 'Workshop on Designing Interactive Lighting', Newcastle, UK, June 2012.

Powell, K. (2000) *The Jubilee Line Extension*, London: Lawrence King.

Public Meeting 2 (October 21, 2010) Philadelphia Pedestrian and Bicycle Plan, Phase 2: Southwest

Putnam, R. D. (2000) *Bowling Alone. The Collapse and Revival of American Community*, New York: Touchstone Books.

Rendgen, S. (2012) *Information Graphics*, Köln: Taschen.

Ritzer, G. (1999) *Enchanting a Disenchanted World. Revolutionizing the Means of Consumption*, Thousand Oaks: Pine Forge Press.

Ritzer, G. (2001) *Explorations in the Sociology of Consumption. Fast Food, Credit Cards and Casinos*, London: Sage.

Road Directorate (2002) *Beautiful Roads. A Handbook of Road Architecture*, Road Directorate, Ministry of Transport, Denmark.

Sadler, S. (1998) *The Situationist City*, Cambridge, Mass.: The MIT Press.

Schumacher, P. (2010) Parametric Diagrams, in Garcia, M. (ed.) (2010) *The Diagrams of Architecture*, Chichester: Wiley, pp. 260-269.

Schwarzer, M. (2004) *ZoomScape. Architecture in Motion and Media*, New York: Princeton University Press.

Schön, D. A. (1983/2001) *Den reflekterende praktiker. Hvordan professionelle tænker, når de arbejder*, Århus: Klim.

Scollon, R. and Scollon, S. (2003) *Discourses in Place. Language in the Material World*, London: Routledge.

Scott, J.C. (1998) *Seeing Like a State. How Certain Schemes to Improve the Human Condition Have Failed*, New Haven: Yale University Press.

Seiler, C. (2008) *Republic of Drivers. A Cultural History of Automobility in America*, Chicago: University of Chicago Press.

Sennett, R. (1994) *Flesh and Stone. The Body and the City in Western Civilization,* New York: W. W. Norton & Company.

Shane, D. G. (2005) *Recombinant Urbanism. Conceptual Modelling in Architecture, Urban Design, and City Theory*, Chichester: Wiley.

Shane, D. G. (2010) Urban Diagrams and Urban Modelling, in Garcia, M. (ed.) (2010) *The Diagrams of Architecture*, Chichester: Wiley, pp. 80-87.
Shane, D. G. (2011) *Urban Design Since 1945 – a global perspective*, Chichester: Wiley.
Shared Space (2005) *Shared Space: Plads til alle – en ny vision for det offentlige rum*. Leeuwarden: Interreg IIIB project Shared Space, Province Fryslân.
Sheller, M. (2004) Automotive Emotions. Feeling the Car, *Theory, Culture & Society*, vol. 21 (4/5): 221-242
Sheller, M. & J. Urry (Eds.) (2006) *Mobile Technologies of the City*, London: Routledge.
Shepard, M. (ed.) (2011) *Sentient City. Ubiquitous computing, architecture, and the future of urban space*, Cambridge, Mass.: MIT Press.
Shields, R. (1991) *Places on the Margin. Alternative Geographies of Modernity*, London: Routledge.
Simmel, G. (1903/50) The Metropolis and Mental Life, in K.H. Wolff (ed.) (1950) *The Sociology of Georg Simmel*, New York: The Free Press, pp. 409-424.
Sieverts, Th. (2003) *Cities without Cities. An interpretation of the Zwischenstadt*, London: SPON Press.
Skovmand, S. (red.) (2000) *Manhattan på Amager. Sagen om Ørestaden*, København: Aschehoug.
Sloterdijk, P. (2011) Society of Centaurs: Philosophical Remarks on Automobility, *Transfers* 1(1), spring 2011:14-24.
Smith, S. (2003) *Beyond Big - an examination of contemporary space*, Ph.D. dissertation, Aarhus: Aarhus School of Architecture.
Soja, E. W. (2000) *Postmetropolis. Critical Studies of Cities and Regions*, Oxford: Blackwell.
Soja, E, W. (2002) Sprawl is no longer what it used to be, in Gent Urban Studies Team (GUST) (ed.) (2002) *Post, Ex, Sub, Dis. Urban Fragmentations and Constructions*, Rotterdam 010 Publishers, pp. 76-88.
Soja, E. W. (2010) *Seeking Spatial Justice*, Minneapolis: University of Minnesota Press.
Sommer, R. (2007) *Personal Space. The behavioral basis of design,* Bristol: Bosko Books.
Sorkin, M. (ed.) (1992) *Variations on a Theme Park. The New American City and the End of Public Space*, New York: Hill and Wang.
Statistikbanken (2010) Folketal pr. 1. januar fordelt på byer. In: http://www.statistikbanken.dk/BEF44.
Steen & Strøm (2010*) Friis Bycenter Aalborg. Tracking Report*, December 2010.
Steinbeck, J. (1961) *Travels with Charley. In search of America*, New York: Penguin Books.
Stevens, G. (1998) *The Favored Circle. The Social Foundation of Architectural Distinction*, Cambridge, Mass.: The MIT Press.
Stoffers, M. (2011) Cycling Cultures: Review Essay, *Transfers* 1(1), spring 2011: 147-154.
Svenstrup, M., T. Bak, O. Maler, H. J. Andersen & O. B. Jensen (2008) *Pilot Study of Person Robot Interaction in a Public Transit Space*, Paper for the Eurobot 2008 Conference, Heidelberg, May 21-25 2008.
Sucher, D. (2003) Getting Around, in M. Larice & E. Macdonald (eds.) (2007) *The Urban Design Reader*, London: Routledge, pp. 392-404.
Sudjic, D. (1992) *The 100 Mile City*, Florida: Harcourt Brace & Company.
Suenson. V. (2012) *Konstruktioner & Aktiviteter: En RFID undersøgelse af sociale aktiviteter i danske kulturhuse*, Ph.D. Afhandling, Aalborg: Inst. For Arkitektur, Design og Medie Teknologi, Aalborg Universitet.
Suenson, V. & H. Harder (2011) *RFiD tracking af brugeres adfærd i bygningsrum*, Geoforum Perspektiv, nr. 19, april 2011, pp. 29-38.

Tait, M. & O. B. Jensen (2007) Travelling Ideas, Power and Place: The Cases of Urban Villages and Business Improvement Districts, *International Planning Studies*, vol. 12, no. 2, pp. 107-127.

Thomsen, T. U. (2001) *Persontransportens betydning for individet i et identitetsperspektiv – med focus* på transportmiddelvalg, Aarhus: Handels Højskolen i Aarhus, Ph.D. afhandling.

Thrift, N. (2004) Driving in the City, *Theory, Culture & Society*, vol. 21 (4/5): 41-59.

Thrift, N. (2008) *Non-Representational Theory. Space. Politics. Affect*, London: Routledge.

Trafitec (2004) *Undersøgelse af bilisters adfærd ved passage af reklamefly ved motorvej – distraktorer I trafikken*, København: Trafitec Aps, juni 2004.

Trip, J. J. (2007) *What Makes a City? Planning for 'quality of place'. The case of high-speed train station area development*, Delft: Delft University of Technology.

Tschumi, B. (1994) *The Manhattan Transcripts*, New York: Academy Editions.

Tschumi, B. (2010) The Diagrams of Bernard Tschumi, in Garcia, M. (ed.) (2010) *The Diagrams of Architecture*, Chichester: Wiley, pp.194-209.

Urry, J. (1990) *The Tourist Gaze. Leisure and Travel in Contemporary Societies*, Sage: London.

Urry, J. (2000) *Sociology beyond societies. Mobilities for the twenty-first century*. London: Routledge.

Urry, J. (2003) *Global Complexity*, Oxford: Polity.

Urry, J. (2004) The 'System' of Automobility, *Theory, Culture & Society*, vol. 21 (4/5): 25-39.

Urry, J. (2007) *Mobilities*, Cambridge: Polity.

Van Berkel, B. & C. Bos (2010) Diagrams, in Garcia, M. (ed.) (2008) *The Diagrams of Architecture*, Chichester: Wiley, pp. 222-227,

Vanderbilt, T. (2008) *Traffic. Why We Drive the Way We Do (and What It Says About Us)*, London: Allen Lane.

Vannini, P., L. Budd, O. B. Jensen, C. Fisker & P. Jirón (2012) Technologies of Mobility in the Americas: Introduction, in Vannini, P., L. Budd, O. B. Jensen, C. Fisker & P. Jirón (Eds.) (2012) *Technologies of Mobility in the Americas*, New York: Peter Lang, pp.1-20.

Varnelis, K. (ed.) (2008) *The Infrastructural City. Networked Ecologies in Los Angeles*, Barcelona: Actar.

Veblen, T. (1889/1994) *The Theory of the Leisure Class: An Economic Study of Institutions*, New York: Penguin

Venturi, R. & D. Scott-Brown (2004) *Architecture as Signs and Systems. For a mannerist time*, Cambridge, Mass.: The Belknap Press.

Venturi, R., Brown, D. S. & Izenour, S. (1972) *Learning from Las Vegas: The Forgotten Symbolism of Architectural Form*, Cambridge, Mass.: MIT Press.

Vitruvius (2009) *On Architecture*, London: Penguin.

Votolato, G. (2007) *Transport Design. A Travel History*, London: Reaktion Books.

Wall, A. (2005) *Victor Gruen. From Urban Shop to New City*, Actar: Barcelona.

Walzer, M. (1986) Pleasures and Costs of Urbanity, in Kasinitz, P. (ed.) (1995) *Metropolis. Center and Symbol of Our Times*, New York: New York University Press, pp. 320-330.

Web1 (2012) Hedensteds Kommunes Hjemmeside, http://www.hedensted.dk/page30851.aspx.

Weber, M. (1978) *Economy and Society. An Outline of an Interpretative Sociology*, Berkeley: University of California Press.

Weiss, S. J. & S. T. Leong (2001) Escalator, in Chung, C. J., J. Inaba, R. Koolhaas & S. T. Leong (eds.) (2001) *Project on the City 2. Harvard Design School Guide to Shopping*, Köln: Taschen, pp. 336-365.

Whitelegg, J. (1997) *Critical Mass. Transport, Environment and Society in the Twenty-First Century*, London: Pluto Press.

Whyte, W. H. (1988) *City. Rediscovering the Centre*, Philadelphia: University of Pennsylvania Press.

Wittgenstein, L. (1953) *Philosophical Investigations*, Oxford: Rhees and Anscombe.

Wouter, D. & U. Garritzmann (2010) Diagramming the Contemporary, in Garcia, M. (ed.) (2010) *The Diagrams of Architecture*, Chichester: Wiley, pp. 228-235.

Xue, C., M. Loming & K. C. Hui (2012) Indoor 'Public' Space: A study of atria in mass transit railway (MTR) complexes of Hong Kong, *Urban Design International*, vol. 17, 2, pp. 87-105.

Yan, H. H. Yi & Z. Pang (2003) *Beijing Ring Roads*, in Houben, F. & L. M. Calabrese (eds.) (2003) *Mobility: A room with a view*, Rotterdam: NAi Publishers, pp. 186-211.

Zacharias, J., T. Zhang & N. Nakajima (2011) Tokyo Station City: The railway station as urban place, *Urban Design International*, vol. 16, 4, pp. 242-251.

Zera-Polo, A. (2010) Between Ideas and Matter. Icons, Indexes, Diagrams, Drawings and Graphs, in Garcia, M. (ed.) (2010) *The Diagrams of Architecture*, Chichester: Wiley, pp. 236-243.

List of illustrations

Cover photos: Jacob Bjerre Mikkelsen

Chapter one: Chapter photo by Jacob Bjerre Mikkelsen

Fig. 1.1: Jensen, O. B. (2013a) *Staging Mobilities*, London: Routledge

Chapter two: Chapter photo by Ole B. Jensen

Fig. 2.1 and 2.2: Courtesy of Anne-Marie Sandvig Knudsen

Fig. 2.3: Tschumi, B. (1994) *The Manhattan Transcripts*, New York: Academy Editions

Chapter three: Cover photo by Ole B. Jensen, diagrams developed by Ole B. Jensen

Chapter four: Photos and illustrations by Simon Wind

Chapter five: Photos and illustrations by the Bikeability Project

Chapter six: Photos and illustrations by Jacob Bjerre Mikkelsen and Janni Toft

Chapter seven: Photos and illustrations by Jacob Bjerre Mikkelsen

Chapter eight: Photo by Janni Nesager Toft

Appendix: Unless otherwise noted, pictures are under the Creative Commons licens. More information about the licens at: http://creativecommons.org/licenses/